FINANCIAL ACCOUNTING

Visit the *Financial Accounting,* fifth edition, Companion Website at **www.pearsoned.co.uk/britton** to find valuable **student** learning material including:

- Multiple choice questions to test your learning
- Annotated links to valuable resources on the web
- Glossary to explain key terms

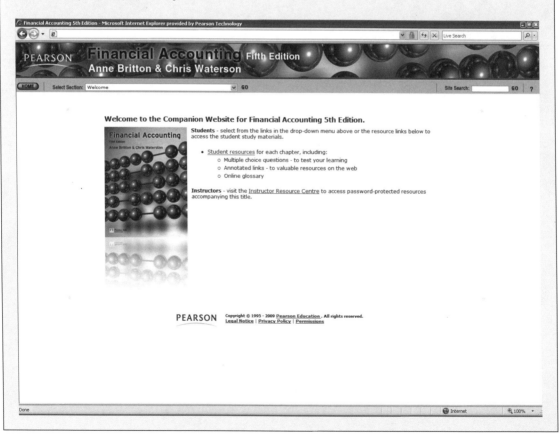

We work with leading authors to develop the
strongest educational materials in accounting,
bringing cutting-edge thinking and best
learning practice to a global market.

Under a range of well-known imprints, including
Financial Times Prentice Hall, we craft high quality
print and electronic publications which help readers
to understand and apply their content, whether
studying or at work.

To find out more about the complete range of our
publishing, please visit us on the World Wide Web at:
www.pearsoned.co.uk

Fifth edition

FINANCIAL ACCOUNTING

Anne Britton
Leeds Metropolitan University (retired)

Chris Waterston
Newcastle University

FT Prentice Hall
FINANCIAL TIMES

An imprint of **Pearson Education**
Harlow, England • London • New York • Boston • San Francisco • Toronto • Sydney • Singapore • Hong Kong
Tokyo • Seoul • Taipei • New Delhi • Cape Town • Madrid • Mexico City • Amsterdam • Munich • Paris • Milan

Pearson Education Limited

Edinburgh Gate
Harlow
Essex CM20 2JE
England

and Associated Companies throughout the world

Visit us on the world wide web at:
www.pearsoned.co.uk

———————————

First published 1996
Second edition published 1999
Third edition published 2003
Fourth edition published 2006
Fifth edition published 2010

ISBN: 978-0-273-71930-4

British Library Cataloguing-in-Publication Data
A catalogue record for this book is available from the British Library

Library of Congress Cataloging-in-Publication Data
A catalog record for this book is available from the Library of Congress

10 9 8 7 6 5 4 3
13 12

Typeset in 9.5/12.5pt by 30
Printed by Ashford Colour Press Ltd, Gosport

Brief Contents

Contents

Supporting resources

Visit **www.pearsoned.co.uk/britton** to find valuable online resources

Companion Website for students
- Multiple choice questions to test your learning
- Annotated links to valuable resources on the web
- Glossary to explain key terms

For instructors
- Additional long exercises complete with solutions
- Solutions to all the questions posed in the text
- PowerPoint slides that can be downloaded and used as OHTs
- Glossary

Also: The Companion Website provides the following features:
- Search tool to help locate specific items of content
- E-mail results and profile tools to send results of quizzes to instructors
- Online help and support to assist with website usage and troubleshooting

For more information please contact your local Pearson Education sales representative or visit **www.pearsoned.co.uk/britton**.

Preface

Welcome to your studies of financial accounting. Here we suggest how to use this book to gain the maximum benefit from your studies.

This fifth edition has been revised to introduce new topic areas, notably incomplete record accounting, accounting for partnerships and an introduction to group accounting, corporate governance and corporate social responsibility. All lists of key terms and self-assessment questions have been revised and updated. As before, the whole book is supported by a dedicated website, containing further questions, with answers available to tutors, and self-marking multiple-choice questions. The website also contains overhead transparency masters of key topics, for use by tutors, and an updated list of suggested web links for use by all users.

The book is divided into 16 chapters, each dealing with a separate area of financial accounting. The sequence of chapters is important, and you should normally work through the book following the chapter order. If you try to jump ahead, you may find that the material doesn't make much sense because you haven't yet picked up the necessary underpinning knowledge and skills.

Each chapter starts with a brief list of its objectives. This is a checklist of the things you should be able to do by the time you have worked through that chapter. Check back to this list when you finish each chapter to ensure that you have understood it all. If you are unsure about one or more aspects, don't leave the chapter, but have another look at the relevant part. You may also find it helpful to review the list of key terms towards the end of each chapter.

It is very tempting to forget this advice and to move on. However, we also know that the next topic will be much easier if you have thoroughly covered the previous one.

At a number of points in the book we suggest that you jot down your own ideas about a question raised, or that you calculate a figure, prepare an account, etc. You should therefore have pen, paper and a calculator at your side when you read this book.

Where an activity is designed to help you to learn the material, an answer is given in the text immediately following. It can be difficult to discipline yourself to make the effort to do the suggested activity instead of just reading ahead to the answer, but it is well worth the effort.

Notice that in each case we have provided *an* answer, not necessarily *the* answer. As you will see as you explore accountancy, it is not the exact science that many people suppose it to be. Almost all the answers in accountancy, at least in the UK, are contingent and dependent on ideas of what is to be achieved – which is why Chapter 1 is concerned with such fundamental issues. We must be clear about what we are trying to achieve before we start on the mechanics of doing it.

Self-assessment questions can be found at the end of each chapter and the relevant answers are at the end of the book. These are a selection of questions providing practice in the topics covered in the chapters. Don't forget that there is also a website to support this book at **www. pearson.co.uk/britton/**.

Remember, if you work through the issues for yourself, you will learn and retain them much more effectively than if you just read about them. Ultimately, it is your choice as to how much benefit you derive from studying this book.

A few words about current changes in accounting

The general public have tended to view accounting as a traditional, never-changing subject. This is not true; despite common appearances, accounting is a dynamic subject. The big change in recent years has been the gradual move in the UK from domestic accounting rules to international rules. Specifically, the rules that have been developed in the UK since 1970, known as Statements of Standard Accounting Practice (SSAPs) and Financial Reporting Standards (FRSs), are effectively being phased out. Coming in their place are International Accounting Standards (IASs) and International Financial Reporting Standards (IFRSs).

This change is being introduced gradually, with all companies across the European Union (EU), including the UK, that are listed on a stock exchange in the EU, using the international set of standards from 2005. Other companies, broadly the small and medium-sized ones, will continue to use the old UK standards for the time being. However, it seems likely that all companies will move to using the international standards in the medium term and the UK standards will then fade away. Indeed, the UK's standard setters are currently working on convergence of UK and international rules.

This means that UK accounting is currently in the middle of a major transition and this book reflects that. The book is based on the jargon and rules in the new international standards. However, we have also made reference to the older jargon and rules at the appropriate points. For example, what is now properly called the 'statement of comprehensive income' was previously known as the 'income statement' and before that was traditionally known as the 'profit and loss account' in the UK. This is a problem because everyday usage still commonly refers to the statement as the profit and loss account. Nevertheless, in this book, we have used the up to date terms. For reference, new and old terms for the main financial statements are set out below. We'll look at all these statements in more detail in the coming chapters.

Current name	Previous name	Pre-previous name, if any
Statement of comprehensive income/statement of income	Income statement	Profit and loss account
Statement of financial posititon	Balance sheet	
Statement of cash flows	Cash flow statement	
Statement of changes in equity	Same	

It's not just the names of the main statements which have changed. When we explore the format of the statement of cash flows in Chapter 10, we'll use the layout specified by the international standard rather than the layout required by the UK standard. Furthermore, the terms used for some individual items within the financial statements have also changed. In particular, people who owe us money have traditionally been called debtors, but the more correct, up-to-date name is 'trade receivables', and people we owe money to have traditionally been called creditors but we should now be calling them 'trade payables'. The original terms are likely to remain in wide use, of course, for the foreseeable future, but we should try to get used to the new terms.

We know this is confusing (it is for all accountants during the current transition!) but we believe that following the rules and jargon which will increasingly become the norm over the next few years will best prepare you for those years and beyond.

Guided tour of the book

6

Adjustments, including entries in ledger accounts

Objectives

By the end of this chapter you should be able to:
- Identify the need for adjustments to ledger accounts.
- Understand the nature of prepayments and accruals.
- Describe the necessity for adjustments for bad and doubtful debts.
- Define depreciation.
- Carry out the required ledger entries for depreciation.
- Balance off all ledger accounts after adjustments.
- Understand the nature of any balance remaining.

Introduction

Chapter 5 introduced you to the double entry system of bookkeeping. This chapter intends to build on that knowledge and expertise gained and also to further develop the concepts and conventions of accounting in relation to this double entry system.

So far we have assumed, with the exception of the inventory adjustment that we looked at in Chapter 5, that all entries made in the ledger for assets, liabilities, expenses and income relate to the period for which you wish to extract a statement of comprehensive income and a statement of financial position and that no items are missing. This is an incorrect assumption!

Accruals and prepayments

In the previous chapter all the expenses for Mr Bean's business entered the ledger accounts via the cash or bank account and the assumption was made that these related to sales, and were used up by Mr Bean in achieving those sales.

However, many expenses may be recorded as they are paid but may not relate, match, to the period in question. This was true in the case of purchases.

Objectives – Bullet points at the start of each chapter show what you can expect to learn from that chapter, and highlight the core coverage.

Activities – Appearing throughout every chapter, each activity is purposefully designed to help you learn the material, with the answer given in the text immediately following. Try not to look at the answer before trying the activity!

Key terms – The key concepts and techniques in each chapter are highlighted in colour where they are first introduced, listed at the end of each chapter, and fully explained in the comprehensive glossary.

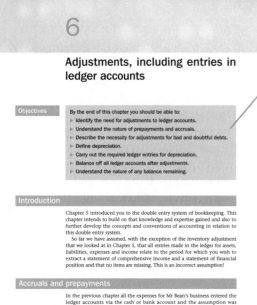

18 Financial Accounting

Activity 2.1 List three sources of funds for a typical business. You may find it helpful to think about your present or past employer, or another business you know of.

Answer Our list would include the following:

1 Money borrowed from an outsider, often a bank. Money borrowed is known as 'debt finance'.

2 Money invested by the owners. For a sole trader or a partnership this is known simply as 'capital'. For a limited company, such money is called 'share capital'.

3 Once a business is up and running it will hopefully make profits. Profit is then another source of funds, and can be used in the business as soon as it is received. The total of capital or share capital, together with such profit, is then called 'equity finance'.

4 More subtly, the credit allowed to an entity by a supplier is also a source of funds. If I agree to supply you with goods and accept payment next month, what I am effectively doing is lending you the goods for a month. Such a loan in kind is analogous to the loan in money that we listed at point 1 above.

There are thus two broad classifications of funding sources: equity (otherwise known as capital) and debt. These are both liabilities of the business because the business has an obligation to repay them eventually. Loans will have to be repaid and even the capital invested by the owners of the business will have to be repaid to them if and when the business comes to an end. Similarly, the profits ultimately belong not to the business, but to the owners, since the whole business belongs to them. The profits will therefore have to be paid by the business to the owners. In other words, the profits made in the past and retained by the business are a liability of the business.

In the meantime, the business can spend the equity and debt funds on buying a range of goods and services. Some of the things it buys will have a transitory existence, such as the labour of the workforce. The immediate benefit that comes from buying one hour of an employee's time ends at the end of that hour. Similarly, there will be nothing to show for money applied to paying the electricity bill. Note that the labour and the electricity may well have been used to produce the business's product, and any inventory (stock) of that product will have a continuing existence. The distinction we are aiming for, however, is that the labour and the electricity no longer exist as labour and electricity, but as part of the inventory value.

For comparison, some of the things the business applies its funds to will have a continuing existence. We have already seen that one such example could be inventory. Others could be, for example, buildings, vehicles or machinery. Items like this which have a continuing existence in themselves, and are of future benefit to the business, are called assets.

In Chapter 1 we defined assets as things we own and liabilities as things we owe. We can now adopt more accurate definitions, namely:

Summary

This chapter has introduced you to the double entry system of accounting. Within it we:

▸ have identified the need for the system when a business has several transactions to account for
▸ saw that it was based upon the concept of duality
▸ have taken you through the workings of the ledgers
▸ have balanced them off
▸ have extracted a trial balance
▸ have learnt that the statement of comprehensive income was in fact part of the double entry system and that income and expense accounts were cleared by being transferred to the statement of comprehensive income, recognising that the concept of matching must be applied, and
▸ have illustrated the matching concept within the context of cost of sales.

The remaining balances in the ledgers then formed a statement of financial position at the end of the financial period. The two main statements extracted from all this double entry, the statement of comprehensive income and the statement of financial position, have also been written in what is regarded as a 'user friendly' manner, i.e. vertical format. The statement of financial position format also reflected the equation assets = equity + liabilities

All this has been rather 'long winded' and the accounts take time to enter up. However, practice makes perfect, so we have provided several questions below.

Key terms

double entry (p. 73)
account (p. 73)
credit transactions (p. 78)
accounts payable (p. 78)
accounts receivable (p. 78)

ledger (p. 79)
balance off (p. 80)
trial balance (p. 84)
closing inventory account (p. 87)

Self-assessment questions

1 On 1.4.20X1 H. Britton commenced a business dealing in subaqua equipment. He paid £20,000 into the business bank account and the following transactions took place during the month of April.

Bullet point chapter summary – Each chapter ends with a 'bullet point' summary. This highlights the material covered in the chapter and can be used as a quick reminder of the main issues.

Self-assessment questions – At the end of each chapter you will encounter these questions, allowing you to check your understanding and progress. Solutions are provided in the Appendix.

Guided tour of the website

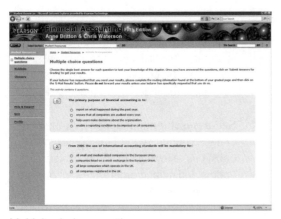

Multiple choice questions

Weblinks

Glossary

1

What is accounting?

Objectives

By the end of this chapter you should be able to:

▶ Discuss the need for, and purposes of, accounting.

▶ Outline the nature and types of accounting.

▶ Describe the major formats in which accounting information is presented.

▶ List the users of accounting and describe their particular informational needs.

Introduction

This chapter aims to introduce the purposes and the types of accounting, and to consider who might be interested in a knowledge of accounting. Since you are reading this book, you presumably have some interest in accounting, or at least a need to study it. Nevertheless, you may not be aware of the range of activities that make up accounting, nor be quite sure about what, and who, accounting is for. In this chapter we look at these issues under three headings – the purposes, the types and the users.

If you have done some accounting before, you may be tempted to skip over this chapter. Don't. The last few years have seen a strong trend towards accounting for the spirit of transactions, rather than the letter. If you are to understand what the spirit of a transaction is, then you must be clear about the fundamental issues dealt with in this chapter.

Purposes of accounting

Before we look at the purposes of accounting, it is helpful to review briefly the contexts in which accounting occurs. In other words, we examine the different types of organisation that need accounting.

Activity 1.1

What types of organisation can you think of? Jot them down and then put a cross against any that you think have no need of accounting.

Answer

The following list of organisations covers the main types. You may have included others, or have expressed the same ones in different words.

▶ *Sole trader*. This means one person who runs a business on their own, or perhaps with a few employees. The main aim is to make a profit.
▶ *Partnership*. This is two or more people who carry on a business in common, intending to make a profit.
▶ *Limited company*. In the UK, a limited company is a legal organisation set up under the Companies Act 2006. The owners are called the shareholders, and it is run by directors, who are appointed by the shareholders. In small companies it is common for the shareholders to appoint themselves as directors. Larger companies are often public limited companies, or plcs. You will find out more about limited companies in Chapter 8.
▶ *Public sector bodies*, such as local councils or the National Health Service. Traditionally, these bodies have not existed to make a profit, but exist to provide a service.
▶ *Clubs and societies*, such as a local cricket club. Again the intention is not to make a profit but to provide services for members.

All of these organisations require some form of accounting, however simple. Our next task is to explore why this should be so.

Activity 1.2

Accounting is undertaken by organisations for a variety of reasons. What do you think they are? Jot down at least three reasons before you read on.

Answer

This is probably the most fundamental question in accountancy. Nevertheless, there are no agreed, clear answers to it. In principle, therefore, your answers are as valid as any others, but we would expect you to include some or all of the following:

1 To record what money has come into the organisation and what has gone out.
2 To help managers make decisions about how to run the organisation.
3 To tell other people about the activities and consequent profit or loss of the organisation during the past year, or other period.
4 To tell other people about the present financial state of the organisation.
5 To provide a basis for taxation.
6 To help assess whether the organisation is beneficial to society as a whole.
7 To control the organisation, by controlling the finances.
8 To provide a basis for planning future activities.
9 To support legal relationships, for example how much one business owes another.

This is not a comprehensive list: you may have listed other items, or expressed similar points in different ways. Points 2 and 8 in the list arguably overlap. However, if you look at our list and your own, you should see that the purposes are broadly of two types.

First, there are purposes that relate to the running of the business, that is, those that form a basis for decision making. In Chapter 11 you will see that part of the regulatory framework of financial accounting is a document called the 'Framework for the Preparation and Presentation of Financial Statements' (hereafter just called the Framework). This is a publication by the International Accounting Standards Board (IASB), which is itself an authoritative international group of accountants. The Framework is dealt with in more detail in Chapter 4; briefly, it states that the prime objective of financial statements is to aid decision making.

Second, there is a group of purposes that can be classified as 'stewardship'. This term means that accounting is used to keep track of what has been done with the financial resources entrusted to its managers. Historically, this was the original purpose of financial accounting, whereby managers ('stewards') had to account to the owners for their stewardship of the owners' money. The Framework is clear that stewardship is secondary to decision making as a general aim of financial accounting. This means that accounting is now less a matter of keeping track of the money, and more a matter of using the resulting information to actively manage the organisation, and for outsiders to make decisions about the organisation.

A brief history

We've seen that the primary purpose of accounting is now seen as the provision of information to help those interested in the organisation (the 'stakeholders') make decisions about it. This is a more active use of accounting information than was originally the case.

Keeping track of economic data, i.e. stewardship, has been a main purpose of accounting for many years. Modern accounting is usually dated to 1494, when one Luca Pacioli codified the accounting that had developed during the Renaissance to keep track of the increased trading that was occurring. For a long time afterwards it was still about stewardship, but early in the twentieth century a more proactive use started to be made of accounting. As we've seen, this more modern view sees accounting as primarily a way of helping us make decisions about the future, rather than simply keeping track of what happened in the past.

If this is what accounting is for, what does that imply for the present nature of accounting? Well, for one thing, it means that accounting is not just a matter of recording data, or even of processing them in an organised way. It is both these things, but an increasingly large part of accounting is concerned with subsequently presenting the resultant information to those who are interested in the welfare of the organisation. The next section looks in more detail at the consequent nature of today's accounting.

Types of accounting

Accounting can be divided very roughly into two areas, financial accounting and management accounting. Bear in mind that the division is a rather arbitrary one, and many functions in the accountancy world spread across both areas. Nevertheless, it is a distinction that is often made, and which can help to make accountancy as a whole more manageable.

Financial accounting is concerned with the recording, processing and presentation of economic information after the event to those people outside the organisation who are interested in it. By contrast, management accounting deals with similar activities, but is geared to providing information about the organisation to its managers to help them run it. In other words, the heart of the distinction is the *purpose* of the accounting, rather than what is done. This may become clearer if we look at each of the three functions of recording, processing and presentation.

Recording

All accounting requires the prior collection of raw data and their organisation into some form of structured record. In principle, this could be as crude as writing down each transaction in a single book, as it occurs. It should be obvious, however, that it would not be easy to get information out of this book. You may be aware that, in fact, almost all accounting systems across the world rely on 'double entry' recording in some form. This method has been so successful over the past 500 years since it was codified precisely because it is relatively easy to get information out of it. In Chapter 5 you will start to learn about this system.

Before we can start on the practicalities of recording data, however, there remains one major question to be answered.

Activity 1.3	What sorts of transaction does an accountant record? Note down at least four.

Answer	There are many kinds of transactions, and you may have noted others than those listed below, or expressed similar items in different ways.

1 Sales made.

2 Money received for the sales – remember that you don't always get paid as soon as you sell something.

3 Production materials bought.

4 Expenses incurred, for example electricity used.

5 Production materials and expenses paid for – again, we don't always pay for something as soon as we buy it.

6 Borrowing money from the bank.

7 Persuading other people to put money into our organisation.

8 Buying big items that we intend to keep, such as buildings or machinery.

Note that what accountants therefore record is almost always restricted to what can be valued reasonably objectively in money terms. In other words, if you can't attach a currency symbol, such as a £ sign, to it, accountants ignore it. Furthermore, accountants tend to focus on the organisation, rather than taking a broader societal view.

Activity 1.4

List three things about an organisation that accountants might not record, but which you would regard as useful things to be told about.

Answer

As with most of the questions raised in this chapter, there is no single, correct answer. Some of the things we consider to be currently important are:

1 The value added to the economy by the activities of the organisation.

2 The measurement and inclusion of human resources. Some football clubs, for example, include a valuation of their players in their statement of financial position (balance sheet), that is, the summary of what the organisation owns and owes. Others claim that it is impossible to say objectively what a player is worth, and so omit them from the statement of financial position. Which approach do you think gives the best picture of what the organisation owns? We think this area of accounting is one of the more interesting ones, and it is dealt with more fully in the next chapter and in Chapter 13.

3 Environmental accounting, which tries to report the impact of the organisation on the environment, perhaps in terms of tonnes of pollutants emitted, compared with previous years, other similar organisations, or standards of some sort.

4 Social accounting, which provides information about the social impact of the organisation. This could include looking at, say, the employment of minority groups, or the effect of purchasing policies, especially where supplies come from the Third World. In the UK, The Body Shop plc is one of the more notable companies already moving down this road.

The above possibilities are not part of generally accepted accounting practice at the moment. However, there are signs that this is changing. Ethical investment is a growing force in the UK, with around £9 billion invested by investment funds which claim some ethical basis. An organisation trying to attract such investment could find that providing some of the information suggested above could help. Against this, there is a view that organisations in the UK, especially limited companies, already have to provide so much information that the costs of doing so prevent them from concentrating on their core business. All we can do here is note that accounting is constantly changing, and that there are signs that it is moving towards some of the issues indicated above. This is discussed in more detail under 'The future of financial accounting' later in this chapter.

Chapter 5 will start to explore exactly how organisations record data and turn them into useful financial statements of various sorts. For the moment all we need to consider is what data should be recorded and why. To consolidate your knowledge so far, try putting a tick in the correct box in the table shown in Activity 1.5.

Activity 1.5

In conventional accounting, which of the events listed in the table would usually be recorded and which would be ignored?

	Recorded	Ignored
1 Selling one of the organisation's cars		
2 Paying the wages		
3 Making the tea		
4 Moving staff between jobs in the office		
5 Incurring a fine for polluting a local river		
6 Paying the fine		

Answer

You should have ticked the 'recorded' column for items 1, 2, 5 and 6, since all these result in objectively measurable resources coming into or leaving the organisation. On the other hand, items 3 and 4 do not change the economic relationship with the outside world, and would therefore not be recorded in a financial accounting system. You should therefore have ticked the 'ignored' column for these two.

You might expect the law to specify what records are required. In fact, in the UK the Companies Act is quite vague about exactly what records need be kept, and say only that they should be 'sufficient to show and explain' the transactions and consequent position of the company. This means that the records differ between companies, each organising the recording as it thinks best. It need not be like this. In France, for example, the *plan comptable*, that is, the government's accounting plan, specifies exactly which ledger accounts must be kept, and exactly what can and can't be recorded in each. Ledger accounts are explained in Chapter 5.

Activity 1.6

Which approach, the UK or the French, do you think is better? Why?

Answer

As usual, the answer depends on what you think accounting is for. The UK system has the benefit of flexibility, in that it allows each organisation to set up an accounting system that best suits its own circumstances and needs. If we are aiming to present information for users to make decisions about that organisation, then gearing the system to the peculiarities of the organisation is most likely to result in relevant information.

On the other hand, allowing each organisation to design a different system is unlikely to result in information that is comparably prepared and presented between organisations. Despite rules set down by the Companies Acts and by the IASB in accounting standards, lack of comparability is a major problem in the UK. We leave it to you to judge whether state control of accounting would be politically and culturally acceptable in the UK. Nevertheless, as we've seen, it is becoming the case that UK accounting is increasingly subject to international accounting standards published by the International Accounting Standards Board. Ultimately, we get the accounting that reflects our society.

Processing

Processing means turning the raw data that we have recorded into useful information that can be presented to those interested in knowing about the organisation. As we have already seen, the processing will be determined by what information we want from our accounting system, and by the underlying method of recording that we have adopted. Given these two, the processing is simply the way we turn the recorded data into the required financial information.

Beginning in Chapter 5, you will see how we not only record data but how we then process it so that we can produce the financial statements that most users of the information require. Having looked at the essential features of recording, it may help to appreciate what is involved in processing if we now turn our attention to the end product. In other words, it is time to look at the ways in which financial information is most usually presented.

Presenting

We saw above that there are very lax rules in the UK about what records need be kept and how the data in them are then processed. However, as you will see as we progress through this book, limited companies in the UK are closely governed with respect to the presentation of information to the users of the accounts. The Companies Act requires a statement of comprehensive income (income statement) and a statement of financial position (balance sheet). Furthermore, accountants' own rules, the accounting standards, also require a statement of cash flows and a statement of changes in equity.

Overall, what we have here is an accounting system, that is a series of inter-connected entities, together making up the total system. It may be best to present this idea as a diagram.

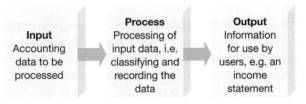

In the diagram above, the data we identified earlier as being appropriate for accounting form the input to our system. We then process this data, usually using some form of double entry bookkeeping. In practice, of course, this processing will normally be computer based. Once we've put the input data into a form that users can access to help them make decisions, we call this organised data 'information'. In financial accounting, this information takes the form of the four financial statements we listed above. We'll look at them in much more detail later in the book – indeed, you will learn to prepare them yourself – but they are so fundamental to accounting that it is worth taking a brief look at them now.

The statement of comprehensive income

This is a list of the expenses incurred by the organisation, set against its revenues, the net result being a profit if revenues are more than expenses, and a loss if the reverse is true. It covers a specific period, usually one year. Note that this used be known as the income statement until 2009, and before that, in the UK at least, this statement used to be known as the profit and loss account. Many accountants will no doubt continue to refer to the statement as an income statement or as a profit and loss account, especially for smaller companies, for a few years yet. There's more information about this change in Chapter 11.

In fact, the new statement of comprehensive income, as the name suggests, actually reports more than the income statement used to. Specifically, the new statement reports the trading profit, exactly as the income statement did, but then adds on a section reporting non-trading gains, such as changes in the value of our property. This is all covered in detail in Chapters 3 and 13.

The statement of financial position

This is a summary of the assets and liabilities of the organisation at a specific time. With effect from 2009, the IASB now refers to this as a 'statement of financial position', although it was previously called the balance sheet, and this term is likely to be more commonly used for a while yet. In simple terms, assets are what the organisation owns and liabilities are what it owes. As you will see in the next chapter, these definitions are not strictly true, but they are good enough for a basic understanding.

The statement of cash flows

Like the statement of comprehensive income, the statement of cash flows covers a specific period, but it differs by listing the actual cash received and paid out. The statement of comprehensive income, by contrast, lists the amounts incurred. For example, if we sell goods for £10,000 but are paid only £8,000 immediately, with the other £2,000 to be paid to us next month, the statement of comprehensive income would record the sale of £10,000 but the statement of cash flows would record only the cash event of the receipt of £8,000. The difference will become clearer when you look at the statement of comprehensive income adjustments in Chapters 6 and 7.

For the time being, however, we should note that the statement of cash flows is usually regarded as a more reliable statement of activity in that it deals only with actual cash in and out, and those cash flows are normally an objective fact. The sale recorded in the statement of comprehensive income, by contrast, is less objective since it inherently contains an element of uncertainty. For example, in the example above, it is possible that some goods, say £1,000's worth, will yet be returned to us as unsuitable and the final sale could then be seen as only £9,000. This greater objectivity of cash flows, and hence of the statement of cash flows, has led some accountants to regard the statement of cash flows as a more useful and reliable statement than the statement of comprehensive income. You will see these differences in more detail when we look at the preparation of statement of cash flows in Chapter 10.

Statement of changes in equity

As we saw above, the statement of comprehensive income lists revenues and expenses, that is, amounts we are entitled to and have to pay, respectively, as a result of our routine operations, usually from our trading. However, organisations can also gain or lose wealth from causes other than trading.

For example, what if the value of our buildings rises – is that a gain? The gain hasn't arisen from anything we have done (except buy the building in the first place and keep it), so it presumably can't be seen as a trading gain. On the other hand, aren't we richer because the value of our building has risen, and shouldn't we then report this increase in wealth? This is exactly what a statement of changes in equity does – it reports gains and losses, including those that have arisen other than from operations, and so reconciles the opening and closing equities, i.e. the owners' stake in the business.

It may have occurred to you that all four of these statements are summaries of different aspects of the organisation, prepared for those outside the business. They therefore fall within the area of *financial* accounting. The presentation of *management* accounting information is not governed by the Companies Acts or the accounting standards. This means that management accounting statements vary between organisations. Nevertheless, most organisations of any size will produce some or all of the following, and these would normally be regarded as management accounting statements:

▶ A structured guess about what revenues and expenses will be in the future. This is usually called a budget.

▶ A comparison of the previously estimated revenues and costs with the actual revenues and costs. Such a statement allows managers to see where things have not gone according to plan, by highlighting the variances between estimated and actual figures. It is therefore sometimes known as a variance report, or variance analysis report.

▶ An analysis of the cost of a particular product or service provided by the organisation, showing the cost of each item that has gone into that product or service.

▶ An estimate of what money will come into and flow out of the organisation over the coming months. This is usually known as a cash flow forecast.

*A*ctivity 1.7

Earlier in this chapter we referred to the statement of cash flows. This is not the same thing as a cash flow forecast. To ensure that you appreciate the difference, and hence something of the difference between financial and management accounting, state the difference in your own words.

Answer

A statement of cash flows is a summary of what cash flow actually occurred during the past accounting period. It is a record of what happened, prepared primarily for those outside the business. It would therefore normally be regarded as part of financial accounting. The cash flow forecast is an educated, structured guess about what we think the cash flows will be in the next accounting period(s). It is mainly prepared for managers, to help them plan the activities of the organisation in the future. It is thus probably best classified as management accounting.

As you may have guessed from its title, this book is only about financial accounting. We will therefore not be dealing with management accounting topics any further.

Who cares anyway? The users

You should have noticed in our discussion above that what accounting is ultimately depends largely on who we think the end users will be. If, for example, you think that the information produced by the accounting process is primarily for the managers of the organisation, you would probably want to focus on recording and processing data about, say, the estimated and actual costs of products, and estimates of future revenues and costs. You could then present the resulting information to managers in the form of comparisons of estimated and actual costs for making each product.

Alternatively, if you think those with the greatest need of information about the organisation are those who work there, you might be more concerned to record and process information about changes in rates of pay, health and safety records, emission levels of toxic products, or employment of minority groups. Think for a moment about how such a perspective would change the nature of accounting.

*A*ctivity 1.8

As a way of getting to grips with the various groups who are usually held to need financial information, and why they need it, try completing the following table. To get you started, we have already filled in some of the table. Don't look ahead to the completed table which follows until you have tried this for yourself.

User group	*User needs*
1 Investors	Return on capital. Growth in the total value of the organisation.
2	Security of employment. Wage rates, and the share of generated wealth going to the employees, compared with owners and the Revenue.
3 Lenders	
4 Suppliers and other trade creditors	
5 Customers	
6	Tax assessments and trade statistics.
7 Public	

Answer

At this point, we should admit that we have cheated a little here, and based the list of users on the 'Framework for Preparation and Presentation of Financial Statements'. You may recall that we came across the Framework earlier, where it gave us an authoritative statement about the purposes of financial accounting. The list is very similar to other lists, notably that in the 'Statement of Principles', which was developed independently in the UK through the 1990s. The suggested user needs are our own. The completed table is as follows:

User group	User needs
1 Investors	Return on capital. Growth in the total value of the organisation.
2 Employees	Security of employment. Wage rates, and the share of generated wealth going to the employees, compared with owners and the Revenue.
3 Lenders	Ability to make repayments of capital and interest. Security, in the event of non-repayment.
4 Suppliers and other trade creditors	Credit worthiness of the organisation. Time typically taken to pay suppliers.
5 Customers	Security of supply, i.e. will the organisation still be in business next year?
6 Government and its agencies	Tax assessments and trade statistics.
7 Public	A 'catch-all' category covering local communities, pressure groups and industry watchers.

As a final point on users, note that they will not only be interested in commercial businesses. You saw at the start of this chapter that accounting is required by all organisations, not just commercial ones. We have therefore used the term 'organisations' in this chapter to cover not only businesses, but also charities, public sector organisations such as the NHS, voluntary bodies and social clubs. Each will have a different weighting of users, and different information needs.

The future of financial accounting

If nothing else, you should be finishing this chapter with the idea that accounting is a dynamic subject. This means that it is constantly changing to reflect changing practices and the requirements of competing user groups. It may be helpful to conclude this first chapter with a brief exploration of where financial accounting may be going over the next few years.

Notice what the table of users above is suggesting. A single set of financial statements has to meet all the user needs in the list above. This is an ambitious aim. Is it likely that it is achievable? If not, are we to try to satisfy all users partially, or to put the needs of some users above the needs of others? Who decides? Would it be acceptable to produce a number of financial statements, each one geared to the needs of a different user? If we did, what would happen to comparability, and who would pay for all the extra reports? You should be getting used to the idea that there are few definite answers to many of the questions in accounting, and the questions we have raised here are simply more examples of such questions. All we can suggest is that you think about them in the light of what you have learned in this chapter, and bear them in mind for later chapters.

For a specific example of how accounting is currently changing, we could take the growing area of social and environmental accounting. We touched on what is involved in this form of accounting earlier in the chapter. All we want to emphasise here is that it constitutes an extension – some would say an alternative – to existing generally accepted accounting practice. It has arisen because of changing societal concerns over the environment and over the impact of business on social issues. In turn, the more responsible and responsive businesses have reacted to the changed context by changes in their commercial practices. This is resulting in some, so far limited, changes in accounting.

Nevertheless, social and environmental accounting is not only a good example of the way financial accounting changes, but is also an increasingly important topic in its own right. What follows is therefore a brief summary of some of the main features of this new form of accounting.

It should be said to begin with that there are currently no legal or accounting rules which require such accounting. Why, then, do some companies do it? There is a complex range of views on this but we can distinguish three broad categories.

First, there are those companies, and other organisations, that do it because their core values are tied up with social and environmental concerns. They therefore regard it as important to gather and present information about their activities in these areas. It must be said that there are not many such companies in the UK, but The Body Shop and Traidcraft would perhaps fall into this category.

Second, there is a fast-growing range of companies that are entering social and environmental reporting because they foresee that such concerns are becoming an increasingly significant issue in business. In other words, while there may be some concern, as with the first group, the main motivation is more probably commercial. This is a growing group in the UK and elsewhere, and could be said to include such companies as BT, Scottish Power, Shell and CIS. In Europe, environmental reporting is strongly supported by Norsk Hydro, Daimler Benz and Volvo among others.

Third, there is a large group of companies that undertakes little or nothing in the way of social and environmental reporting.

You may have noticed that activity focuses on environmental reporting rather than social. Why this should be is an interesting question, and we can identify two possible causes. First, reporting on such environmental matters as tonnes of sulphur dioxide emitted, or kilometres of copper cable recycled, is a significant shift from traditional accounting. As we saw earlier in this chapter, the traditional approach in financial accounting has been to ignore an event unless it can be objectively measured in some unit of currency. Even so, with environmental reporting there is still a reasonably objective unit of measurement. However, this is unlikely to be the case if we are reporting on such social issues as the impact of making 500 employees redundant, or seconding 20 of our staff to work on local community projects. In other words, environmental accounting is proving technically easier than social accounting. Second, social reporting can be seen as more politically charged than identifying our impact on the physical environment – we are all green now.

Activity 1.9

Look back at the user groups we identified earlier in this chapter. Which three groups do you think would benefit most from environmental (not social) reporting? Give a couple of reasons to justify each of your choices.

Answer

This is another of those questions to which there is no unarguably correct answer. Nevertheless, our answer is:

Investors
▶ Environmental liabilities are becoming an ever-greater commercial issue. Unless they are reported, an investor is unable to fully assess the worth of the reporting company.
▶ Environmental action can prove good business sense, for example where cutting waste cuts costs.

Employees
▶ Many environmental issues have a health and safety impact, of obvious concern to an employee.
▶ Many employees want to feel that they work for an environmentally responsible employer.

Customers
▶ As more well-respected companies undertake environmental accounting, environmental responsibility can be taken as a measure of a well-run company, so helping to ensure stability of supply.
▶ Increasingly, firms are asking their suppliers to verify that what they supply comes, as far as possible, from renewable sources.

Summary

This first chapter asks what accounting is all about. We saw that it is concerned with:

▶ the recording, processing and presentation of economically measurable information
▶ the law, especially the Companies Act
▶ the international accounting standards set by the IASB.

These issues are themselves a reflection of what users want to know about the organisation. Where the users are primarily concerned about information for the internal running of the organisation, the resultant accounting systems and reporting would usually be classified as management accounting. Otherwise, it will be the subject of this book, financial accounting.

Many textbooks simply describe accounting as it is, while this chapter has tried also to suggest how accounting might be. After all, if you continue with your studies of accountancy, you will one day be one of those who will determine the nature and purposes of accountancy.

Before you can tackle such issues seriously, however, you should be competent in the existing practice of financial accounting. The rest of this book will help you achieve that competence, but always remember that all accounting is ultimately determined by the issues we have covered in this chapter.

Key terms

decision making (p. 3)
stewardship (p. 3)
recording (p. 4)
processing (p. 7)
presentation (p. 7)
income statement (p. 8)
statement of comprehensive
   income (p. 8)

profit and loss account (p. 8)
balance sheet (p. 8)
statement of financial position
   (p. 8)
statement of cash flows (p. 8)
statement of changes in equity
   (p. 9)

Self-assessment questions

For each of the following questions, choose the single most appropriate answer.

1 The main purposes of financial accounting and reporting are:

  (a) for stewardship and to aid decision making, in that order.
  (b) to aid decision making and to comply with company law, in that order.
  (c) to aid decision making and for stewardship, in that order.
  (d) for stewardship, and to comply with company law, in that order.

2 The main purpose of management accounting and reporting is to:

  (a) provide information for internal decision making.
  (b) determine costs of production processes.
  (c) set budgets against which actual costs can be compared.
  (d) none of the above.

3 Which two of the following events would not normally result in an immediate accounting transaction?

  (i)   Buying goods, agreeing to pay next month.
  (ii) Selling goods for cash, payable immediately.
  (iii) Taking on a new employee.
  (iv) Announcing a new product line.

  (a) (i) and (iii)
  (b) (iv) and (i)
  (c) (ii) and (iv)
  (d) (iii) and (iv)

4 The main purpose of a statement of cash flows is to:

(a) summarise short-term assets and liabilities at a point in time.
(b) summarise the cash in hand at a point in time.
(c) summarise cash paid and received over a period.
(d) summarise cash paid and payable, and received and receivable over a period.

5 Which user group is likely to be most interested in the growth in wealth of the organisation, and the profit relative to the money tied up in the organisation?

(a) lenders
(b) Investors
(c) Employees
(d) None of the above

6 Accounting standards are:

(a) broad statements of guidance on accounting practice.
(b) effectively mandatory statements of acceptable accounting practice.
(c) rules set out in the Companies Act governing accounting practice.
(d) the same thing as the French *plan comptable*.

7 Social and environmental accounting is:

(a) a mandatory part of UK financial accounting.
(b) a possible extension to UK financial accounting.
(c) a particular form of management accounting.
(d) none of the above.

8 The essential difference between the UK and French systems of financial accounting is that:

(a) The UK system specifies more precisely the form of recording and presentation.
(b) The French system specifies more precisely the form of recording and presentation.
(c) There is no significant difference.
(d) They are recorded in different units of currency.

9 Match the statements listed in the left-hand column against the correct definition in the right-hand column. Note that there will therefore be two definitions that are not applicable.

Statement of comprehensive income	A summary of the environmental impacts of the organisation ·
Statement of financial position	A summary of liquid funds that flowed in and out of the organisation in the past year
Statement of cash flows	A summary of why the organisation has become richer or poorer during the past year
	A summary of gains and losses made by the organisation during the past year
	A summary of the assets, liabilities and capital applicable to the organisation at the end of the year

▶

10 The IASB Framework outlines two rationales for financial accounting, namely decision making and stewardship. It suggests that accounting is done to help users make decisions (decision making) and to confirm what has happened (stewardship). Which of these two purposes do you consider to be the more important? Give reasons for your answer.

Your answer should be in the form of a short essay, of about 300 to 500 words, or at least in the form of comprehensive notes for such an essay. There is no single right answer, nor will you find the answer by looking it up in this chapter. You will have to apply the ideas and facts introduced in this chapter to formulate your own answer – indeed, requiring you to work through the issues like this is the point of this question. Our answer is at the back of the book, and is based on the Framework, and lists the main points that you should have covered.

Answers to these questions can be found at the back of this book.

2

The statement of financial position

Objectives

By the end of this chapter you should be able to:

▶ List and explain the major sources and applications of funds for a commercial entity.

▶ Construct a simple statement of financial position.

▶ Outline the alternative methods of valuing assets and liabilities.

Introduction

In Chapter 1 we looked at the purposes of accounting, and saw how accounting information is conventionally presented. One of the main methods of presentation was the statement of financial position, which we saw is the new name for what has traditionally been called the balance sheet. Whatever it's called, this is a statement of the financial position of the undertaking at a specific point in time. In this chapter we look at the statement of financial position in more detail, and you will learn how to prepare one.

Before we tackle the construction of a statement of financial position, however, we need to turn our attention to where the money typically comes from and where it is spent. You discovered in the previous chapter that a statement of financial position is simply a list of the assets and liabilities of an entity. The entity must have got the assets by spending money on them, and must have got that money in the first place by incurring a liability to third parties. This should become clearer if we now examine what are more formally known as the sources and applications of funds.

The sources and applications of funds

The starting point is to consider where an entity gets its money from. Some entities will have unusual sources. Charities, for example, receive donations, whereas most other entities do not. Furthermore, public sector bodies, such as local authorities and the police, receive government funds. Nevertheless, we can identify some sources of funds which will be widely applicable, especially to commercial organisations.

*A*ctivity 2.1   List three sources of funds for a typical business. You may find it helpful to think about your present or past employer, or another business you know of.

Answer   Our list would include the following:

1 Money borrowed from an outsider, often a bank. Money borrowed is known as 'debt finance'.

2 Money invested by the owners. For a sole trader or a partnership this is known simply as 'capital'. For a limited company, such money is called 'share capital'.

3 Once a business is up and running it will hopefully make profits. Profit is then another source of funds, and can be used in the business as soon as it is received. The total of capital or share capital, together with such profit, is then called 'equity finance'.

4 More subtly, the credit allowed to an entity by a supplier is also a source of funds. If I agree to supply you with goods and accept payment next month, what I am effectively doing is lending you the goods for a month. Such a loan in kind is analogous to the loan in money that we listed as point 1 above.

There are thus two broad classifications of funding sources: equity (otherwise known as capital) and debt. These are both liabilities of the business because the business has an obligation to repay them eventually. Loans will have to be repaid and even the capital invested by the owners of the business will have to be repaid to them if and when the business comes to an end. Similarly, the profits ultimately belong not to the business, but to the owners, since the whole business belongs to them. The profits will therefore have to be paid by the business to the owners. In other words, the profits made in the past and retained by the business are a liability of the business.

In the meantime, the business can spend the equity and debt funds on buying a range of goods and services. Some of the things it buys will have a transitory existence, such as the labour of the workforce. The immediate benefit that comes from buying one hour of an employee's time ends at the end of that hour. Similarly, there will be nothing to show for money applied to paying the electricity bill. Note that the labour and the electricity may well have been used to produce the business's product, and any inventory (stock) of that product will have a continuing existence. The distinction we are aiming for, however, is that the labour and the electricity no longer exist as labour and electricity, but as part of the inventory value.

For comparison, some of the things the business applies its funds to will have a continuing existence. We have already seen that one such example could be inventory. Others could be, for example, buildings, vehicles or machinery. Items like this which have a continuing existence in themselves, and are of future benefit to the business, are called assets.

In Chapter 1 we defined assets as things we own and liabilities as things we owe. We can now adopt more accurate definitions, namely:

▶ The essence of an asset is the right to receive future economic benefit as a result of past transactions or events.

▶ A liability is the obligation to transfer economic benefits as a result of past transactions or events.

Both of these definitions are based on definitions in the International Accounting Standards. In Chapter 11 we will look at the significance of these standards and at how they are replacing the UK's own Financial Reporting Standards, but for the moment you only need to be aware that they are very authoritative in the world of financial accounting.

The situation we have arrived at may become clearer if we look at an activity.

Activity 2.2

A new business starts up as a limited company called Sunrise Ltd by raising £10,000 from its owners, i.e. its shareholders. It puts this money into a new bank account. What would be the asset(s) and liability(ies)?

Answer

The asset would be a bank account with £10,000 in it, and the liability would be share capital of £10,000. Remember that the share capital is a liability because it represents money that has been contributed to the company by the shareholders. It is a liability of the company to the owners, that is, the company is distinct from the owners.

Activity 2.3

Sunrise Ltd then uses £6,000 of its bank account to buy a delivery van. List the asset(s) and liability(ies) after this transaction.

Answer

The list should have been fairly easy to construct, i.e.:

Assets:	Delivery van	£6,000
	Bank account	£4,000
Liability:	Share capital	£10,000

What you may not have noticed is that you have just constructed your first statement of financial position. In other words, a statement of financial position is simply a listing of all assets and liabilities. As we saw in Chapter 1, the actual layout of the statement of financial position is presented in a specific, detailed format, especially for limited companies, but its basic nature is no more than you have just done.

Activity 2.4

Finally, Sunrise Ltd buys some inventory for £3,000 but does not yet pay for it. That is, it buys on credit from Daytime Suppliers, agreeing to pay them the £3,000 next month. List the asset(s) and liability(ies) after this transaction.

Answer   Our answer is shown below:

Assets:	Delivery van	£6,000
	Inventory	£3,000
	Bank account	£4,000
Liabilities:	Share capital	£10,000
	Creditor	£3,000

Note one very important matter – the total assets equal the total liabilities. This is not a coincidence, or just a feature of this example. It is inevitable because the liabilities are providing the funds that we are then spending on these assets. This equality is fundamental to all financial accounting, and is often expressed as the balance sheet equation. (We're still using the traditional term for this equation, even though the balance sheet is now more properly known as the statement of financial position.) This equation is usually set out so as to make a distinction between the capital liability and all other liabilities. This is done in order to maintain the distinction we saw earlier between equity and debt. In the case of Sunrise Ltd, for example, the equity is the share capital, while the debt is the creditor. After all, giving us goods with only a promise to pay in return could be thought of as a loan in kind.

The balance sheet equation thus becomes:

ASSETS = CAPITAL + LIABILITIES

Note that the equation can be re-expressed in a number of different ways, including:

CAPITAL = ASSETS – LIABILITIES

Bear in mind that capital can also be referred to as equity – it's one of the slightly confusing cases where accounting jargon can be imprecise, so you need to be aware of the alternatives. It is also worth noting here that this equality forms the basis of double entry bookkeeping, which we will deal with in Chapter 5.

The format of the statement of financial position

We have seen that a statement of financial position is no more than a list of assets and liabilities (including capital) at a particular point in time. However, we have also noted that there is a specific format for the statement of financial position. In the case of limited companies in the UK, this format is specified by law, in the Companies Act, which refers to the accounting standards. The next step in learning to construct a statement of financial position is therefore to apply the standard format to a list of assets and liabilities.

A few days later, on 30 June 20X6, Sunrise Ltd has the following assets and liabilities (the use of dates such as '20X6' is a standard way of expressing a generic date, commonly used in textbooks):

Assets: Delivery van £6,000; Inventory (i.e. stock of goods for sale) £3,000;
                Bank £500; Machinery £2,200; Debtors £700.

Liabilities: Share capital £10,000; Creditors £400; Loan repayable in five
                years £2,000.

The first step is to divide the assets into 'non-current assets' and 'current
assets'. Non-current assets are those where the expected life, i.e. how long
we think the asset will last in our business, is more than one year. (Note
that 'non-current assets' is the term for such assets under the new international accounting standards; they used to be known as 'fixed assets' in the
UK, and many accountants will probably continue to use the latter term
for a while yet.) Current assets are then those that we do not expect to still
have one year from now. This is a rather crude pair of definitions, and we
will see in Chapter 8 that it will not always be valid, but is nevertheless
acceptable for our present purposes.

Activity 2.5   List the non-current assets and subtotal them. Then list the current assets beneath
                the non-current assets, sub-total each group, and add the two subtotals.

Answer   Your answer should look like the one below. There is a number of specific points relat-
                ing to our layout, which are explained below.

Non-current assets		
Machinery		2,200
Delivery van		6,000
		8,200
Current assets		
Inventory	3,000	
Trade receivables	700	
Bank	500	
		4,200
		12,400

Note the following points about the layout above. These are not optional
issues, but matters you must normally comply with.

▶ There are two columns of figures, with the current assets being inset to
   provide for a sub-total for the current assets.

▶ Both the non-current and current assets are listed in reverse order of liquidity. This means that both lists start with the asset that is likely to be
   hardest to turn into cash. We have assumed, for example, that a van is
   easier and quicker to sell than machinery, and that trade receivables are
   more liquid than inventory. The bank account is obviously the most
   liquid asset and therefore comes last in the list of current assets.

▶ There is a subtotal for each group of assets.

▶ The total of all assets is double-underlined to show that the £12,400 is a final total for the first half of the statement.

The next step is to list and add up the equity and the liabilities.

Activity 2.6	Extend your statement of financial position to list the equity (capital) and the liabilities, and then total your figures, and double underline the total.

Answer	Your completed statement of financial position should now look as follows. As before, there is a number of important points relating to the layout, which are explained below.

SUNRISE LTD
STATEMENT OF FINANCIAL POSITION AS AT 30 JUNE 20X6

Non-current assets		
Machinery		2,200
Delivery van		6,000
		8,200
Current assets		
Inventory	3,000	
Trade receivables	700	
Bank	500	
		4,200
		12,400
Share capital		10,000
Non-current liability		
Loan, repayable in five years		2,000
Current liability		
Trade payables		400
		12,400

▶ The completed statement of financial position must be headed by the name of the reporting entity and the date of the statement of financial position. Remember that the statement of financial position only reports the entity's state of affairs at a single moment.

▶ The division of liabilities into current and non-current is done on the same basis as the split of assets into non-current and current. That is, current liabilities are those we expect to have cleared within a year, while non-current liabilities are those we expect to still owe one year from the date of the statement of financial position.

▶ If we subtract the current liabilities from the current assets then the net figure, £3,800 in the example above, is what is known as the working capital of the organisation.

▶ If we subtract the non-current liabilities (£2,000) and the current liabilities (£400) from the total assets (£12,400) it will, of course, equal the share capital or equity (£10,000). This £10,000 can be also be thought of as the net worth, i.e. what the organisation is worth, assuming that the statement of financial position reflects something close to the true values of assets and liabilities.

A few words about non-commercial organisations

All we've said above has assumed that the organisation we're accounting for is commercial, i.e. it is owned by one or more people who aim to make a profit from it. Where this isn't true, for example government authorities, the National Health Service, charities, or social organisations, then the format of the statement of financial position will be a little different.

The first half will often be the same as above, since most organisations will have buildings, bank accounts and other assets, even where the object of their activities is not to make a profit. However, the second half of the statement of financial position will include liabilities as before, but will not include owners' equity but, instead, the stake in the organisation held by government, trustees or members. These people don't own the organisation in the same way that shareholders own a company, but they caretake the funds so that the organisation can provide the services it was set up to provide.

In terms of the format of the statement of financial position, the capital will consist not of 'owners' equity' but of 'funds'. These may be divided into a number of individual funds, depending on the nature and needs of the organisation, but in total will constitute the funding for the net assets listed in the statement of financial position. We'll explore this further in Chapter 8.

What the statement of financial position tells the user

Having now prepared a statement of financial position, it is worth considering what it tells us. In other words, what does a statement of financial position mean? We already know that it provides a list of assets and liabilities at a particular point in time, and you saw above that the total of the statement of financial position represents, in principle, what the entity is worth. Knowing the state of affairs of an entity would obviously be a useful thing to know, but it is not necessarily true that this is what the statement of financial position tells us.

Activity 2.7	Look at the statement of financial position for Sunrise Ltd, on page 22.

1 We have included the delivery van at what we paid for it. List at least two other ways we could have valued it.

2 Note down one reason why the trade receivables may not actually result in a benefit to the business of £700.

Answer

Sorting out alternative valuations of assets, and indeed liabilities, is one of the major difficulties in financial accounting and reporting. As you have seen in the statement of financial position above, the usual practice is to record assets at what the business paid for them. This is known as the historical cost. Nevertheless, alternatives are possible, and you could have listed any or all of the following:

▶ Historical cost less an allowance for using up the asset to date. Such an allowance is called depreciation, and is dealt with in more detail in Chapter 6. This valuation is, of course, still simply a refinement of the historical cost valuation.

▶ Selling price, i.e. what the van could be sold for. This is usually called the realisable value. Normal practice when considering realisable value is to deduct any costs of sale, such as advertising. In this case the net figure is known as the net realisable value, or NRV.

▶ Replacement cost, i.e. the cost of replacing the van if, for example, it were stolen this afternoon. In a perfect market (i.e. one of zero transaction costs, perfect competition and perfect knowledge of the market by all concerned) this should be the same as the realisable value.

▶ A refinement of the replacement cost approach would be to use the cost of replacing the asset, not with another identical one, but with something that will do the same job. This may be particularly relevant in times of rapidly changing technologies, such as computing.

▶ Finally, we could take a more complex view, and say that the van's value is the economic benefit that it will bring to the business. This is in line with the definition of an asset that we looked at earlier in this chapter. Arriving at this valuation will involve estimating the additional net revenues that the business will earn because of its use of the van. Such additional net revenues will be difficult to determine, but might be the profit on the orders that we only got because we were able to deliver directly and quickly to the customer. This is conceptually and practically the most difficult approach to valuation, and we will therefore examine it more thoroughly later in this chapter and in Chapter 13.

As far as the trade receivables are concerned, their statement of financial position valuation will not turn out to be what they are worth if the debtor does not, in fact, pay us. We have, after all, previously defined the essence of an asset as being control of future economic benefit. If there is no payment, we will receive no economic benefit, and the debtor will therefore not turn out to be an asset. It should therefore not be shown as an asset in the statement of financial position, but as an expense in the statement of comprehensive income, usually described as something such as 'Bad Debt Written Off'. We will look at expenses in the statement of comprehensive income in more detail in Chapter 3.

Alternatively, the debtor may only be expected to pay us part of what is owed, perhaps £500 of the total £700. In this latter case it would seem to be sensible, and consistent with the definition of an asset, to value the debtor in the statement of financial position at £500. The remaining £200 would then be written off as an expense.

Valuation in the statement of financial position, especially of assets, is thus a problematic area of financial accounting and reporting. The final part of this chapter therefore considers each of the suggested alternative methods of valuation in the statement of financial position more fully.

The alternative valuation methods

We have seen that the obvious way to value an asset is at what we paid for it, that is, at its historical cost. This is obviously simple and unambiguous as a method. In other words, it has the advantage of objectivity.

Activity 2.8

List at least two disadvantages that you can see with the use of historical cost as a method of valuing an asset.

Answer

The most obvious problem with historical cost is that it will gradually become more and more out of date. It will describe the value of an asset as it was several years ago. This is inappropriate when we have already said that a statement of financial position is supposed to give us a picture of the entity today. Furthermore, the higher the level of inflation then the more inappropriate the historical cost valuation will become, as the difference between today's cost and the historical cost gets wider.

Second, and more subtly, adding together assets in the statement of financial position which were bought at different dates is implicitly adding together items expressed in different £s, since the real value of the £ will fall during times of inflation. The meaning of the aggregate amount is then highly questionable.

If the deficiencies of historical cost stem from the fact that it becomes more and more out of date, perhaps we should use a current method of valuation. One possibility would be to value an asset at what it would cost today, that is its *current cost*. One way of looking at this is to say that we will value each asset at what it would cost if we were to buy it today, as a replacement for the existing asset. This is known as the replacement cost.

Activity 2.9

Which of the following statements about a method of valuing assets are true? Mark each with a T for true, or an F for false.

1 Replacement cost represents a current valuation of what the entity is worth _____
2 Replacement cost is usually simpler to determine than historical cost _____
3 Replacement cost is more objective than historical cost _____
4 Historical cost is the more true and fair valuation _____
5 Historical cost is a more useful method of valuation than replacement cost _____

Answer	Our suggested answer is set out below. Note that some of our answers are debatable, especially the last two. Whether historical cost is the more true and fair valuation or not depends on what we mean by true and fair. There is no agreed definition of this key phrase, which appears in the Companies Act as the over-riding requirement for financial statements in the UK. Nevertheless, we think that replacement cost comes closer to providing a true and fair valuation, if only because it is a better representation of the position at the statement of financial position date.

Similarly, statement 5 depends on your definition of useful – an issue that we looked at in the previous chapter. This is a very contentious statement, and our answer depends on seeing objectivity as a very important quality of accounting. We think it is because it improves the comparability and the understandability of financial accounting, as well as its reliability. We have therefore marked this question as true. However, you could think that the more up-to-date nature of replacement cost makes that valuation method the more useful.

1 Replacement cost represents a current valuation of what the entity is worth   T

2 Replacement cost is usually simpler to determine than historical cost   F

3 Replacement cost is more objective than historical cost   F

4 Historical cost is the more true and fair valuation   F

5 Historical cost is a more useful method of valuation than replacement cost   T

Replacement cost is a current valuation, but it is not the only one. Net realisable value is also a current valuation, one that values an asset at what it could be sold for, rather than at what it could be bought for. You might expect these two valuations to be the same, or certainly very similar. In perfect market circumstances, that is, where all buyers and sellers have the same information and competition is universal, you would be right. However, you should note that buying and selling costs, and imperfections in the market, for example through poor information being available to one party to the deal, will often mean that what we could sell for, net of selling costs, is not the same as what we could buy for.

Furthermore, you should note that using net realisable value could be held to be inappropriate to a business that has no intention of selling one or all of its assets. After all, selling all the assets would probably only be the case if the entity were being wound up. For an entity that is a going concern, replacement cost might be held to be more suitable as a method of valuation, although not all accountants would agree with this view. Going concern is a concept that we will return to in Chapter 4.

Finally, as we noted above, the economic value method is both conceptually and practically the most difficult method, and we will therefore leave a detailed exploration of that method until Chapter 13.

Statement of changes in equity

If we do decide to show a valuation other than the existing historical cost in our statement of financial position then the issue arises of reporting that change. In Chapter 1 we briefly considered the statement of changes in equity, and saw that it is, indeed, largely a summary of any gains and/or losses we may make when the value of our assets and liabilities changes. If we regard those changes as substantial and for the long term, then we could reflect such a change in a change in the valuation of the asset or liability in the statement of financial position. This would be one way to obtain a more up-to-date valuation.

For example, if we decide to reflect a rise in the value of a building from its historical cost of £300,000 to a current valuation of £400,000, then the asset side of the statement of financial position would rise by £100,000 to reflect this, and the capital side must also rise so that the statement of financial position still balances. The rise on the capital side is shown in a 'revaluation reserve' of £100,000, showing that the organisation is now richer by £100,000. This gain is not a trading gain so would not be reported as trading income, but would appear in the 'other comprehensive income' part of the statement of comprehensive income and in the statement of changes in equity, so that the gain is reported as an event of the year. We will look at the preparation of statements of comprehensive income in the next chapter, and at statements of changes in equity in more detail in Chapter 13.

Uncertainty

At this point you may be beginning to feel that there are no clear answers in accounting, and that it is not the straightforward process you thought it was. We know that this may be unsettling, and that you may be asking whether there is any point to accounting when the answer always seems to be 'it depends . . .'. Nevertheless, for better or worse, this is the position of UK accounting.

At anything above a very basic level, accounting is not a mechanistic exercise, because it has to reflect the uncertainties and complexities of the transactions it describes. We have deliberately started this book with a consideration of fundamental questions about the nature and purposes of accounting for two reasons. First, you can only learn to do good accounting if you understand why you are accounting in the way you are. Second, we think that sorting out these issues is one of the more interesting aspects of accounting.

To check your understanding of what we have covered in this chapter you should now attempt the following question. It brings together many of the points from Chapter 1 as well as from this chapter, so you will help yourself if you attempt it seriously. We have provided an answer after the question, but try not to simply read through our answer.

Activity 2.10

Dayspring Ltd undertakes the following activities in its first week of existence:

1 Starts its activities by raising £50,000 from the issue of 50,000 £1 shares, and putting this money into a new bank account.

2 Buys a workshop for £30,000, paying by cheque.

3 Buys two delivery vans for £8,000 each, paying by cheque.

4 Interviews and appoints two employees, to start work next week.

5 Borrows £10,000, agreeing to repay it in one lump sum, with interest, in two years' time. Puts the money into the bank account.

6 Buys machinery for £15,000 on credit from Hartford Supplies.

7 Decides that it does not need two delivery vans, and sells one of them on credit to Sunset Garages for £8,000.

Required

There are three questions for you to deal with:

1 Prepare the statement of financial position at the end of the week. You could do this by preparing successive statements of financial positions after each relevant transaction, but this would be rather clumsy and time-consuming. For a fairly small set of transactions like this, it is probably better, therefore, to simply keep a rough record of the balance of each item. The workshop, for example, starts at £30,000 and then does not change, and so will appear in your statement of financial position at £30,000. The bank account will take more analysis.

You may find it helpful to use the Sunrise Ltd statement of financial position (page 22) as a guide to the correct layout.

2 Justify your treatment of transaction (4).

3 Suggest two groups who would probably be particularly interested in the statement of financial position you have prepared. Briefly note down why each would be interested.

Answer

Our suggested answers are set out below. Make sure that you understand all parts of them before you leave this chapter.

1   **DAYSPRING LTD**

STATEMENT OF FINANCIAL POSITION AT END OF FIRST WEEK

Non-current assets

Workshop		30,000
Machinery		15,000
Delivery van		8,000
		53,000
Current assets		
Trade receivables	8,000	
Bank	14,000	22,000
		75,000
Share capital		50,000
Non-current liability		
Loan, repayable in five years		10,000
Current liability		
Trade payables		15,000
		75,000

2 There is a number of reasons why the appointment of two employees should not be reflected in the statement of financial position. If you have done some accounting before, you may have mentioned the accruals, or matching concept. In terms of what we have covered so far in this book, you could have justified the exclusion of transaction (4) by reference to the definitions of assets and liabilities.

We know that only assets and liabilities (including capital) appear in a statement of financial position. Does the appointment of employees to start next week result in an asset or liability as defined? An employee will normally result in future economic benefit to the business, and will in principle, therefore, be an asset. However, quantifying this benefit with reasonable objectivity will usually be impossible. In these circumstances, an employee should therefore not be recognised as an asset in a statement of financial position.

3 It is possible to make out a case for virtually any user group having some interest in the financial statements of any organisation. However, it is likely that the shareholders and the lender will be particularly interested in the statement of financial position of Dayspring Ltd, since it has substantial sums at stake in the company. Additionally, you could have made out a good case for saying that Hartford Supplies would be especially interested, given that they have effectively lent Dayspring Ltd £15,000.

Summary

This chapter has been about the statement of financial position. We have seen that it is:

► essentially just a listing of assets and liabilities

► in a specified format.

You have also prepared a simple statement of financial position for yourself. However, what ultimately determines the nature and usefulness of the statement of financial position are:

► the definitions of the assets and liabilities (these definitions are worth learning and remembering)

► the different bases on which assets and liabilities can be valued; the usual method – historical cost – is not necessarily the best basis.

In Chapter 3 we continue our review of the basic accounting statements with an exploration of the statement of comprehensive income.

Key terms

sources and applications of funds (p. 17)
assets (p. 18)
liabilities (p. 18)
balance sheet equation (p. 20)
non-current assets (p. 21)

net worth (p. 23)
working capital (p. 23)
alternative methods of valuation (p. 25)
replacement cost (p. 25)
net realisable value (p. 26)

Self-assessment questions

Select the most appropriate answer for each of the following multiple choice questions.

1 Non-current assets are:

   (a) Assets the organisation expects to keep for more than one year.
   (b) Assets worth more than £1m.
   (c) Assets that can't normally be physically moved.
   (d) Assets specified as fixed by the organisation.

2 Liabilities are:

   (a) The capital of an organisation.
   (b) The total of assets and capital.
   (c) The obligation to transfer economic resources.
   (d) The total an organisation would have to pay if it were wound up.

3 The total of a statement of financial position represents:

   (a) What the organisation would sell for if someone took it over.
   (b) The original historical cost of the assets, amended by revaluations.
   (c) The total replacement cost, net of liabilities.
   (d) What the directors believe the organisation should be valued at.

4 The difference between debt and equity is that:

   (a) Debt is what the organisation owes its shareholders and equity is what it owes government.
   (b) Debt is what the organisation owes its lenders and equity is what it owes government.
   (c) Debt is what the organisation owes its lenders and equity is what it owes shareholders.
   (d) Debt is what the organisation owes its shareholders and equity is what it owes lenders.

5 'Working capital' is the difference between:

   (a) Non-current assets and current liabilities.
   (b) Share capital and non-current assets.
   (c) Current assets and current liabilities.
   (d) Non-current liabilities and current assets.

6 'Historical cost valuation' means valuing an asset at:

   (a) What it was worth one year ago.
   (b) What it is worth at the statement of financial position date.
   (c) What it would cost to replace.
   (d) What was paid for it.

7 Mortlake Ltd owned a building that had cost £42,000 just before the end of the current accounting year on 31 December, and a vehicle bought for £13,000 at the same time. A new access road was announced on the statement of financial position date, perhaps making the building worth about £50,000 on the open market. Inventory existing at the statement of financial position date had been bought for £7,000, but had deteriorated in storage and was now valued at £6,000. Trade receivables and trade payables at the statement of financial position date were £4,000 and £5,000 respectively.

You are required to prepare the statement of financial position, including the equity figure as the amount needed to make the statement of financial position balance. For each item where there is a choice of valuation, you should briefly note down why you have chosen the valuation you have.

8 Hammerstein Ltd has a number of assets with the following details. For each asset you are required to state the most true and fair valuation, and to justify your choice. In all cases you should ignore depreciation. (Depreciation is a topic that we will deal with in Chapter 6.)

(a) A building cost £300,000 four years ago. Since then the company has spent £80,000 on an extension to the building and £45,000 on repairs. The current market price of a similar building next door is £400,000.

(b) Two cars were bought last month for use by the company's sales force. The first cost £12,000 and the second £15,000. The first was written off in an accident just after the statement of financial position date and insurance proceeds are expected to be £10,000.

(c) Computing equipment was acquired for £19,000 one year ago. The same equipment is no longer made, but could be bought for about £8,000 on the second-hand market. Equipment that would do much the same job could be bought new and would cost around £15,000.

(d) We have three trade receivables (debtors) at the statement of financial position date. The first owes £2,000 and has always paid on time in full. The second owes £700 and has disappeared. The third owes £800 and has been promising to pay for the last three months, but has so far paid nothing.

9 Prepare the statement of financial position at 31 December 20X9 for Yeovil Electronics, in each of the following situations. The capital is not given, so you should calculate it as being the figure needed to make the statement of financial position balance, in accordance with the balance sheet equation.

(a) First, the accountant has extracted the following balances from the books at 31 December, all balances being at the traditional historical cost valuation.

Premises	345,000
Plant and machinery	104,800
Inventory	67,250
Trade receivables	46,200
Bank overdraft	15,000
Trade payables	56,780
Non-current loan	120,000

Prepare the historical cost statement of financial position.

(b) Second, the managers of Yeovil Electronics are concerned that the historical cost figures do not represent the 'true' worth of the company and are accordingly a poor basis for their decision making. They have therefore estimated the replacement cost of the assets and liabilities. Specifically, the balances that differ significantly from historical cost are:

Premises	480,000
Plant and machinery	95,000
Inventory	61,000
Trade payables	53,600

All other figures may be assumed to be at historical cost. Prepare a replacement cost statement of financial position.

(c) Third, the major lender has expressed a wish to wind up the company, sell the assets, and use the proceeds firstly to repay her loan of £120,000. Her estimates of what the assets would sell for and what the liabilities could be settled for are set out below. Draft a statement of financial position using these net realisable values.

Premises	450,000
Plant and machinery	40,000
Inventory	83,650
Trade receivables	44,000
Bank overdraft	15,000
Trade payables	56,780

(d) Which statement of financial position gives the most true and fair view of the state of affairs of Yeovil Electronics? Justify your decision.

Answers to these questions can be found at the back of this book.

3

The statement of comprehensive income

Objectives

By the end of this chapter you should be able to:

- ▶ List the main trading transactions.
- ▶ Identify major non-trading events that result in gains or losses.
- ▶ Prepare a simple statement of comprehensive income, including the treatment of opening and closing inventory.
- ▶ Account for non-commercial organisations.

Introduction

This chapter introduces the second of the main financial statements typically used in the UK, that is, the statement of comprehensive income, along with the associated statement of changes in equity. The advent of international accounting standards to the UK has resulted in changes in jargon here as well as in the statement of financial position. Specifically, what is from 2009 properly called the statement of comprehensive income used to be called the income statement, and before that was known as the profit and loss account. It's likely that all terms will be used in the UK for the immediate future.

The statement of financial position that we explored in the previous chapter tells us something about the state of affairs at a point in time, usually the last day of the accounting year. The statement of comprehensive income tells us something about what happened during that year. In its simplest form, the statement of comprehensive income is just a list of the revenues and expenses that arose during a particular period. In practice, it can be complicated. This chapter looks first at the basics of statement of comprehensive incomes, and then goes back to pick up some of the complications. In this way you should be able to grasp the essentials without being distracted by the intricacies.

Structure of the statement

The **statement of comprehensive** income has two distinct parts. The first is a summary of the trading results, usually for the past year. This is equivalent to the old income statement or profit and loss account. Indeed, for ease of reference, this part of the statement can still be called the 'income statement'.

The second part is a summary of non-trading gains and losses and this section is entirely new. A common example of the sort of thing that might go in this section could include gains and losses on revaluations of property. We saw in the last chapter that, initially at least, we normally value property at what we paid for it, i.e. at its historical cost. If we later decide to recognise the fact that our property has risen in value since we bought it, then is that a profit? The gain hasn't come from trading, and we haven't even sold the property, so it seems right not to include it with trading gains and losses. On the other hand, the rise in the value of the property has made the business richer and surely we should report that? The new statement of comprehensive income resolves this dilemma by including such gains and losses, but separately from the trading gains. This means that a typical statement of comprehensive income will be structured like this:

Revenues	1,000	Part 1:
Cost	600	'income statement'
Profit from trading	400	
Gain from revaluation of property	*150*	*Part 2:*
Total comprehensive income	*550*	*'Other comprehensive income'*

As we'll see in Chapter 13, gains from revaluations of property aren't the only possible sources of non-trading gains, but they are probably the most common, so we've used them to illustrate the structure. What this structure does is show the profit or loss from trading – £400 in our example above – and then combines that with non-trading gains, to show the total increase in wealth that's arisen in the past year – £550 in the example above.

Finally, note that the rules in International Accounting Standard 1 'Presentation of Financial Statements' allow us to present the two parts of the statement separately, but in this book we'll use the combined presentation above.

Having seen that there are two distinct parts to the statement of comprehensive income, we'll explore the statement in this chapter by looking at each part in turn.

The income statement part

To recap, this part of the statement only reports trading transactions. Furthermore, bear in mind that the statement of comprehensive income as a whole does not tell us about everything that happened during the year. Specifically, it does not tell us about events that cannot be objectively quantified. This exclusion is one that we have already come across in relation to the statement of financial position.

Activity 3.1

Note down at least three specific events that will therefore not usually be included in the first, income statement, part of a statement of comprehensive income.

Answer

There are many examples that you could have chosen, but they should all be either events:

▶ the effect of which cannot be quantified with reasonable certainty, such as the employment of a new manager, or the introduction of a new manufacturing process, or

▶ which do not relate to trading, such as the purchase of an asset, or the issue of new shares (both of these would, however, be reflected in the statement of financial position instead).

So, what does go in the first, income statement part of a statement of comprehensive income? There are three distinct elements to this, and we can deal with each of these elements in turn.

The first section of the income statement part can be called the trading account, and it details the core trading of an organisation. For example, for a supermarket, this would deduct the cost of purchasing the goods sold from the proceeds of the sales, to calculate the profit on trading. This profit is more properly called the 'gross profit'.

Activity 3.2

Mr Tate owns a supermarket, which trades as Lowprice Supermarkets. In June, Lowprice Supermarkets buys goods from its suppliers costing £220,000, and makes sales of £300,000. Prepare the trading account.

Answer

LOWPRICE SUPERMARKETS
TRADING ACCOUNT FOR THE MONTH ENDED 30 JUNE

Sales	300,000
Cost of goods sold	220,000
Gross profit	80,000

You should note that the trading account is headed by the name of the entity, just as the statement of financial position was in the previous chapter. It is also good practice to head the trading account not only with the fact that it is a trading account, but also to specify which period it covers.

It is unlikely, of course, that the supermarket sells all the inventory it has on its shelves. ('Inventory' is accounting jargon for 'stock', introduced by the advent of international accounting standards into the UK in 2005. We'll no doubt continue to talk about 'stock' alongside 'inventory' for a few years yet, but note that 'inventory' is technically the correct term now.) There will almost certainly be a closing inventory of goods left over at the end of the month. This inventory represents goods that have been bought but not sold. If we are to compare the selling price of the goods sold with their cost, then we should deduct the cost of any goods not sold from the purchases' cost. This net amount, which we then deduct from sales to calculate the gross profit, is called the 'cost of goods sold' or the 'cost of sales'. These are both good names, because they accurately describe exactly what this net figure represents, i.e. the cost to Lowprice of the goods it has sold to its customers.

If, for example, the supermarket staff do a stocktake at the end of June – i.e. they physically count it – and find that there are goods left which cost Lowprice £55,000, then the trading account will look like this:

LOWPRICE SUPERMARKETS
TRADING ACCOUNT FOR THE MONTH ENDED 30 JUNE

Sales		300,000
Purchase	220,000	
Less: Closing inventory	55,000	
Cost of sales		165,000
Gross profit		135,000

Notice the technique we used above of insetting a subsidiary calculation into a left-hand column, and carrying the total out into the main, right-hand column.

Before we move on, we should look at how we cope if there was inventory at the beginning of June as well as at the end. If a stocktake at the start of June had shown an **opening inventory** for the month of, say, £48,000, think what must have happened to this inventory. Assuming it was neither lost nor stolen, then this inventory must have been sold during the month. In other words, it is part of the cost of sales for June, and should therefore be added to the purchases in the trading account. True, some of it might still be inventory as part of the £55,000 at the end of the month, but this does not change the fact that what has been sold should be added to the purchases.

Activity 3.3   Use the opening inventory figure of £48,000 to revise the trading account above.

Answer

LOWPRICE SUPERMARKETS
TRADING ACCOUNT FOR THE MONTH ENDED 30 JUNE

Sales		300,000
Opening inventory	48,000	
Add: Purchases	220,000	
	268,000	
Less: Closing inventory	55,000	
Cost of sales		213,000
Gross profit		87,000

In our examples above we have put a double underline under the gross profit to indicate that this is the end of the financial statement. This is correct so long as we are only preparing a trading account. Usually, however, the user of the financial statements will also want information about other expenses, such as insurance, wages, rent and so on. Such information is provided by the second section of the income statement part of the statement of comprehensive income.

Operating costs

The second section of the income statement part of the statement of comprehensive income starts where the trading account left off, that is, with the gross profit. There will then be no need to underline the gross profit, since we will construct what will effectively be a single financial statement. What is therefore happening is that the trading account presents the 'raw' profit on direct trading, and the second section shows what expenses are then paid out of the gross profit. The net result is called the 'net profit'.

Activity 3.4

Assume that the other expenses for June were wages of £32,000, insurance of £4,000, heat and light expenses amounting to £17,000, and telephone costs of £2,000. Draft the income statement part of the statement of comprehensive income for June. (You can use the same insetting technique that we saw above to provide a subtotal of the overhead expenses.)

Answer

LOWPRICE SUPERMARKETS
INCOME STATEMENT FOR THE MONTH ENDED 30 JUNE

Sales		300,000
Opening inventory	48,000	
Add: Purchases	220,000	
	268,000	
Less: Closing inventory	55,000	
Cost of sales		213,000
Gross profit		87,000
Wages	32,000	
Insurance	4,000	
Heat and light	17,000	
Telephone	2,000	
		55,000
Net profit		32,000

As we noted at the beginning of this chapter, this first look at the income statement will avoid complications. We will pick up some of the more important ones later in this chapter, and others in later chapters, particularly in Chapters 7 and 8. Nevertheless, the income statement above is valid for non-company accounting, where the net profit is simply added to the owner's capital account. For limited companies, it only remains to consider what will happen to the £32,000 profit and to report those happenings. Such a report is the third and final section of the income statement part of the statement of comprehensive income. This is traditionally referred to as the appropriation account.

The appropriation account

As the name suggests, the appropriation account details the various appropriations of profit. In simpler language, it lists what has happened to the profit made by the entity in the past year. There are normally only three things that can happen to the profit.

Activity 3.5

Think about who is likely to be entitled to a share of a limited company's profit, and so suggest what these three appropriations will be.

Answer

You may have expressed your ideas in different ways, but your suggestions should have fallen into the following groups:

1 *Tax*. The Revenue, or equivalent authority in other countries, will want the first slice of a limited company's profit. We will look at tax in more detail in Chapter 8.

2 *Owners' share*. In a limited company this share will be in the form of dividends – again we will look at dividends in more detail in Chapter 8. More generically, this slice of profit will more usually be called the distribution.

3 *Retained profit*. By default, this is the amount left over after the other appropriations. In a sole trader or partnership business, this amount will simply be added to the capital of the sole trader or shared out to the capitals of the partners. In a company the procedure is more formal, and the retained profit will be transferred to one or more 'reserves'. Once again, Chapter 8 will examine this transfer in greater detail.

Traditionally each of these three appropriations was subtracted in turn from the net profit. However, current practice under International Accounting Standard 1 'Presentation of Financial Statements' subtracts the tax from net profit to leave the retained profit, but the dividends are seen as what we do with the profit after tax, rather than part of the calculation of profit, so we now show them in a separate statement, the 'Statement of Changes in Equity'. We'll look at this later in this chapter.

The presentation of the appropriation account within the income statement section of the statement of comprehensive income is relatively simple. All we need to do is subtract the tax from the net profit, and we'll worry about the dividends later in the statement of changes in equity.

Activity 3.6

Assume that Lowprice Supermarkets is a limited company. It calculates its tax liability on the profit for June at £11,000. Any retained profit is to be transferred to the company's reserves. Draft the appropriation account for June.

Answer

LOWPRICE SUPERMARKETS LTD
APPROPRIATION ACCOUNT FOR THE MONTH ENDED 30 JUNE

Net profit before tax	32,000
Tax	11,000
Profit after tax	21,000

Statement of changes in equity

We have now seen all the elements of the income statement part of the statement of comprehensive income, but we have still to look at the associated statement of changes in equity. This is simply a summary of why the equity, i.e. the shareholders' stake, has changed during the year. We know from previous studies that equity may rise because we revise the value of our buildings upward. However, in the absence of such capital gains, the change in equity will typically be due to the profit after tax that we've just worked out, less any dividends paid out to the shareholders, so it will look like this:

LOWPRICE SUPERMARKETS LTD
STATEMENT OF CHANGES IN EQUITY FOR THE MONTH ENDED 30 JUNE

Retained earnings at 1 June	10,000
Profit after tax	21,000
Less: Dividends	(8,000)
Retained earnings at 30 June	23,000

We should now have a fair understanding of the income statement, ie the trading, part of the statement of comprehensive income. Our next step is to look at the 'other comprehensive income' part. Before we do this, however, you should try the following activity. It brings together all we have covered in this chapter, and is intended to consolidate your knowledge and understanding of the basics.

Activity 3.7

Suraya Ltd prepares accounts for a calendar year. On 31 December 20X7 the following balances were taken from the company's books, and from a final stocktake:

Sales	296,483
Heat and light	26,730
Insurance	11,978
Wages	36,389
Opening inventory	15,450
Closing inventory	16,070
Purchases	175,962
Dividend	18,400
Rent	6,397
Retained earnings balance at start of period	55,000

The tax liability on the profit for the year was estimated at £7,360. Any retained profit is to be transferred to the company's reserves.

Prepare the statement of comprehensive income and the statement of changes in equity for the year ended 31 December 20X7. The statement of comprehensive income will incorporate the trading, operating costs and appropriation sections, but the whole thing can be entitled simply 'Statement of comprehensive income'.

Answer

Your answer should look like the following. Check your answer against ours, noting not just the numbers, but also the narration in the title and in how each number is labelled. Accounting is about communication, and the words matter.

SURAYA LTD
STATEMENT OF COMPREHENSIVE INCOME
FOR THE YEAR ENDED 31 DECEMBER 20X7

Sales		296,483
Cost of sales:		
Opening inventory	15,450	
Purchases	175,962	
	191,412	
Closing inventory	16,070	
		175,342
Gross profit		121,141
Heat and light	26,730	
Insurance	11,978	
Wages	36,389	
Rent	6,397	
		81,494
Net profit before tax		39,647
Tax		7,360
Profit after tax		32,287

We can now draft the statement of changes in equity.

SURAYA LTD
STATEMENT OF CHANGES IN EQUITY
FOR THE YEAR ENDED 31 DECEMBER 20X7

Retained earnings balance at 31 December 20X6	55,000
Profit for the period	32,287
Less: Dividends	(18,400)
Retained earnings balance at 31 December 20X7	68,887

Other comprehensive income

Having arrived at the net trading profit, the remainder of the statement of comprehensive income is relatively brief. All we need to do is list any gains that come from non-trading sources. There are a few of these, but we'll consider just two:

▶ gains from revaluing non-current assets

▶ gains on holding foreign currency.

We'll look at revaluations of non-current assets in more detail in Chapter 13, but, for now, we can simply add any such gains to the trading profit. Gains and losses on foreign currency are a bit more complex to deal with.

Let's say we place £1,000 on deposit at a bank, but we choose the Paris branch of a French bank. The deposit will presumably be held in euros, so our £1,000 is changed into euros at whatever the exchange rate is at the time, say €1.20 = £1, so €1,200. Note that our asset is then no longer £1,000 (although that's how it's recorded in our books) but €1,200. When we next prepare a statement of financial position we need to include this asset, of course, at its current value. Remember that the asset is now €1,200, so we need to include it at the current sterling equivalent. If the exchange rate is now, say, €1.10 = £1, then the sterling equivalent will be 1,200/1.10 = £1,091. In other words, we've made a gain of £91 simply by holding our money in a foreign currency. This isn't a trading gain so we report it in the 'other comprehensive income' part of the statement of comprehensive income.

Example 3.1

Harper Industries Ltd has calculated its net profit after tax as £200,000. During the year it revalued its non-current assets from £420,000 to £550,000. Finally, it bought an investment in Germany costing £60,000, but which is held in euros. At the date of purchase the exchange rate was €1.25 = £1, but at the accounting year end the rate has moved to €1.20 = £1. We are required to prepare extracts from the statement of comprehensive income.

There are three elements to be reported, namely the trading profit from the income statement part (200,000), the gain on the revaluation of the non-current assets (550,000 − 420,000 = 130,000), and the gain on exchange. Since we spent £60,000 at €1.25 = £1, we must hold 60,000 × 1.25 = €75,000. At the new exchange rate this will be worth 75,000 /1.20 = £62,500, so we've gained £2,500. The relevant extract from the statement of comprehensive income will therefore be:

Example 3.1
continued

Net profit after tax	200,000
Gain on revaluation of non-current asssets	130,000
Gain on exchange	2,500
Total comprehensive income	332,500

The rest of this chapter is now concerned with three refinements which you need to be aware of before we leave the statement of comprehensive income. These are inventory valuation, non-trading organisations, and the particular presentation of statements of comprehensive income for limited companies.

Inventory valuation

We have seen how the purchases figure has to be adjusted by adding on the opening inventory and deducting the closing inventory to arrive at the cost of the sales figure. However, we have not yet given any thought to where the inventory figure came from, other than to say it resulted from a stocktake.

A stocktake involves counting all the inventory items that we hold at a particular time. While this will give us the number of each inventory line we hold, it will not attach a value to that number. Counting the inventory of bags of sugar held by Lowprice Supermarkets at the end of June, for example, will tell us that we have, say, 60 bags in stock, but not what each is worth. There is a number of different bases of inventory valuation that we could use, such as:

▶ *Historical cost*, that is, what Lowprice Supermarkets paid for each bag.

▶ *Replacement cost*, that is, what it would cost Lowprice to buy the inventory again today. This will often be more than the historical cost, especially when prices are rising quickly.

▶ *Net realisable value*, which is what Lowprice could sell each bag of sugar for, less any immediate costs of sale. In these circumstances, this would be the selling price on the shelf, and would normally be more than either cost above.

We shall see in Chapter 13 that there are other bases of valuation, and we will look at the relative merits of each in that chapter. For the moment we can take a pragmatic approach, and all we need to know is what International Accounting Standard 2 (IAS 2) 'Inventories' says. In Chapter 11 we shall examine the nature and purposes of such accounting standards, but note for now that their regulations should be followed when preparing financial statements. IAS 2 specifies that inventory should be valued at 'the lower of cost and net realisable value'.

As with the bags of sugar in Lowprice Supermarkets, the lower of these alternatives will normally be cost. Net realisable value will only be lower in relatively rare cases, such as when the inventory has gone out of fashion, or is close to its sell-by date. In such circumstances the owner might be prepared to sell for less than he or she paid for it, in order to be able to sell it.

However, this is not the end of the matter, because identifying what we paid for the inventory, that is, its historical cost, is not always straightforward. Look, for example, at the following case.

Lowprice Supermarkets had the following transactions in bags of sugar during June:

1st	Bought 300 bags from the supplier for 60p each
14th	Sold 160 bags for 95p each
19th	Bought 100 bags for 65p each
26th	Sold 200 bags for 95p each

If we now try to work out the profit on our trading in sugar, we must follow through the sales transactions. The first sale was of 160 bags at 95p, i.e. £152, and the cost of this sale is clearly 160 bags at the 60p we paid for them, i.e. £96. There was thus a gross profit of £56 on the first sale.

The sales value of the second batch of sales is also fairly easy to calculate, that is, 200 bags at 95p, i.e. £190. However, the cost of these sales is problematic. Have we now sold the remaining 140 bags from those we bought on 1 June, and 60 from those bought on 19 June? If so, the cost of sales will be 140 at 60p plus 60 at 65p, i.e. £123.

One way to decide which batch of purchases is being sold for any given sale is to consider the physical reality. Normal supermarket practice would be to sell the older inventory first, so that they are not left with inventory past its sell-by date. In other words, the first inventory that came in is the first to go out. This method is called 'first in, first out', usually abbreviated to 'FIFO'. In our example above, this is what we did, which resulted in a cost of sales of £123. FIFO is widely used in practice, largely because it does reflect normal inventory rotation practice.

Alternatively, have we sold all the 100 bought on 19 June and thus 100 from those left from the batch bought on 1 June? In this case, the cost of sales will be 100 at 65p plus 100 at 60p, i.e. £125. This is certainly not a large difference from the other calculation of £123, but replicated over all product lines in the supermarket it is clear that we potentially have a significantly different cost of sales figure, and hence a different gross profit reported. Notice that, if we adopt a FIFO approach, any inventory left over is assumed to be from the later delivery.

Some traders, however, do not deal in inventory which has a short sell-by date, but do have inventory which is difficult to handle. An example would be a steel stockholder, dealing in girders, RSJs and so on. When a new delivery arrives from the steel mill, the stockholder is unlikely to move the existing inventory to store the new delivery underneath the old. When he then sells to a customer, he will usually take the steel from the top of the pile, and will thus be selling the newer inventory. In other words, the last inventory that came in is the first to go out. An inventory system that rests on this model is known as 'last in, first out', or 'LIFO'. This is the approach implicitly adopted by the second alternative in our example above, and resulted in a cost of sales of £125.

However, there's a major problem with LIFO, in that IAS 2 'Inventories' does not allow it as a valuation method. Rightly or wrongly, the view taken is that examples such as the steel one above are relatively rare in practice, so as LIFO will not normally reflect practice, it is not permitted. Accordingly, we'll say no more about LIFO.

There is, however, one more possibility for our inventory valuation. Consider the position of a garage that takes a new delivery of petrol into a tank already part full from a previous delivery. When a customer draws off a few litres what she takes will be a mixture of the old and new inventory. Neither FIFO nor LIFO will now be wholly appropriate – what we need is a mixture, to reflect the mixture that has been taken as the cost of sales. This third method is called average cost, abbreviated to AVCO, and calculated as follows.

Suppose customers in Lowprice Supermarkets could help themselves to sugar from the total inventory, and took some of the old delivery and some of the new. The sales on 14 June must have been from the inventory bought on 1 June for 60p, since we had no other inventory at that time. The cost of sales must therefore have been 160 at 60p, i.e. £96 again. However, the sale on 26 June of 200 is now deemed to come partly from the 140 bags remaining from those delivered on 1 June (cost 60p), and partly from the 100 delivered on 19 June (cost 65p). The way to work out the average cost to Lowprice of the bags sold on 26 June is:

140 bags at 60p	=	84
100 bags at 65p	=	65
240		149

The average cost of each bag sold on 26 June must therefore have been 149/240, i.e. 62p. This would then be the AVCO valuation of the remaining inventory of 40 bags, so that the closing inventory under AVCO would be shown in the trading account at 40 times 62p, i.e. £25, to the nearest £.

Activity 3.8

Anne, a trader, had the following dealings during August in her only item of inventory. There was no opening inventory.

1st	Bought 40 for £28 each
5th	Bought 25 for £30 each
10th	Sold 50 for £45 each
21st	Bought 30 for £32 each
27th	Sold 35 for £45 each

Draft the trading account for the month, assuming:

▶ a FIFO basis of inventory valuation

▶ an AVCO basis of inventory valuation.

Answer

We have used a tabular layout for our answer, which we think allows for a better comparison of the methods.

	FIFO		AVCO	
Sales		3,825		3,825
Purchases	2,830		2,830	
Closing inventory	320		309	
Cost of sales		2,510		2,521
Gross profit		1,315		1,304

Notice that the sales and purchases figures do not alter. What gives the different gross profit figure is the different inventory valuation. Under FIFO the remaining ten items are valued at £32, since the earlier inventory has been sold and what is left as the closing inventory is priced at what came in last. Under AVCO, the closing inventory is calculated like this:

Sale on 10 August		
40 at £28	=	1,120
25 at £30	=	750
65		1,870

Cost of sale = $50/65 \times 1,870 = 1,438$
Inventory remaining = $15/65 \times 1,870 = 432$

Sale on 27 August		
15 at average cost, as above	=	432
30 at £32	=	960
45		1,392

Cost of sale = $35/45 \times 1,392 = 1,083$
Inventory remaining = $10/45 \times 1,392 = 309$

We thus have two bases on which we can arrive at a cost for our inventory, and the question that should occur to you is which one is right? As you may be beginning to suspect by now, the answer is that there is no single right choice. It would seem reasonable to choose the method that best reflects our inventory management in practice, using FIFO, for example, where strict inventory rotation is a feature of our business. Many businesses do, in fact, use FIFO. However, it is important to note that many accountants would argue that the accounting treatment need not necessarily reflect the physical reality – certainly, there is no obligation for it to do so, either in law or in any accounting standard. Hence, there is no absolutely correct method, but bear in mind that IAS 2 no longer allows the use of LIFO, as it argues that the inventory value under this method is unlikely to bear a reasonable relationship to actual costs incurred in the period.

Non-commercial organisations

So far in this chapter we have been looking at organisations whose aim is to trade for a profit. While this will be true of the great majority of organisations for whom accounts are prepared, it is not universal. Some organisations exist for more fundamental purposes. Examples are charities, social clubs and religious bodies.

Such organisations will not usually prepare a statement of comprehensive income, because they typically do not trade, and because a financial statement that reports on the profit or loss is inappropriate for bodies that do not aim at a profit. There are two possible alternatives to the statement of comprehensive income for such bodies. These are the 'receipts and payments account' and the 'income and expenditure account'.

The receipts and payments account is, in fact, sometimes also used for reporting the activities of very small trading organisations, but is more often found in non-trading bodies. As the name suggests, it is simply a list of what money has been received and what has been paid out. In other words, at its simplest, it is just a summary of the bank account. There will thus be no inventory adjustment, such as we have just looked at above for the trading account. Nor will there be any of the other adjustments that we will come across in Chapter 6, and which are involved in the preparation of a commercial statement of comprehensive income.

The receipts and payments account for an athletics club might look like this:

MOORTOWN ATHLETICS CLUB
RECEIPTS AND PAYMENTS ACCOUNT
FOR THE MONTH ENDED 31 JANUARY

Subscriptions from members		120
Life memberships		45
		165
Rent of clubhouse	75	
Publicity	10	
Travel	20	
Furnishings	40	
		145
Excess of receipts over payments		20

The 'subscriptions from members' is a typical source of funds for a non-profit-making organisation. It will usually cover the whole of the forthcoming year. 'Life memberships' may be a feature of some clubs. They represent lump sums paid by members which entitle them to life membership without paying any further subscriptions.

Notice also that the payments include a non-current asset, 'furnishings'. Everything, including non-current assets that would normally be shown separately in the statement of financial position, is included in the receipts and payments account.

By contrast, an income and expenditure account is prepared using all the adjustments, such as the inventory adjustment, that are used in preparing the statement of comprehensive income. The difference between the income and expenditure account and the statement of comprehensive income is one of terminology. The former title seems more appropriate than the latter when the statement is reporting on a non-profit-making organisation. In all other respects an income and expenditure account is identical to a statement of comprehensive income.

If, for example, Moortown Athletics Club decides to prepare an income and expenditure account instead of a receipts and payments account, it will use exactly the same techniques that a commercial organisation would use to prepare a statement of comprehensive income. It will therefore need to determine its trade receivables, trade payables and inventory, and to distinguish between capital and revenue items.

Activity 3.9

Suppose that the subscriptions from members of the Moortown Athletics Club (see above) are for the year to 31 December, but were all received in January, and that the rent of the clubhouse was paid in January for the first three months of the calendar year. There is a stock of publicity materials left at the end of January valued at £5. Amend the receipts and payments account above to turn it into an income and expenditure account. To do this, you will need to adjust the cash flows by the amounts outstanding in order to arrive at the amount that relates to January alone. Life memberships are awkward because they relate to an uncertain future period, i.e. the lives of the relevant members. It will therefore often be regarded as acceptable for the club to account for these wholly in the period when they are received.

You may find this a difficult activity, but, as always, do try it before you look at the answer.

Answer

MOORTOWN ATHLETICS CLUB
INCOME AND EXPENDITURE ACCOUNT
FOR THE MONTH ENDED 31 JANUARY

Subscriptions from members (£120/12 months)		10
Life memberships		45
		55
Rent of clubhouse (75/3 months)	25	
Publicity (10 − 5)	5	
Travel	20	
Furnishings	40	
		90
Excess of expenditure over income		35

Our answer above includes calculations of the adjustments we have made. Make sure you at least understand the answer before you move on. Notice that the cash surplus reported by the receipts and payments account indicated a positive view of the club's finances, but the income and expenditure account gives a very different view of its financial health. This is primarily because the income and expenditure account allows for the fact that the subscriptions received in January will have to last the club for the whole year.

Limited companies

This is a topic that we will deal with in more detail in Chapter 8. However, if you have seen any statement of comprehensive income published by limited companies, you may have noticed that they do not look exactly like the one you prepared for Lowprice Supermarkets. This is because the Companies Act, in conjunction with the international accounting standards, specifies a more aggregated layout, where the expenses are grouped, not by 'purpose' as we have done (cost of sales, heat and light, insurance, wages, rent), but by 'function'. The three broad functional areas that are specified are:

▶ cost of sales

▶ selling and distribution expenses

▶ administration expenses.

There are other changes, as we will see in Chapter 8, but this regrouping of expenses is perhaps the most striking. For now, all you need to be aware of is the different presentation of the statement of comprehensive income imposed by the law. Note that it is purely a matter of different presentation – the final net profit will be exactly the same, whichever method of presentation is used.

Information technology and accounting

Before we leave the statement of comprehensive income and the statement of financial position that we considered in the previous chapter, it is worth briefly looking at the role of information technology in all this accounting. It is a topic that we will return to in more detail in Chapter 15, but has become so central to accounting that we should introduce it before moving on.

All the accounting that you have done in the past couple of chapters has been manual, that is, you used pen and paper to keep track of changes to the bank account, summarise the expenses in the statement of comprehensive income, and so on. In practice much or all of this work tends to be done using computers. This should not be surprising given that you have seen that accounting is largely concerned with recording and summarising routine transactions. Since computers are good at dealing with large numbers of well-defined routine events, accounting has used computers since the earliest days of information technology.

Recording the purchase of inventory for £3,000 on credit from Daytime Suppliers, as Sunrise Ltd did in Chapter 1, for example, would be a very typical transaction. In a manual system, we would record the asset as inventory and also record our liability towards Daytime. This implies two entries, and we may forget one, or enter one twice, or enter both but for the wrong amount. In Chapter 5 we will look at how this works in more detail and at how we can control for such errors, but for now note that the possibility of such errors is inherent in manual systems. If uncorrected, the inventory and/or the creditor figure that we report in the statement of financial position would be wrong.

In a computer-based system the entry of the inventory purchase will require us also to record the liability towards Daytime. In other words, the software will not let us record the transaction at all unless we record both aspects for the same amount. This is not fool-proof – we could record both the inventory and the liability at £300 instead of £3,000, for example, but it is an improvement.

Perhaps more importantly, information technology is able to sort and extract the information we want from very large amounts of data extremely quickly. This means that more, and more flexible, information can be extracted from the data that we already hold.

These are all issues that we will return to in Chapter 15. For now, all you need be aware of is that accounting usually relies heavily on information technology, even though the exercises in this book inevitably require you to use a manual approach.

*A*ctivity 3.10	List three advantages for a business having its accounting carried out using information technology. (There are a couple inherent in what we have said above, but try to come up with at least one other for yourself.)
Answer	1 Accounting software can impose a certain amount of control on the accuracy and completeness of our accounting. 2 Information can be extracted both more quickly and in a wider variety of formats than would usually be possible with a manual system. 3 Computer-based systems can reduce the overall level of understanding of accounting required by staff, and so reduce training costs. 4 Business partners, including our auditors, expect to be able to exchange data with us so that, for example, they can place orders with us through the internet.

Summary

This chapter has introduced you to what is usually just called the statement of comprehensive income. You have seen that it is actually made up of two parts, that is:

▶ an income statement reporting trading results

▶ other comprehensive income, which reports non-trading results, such as gains from revaluations of non-current assets.

In turn, we broke the income statement down into three elements, namely:

▶ the trading account
▶ the operating costs account
▶ the appropriation account.

Each of these parts has been examined in turn, and you have now covered the essentials of financial reporting, specifically:

▶ a simple statement of comprehensive income, including an inventory adjustment
▶ a simple statement of financial position in the previous chapter
▶ some of the problems surrounding the question of how to value inventory, distinguishing between, and calculating, the FIFO, LIFO and AVCO bases.

One of the points that has hopefully struck you is that each of these inventory valuation bases results in a different profit figure. Furthermore, we saw in Chapter 2 that there is a number of different ways to value assets, and each results in a different statement of financial position being reported. There is obviously a problem looming here, which is the range of possible accounting results from given data. Before looking at any more of the techniques of accounting, we will therefore look in some detail at what theory of accounting has been developed to help us tackle this problem. The next chapter is therefore concerned with the concepts and characteristics of accounting.

Key terms

statement of comprehensive income (p. 34)
trading account (p. 35)
closing inventory (p. 35)
opening inventory (p. 36)
appropriation account (p. 38)

statement of changes in equity (p. 39)
inventory valuation (p. 42)
receipts and payments account (p. 46)
income and expenditure account (p. 47)
information technology (p. 48)

Self-assessment questions

1 The following details relate to the trading activities of Anarkhi Ltd for its first year of trading, to 30 June:

Purchases	531,946
Sales	794,062
Wages	218,470
Transport	54,475
Rent and insurance	30,775
Tax	3,900

All purchases may be considered as part of cost of sales. All other costs should be allocated 40% to cost of sales, 40% to selling and distribution expenses, and 20% to administration expenses.

Anarkhi Ltd uses the FIFO method of inventory valuation. On 23 June there was no trading inventory. During the last week of the year, inventory transactions were:

5,000 units delivered at £12 each
2,000 units delivered at £13 each
3,000 units sold at £19 each

You are required to draft the statement of comprehensive income for the year, adopting the Companies Act format as far as possible. You will need to calculate the value of the closing inventory and to allocate the expenses as listed above to their Companies Act categories before you can construct the statement of comprehensive income.

2 This question requires you to prepare an statement of comprehensive income, but then also brings in the preparation of the associated statement of financial position. In this way it aims to integrate your study of Chapters 2 and 3. Note that any retained profit you calculate in the statement of comprehensive income should appear in the statement of financial position as 'Reserves', included immediately after share capital.

Use the following balances of Tayside Glass Ltd to prepare an statement of comprehensive income for its first year of trading, which ended on 31 March 20X9 and the associated statement of financial position at that date. You will first need to identify which items relate to the statement of comprehensive income and which to the statement of financial position.

Sales	80,007
Purchases	62,419
Trade receivables	1,215
Trade payables	1,630
Rent	4,600
Telephone	627
Delivery van	4,000
Wages	9,650
Share capital	10,000
Light and heat	1,629
Office expenses	1,127
Bank – positive balance	370
Shop fittings	6,000

There was no opening inventory, since this was the first year of trading. The closing inventory was valued at £4,200.

3 Marsden Computing buys end-of-range computers and sells them to the general public at monthly auctions. Its transactions for the past three months have been as follows (on 1 January it held 20 computers which had cost £550 each):

January   Bought 300 computers at £550 each and sold 260 for £700 each
February Bought 240 computers at £650 each and sold 280 for £700 each
March   Bought 300 computers at £600 each and sold 290 for £680 each.

Prepare the trading account for the three-month period, assuming

(a) a FIFO inventory valuation method

(b) an AVCO inventory valuation method.

4 Hambleton Players is a cricket club which exists primarily to play cricket but incidentally carries out some fund-raising activities. As accountant for the club, outline the arguments for producing a receipts and payments account, compared with the arguments for preparing an statement of comprehensive income, to report the activities of the club for the past year.

Answers to these questions can be found at the back of this book.

4

Concepts and characteristics

Objectives

By the end of this chapter you should be able to:

▶ Outline the generally accepted concepts and conventions of financial accounting.

▶ Explain the four major characteristics of financial reporting.

Introduction

At this stage, it is worth taking stock of where we have got to. Chapter 1 explored the nature and uses of accounting, and then Chapters 2 and 3 looked at the two major statements conventionally used in financial accounting, that is, the statement of financial position (previously known as the balance sheet) and the statement of comprehensive income. One of the points that should have struck you is that accounting is far from being the exact science many people believe it to be.

In particular, we have already seen how both the statement of financial position and the statement of comprehensive income can vary according to the basic assumptions we make about how and what we should measure. For example, statements of financial position would look very different if all companies did what some football clubs currently do, and showed the value of their employees – the players, valued at their transfer fees – on the statement of financial position. Again, we saw in the previous chapter that the gross profit will vary if we change our assumptions about inventory rotation, and use FIFO instead of AVCO as a basis of inventory valuation. As you will see as we work through this book, there are many other examples.

What we seem to have in accounting is a situation where the statement of financial position and the statement of comprehensive income, taken together, present a different picture of the state of affairs and the performance of an entity, respectively, depending on what fundamental assumptions we make. In other words, the economic health of an entity can apparently vary not only with the reality of economic changes, but also with how we choose to account for that reality. How, then, can any user place any reliance on the financial statements?

The approach that accountants in many countries, including the UK, have chosen as their way forward is a two-stage technique:

▶ to agree on explicit underlying assumptions, and then

▶ to develop accounting practices that are consistent with those generally accepted assumptions, and hence lead towards 'a true and fair view'.

We have come to accept this approach in the UK as being so obviously correct that it can be hard to think of any alternative. However, it is instructive to look at what, say, the French approach has been. The French approach is to specify in great detail exactly what sort of transactions go under each heading or account, and then to further specify how those accounts shall be presented. The set of rules that specify these headings and presentations is known as the *plan comptable* – the plan of accounts. There is thus, for example, no choice about whether to use FIFO or AVCO, since the single, 'correct' method is laid down in the *plan comptable*.

The French equivalent of the UK idea of a true and fair view is the *image fidèle*. A rough translation would be 'faithful picture', and it is notable that the French first specified the 'plan', as the way to produce accounts, and only subsequently imposed the aim of an *image fidèle*. In other words, the attainment of an *image fidèle* is not central to French accounting in the same way as the attainment of 'a true and fair view' is central to UK accounting.

Activity 4.1

Complete the following table, by making at least one entry under each heading. You may find it helpful to think in terms of the relative disadvantages of the UK system, rather than of the relative advantages of the French system. You will be addressing much the same issues.

	UK approach	French approach
Relative advantages		

Answer

Any answers to this activity will be a matter of debate, but our views are that the UK approach has advantages in terms of relevance. By allowing some choice of method, it can be argued that UK accounts can be prepared according to methods which are geared to the particular needs of the entity, rather than being geared to a mythical 'national average' entity. Furthermore, it may be that the need to consider the most appropriate treatment of a given accounting issue, rather than to simply follow the specified treatment, results in a more lively and participative accounting profession.

On the other hand, the French approach does have the key benefit of consistency. All entities will, in principle at least, treat the same item in the same way, so improving comparability between the accounts of different entities. In addition, the prescription of practice should result in less debate and therefore in faster preparation, and faster will mean cheaper.

You may have had your own, equally valid, ideas. We hope so, because, as you have just seen, accounting in the UK is ultimately determined by some minimum agreement on fundamental underlying assumptions. If you have no ideas then you can't engage in this fundamental debate. The rest of this chapter presents the current state of the more important parts of this debate. It is divided into two main sections. The first part, concepts, covers fairly well-established ideas. The second part, characteristics, deals with more recently developed thinking about what makes a set of financial statements 'good' – whatever that means.

Concepts and policies

To reiterate, concepts are the underlying ideas of accounting. They have usually been implicit and understood as a common culture of accounting, rather than being made explicit, even though we have seen above how important they are. Given that such underlying theoretical principles can radically change the view the financial statements give of an entity, it should be obvious that preparers and users of those statements should be very clear about the particular principles that have been applied to any given set of statements. Requiring such an explicit declaration of the accounting practices they result in for a given entity is a large part of the purposes of International Accounting Standard 8 (IAS 8), 'Accounting Policies, Changes in Accounting Estimates and Errors'.

We will consider the nature and authority of accounting standards in more detail in Chapter 11, but for the moment you need only be aware that they are generally held to be effectively mandatory in almost all cases. At the heart of IAS 8 is the assumption that all financial statements will be consistent with a few basic, specified principles, known as the concepts. Linked to this, International Accounting Standard 1 (IAS 1) 'Presentation of Financial Statements' highlights two concepts, going concern and accruals, as being pervasive. In other words, these two ideas are held to be so important that they should underpin all accounting.

You should note that this is a change from the UK position before 2001, when the standard in force was SSAP 2 'Disclosure of accounting policies', which specified four basic concepts, namely going concern and accruals again, but also consistency and prudence. What has happened to the latter two is an instructive story, and one that we will consider later in this chapter.

IAS 8 is concerned that the accounting policies it uses should be both explicitly stated and appropriate for the organisation to achieve a true and fair view. Policies are defined as 'the specific principles, bases, conventions, rules and practices applied by an entity in preparing and presenting financial statements'. Put simply, policies are how an organisation chooses to account for transactions and events given the range of different methods available to it. We have already seen that an organisation has some choice in how it accounts for inventory, for example. However, this is not an entirely free choice, since IAS 8 requires that the accounting an organisation chooses should be based on a few basic policies, principally, as we have seen, going concern and accruals, but also realisation. It is therefore time to turn our attention to a more detailed consideration of the ideas of accounting.

Going concern

There is an assumption that the business will continue to operate for the foreseeable future. The application of this policy could make a difference, for example when we consider asset valuations. We have seen that the usual basis is historical cost, but if the entity is no longer a going concern and will be wound up, it is arguably more appropriate to value the assets at selling price, since they will soon be sold.

Accruals (or matching)

When preparing the statement of comprehensive income, revenue and profits are matched with the associated costs and expenses incurred in earning them (known as accruals or matching). This means that revenues and expenses are recognised when they are incurred, rather than when the related cash is received or paid. A sale will thus be accounted for when the contract is agreed, and not when the goods or services are paid for.

Realisation

Realisation is an idea that we touched upon in Chapter 3 when we explored the two parts of the statement of comprehensive income. We saw then that one of the critical differences is that the first, trading, part of the statement of comprehensive income deals only with transactions that are realised; that is, ones where the money has changed hands, or is almost certain to do so in the near future, whereas the second 'other comprehensive income' part deals with unrealised transactions. This is an increasingly important issue in accounting, and we will return to it later in this chapter under 'Revenue recognition'.

The characteristics of good accounting

The question which then arises is how do we select and apply these policies in practice? If there is a range of possible accounting policies, how can we judge which represent good accounting? Certainly, the policies we choose should be in line with the three concepts above, but that could still leave us with a range of possible policies from which to choose. In other words, what are the characteristics of good accounting? This question is dealt with in the 'Framework for the Preparation and Presentation of Financial Statements', which specifies four such characteristics, namely relevance, reliability, comparability and understandability. We'll explore the nature and authority of this 'Framework' later in the chapter and in more detail in Chapter 11; for now simply note that it is a formal codification, by the International Accounting Standards Board, of the ideas we've been discussing in this chapter.

Briefly, relevance asserts that good financial information is information which is relevant to helping users to make decisions about the organisation being reported on. Reliability is essentially a matter of freedom from bias and material error. Comparability simply means that accounting policies should normally be the same from one year to the next, and ideally also between organisations, so that comparisons aren't distorted by different methods of accounting. Finally, understandability makes the seemingly obvious point that financial information should be understandable by users. However, we shall see when we look at the Framework that it isn't always that simple.

Activity 4.2

In the list below, two definitions are given. Identify which definition relates to which two of the three policies we explored above, i.e. accruals, going concern and realisation.

A The non-cash effects of transactions and other events to be reflected, as far as is possible, in the financial statements for the accounting period in which they occur.

B The information provided by financial statements is usually most relevant if prepared on the hypothesis that the entity is to continue in operational existence for the foreseeable future.

Answer

The correct answer is that A is an extract from the definition of accruals, and B from that for going concern.

In addition to the well-established ideas outlined above, there is also a number of implicit ideas that are generally accepted. You will find that these are referred to both in books and, less commonly, in practice, so it is worth being aware of them.

Consistency concept

There should be consistency of treatment of like items within each accounting period and from one period to the next. In other words, once you have chosen an accounting treatment, you should stick with it from one year to the next. The key reason for this is to promote comparability, which we identified above as a key characteristic. That is, it helps the user to make comparisons over time, and so to pick out useful trends. Having decided, for example, to value our buildings at historical cost, rather than at, say, replacement cost, consistency requires that we will normally continue to adopt historical cost for the buildings.

Prudence concept

In the UK tradition of accounting, prudence was regarded as one of the major ideas. In recent years it has been significantly downgraded, so that it is now simply one approach to help achieve the characteristic of reliability.

When we have to choose between two or more accounting treatments of an economic event, prudence dictates that we should always aim to show a treatment free from bias and/or the result we would like to present. The logic is that explicitly avoiding overstatement under conditions of uncertainty results in more reliable accounting. For example, we saw in Chapter 3 that inventory is valued at the lower of cost and net realisable value, rather than at the normal selling price. The justification for this lower valuation has been the prudence concept. Note that prudence doesn't mean erring on the low side, but it does mean not erring on the high side.

Separate valuation

This concept is best explained by an example:

> Assume that A has sold goods on credit to B worth £600, so that, in A's books, B shows up as a trade receivable for £600. Meanwhile, B has sold goods on credit to A for £400. In A's books, B also therefore appears as a trade payable for £400. No agreement has been made about setting off one amount against another. What should we show in A's statement of financial position in relation to B?

You could argue that we should simply show the net trade receivable of £200 as a current asset. However, there is a counter-argument that holds that showing just the net trade receivable does not give a full picture of the total situation, and thus does not give a true and fair view. After all, in the absence of an explicit agreement between A and B to legally set off the £400 against the £600, the position is that B must pay the full £600. This being so, the correct presentation in A's statement of financial position would be to show a trade receivable of £600 and a trade payable of £400. In other words, the trade receivable and the trade payable should be separately valued, and disclosed as such.

Business entity

We have come across this concept already, in relation to capital in the statement of financial position. The business has an identity and existence distinct from the owners, so that the business can and should record an amount owing to its owner, i.e. the capital. Transactions of a business are recorded as they affect the business, not as they affect the owner.

Duality

Again, we have already seen this concept in action, when we looked at sources and applications of funds in Chapter 2. In relation to any one economic event, two aspects are recorded in the accounts, that is, the source of funds and the related applications. The balance sheet equation is an application of the duality concept. In Chapter 5 we will see that it also underpins double entry bookkeeping.

Monetary measurement

Only those events and situations that can be reasonably objectively measured in money terms are recorded. This means, for example, that 'happy and skilled workforce' is not an asset that you will see on a statement of financial position, even though most managements routinely say that their workforce is the company's greatest asset, and it may even be true. It does not appear because the value of this asset cannot normally be objectively quantified.

Objectivity

This concept is obviously closely linked to money measurement. More generally, however, and more formally, it is a required attribute of accounting that competent individuals working independently should arrive at the same or very similar measures of given economic events or situations.

Historical cost

The usual method of arriving at an objectively agreeable quantification of an event is to value it at what the item in question cost. This is known as its historical cost. It has the huge advantage over any other system of being simple and relatively objective, but we will see in Chapter 13 that it has its own problems, especially in times of significant inflation.

Materiality

A small mistake in the financial statements of an entity will not invalidate those statements. They should still be usable by anyone interested in the entity. However, the key issue is obviously what we mean by 'small'. The concept of materiality applies the test of whether the financial statements still show a true and fair view, and are still of use to users. If the answer is yes, then the error is not material, and we need not spend time and resources trying to find and correct it. If, on the other hand, the mis-statement, or even the total omission, of an item would result in the financial statements as a whole not showing a true and fair view, then that item would be regarded as material. Such an error would have to be corrected if the statements are to comply with the Companies Act 2006 and show a true and fair view.

The materiality of an item is related to the size of the entity. The omission or mis-statement of a £10,000 item would probably not be material in the financial statements of Tesco, but would almost certainly be very material in the financial statements of a one-person business. Note that materiality can be measured against size, as suggested above, but occasionally it may be more appropriate to measure it against profits. If, for example, the profits of Tesco were only £20,000, then a £10,000 item could, perhaps, be considered material.

Activity 4.3 Sam and Louise had £800, out of which they purchased a second-hand van for £500. All their other assets are to be ignored. They estimated that the van will have a life of about another 20,000 miles. Sam and Louise started a light removals business, but were involved in an accident on their first day, and damaged a bicycle. Sam promised to pay for the damage and the rider said he thought the bike could be repaired for between £60 and £100.

▶

At the end of their first day, Sam and Louise were offered £600 for the van. They were also paid £50 cash for a job they did in the morning and £70 for the afternoon's job, payable next week. During the day, they had travelled 50 miles.

List Sam and Louise's assets and liabilities at the start and end of the first day and hence say how much better, or worse, off they are since they started. More importantly, in doing so, clearly indicate which accounting ideas justify your calculations.

This is an important activity, drawing together much of what we have covered so far in this book, so try to do it, and do it conscientiously.

Answer

Given that the ideas involved in any answer to this question are so open ended, what follows should not be regarded as the definitive answer, but rather as a reasonable response that covers all the main points that should be made.

		Relevant ideas
Opening position		
Asset		
Cash	800	Money measurement
Liability		
Capital	800	Business entity
Closing position		
Assets		
Van	500	Historical cost, materiality, reliability, prudence
Trade receivables	70	Accruals
Cash	350	Money measurement
	920	
Liabilities		
Owing for bicycle	100	Accruals, reliability
	820	
Capital		
Opening position	800	Business entity
Increase in wealth	20	Going concern
	820	

What our answer sets out is both the opening and closing statement of financial positions. Notice how the increase in wealth has been calculated by determining the difference between the opening capital position and what the net result of the assets and liabilities tells us must be the closing value of the business. Another way to view this increase in wealth is as the net income for the period. In other words, what we have done above is to calculate the net profit without preparing a statement of comprehensive income. We do not have the detail about revenues and expenses that the statement of comprehensive income provides, but it is an alternative way to calculate profit. This is an idea that we will return to in Chapter 13.

In terms of the concepts that we have listed above, there is a number of points to be made. First, both the opening and the closing cash positions depend on their validity as measures of wealth on the basic assumption that we can measure anything by attaching a number of £s to it. In other words, the whole exercise rests on the money measurement concept.

Second, the valuation of the van is more of a problem. The usual basis would be to value it according to what we paid for it, i.e. at its historical cost, but there are other possibilities. We could, for example, decide that a more relevant and useful valuation would be what we were offered for it, that is, £600. Would this value be any less logical or reasonable than using the old cost? If not, the implication is that the conventional choice of historical cost is at least partly arbitrary. If, on the other hand, the choice of historical cost is more logical and reasonable than any other, we should be explicit about why we believe this. As we saw before, a major advantage of historical cost is its relative objectivity, and the inherent prudence arguably enhances the reliability of the measurement.

Third, this is not the only issue in relation to the valuation of the van, there is also the question of depreciation. This a topic that we will cover in more detail in Chapter 6, but note that if the van is going to be of benefit for 20,000 miles, the accruals concept would suggest that we should allocate some of the cost of £500 against the day's profits. The question of how much benefit can be answered by saying that we have presumably had 50/20,000ths of the benefit, since we have travelled 50 miles out of a total usable mileage of 20,000. Using the historical cost value of £500, this works out to a depreciation charge for the period of £1.25, which hardly seems worth bothering with. In more formal terms, we can invoke the convention of materiality to justify ignoring any charge for the using up of the value of the van, at least for one day.

Fourth, accruals and realisation could be used to justify the inclusion of the amount due for the afternoon's work, that is, the trade receivable of £70.

Fifth, the adoption of prudence would guide our valuation of the trade payable, since showing £100 as being outstanding is a more reliable treatment than only showing £60. Showing £60 would result in a lower total for liabilities and would arguably therefore be an overstatement of our position, contrary to prudence. Further, the amount has not yet been paid, but we conventionally allow for it since it relates to this accounting period. The formal justification for making such allowances is, of course, the accruals concept.

Sixth and finally, the net effect of applying all these concepts and conventions to the opening and closing valuations of Sam and Louise's business is to report an increase in wealth of £20. Unless they withdraw this profit, it will be carried forward to finance their business in future periods. The implication is that we are assuming that the business is a going concern.

This has been a discursive answer to a fairly short activity. However, we have been concerned to demonstrate how even simple accounting practice rests explicitly on fundamental assumptions, usually known as the concepts or principles, or just the ideas, of accounting. If we change the ideas, we will get different accounting. To look in more detail at how the ideas work through into practical accounting, we need to consider estimation and measurement bases.

Accounting estimation and measurement bases

In the conventional understanding of the conceptual framework, estimation builds on the policies, and measurement bases then build on the estimation. Estimation is concerned with how the policies can be applied to economic transactions and events in order to attach a number of £s to an accounting item. For example, the accounting policy of accruals applied to inventory implies that we should allow for opening and closing inventory in the calculation of gross profit. However, this still leaves the question of how to value that inventory, and estimation is the particular method that we select. As we saw in the previous chapter this could be FIFO or AVCO, and our particular choice is then our estimation technique.

To continue the example, we have decided to apply the policy of accruals and so chosen to allow for inventory in the profit calculation, and have further chosen, say, FIFO as the estimation technique for inventory. There remains just one final step before we have an amount to enter into the statement of comprehensive income for the inventory adjustment, and that is to measure the value on our FIFO basis. The final step is thus to select the measurement basis.

We already know that there are alternative measurement basis such as historical cost, replacement cost and net realisable value. We choose one of these, and then stick with it to provide consistency and hence comparability, and this choice is our measurement basis.

Accounting practice is thus determined by the policies the entity chooses. If it had chosen different policies then the practices would have been different, and the statement of comprehensive income and statement of financial position would present a different view of the entity. If users are to be able to make allowances for differing policies between entities they are looking at, then they must at least know what the policies are. Finally, therefore, IAS 8 requires that the accounting policies and associated estimation techniques should be disclosed as a note to the financial statements. If we change the estimation basis then the figures will change, of course, so IAS 8 also requires explicit disclosure of any such change.

Revenue recognition

This is a topic that we have touched on earlier, especially in relation to the realisation concept. That introduced the idea that we should only take account of revenues and expenses when the associated cash flow has happened, or at least become reasonably certain. However, this is not always easy to apply in practice and the idea has recently been developed into the broader area of revenue recognition.

There has been an international accounting standard, IAS 18 'Revenue Recognition', in the area for a number of years. The standard starts with a consideration of what we mean by revenue, and asserts that it is an inflow of economic benefits arising from ordinary activities. This seems like an obvious definition, but note two points about it. First, the reference to economic benefits is an echo of the definition of an asset, that is, the revenue associated with it is what makes an asset worth something. Second, revenue only arises from ordinary activities, so selling a major asset, for example, is not revenue.

This leads on to the next major issue which is how we measure the amount of the revenue. The approach adopted is to take the fair value of the consideration received. In other words, the value of revenue is not the value to us of what we gave up, but the value of what we received from our customer.

So far this all appears to be fairly obvious and you may be wondering why we need an accounting standard on such a simple topic. However, the recognition and measurement of revenue is not always so simple. For example, consider the following activity.

*A*ctivity 4.4

Markham Publishing plc sells books to bookshops worth £200,000 just before the accounting year end. The agreement is that any book not sold may be returned to the publisher. None are returned in this accounting year, but past experience is that about 10% will be returned next year. The right of return expires after two years. Is the revenue to be entered in this year's Markham statement of comprehensive income £200,000 or £180,000 or something else?

Answer

The approach adopted by the standard setters is that one of two accounting policies will be appropriate, depending on the circumstances. (The fact that there is no right way to deal with this situation is an indication that revenue recognition is not as simple a topic as it first appears.) One policy would be to recognise £180,000, being the books sold that are likely to stay sold, that is, to allow for returns as best we can given the inherent uncertainty.

The other policy put forward by the standard setters is to only recognise the sale after the possibility of any returns has expired. This would imply not recognising any revenue until two years have passed. This latter approach might be considered inappropriate in the circumstances, and the decision about which policy to adopt would rest on a consideration of the policies and characteristics set out in IAS 8 and which we explored earlier in this chapter. Ultimately, we would have to decide, as always, which of the alternatives produces the most true and fair view. In other words, there's no single correct answer, and we would have to assess how sure we are of our estimate that about 10% of books will be returned. Only if we have evidence from prior experience that our estimate is sound should we account for sales of £180,000. If we have little idea of returns then it would probably be best not to recognise any revenue until the situation becomes more certain, presumably next year.

A true and fair view

As a final element in our survey of the ideas of accounting we should consider a true and fair view. This phrase comes from the Companies Act, and is the over-riding legal requirement for financial statements in the UK, that is, they must show a 'true and fair view'. The phrase is not then defined in the Act so is implicitly left to accountants to define in practice. It is held to be achieved primarily through adherence to the accounting standards, which implies that the ideas we have considered in this chapter do have legal impact.

The 'Framework'

To give it its full title the 'Framework' is properly called The Framework for the Preparation and Presentation of Financial Statements. We introduced it earlier in this chapter, where we noted that it is a codification of many of the ideas of accounting that we've been considering. It can be seen as the International Accounting Standard Board's attempt at a conceptual framework for accounting. Alternatively, we could regard it as a standard for setting standards, in that it provides guidance on what constitutes good accounting.

It is divided into a number of sections, each dealing with a specific theoretical topic. The next page or so explores each of these sections in some detail.

First, the Framework deals with who are the users of financial information. This is a topic that we considered back in Chapter 1, so we needn't consider it again here. Second, the Framework goes on to address the question of why we do accounting. Again, this is something we explored back in Chapter 1, where we decided that it's primarily 'decision usefulness' – the main purpose of accounting is to help users make decisions about the organisation.

The Framework then goes on to consider the characteristics of good accounting. We've already touched on these, but they're such an important issue that we'll leave them for now and explore them as a separate topic later in this chapter, under the 'Characteristics' heading.

The next part of the Framework identifies and defines the basic building blocks of financial accounting. These are identified as being assets, liabilities, equity, gains and losses, and contributions from, and distributions to, owners. These classifications will be familiar to you from our exploration of the statement of financial position in Chapter 2. The significance of their formal declaration in the Framework is that they now define the scope of financial accounting. All items that appear in financial statements must fall into one of the specified categories. The question of whether a key employee should be shown as an asset of the company in the statement of financial position, for example, should be answered, at least partly, by reference to the definition of an asset in this part of the Framework. In such a case, the issue would be whether the employee represents 'future economic benefit' controlled by the company, since that phrase is the heart of the definition of an asset. Presumably, the answer would be yes, given that it is likely that the net revenues generated by such a key employee would exceed the cost of his or her wages. However, the question does not rest there, because the material in the framework on elements has to be seen alongside the issue of recognition.

Accordingly, the framework goes on to deal with the circumstances in which these elements should be recognised in the financial statements. It should come as no surprise to find that it requires items to be recognised only if they are elements as defined. We have already accepted that our key employee probably fits the definition of an asset. However, the framework also imposes the further condition that the element must also be capable of being objectively quantified. In other words, we need to be able to objectively quantify the 'future economic benefit' that our employee represents. One approach could be to sum the net revenues after wages costs that the employee will bring in during his or her time with the company.

Activity 4.5

Briefly, note down at least one practical problem that you foresee with such an approach to valuation. As always, you will learn more and faster if you think about the issue raised in the activity than if you simply skip ahead to the answer.

Answer

Our view is that the main problem is the uncertainty inherent in any estimate of future revenues and expenses. It would be highly questionable, for example, whether our guesses about the net revenues or the number of years the employee will stay with us will turn out to be accurate. If we cannot objectively quantify an element, then the Framework requires that we do not recognise it, that is, we should not include it in the financial statements.

More subtly, such an approach to valuation is not historical cost, and we have already seen that historical cost is the most widely used and accepted method of valuation. If we use some estimate of future value for an employee, and historical cost for another asset, such as a building, it is hard to see what the total of the two assets represents or means. We looked at valuation problems in Chapter 2, and will return to the topic in greater depth in Chapter 13. In the meantime, the Framework goes on to address the issue of valuation.

Specifically, the next section of the Framework deals with the alternative bases on which we could quantify financial items. So far we have only looked seriously at historical cost, but we will explore other possibilities in Chapter 13. As you may be beginning to realise from the brief discussion above, valuation is a complex topic.

Finally, the last main topic dealt with by the Framework is an exploration of capital maintenance. This means looking at what we understand by the 'wealth' or 'net worth' of an organisation. It's something we touched on back in Chapter 2, and something that we'll return to in Chapter 13.

In the rest of this chapter we will consider the characteristics in more detail, that is, the conventional wisdom on what constitutes good accounting. This topic therefore represents guidelines for everything else we do in this book.

The characteristics

As we briefly saw earlier in this chapter, the Framework identifies the qualitative characteristics of good financial reporting as relevance, reliability, comparability and understandability.

Activity 4.6   Write two sentences of your own to define each of the characteristics, 'relevance' and 'reliability'. In other words, what do you think these words mean in accounting terms?

Answer   Our answer is based closely on the Framework, which says that the relevance of financial information is primarily related to its predictive role, that is, the extent to which the information helps users to predict the organisation's future and so to make decisions about it. For example, the attempt by a potential investor to predict future profitability and dividend levels will be at least partly based on the financial statements. Relevance also relates to the use of financial information to confirm past predictions, e.g. about returns on a particular capital project.

In relation to reliability, the Framework asserts that reliability of financial information is deemed to be achieved by producing information that has a series of characteristics. There are five of these, but most should already be familiar from your studies earlier in this book.

1   *Faithful representation*. This consists of valid description, free from error, although it should be taken together with a suitable 'choice of aspect', i.e. a decision of which properties of a transaction we should disclose. Achievement of faithful representation also depends on the idea of 'substance over form'.

2   *Substance over form*. Briefly, this idea says that where there's a difference between the strict form of the legal position and the economic substance of an event then we should always account for the substance rather than the form. This is a very important, and quite complex, idea in accounting, and so we'll consider it as a topic in its own right later in this chapter.

3   *Neutrality*. The information presented must be free from bias. There is a very close link here to the prior concept of objectivity.

4   *Prudence*. This principle is restated. While we should aim to reflect an unbiased view of an event or transaction, in accordance with neutrality, under conditions of uncertainty it will be helpful to select a prudent view of the possible outcomes.

5   *Completeness*. The more complete the information is the better, but the benefits of completeness should be weighed against the costs of the time and money needed to prepare full information.

Activity 4.7   The other characteristics are comparability and understandability. Repeat the previous activity, this time jotting down a couple of your own sentences to define each of these terms.

Answer   Once again, our answer draws heavily on the points made in the Framework. Specifically, the achievement of comparability implies the presentation of financial information in a consistent way from one year to the next, and between enterprises. One important feature of this will be the disclosure of and adherence to accounting policies. The presentation of comparative figures for the previous year will also help to achieve this characteristic.

Understandability requires a prior consideration of who the users of the information are held to be. The presentation of the information should then be such that those users will normally be able to make substantial use of that information. It will, however, be acceptable to assume that users are reasonably well-informed about basic accounting and economic matters.

Finally, the Framework insists that all the above characteristics are subject to a minimum threshold of quality. The main consideration here is materiality, which provides a cut-off point for the disclosure or non-disclosure of particular events. Furthermore, you should bear in mind that in the UK everything in the Framework is subject to the over-riding legal requirement to show a true and fair view.

Activity 4.8

Global Trading is currently preparing its annual report and accounts. As its name suggests, it is a very big enterprise, with very complex accounting procedures and reports. Currently, it publishes an statement of comprehensive income and a statement of financial position. The directors are considering a proposal to produce a more simplified set of financial statements, either in addition to, or even instead of, the usual, more complex statements. One possibility, for example, would be to produce simply a summary of monies in and out of the bank account.

Taking each of the four characteristics in turn, assess whether the proposal is sound. You may ignore any legal requirements.

Answer

As with many of the questions in this fundamental area of accounting, there is no single correct answer. However, we think the following suggested answer covers most of the main points.

Relevance

The Framework says that relevance rests on whether the financial statements are of significant use for predicting or confirming economic events. Whether the proposal improves relevance depends on who the users are, and what they want to predict or confirm. A lender, for example, would probably find a summary of cash movements relevant, since he or she would be concerned about the ability of Global Trading to make repayments. A shareholder, on the other hand, would probably be most concerned about the profit made, and would accordingly find the statement of comprehensive income more relevant, and the proposal would therefore not be as sound.

Reliability

This characteristic is to be judged according to faithful representation, substance over form, neutrality, prudence and completeness. These points seem to be as valid for either approach to accounting, but they at least do not suggest that the proposal should be rejected on the grounds of reliability. Indeed, in terms of neutrality (objectivity) the proposal could be seen as positive, in that the amounts passing through the bank account are a more objective measure of events than, say, the measure of profit. In terms of completeness, the provision of the suggested statement in addition to existing statements is likely to be positive. Note, however, that provision of an extra statement will take time, so delaying the publication of the statements and so making them more out of date.

▶

Understandability

A summary of monies in and out of the bank account will probably be understandable to a wider group of users than will a conventionally complex set of financial statements. On these grounds the proposal seems sound. However, we need to balance this against the difficulties we have already noted in relation to relevance and reliability. Arguably, it is more important that the accounts be 'right' than that they be understandable.

Comparability

This refers to a user's ability to make comparisons both with Global Trading's own accounts in previous years, and with the accounts of other similar companies. Comparability with previous years will be poor, unless the company retrospectively prepares a similar cash summary for those years. This is possible, but would be expensive. Comparability with other companies will only be possible if other companies produce a similar statement.

Overall, it is not possible to make a clear recommendation to the directors, without knowing more about the circumstances. What we can say is that the four characteristics seem to provide criteria by which we can start to judge the validity of both current and proposed accounting practices.

Substance over form

You'll remember that the idea of 'substance over form' is part of how we achieve reliability. It's a fundamental part of the conceptual framework so we've separated it out here to deal with it as a topic in its own right.

In essence, the idea says that there can be a difference between the economic substance of a transaction – what's really happening – and the strict legal form. An example is probably the best way to explain how the idea works. If we buy a car and use it in our business then there's no difference. The economic substance is that the car is our asset, since we receive any economic benefits associated with its use. Similarly, since we bought the car the legal form is also that its our car. However, compare this with the situation where we lease the car for most or all of its expected life.

We will again physically have the car, we'll use it to earn economic benefits for our business, we'll control who can drive it, and we'll pay for the running costs. In substance, it appears to be our asset, and so we'll presumably show it in our statement of financial position. However, legally the car doesn't belong to us, but belongs to the lease company. Accordingly we shouldn't show it in our statement of financial position. There's a conflict between what the economic substance of the lease suggests we do and what the legal form suggests is the correct accounting. The concept of substance over form says that in those situations where we have such a conflict then we account according to the economic substance rather than the legal form. In this case we would therefore show the car in our statement of financial position, and then depreciate it, even though it belongs to someone else. Note that the idea of substance over form applies to all accounting, not just to leases. It's therefore a very powerful idea in accounting.

Summary

This chapter has dealt with three topics:

▶ the concepts of accounting, the most important of which are set out in the Framework, complemented by IAS 1 and IAS 8

▶ IAS 8, which sets up a structure of policies for determining accounting practice in a reasonably coherent way

▶ the Framework, which attempts a definition of what constitutes good accounting. In other words, it provides a target for all our accounting to aim at.

This chapter concludes the first part of this book. So far, we have explored the nature of accounting, looked at the two main statements by which accounting reports to the outside world, and started to look at some of the theoretical underpinning to accounting. We will return to the theory in Chapter 13. In the meantime, however, we should turn our attention to the everyday practicalities of accounting. Chapter 5 therefore starts our study of double entry bookkeeping.

Key terms		
concepts (p. 55)	characteristics (p. 56)	
going concern (p. 56)	measurement bases (p. 62)	
accruals (p. 56)	revenue recognition (p. 62)	
matching (p. 56)	true and fair view (p. 63)	
realisation (p. 56)		

Self-assessment questions

Select the most appropriate answer for each of the following multiple choice questions.

1 The assumption that an organisation will continue to operate indefinitely is a fair description of which concept?

(a) Accruals
(b) Going concern
(c) Consistency
(d) Prudence

2 The concept of materiality implies that an organisation will:

(a) Only account for items which don't affect the overall view gained from its accounts.
(b) Not account for non-current assets which are due to be sold in the next accounting year.

▶

(c) Only account for non-current assets and those current assets costing more than £1,000.

(d) Not account for items which don't affect the overall view gained from its accounts.

3 The concept of money measurement means:

(a) Accounts cost a material amount of money to prepare.
(b) Only items that can be objectively measured in money terms are accounted for.
(c) Accounts are only ever prepared in one currency.
(d) Items in accounts are recorded at the amount of money they originally cost.

4 The recognition that an organisation is distinct from its owners is a fair description of which concept?

(a) Duality
(b) Separate valuation
(c) Business entity
(d) Objectivity

5 The concept of realisation means that:

(a) Items are accounted for in the period in which the associated cash flow occurs.
(b) Items are recognised when the directors realise that a cost has been incurred.
(c) Items are accounted for when only they can be objectively measured.
(d) Items are recognised when the associated cash becomes reasonably certain of being received or paid.

6 'The International Accounting Standards Board (IASB) should spend less time on developing a vague set of principles and more time on specifying clear accounting practices.' To what extent do you agree with this statement?

As in the self-assessment question for Chapter 1, you should justify your response and construct your answer as an essay of 300 to 500 words, or as comprehensive notes for such an essay. Again, we have provided feedback as a list of points that you should have covered.

7 Back in Chapter 1 we asked you to identify the relative merits of the UK and French approaches to financial reporting. To recap, the French system is based on the *plan comptable*, a specification of exactly which accounts must be kept to record which transactions and how those details are then to be presented in the statement of comprehensive income and in the statement of financial position. This can be contrasted with the less directed approach used in the UK and outlined in this chapter.

For each of the characteristics of good accounting that you have now explored (relevance, reliability, comparability and understandability), suggest one reason to prefer the UK system and one reason to prefer the French system. You may like to set out your answer as a table – we have.

8 Outline the purposes and main features of the Framework for the Preparation and Presentation of Financial Statements. Your answer should be in the form of an essay of around 500 words, briefly covering both the content and the purposes of the Framework.

Answers to these questions can be found at the back of this book.

5

The double entry system

Objectives

By the end of this chapter you should be able to:

▶ Identify the need for a system of double entry.

▶ Relate the duality concept to this system.

▶ Prepare ledger accounts.

▶ Balance off ledger accounts.

▶ Extract a trial balance and understand its importance within the system.

▶ Prepare simple statements of comprehensive income (income statements) and statements of financial position (balance sheets) from a trial balance.

Introduction

This chapter is intended to introduce you to the basics of the double entry bookkeeping system that was codified by Luca Pacioli in the fifteenth century. As an accountant you may not be involved in the actual recording within the double entry bookkeeping system as this is carried out by bookkeepers or indeed a computer. You must, however, understand the system as you, as an accountant, will be called on to ensure the system is operating effectively and to complete year-end entries to enable relevant and reliable financial statements to be prepared for an organisation.

The need for a double entry system

You have seen in previous chapters that it is possible to construct a statement of financial position (a balance sheet), to show the position of a business at a point in time, and a statement of income to identify the profitability of a business for a period of time. How did you do this? Refresh your memory with the following activity.

Activity 5.1

Mr Bean intends to set up in business as an antiques dealer. He places £20,000 of his own money into a business bank account then purchases items for resale for £12,000 and a van for £5,000. He rents a shop for £3,600 per annum paying the first monthly instalment of rent. At the end of his first month of trading he is able to identify the fact that he has sold for cash two items, one costing £2,000 for £3,500, and one costing £500 for £800.

Draw up the statement of financial position for Mr Bean as at the end of the first month's trading and a statement of comprehensive income for the period.

Answer

MR BEAN
STATEMENT OF FINANCIAL POSITION (BALANCE SHEET) AS AT END OF FIRST MONTH

Non-current assets

Van		5,000
Current assets		
Inventory	9,500	
Bank	7,000	16,500
		21,500
Capital		
Opening	20,000	
Profit	1,500	21,500

MR BEAN
STATEMENT OF COMPREHENSIVE INCOME STATEMENT FOR THE PERIOD ENDED FIRST MONTH

Sales	4,300
Cost of sales	2,500
Gross profit	1,800
Rent	300
Net profit	1,500

How did you construct the above? Probably by doing calculations on a piece of paper to arrive at sales, cost of sales, inventory and bank figures.

Would the above have been as simple though if Mr Bean had made 100 sales during the month? Obviously the answer is no. Thus you have identified that there is a need for a record of all Mr Bean's transactions that will enable a statement of financial position and a statement of comprehensive income to be drawn up at the end of any given period. We have dealt here with a sole trader business, that of Mr Bean. However, all types of organisations, companies both private and public limited (plcs), partnerships, charities, public sector, use double entry bookkeeping to record their transactions.

Double entry system – duality

You learnt in Chapter 4 about the concept of duality.

Activity 5.2

Identify for Mr Bean the duality involved in the introduction of his capital into the business and the purchase of his van.

Answer

This was fairly straightforward. In the first case you created a liability of capital and the asset of bank, in the second you reduced the asset of bank and created an asset of van. There was a dual effect of each transaction to maintain the accounting equation:

$$ASSETS = CAPITAL + LIABILITIES$$

Double entry system – account

When you calculated the bank figure in Activity 5.1 you made a list of additions to and subtractions from the bank probably similar to the following:

Additions		Subtractions	
Capital	20,000	Van	5,000
Sale 1	3,500	Purchases	12,000
Sale 2	800	Rent	300
	24,300		17,300

Additions were sources of funds to the business and subtractions applications of those funds from the business.

The above can be represented as an **account** in a **double entry** system as follows:

BANK ACCOUNT

Capital	20,000	Van	5,000
Sale 1	3,500	Purchases	12,000
Sale 2	800	Rent	300

The left-hand side of this account is referred to as the debit side (debit means 'to give' – I give (place) £20,000 to the bank account); the right-hand side as the credit side (credit means to receive – I receive £5,000 from the bank to buy a van).

This bank account has enabled you to make a very neat recording of Mr Bean's dealings with the bank but has not recorded the *duality* of the above transactions. Looking at the transaction of purchasing the van, you have credited the bank account with £5,000, so to comply with duality it would seem reasonable to suggest that you should debit another account with £5,000.

Thus:

VAN ACCOUNT

Bank	5,000

Activity 5.3   Complete the duality for the other transactions in the bank account.

Answer

PURCHASES ACCOUNT

Bank	12,000

RENT ACCOUNT

Bank	300

SALES ACCOUNT

	Bank sale 1	3,500
	Bank sale 2	800

CAPITAL ACCOUNT

	Bank	20,000

The pattern of the above accounts is that of *double entry*. For each transaction we have made a debit and a credit entry for the same amount, the description (narrative) referring always to the other double entry account.

Using your knowledge of the duality concept, the accounting equation and with reference to the double entry accounts used above you should be able to complete the following activity without too much trouble.

Activity 5.4   Complete the following table:

Account	Transaction	Entry to account
Asset	Addition	Debit
Asset	Subtraction	(a)_____
Liability	Addition	(b)_____
Liability	(c)_____	Debit
Capital	(d)_____	Credit
Capital	Subtraction	(e)_____
Expense	Addition	(f)_____
Expense	Subtraction	(g)_____
Income	Addition	(h)_____
Income	(i)_____	Debit

Answer

The missing entries are as follows:

(a) Credit, (b) Credit, (c) Subtraction, (d) Addition, (e) Debit, (f) Debit, (g) Credit, (h) Credit, (i) Subtraction.

Fairly easy we know, but we hope you thought about the activity rather than just following the pattern.

Activity 5.5

The following question is similar to Activities 5.1 and 5.3 and completing the question will ensure that you have understood the concepts so far.

Miss Coffee intends to set up in business as a retailer of ladies' high-class fashion. She places £40,000 of her own money into a business bank account and then purchases a car for £8,000 and inventory for £25,000. She rents property at £12,000 per annum paying the first month's rental. At the end of the first month of trading she is able to identify that she has sold inventory worth £2,000 for £5,000 and paid sundry expenses of £500.

Draw up the statement of financial position for Miss Coffee as at the end of the first month's trading and a statement of comprehensive income for the period together with the double entry accounts for the period.

Answer

MISS COFFEE
STATEMENT OF FINANCIAL POSITION AS AT END
OF FIRST MONTH

Non-current assets		
Car		8,000
Current assets		
Inventory	23,000	
Bank	10,500	33,500
		41,500
Capital		
Opening		40,000
Profit		1,500
		41,500

MISS COFFEE
INCOME STATEMENT OF COMPREHENSIVE FOR THE PERIOD
ENDED FIRST MONTH

Sales		5,000
Cost of sales		2,000
Gross profit		3,000
Rent	1,000	
Sundry expenses	500	1,500
Net profit		1,500

BANK ACCOUNT

Capital	40,000	Car	8,000
Sales	5,000	Rent	1,000
		Purchases	25,000
		Sundry	500

RENT ACCOUNT

Bank	1,000	

SUNDRY ACCOUNT

Bank	500	

SALES ACCOUNT

	Bank	5,000

CAR ACCOUNT

Bank	8,000	

CAPITAL ACCOUNT

	Capital	40,000

PURCHASES ACCOUNT

Bank	25,000	

Activity 5.6

This question is provided for extra practice. Mr Pickup sets up in business as a website designer. He places £25,000 of his own money into a business bank account and then purchases a computer for £2,500 and a car for £10,000. He rents a small office for £6,000 per annum and buys some furniture and other equipment for the office costing £2,200. At the end of the second month of trading Mr Pickup is able to identify that he has sold several website designs for a total of £7,500, he has paid two months' rent on the office and he has paid other expenses of £850.

Draw up the statement of financial position for Mr Pickup as at the end of the second month of trading and a statement of comprehensive income for the period together with the double entry accounts for the period. Note that there will be no cost of sales figure in this example as Mr.Pickup is not buying goods to sell on or manufacture and sell on. It is his own intellectual knowledge that he is selling in the form of his website designs.

Answer

MR PICKUP
STATEMENT OF FINANCIAL POSITION AS AT END OF
SECOND MONTH

Non-current assets		
Car	10,000	
Computer	2,500	
Furniture and equipment	2,200	14,700
Current assets		
Bank		15,950
		30,650
Capital		
Opening		25,000
Profit		5,650
		30,650

MR PICKUP
INCOME STATEMENT OF COMPREHENSIVE FOR THE
PERIOD ENDED SECOND MONTH

Sales		7,500
Cost of sales		0
Gross profit		7,500
Rent	1,000	
Sundry expenses	850	1,850
Net profit		5,650

BANK ACCOUNT

Capital	25,000	Car	10,000
Sales	7,500	Rent	1,000
		Computer	2,500
		Equipment	2,200
		Sundry	850

RENT ACCOUNT

Bank	1,000	

SUNDRY ACCOUNT

Bank	850	

SALES ACCOUNT

	Bank	7,500

CAR ACCOUNT

Bank	10,000		

CAPITAL ACCOUNT

		Capital	25,000

COMPUTER ACCOUNT

Bank	2,500		

EQUIPMENT ACCOUNT

Bank	2,200		

Credit transactions

So far the transactions you have dealt with for Mr Bean have all involved cash as one side of the double entry.

A lot of business is carried out by the use of credit transactions. For example Mr Bean, when he acquired £12,000 of goods, could well have paid only £5,000 immediately and bought the rest on credit. When Mr Bean bought the £7,000 of goods on credit he will eventually have to pay the creditor the amount owed. He will therefore need to create an accounts payable account.

We account for this in the double entry system as follows:

PURCHASES ACCOUNT

Cash	5,000		
Creditor	7,000		

CASH ACCOUNT

		Purchases	5,000

CREDITOR ACCOUNT

		Purchases	7,000

Similarly, sales may be made on credit and a debtor would be created, and Mr Bean will need to use an accounts receivable account. Note that the accounts payable (the creditor) is a liability of the business and the accounts receivable (the debtor) an asset. It is also customary to maintain separate accounts for each account receivable (debtor) and each account payable (creditor) in the double entry system. You will see how these separate accounts are summed and verified by the use of control accounts in

Chapter 14. For now we will use a separate accounts payable for each creditor and accounts receivable for each debtor.

To help reinforce your understanding of the double entry system a full example is provided below for you to work through as a self-check of understanding. The suggested answer is provided at Activity 5.9 so if you feel fairly confident in respect of your understanding so far you could wait and complete Activities 5.7 and 5.9 together. By the way, it is normal in the double entry system to enter the date against each entry made. The place where double entry accounts are recorded is generally known as a ledger. This ledger is divided into sub-ledgers:

► Accounts payable (creditors) ledger – where we record the suppliers accounts (from whom we have purchased supplies)

► Accounts receivable (debtors) ledger – where we record the customers accounts (to whom we have made sales)

► Nominal ledger or impersonal ledger – where everything else is recorded.

We will return to this division of the ledger in Chapter 15.

Worked example of double entry

*A*ctivity 5.7   Enter the following transactions in the ledgers of A. Bate, maintaining separate bank and cash accounts.

				£
March	3	Bate placed £20,000 in a business account	
	3	Bought car for £8,000, paying by cheque	8,000
	4	Bought goods on credit from Hall	6,350
	5	Paid cheque for office expenses	340
	5	Paid cheque for car insurance	195
	8	Cashed a cheque for cash	600
	9	Cash received for sales	2,345
	12	Sold goods on credit to White	1,645
	14	Paid wages in cash	250
	18	Cash received for sales	300
	20	Banked excess cash	
	24	Bought goods on credit from Dunn	1,895
	25	Cheque received from White	850
	26	Cash sales	400
	27	Paid wages in cash	250
	28	Sold goods on credit: White	600
		Black	750
	29	Cash sales	250
	30	Cheque sent: Hall	5,500
		Dunn	1,500
	31	Paid all cash into bank	

Answer   The answer to the above is contained in the answer to Activity 5.9 but we suggest you carry out the exercise now and check your answer later.

Balancing off accounts

You have now learnt how to record business transactions in the books but you also need to know the following data at the end of a period:

▶ what the cash balance is

▶ what the total value of sales is that has been made

▶ how much is owed to the creditors on the accounts payable account

▶ how much debtors owe the business shown on the accounts recoverable account

▶ what the total of expenses is.

To do this we need to balance off the accounts. Looking back at the bank account we derived for you after Activity 5.2 we had:

BANK ACCOUNT

Capital	20,000	Van	5,000
Sale 1	3,500	Purchases	12,000
Sale 2	800	Rent	300

The left-hand side of this account (the debit) totals £24,300 and the credit side (the right) £17,300. The difference is £7,000, the balance at the bank you identified at Activity 5.1, an asset. You should also have noticed that the van, another asset of the business, appeared in its double entry account as a debit which implies that the asset of £7,000 at the bank has to appear as a debit.

The 'balancing off' takes place as follows:

BANK ACCOUNT

Capital	20,000	Van	5,000
Sale 1	3,500	Purchases	12,000
Sale 2	800	Rent	300
		Balance carried down	7,000
	24,300		24,300
Balance brought down	7,000		

To check whether you understand what we did to balance the bank account try the next activity.

Activity 5.8   Identify the sequence that occurred to balance off the above bank account.

Answer   You should have identified a sequence similar to the following:

1 Add up both sides and identify the difference.
2 Enter the difference on the side with the smaller total (the credit side here).
3 Enter the totals for both sides – which are now identical.
4 Complete the double entry in respect of (2) by entering the same figure on the opposite side (in this case the debit side) below the totals.

This balance brought down of £7,000 debit is the balance of cash at bank, an asset of the business. Again it is normal to enter the date in the accounts when balancing off the accounts, the carried-down date being that of the end of the period and the brought-down date that of the start of the next period.

The rest of the accounts for Mr Bean are balanced as follows:

VAN ACCOUNT

Bank	5,000	Balance carried down	5,000
Balance brought down	5,000		

PURCHASES ACCOUNT

Bank	12,000	Balance carried down	12,000
Balance brought down	12,000		

RENT ACCOUNT

Bank	300	Balance carried down	300
Balance brought down	300		

SALES ACCOUNT

		Bank	3,500
Balance carried down	4,300	Bank	800
	4,300		4,300
		Balance brought down	4,300

CAPITAL ACCOUNT

Balance carried down	20,000	Bank	20,000
		Balance brought down	20,000

Notice that when there is only one entry in an account there is no need to enter the total for each side. It is also customary to abbreviate brought down and carried down to b/d and c/d respectively. 'Balance' can also be abbreviated to 'bal'.

Activity 5.9   Balance off all the accounts for Activity 5.7

Answer   The answer below is that for Activities 5.7 and 5.9.

CAPITAL ACCOUNT

Bal c/d	20,000	Bank	20,000
		Bal b/d	20,000

OFFICE EXPENSE ACCOUNT

Bank	340	Bal c/d	340
Bal b/d	340		

CAR ACCOUNT

Bank/loan	8,000	Bal c/d	8,000
Bal b/d	8,000		

INSURANCE ACCOUNT

Bank	195	Bal c/d	195
Bal b/d	195		

LOAN ACCOUNT (note 2)

Balance c/d	5,000	Car	5,000
		Bal b/d	5,000

WAGES ACCOUNT

Cash	250		
Cash	250	Bal c/d	500
	500		500
Bal b/d	500		

PURCHASES ACCOUNT

Hall	6,350		
Dunn	1,895	Bal c/d	8,245
	8,245		8,245
Bal b/d	8,245		

SALES ACCOUNT

		Cash	2,345
		White	1,645
		Cash	300
		Cash	400
		White	600
		Black	750
Bal c/d	6,290	Cash	250
	6,290		6,290
		Bal b/d	6,290

ACCOUNT RECEIVABLE (DEBTOR) – WHITE

Sales	1,645	Bank	850
Sales	600	Bal c/d	1,395
	2,245		2,245
Bal b/d	1,395		

ACCOUNT RECEIVABLE (DEBTOR) – BLACK

Sales	750	Bal c/d	750
Bal b/d	750		

ACCOUNT PAYABLES (CREDITOR) – HALL

Bank	5,500	Purchases	6,350
Bal c/d	850		
	6,350		6,350
		Bal b/d	850

ACCOUNT PAYABLES (CREDITOR) – DUNN

Bank	1,500	Purchases	1,895
Bal c/d	395		
	1,895		1,895
		Bal b/d	395

BANK ACCOUNT

Capital	20,000	Car	3,000
Cash	2,995	Office	340
White	850	Insurance	195
Cash	400	Cash	600
		Hall	5,500
		Dunn	1,500
		Bal c/d	13,110
	24,245		24,245
Bal b/d	13,110		

CASH ACCOUNT

Bank	600	Wages	250
Sales	2,345	Bank (note 1)	2,995
Sales	300	Wages	250
Sales	400	Bank (note 1)	400
Sales	250		
	3,895		3,895

Note 1   At this point the cash account had to be totalled to identify the balance that was then paid into the bank.

Note 2   As the cost of the car was £8,000 but only £3,000 was paid in cash the remaining £5,000 is identified as a loan.

The example we have given above consists of very few sales and purchases but in an actual business or indeed any type of organisation there are likely to be many sales and purchases in a day. For most businesses it is impossible to write up every sale as we have here into the sales ledger but, for now, in our simple examples, we will continue to use the method above. You will see in Chapter 14 how we deal with multiple sales and purchases to minimise the entries in the ledgers.

Trial balance

The double entry system follows the duality concept – for every debit there is an equal credit – thus if the system has been carried out correctly the *total debit balances* should equal the *total credit balances*. This check on the operation of the system is known as a trial balance.

TRIAL BALANCE FOR MR BEAN AS AT (PERIOD END DATE)

	Dr	Cr
Sales		4,300
Capital		20,000
Van	5,000	
Purchases	12,000	
Rent	300	
Bank	7,000	
	24,300	24,300

Activity 5.10   Construct the trial balance in respect of Activity 5.7.

Answer

TRIAL BALANCE AS AT 31 MARCH (A. BATE)

	Dr	Cr
Capital		20,000
Bank	13,110	
Office expenses	340	
Car insurance	195	
Car	8,000	
Wages	500	
Loan		5,000
Purchases	8,245	
Sales		6,290
Accounts payable (creditors):		
Hall		850
Dunn		395
Accounts receivable (debtors):		
White	1,395	
Black	750	
	32,535	32,535

Use of trial balance

If the totals of the trial balance agree, it does not necessarily prove that the books are correct. What it will prove is that you have entered an equal debit for every credit and that the accounts have been added correctly, but there are several errors that could have been made that the trial balance will not identify. It is also worth remembering that the trial balance is not part of the double entry system itself.

Activity 5.11   The following errors have been made in the books of Mr Bean. Identify those errors that the use of a trial balance will reveal and those it will not.

1 The sales account has been incorrectly added.

2 The purchase of goods on credit was entered in the relevant accounts payable (creditor) account but not the purchases account.

3 Wages paid of £92 was debited as £92 to the wages account but as £29 credit to the bank account.

4 The sale of goods for £100 on credit was not entered in the books at all.

5 An electricity bill was correctly credited to the bank account but the debit entry was made to the office expenses account not the electricity account.

6 Goods for £50 were bought on credit and entered in the books as purchases account debit £5 account payable (creditor) account credit £50. Sales made of £50 cash were entered in the cash account as debit £50 but as £5 to the credit of the sales account.

7 A loan made to Mr Bean of £1,000 from Mr Atkinson was debited to the loan account and credited to the bank account.

Answer
A little thought and you should have been able to identify that the trial balance will reveal the following types of error:

▶ Incorrect additions in an account as per item 1.
▶ Posting (entering) one side only of the double entry as per item 2.
▶ Entering a different amount in the debit side than the credit side, for example debit £92 credit £29 as per item 3.

but will not reveal the following:

▶ An entry completely missed as per item 4.
▶ An entry in a wrong account but the double entry still maintained as per item 5.
▶ Where errors cancel each other as per item 6.
▶ Entries where the double entry is completely the wrong way around as per item 7.

Statement of comprehensive income

At the very beginning of this chapter you were able to construct a statement of comprehensive income and a statement of financial position for Mr Bean (see Activity 5.1).

You did this by identifying the expenses to match with the income in the statement of comprehensive income and identifying the assets and liabilities at the end of the period and recording these in the statement of financial position. In effect you made use of the accounting equations:

PROFIT = INCOME – EXPENSES USED UP
ASSETS = CAPITAL + LIABILITIES + PROFIT

If we regard CAPITAL and PROFIT in the above equation as owner's EQUITY it is possible to write this second equation as:

ASSETS = EQUITY + LIABILITIES

The statement of comprehensive income can be treated as part of the double entry system and we can transfer expenses and income to it maintaining the principles of double entry. This would result in a statement of comprehensive income in what is known as 'horizontal format'. This is not the normal format that is used. The normal format is 'vertical format'. We identified this vertical format for you in Chapter 3 and we will return to it again later in this chapter. Whatever format is used, horizontal or vertical, they are still part of the double entry system. We must be careful though that we only transfer that expense used up in generating the income – the accruals or matching concept. Refer back to Chapter 4 here to refresh your memory on the accruals concept. In particular we must be careful how much of the purchase expense we transfer.

Mr Bean, in Activity 5.1, had not sold all of the goods he bought, in fact he has only sold goods costing £2,500. He therefore has goods remaining of £9,500 which is not recorded as yet in the double entry system. This figure of inventory could have been ascertained in one of two ways:

1 By counting the goods remaining in the shop and valuing them at the cost Mr Bean paid.

2 By reducing the figure of purchases, each time a sale is made, by the purchase price of that item sold.

When a business has several sales within a period the easiest method is to count inventory at the end of the period (refer back to Chapter 3 for how we did this).

This inventory figure is then entered in the books by the means of a closing inventory account and the statement of comprehensive income is used to calculate the cost of goods sold. The following demonstrates this. Note we have used a horizontal format for the income statement below.

SALES ACCOUNT

Income statement	4,300	Balance b/d	4,300

PURCHASES ACCOUNT

Balance b/d	12,000	Income statement	12,000

RENT ACCOUNT

Balance b/d	300	Income statement	300

CLOSING INVENTORY ACCOUNT

Income statement	9,500		

INCOME STATEMENT

Purchases	12,000	Sales	4,300
Gross profit c/d	1,800	Closing inventory	9,500
	13,800		13,800
Rent	300	Gross profit b/d	1,800
Net profit c/d	1,500		
	1,800		1,800
		Net profit b/d	1,500

Did you understand what we did here?

Activity 5.12   Identify the sequence carried out above to arrive at the net profit figure of £1,500. For example, the sequence will start:

▶ Transfer balance on sales account to the statement of comprehensive income by debiting sales account and crediting the statement of comprehensive income.

Answer

Your sequence should have been similar to the following:

▶ Transfer balance on sales account to the statement of comprehensive income by debiting sales account and crediting the statement of comprehensive income.
▶ Transfer balance on purchases by crediting this account and debiting the statement of comprehensive income.
▶ Enter closing inventory in the ledgers by debiting closing inventory account and crediting the statement of comprehensive income.
▶ Balance off the statement of comprehensive income but call the balance Gross Profit, i.e. difference between sales and cost of goods sold.
▶ Transfer balance on rent account to the statement of comprehensive income.
▶ Balance off the statement of comprehensive income again calling balance Net Profit.

Let us see if you can do all this now.

Activity 5.13

Given that the closing inventory as at 31 March in Activity 5.9 for A. Bate is £4.500, draw up a statement of comprehensive income using horizontal form for the month ended 31 March.

Answer

STATEMENT OF COMPREHENSIVE INCOME
FOR THE MONTH ENDED 31 MARCH

Purchases	8,245	Sales	6,290
Gross profit c/d	2,545	Closing inventory	4,500
	10,790		10,790
Office expenses	340	Gross profit b/d	2,545
Car insurance	195		
Wages	500		
Net profit c/d	1,510		
	2,545		2,545
		Net profit b/d	1,510

Format of the statement of comprehensive income

In Chapter 3 we discussed the format of the statement of comprehensive income. The above statement of comprehensive income would normally be written as follows:

Sales		6,290
Purchases	8,245	
Less closing inventory	4,500	3,745
Gross profit		2,545
Office expenses	340	
Car insurance	195	
Wages	500	1,035
Net profit		1,510

This is known as a vertical statement of comprehensive income. It is perceived as being easier for users to understand, and avoids the need to insert 'carried down' and 'brought down' figures. From this point on we suggest you always use the vertical format for the statement of comprehensive income.

Balance remaining in the books

Having constructed a statement of comprehensive income for Mr Bean it is possible at this point to extract another trial balance as follows:

	Dr	Cr
Capital		20,000
Inventory	9,500	
Van	5,000	
Bank	7,000	
Net profit		1,500
	21,500	21,500

Again just a minor leap in imagination and the above could be written as follows:

STATEMENT OF FINANCIAL POSITION AS AT 31 MARCH

Assets
Non-current assets

Van		5,000
Current assets		
Inventory	9,500	
Bank	7,000	16,500
Total assets		21,500
Equity		
Capital		20,000
Profit		1,500
Total equity		21,500

Thus the balances remaining in the books, after having extracted a statement of comprehensive income, form a statement of financial position. The statement of financial position records the position of the business at a specific point in time. It is presented in a format that represents the equation we gave you earlier:

$$\text{ASSETS} = \text{EQUITY} + \text{LIABILITIES}$$

Activity 5.14

Draw up the statement of financial position for the information contained in Activities relating to A. Bate after the extraction of the statement of comprehensive income as at 31 March.

Answer

The statement of financial position should look as follows:

STATEMENT OF FINANCIAL POSITION AS AT 31 MARCH

Assets			
Non-current assests			
Car			8,000
Current assets			
Inventory		4,500	
Accounts receivable			
(debtors):			
White	1,395		
Black	750	2,145	
Bank		13,110	19,755
Total assests			27,755
Equity and liability			
Equity			
Capital			20,000
Profit			1,510
Profit			21,510
Non-current liabilities			
Loan		5,000	
Current liabilities			
Accounts payable			
(creditors):			
Hall	850		
Dunn	395	1,245	
Total liabilities			6,245
Total equity and liabilities			27,755

To practice preparing a statement of financial position using the accepted format try the following activity.

Activity 5.15

TRIAL BALANCE AS AT 31 MARCH FOR R. BELL

	Dr	Cr
Capital		45,000
Premises	150,000	
Vehicles	22,000	
Loan		130,000
Profit		15,000
Accounts receivable	4,300	
Accounts payable		5,200
Inventory	9,800	
Bank	8,700	
Cash	400	
	195,200	195,200

Answer

The statement of financial position should be as follows:

STATEMENT OF FINANCIAL POSITION AS AT 31 MARCH FOR R. BELL

Assets		
Non-current assets		
Premises	150,000	
Vehicle	22,000	172,000
Current assets		
Inventory	9,800	
Accounts receivable	4,300	
Bank	8,700	
Cash	400	23,200
Total assets		195,200
Equity and liabilities		
Equity		
Capital	45,000	
Profit	15,000	60,000
Non-current liabilities		
Loan	130,000	
Current liabilities		
Accounts payable	5,200	
Total liabilities		135,200
Total equity and liabilities		195,200

Summary

This chapter has introduced you to the double entry system of accounting. Within it we:

▶ have identified the need for the system when a business has several transactions to account for

▶ saw that it was based upon the concept of duality

▶ have taken you through the workings of the ledgers

▶ have balanced them off

▶ have extracted a trial balance

▶ have learnt that the statement of comprehensive income was in fact part of the double entry system and that income and expense accounts were cleared by being transferred to the statement of comprehensive income, recognising that the concept of matching must be applied, and

▶ have illustrated the matching concept within the context of cost of sales.

The remaining balances in the ledgers then formed a statement of financial position at the end of the financial period. The two main statements extracted from all this double entry, the statement of comprehensive income and the statement of financial position, have also been written in what is regarded as a 'user friendly' manner, i.e. vertical format. The statement of financial position format also reflected the equation assets = equity + liabilities

All this has been rather 'long winded' and the accounts take time to enter up. However, practice makes perfect, so we have provided several questions below.

Key terms

double entry (p. 73)
account (p. 73)
credit transactions (p. 78)
accounts payable (p. 78)
accounts receivable (p. 78)

ledger (p. 79)
balance off (p. 80)
trial balance (p. 84)
closing inventory account (p. 87)

Self-assessment questions

1 On 1.4.20X1 H. Britton commenced a business dealing in subaqua equipment. He paid £20,000 into the business bank account and the following transactions took place during the month of April.

1st	From previous owner bought shop £8,000, fixtures and fittings £5,000 and stock £4,000, paying by cheque £17,000	
2nd	Withdrew cash from bank for shop use	500
	Paid for stationery and other incidentals	175
3rd	Sold goods for cash	450
4th	Sold goods on credit to A. Britton	650
5th	Cash sales	250
	Wages paid in cash	160
8th	Bought goods for resale on credit from R. Sevier	950
	A. Britton returned faulty goods	100
9th	Cash sales	340
	Paid sundry expenses in cash	80
10th	Sold goods on credit to R. Sewell	440
11th	Returned goods to R. Sevier	230
12th	Cash sales	340
	Wages paid in cash	160
	Paid excess cash into bank	
15th	Sold goods on credit to S. Boatman	260
16th	Bought goods for resale from P. Ocean	1,500
17th	Paid cheque on account to R. Sevier	500
	Received cheque on account from A. Britton	400
18th	Cash sales	550
	Office expenses paid in cash	60
19th	Paid wages in cash	160
22nd	S. Boatman paid on account by cheque	50
	Paid P. Ocean by cheque	900
	Cash sales	850
24th	Wages paid in cash	160
	Office expenses paid in cash	50
	Withdrew cash for personal use	400
25th	Paid excess cash into bank account	
	Inventory on hand 30 April cost £3,500	

Required

(a) Record the above transactions in the ledger accounts of H. Britton, maintaining separate cash and bank accounts and separate accounts for returned goods.

(b) Balance off the ledger accounts as at 30 April and extract a trial balance.

(c) Prepare the statement of comprehensive income for the month ended 30 April and close off all revenue and expense accounts.

(d) Prepare a statement of financial position as at 30 April.

2 On 1.6.X1 D. Alex commenced a business dealing in IT software. He paid £50,000 into the business bank account and the following transactions took place during the first week of June.

1 June	Purchased premises for £25,000 from previous owner, including £6,000 for furniture and fittings
	Purchased inventory for £10,000 and further furniture and fittings £2,000
	All transactions above were completed by cheque

▶

2 June	Withdrew cash from bank for shop use	400
	Paid for sundry incidentals	90
	Sold goods for cash	300
	Sold goods on credit to Roberts	100
3 June	Bought goods for resale on credit from Davids	600
	Sold goods for cash	550
4 June	Sold goods for cash	400
	Sold goods on credit to Richards	350
	Paid office expenses in cash	70
5 June	Received cheque from Roberts	60
	Paid cheque on account Davids	250
	Sold goods for cash	200
	Sold goods on credit Martin	480
	Bought goods for cash	250
	Paid all excess cash into bank	
6 June	Stock on hand at cost	9,500

Required

(a) Record the above transactions in the ledger accounts of D. Alex maintaining separate cash and bank accounts.

(b) Balance off the ledger accounts as at 5 June X1 and extract a trial balance.

(c) Prepare the statement of comprehensive income for the week ended 5 June X1 and close off all revenue and expense accounts.

(d) Prepare the statement of financial position as at 5 June X1.

3 Explain why businesses have a need for a system of double entry accounting/ bookkeeping.

4 Complete the following:

The double entry system of accounting is based on the concept of ......

5 What is the accounting equation?

6 A debit balance b/d on a double entry account is:

(a) an asset or expense
(b) a liability or income?

7 Explain the need for a trial balance.

8 What types of errors will the trial balance not reveal?

9 The following trial balance has been extracted from the ledgers of Narn as at 31 March 200X.

	Dr	Cr
	(£)	(£)
Sales		79,000
Purchases	32,000	
Inventory 1st April 200W	2,700	
Salaries and wages	15,600	

Heating and lighting	3,600	
Rent	10,400	
Other expenses	2,300	
Fixtures and fittings	5,600	
Vehicles	10,900	
Motor expenses	4,500	
Trade receivables	6,600	
Trade payables		5,700
Capital injection by Narn		15,000
Bank and cash	5,500	
	99,700	99,700

Required

Prepare the income statement and the balance sheet for Narn as at 31 March 200X given that inventory at 31 March 200X was £4,200.

10 In the trial balance given at question 9 the following issues were discovered.

▶ An item of sale had been correctly entered in the cash ledger but had been entered in the sales account as at £4,500 instead of £5,400.

▶ A debtor had been entered on the ledgers as owing £2,300 instead of £3,200. The sale had been correctly entered in the ledgers.

▶ The bookkeeper had failed to record an office expense of £450 in the ledger although the item had been entered in the cash account.

▶ The bookkeeper had debited £225 to the bank account instead of crediting it.

Required

Correct the trial balance of Narn as at 31 March 200X and redraw the income statement and balance sheet.

Answers to these questions can be found at the back of this book.

6

Adjustments, including entries in ledger accounts

Objectives

By the end of this chapter you should be able to:

▶ Identify the need for adjustments to ledger accounts.

▶ Understand the nature of prepayments and accruals.

▶ Describe the necessity for adjustments for bad and doubtful debts.

▶ Define depreciation.

▶ Carry out the required ledger entries for depreciation.

▶ Balance off all ledger accounts after adjustments.

▶ Understand the nature of any balance remaining.

Introduction

Chapter 5 introduced you to the double entry system of bookkeeping. This chapter intends to build on that knowledge and expertise gained and also to further develop the concepts and conventions of accounting in relation to this double entry system.

So far we have assumed, with the exception of the inventory adjustment that we looked at in Chapter 5, that all entries made in the ledger for assets, liabilities, expenses and income relate to the period for which you wish to extract a statement of comprehensive income and a statement of financial position and that no items are missing. This is an incorrect assumption!

Accruals and prepayments

In the previous chapter all the expenses for Mr Bean's business entered the ledger accounts via the cash or bank account and the assumption was made that these related to sales, and were used up by Mr Bean in achieving those sales.

However, many expenses may be recorded as they are paid but may not relate, match, to the period in question. This was true in the case of purchases.

Mr Bean may have purchased £12,000 of goods during a period but he did not use up all those purchases in achieving his sales. He had some purchases left, i.e. inventory. We accounted for this by making an adjustment to the accounts. An inventory account was debited with the amount of inventory in the warehouse and the same figure was credited to the statement of comprehensive income. The closing inventory also appeared on the statement of financial position as it was a balance remaining after extracting the statement of comprehensive income at the period end. Closing inventory is an example of a **prepayment**. We have acquired the inventory and paid for it or identified the account payable in the ledgers but not yet used it up in generating revenues.

*A*ctivity 6.1

Identify whether the following payments made by Mr Bean during the period 1.1.X5 to 31.12.X5 actually relate (need to be matched) to any income achieved in that period and, if so, how much?

▶ Rent of £200 paid on 1.7.X5 relating to the period 1.7.X5–30.6.X6.

▶ Electricity paid 14.12.X5 relating to the period 1.9.X5–30.11.X5.

▶ Car insurance paid 1.4.X5 relating to the annual premium for the car purchased on that date.

Answer

This was quite tricky if you gave a full answer to the question.

▶ The rent payment related to the year from 1.7.X5 so some of this needs matching to the period in question – six months of it, i.e. £100. The other £100 will need matching to the income of the next year. Mr Bean has in fact *prepaid* his rent.

▶ The electricity amount paid does need matching to the period in question. A very interesting question is what about the electricity expense that was presumably used up in December. Mr Bean will not pay for this until after he receives his next quarterly bill – presumably in March X6 – so there is no reference to this expense within the ledgers as yet. There should be if expenses are to be correctly matched. An accrual of one month's electricity charge is required.

▶ Only nine months of the insurance premium needs matching to the income for the period ended 31.12.X5. The other three months will relate to next year's accounts. Again Mr Bean has prepaid part of his insurance.

The prepayments identified above, for insurance and rent, will need adjusting for in the ledger accounts of Mr Bean in order to correctly match expense with income achieved. The electricity account will also need an adjustment otherwise the 12-month expense for electricity will not be matched, only 11 months. For the electricity an **accrual** is required. Adjustments for accruals and prepayments are necessary to ensure compliance with the matching concept. The adjustments for accruals and prepayments within the ledger accounts can at first sight appear rather confusing but as long as you think very carefully about the *period* an expense relates to rather than its *payment date* you should find no difficulty with it.

Adjustment to ledger accounts

The following example shows the necessary ledger adjustments for accruals and prepayments. An activity then follows asking you to carry out some adjustments. Work through the example and activity carefully.

Example 6.1

Mr Carn has set up in business as a florist and the annual rental for shop premises is £2,000. This rental is paid by Mr Carn as follows:

► £500 5.4.X5

► £500 10.7.X5

► £500 11.10.X5

The remaining £500 Mr Carn expects to pay sometime in January X6.

The three rental payments above will have been entered into the ledger accounts when they are paid, by crediting the bank account and debiting the rent expense account. (See Chapter 5 if you need to refresh your memory on double entry.)

The rent account will appear as follows:

RENT ACCOUNT

5.4	Bank	500
10.7	Bank	500
11.10	Bank	500

Mr Carn wishes to draw up a statement of comprehensive income for the year ended 31.12.X5. To do this you saw in Chapter 5 that the expense accounts were balanced off and the balance transferred to the statement of comprehensive income – a double entry account.

If the rent account as above is balanced off then the balance will be £1,500 and this will be transferred to the statement of comprehensive income. However, this would not be the matched expense for rent for the year. An accrual of £500 needs to be made, i.e. the remainder of the rent that is due for the period but will not be paid until January X6.

RENT ACCOUNT

5.4	Bank	500			
10.7	Bank	500			
11.10	Bank	500			
31.12	Accrual c/d	500	31.12	Statement of comprehensive income	2,000
		2,000			2,000
			1.1	Accrual b/d	500

This account now shows that the expense transferred to the statement of comprehensive income is the matched expense of £2,000 and that there is a balance on the account on the credit side of £500 as at 1 January. This arose because duality had to be maintained. An entry was made on the debit side of the account for the accrual of £500 and duality demands that an equal and opposite entry also be made – this is the

Example 6.1
continued

credit entry below the balance on the account. This credit balance of £500 will appear in the statement of financial position as at 31.12.X5 as a liability, as it is an amount that is owed in respect of the period.

Mr Carn has also made a payment of £600 on 1.4.X5 for his annual car insurance premium.

This again will be entered into the ledger via the bank account and the car insurance account will appear as follows:

CAR INSURANCE ACCOUNT

1.4	Bank	600		

However, only part of this premium relates to the period for which we wish to draw up the statement of comprehensive income. There is a prepayment of £150. This is reflected in the ledger accounts as follows:

CAR INSURANCE ACCOUNT

1.4	Bank	600	31.12	Prepaid c/d		150
			31.12	Statement of comprehensive income		450
		600				600
1.1	Prepaid b/d	150				

The duality concept again gives rise to a balance on the account but this time it is a debit balance b/d as £150 has been paid in advance. This prepayment will form an expense of the next period and will appear on the statement of financial position at 31.12.X5 under current assets.

Activity 6.2

Tom, a greengrocer, wishes to prepare his statement of comprehensive income for the year ended 31.10.X5 and statement of financial position as at that date.

During the year he has made the following payments:

▶ Rent £1,200 for the period 1.1.X5 to 31.12.X5.

▶ Wages £1,020, £20 owing as at 31.10.X5.

▶ General expenses £470, £50 owing as at 31.10.X5.

▶ Electricity for three quarters £900.

▶ Telephone rental, quarterly in advance, £18 paid 1.11.X4, 1.2.X5, 1.5.X5, 1.8.X5 and 28.10.X5.

▶ Telephone calls, quarterly in arrears, £55 1.2.X5, £65 1.5.X5, £60 1.8.X5.

Show the ledger accounts for all these payments and balance them off at the year end, 31.10.X5. Clearly show the matched transfer to the statement of comprehensive income for the period and identify where balances, if any, on these ledger accounts will appear in the statement of financial position.

Answer

RENT ACCOUNT

31.10.X5	Bank	1,200	31.10.X5	Statement of comprehensive income	1,000
			31.10.X5	Bal c/d	200
		1,200			1,200
1.11.X5	Bal b/d	200			

WAGES ACCOUNT

31.10.X5	Bank	1,020	31.10.X5	Statement of comprehensive income	1,040
31.10.X5	Bal c/d	20			
		1,040			1,040
			1.11.X5	Bal b/d	20

GENERAL EXPENSES ACCOUNT

31.10.X5	Bank	470			
31.10.X5	Bal c/d	50	31.10.X5	Statement of comprehensive income	520
		520			520
			1.11.X5	Bal b/d	50

TELEPHONE RENTAL ACCOUNT

1.11.X4	Bank	18			
1.2.X5	Bank	18			
1.5.X5	Bank	18			
1.8.X5	Bank	18	31.10.X5	Statement of comprehensive income	72
28.10.X5	Bank	18	31.10.X5	Bal c/d	18
		90			90
1.11.X5	Bal b/d	18			

TELEPHONE CALLS ACCOUNT

1.2.X5	Bank	55			
1.5.X5	Bank	65			
1.8.X5	Bank	60			
31.10.X5	Bal c/d	60	31.10.X5	Statement of comprehensive income	240
		240			240
			1.11.X5	Bal b/d	60

STATEMENT OF FINANCIAL POSITION EXTRACT AS AT 31.10.X5

	£
Current assets	
Prepayments: Rent	200
Telephone rentals	18
	218
Current liabilities	
Accruals: Wages	20
General	50
Telephone calls	60
	130

Note that the accruals and prepayments b/d will appear as the first item on the ledger account for the next period and will automatically adjust the accounts for the next period. These accrual and prepayment balances must never be ignored! They exist as a liability or asset in the books in the same way as a creditor or a non-current asset. If you ignore them your trial balance will not balance nor will your statement of financial position. The final activity within this section involves providing definitions in your own words for accruals and prepayments.

Activity 6.3   In your own words provide a definition for an 'accrual' and a 'prepayment'.

Answer   Your definitions should have been similar to the following:

▶ *Accrual* – the addition necessary to the cash paid to ensure that all expense used up in generating revenue is matched with that revenue. The accrual will be a liability, an amount owing at the end of the period.

▶ *Prepayment* – the reduction necessary to the cash paid when payments have been made in advance but the expense has not been used up in generating revenue. The prepayment will appear as an asset at the end of the period.

You must also note at this point that accruals and prepayments can also occur in respect of items of income. For example, a business or an organisation may own some property, an asset, which it rents to another business or organisation. This rent receivable will be income to the business owner but could be cash paid in arrears or in advance. If in *arrears* then at the end of the period an adjustment will be made to accrue the rent receivable, if in *advance* an adjustment of a prepayment will be required.

A simple example follows to illustrate this.

Example 6.2

A. Flower rents part of his business premises, which he owns, to A. Carn at an annual rental of £2,400. This rental is payable quarterly in arrears commencing 1.4.X5.

Show the ledger account for rents receivable in A. Flower's books with the year-end adjustments necessary for the year ended 31.12.X5 assuming all payments are received on their due dates.

RENTS RECEIVABLE ACCOUNT

			1.4.X5	Bank	600
			1.7.X5	Bank	600
			1.10.X5	Bank	600
31.12.X5	Statement of comprehensive income	2,400	31.12.X5	Accrued c/d	600
		2,400			2,400
1.1.X6	Accrued b/d	600			

One further point to note is that the main item of revenue for a business, sales income, has already had any revenue owing accrued in the books by the introduction of debtors into the system. So neither accruals nor prepayment adjustments are usually necessary for sales income.

However, other adjustments are required in respect of debtors, but before dealing with this we provide a practice question incorporating accruals and prepayments in respect of both expenses and income.

Activity 6.4

Mr Wong, a sole trader with a year end of 31.12.X1, has the following items of cash paid and received in his ledgers:

▶ Rent paid 10.1.X1 £5,000 relating to the year 1.7.X0 to 30.6.X1 and rent paid 15.12.X1 £6,000 relating to year from 1.7.X1.

▶ Rent received of £12,000 on 1.6.X1 relating to the year from 1.3.X1.

▶ Electricity paid quarterly in arrears: 7.1.X1 £320, 5.4.X1 £300, 3.7.X1 £280, 4.10.X1 £260 and 28.12.X1 £310.

Show the ledger accounts for the above in Wong's ledgers with the year-end adjustments necessary for the year ended 31.12.X1. Note you may also need to make some pre-year adjustments as at 1.1.X1.

Answer

RENTS PAID

10.1.X1	Bank	5,000	1.1.X1	Balance b/d	2,500
15.12X1	Bank	6,000	31.12.X1	Balance c/d	3,000
			31.12.X1	Statement of comprehensive Income	5,500
		11,000			11,000
1.1.X2	Balance b/d	3,000			

RENTS RECEIVED

31.12.X1	Statement of comprehensive income	10,000	1.6.X1	Bank	12,000
31.12.X1	Balance c/d	2,000			
		12,000			12,000
			1.1.X2	Balance b/d	2,000

ELECTRICITY ACCOUNT

7.1.X1	Bank	320	1.1.X1	Balance b/d	320
5.4.X1	Bank	300	31.12.X1	Statement of comprehensive Income	1,150
3.7.X1	Bank	280			
4.10.X1	Bank	260			
28.12.X1	Bank	310			
		1,470			1,470

Adjustments for bad and doubtful debts

The point at which you have recognised sales in the business books, generally at the point of delivery or invoicing of the goods, rather than the point at which cash is received, gives rise to the next lot of adjustments to the year-end accounts.

Recognising sales before cash has been received has introduced debtors, accounts receivable, into the books but there may be a possibility that some of these debtors may not pay the amounts due. In other words the asset, account receivable, becomes impaired (reduces in value) and the full amount will not be recoverable. Under the concept of prudence an allowance for this possibility must be made, but how much does this allowance need to be? This problem can be broken down into two parts.

Bad debts

Some debts can be identified as bad debts, that is, the debtor will never pay what he or she owes as he or she has been declared bankrupt or cannot be traced. These bad debts are a normal part of business today and like all other expenses of a business must be charged as an expense to the statement of comprehensive income.

See if you can complete the following activity without an example first.

Activity 6.5

A. Flower has several accounts receivable within his books. Two of these debtors, A. Carn and P. Rose, who owe respectively £250 and £130, have both been declared bankrupt and there is no possibility that these debts will be paid. Show the adjustments necessary in the accounts of A. Flower as at the year end, 31.12.X5, to deal with these bad debts.

Hint – use a ledger account entitled bad debt account to make the required adjustments.

Answer

A. CARN ACCOUNT

31.12.X5 Balance		250	31.12.X5 Bad debts	250

P. ROSE ACCOUNT

31.12.X5 Balance		130	31.12.X5 Bad debts	130

BAD DEBTS ACCOUNT

31.12.X5 A. Carn	250			
31.12.X5 P. Rose	130	31.12.X5 Statement of	380
		comprehensive	
		income	
	380		380

As you can see, a bad debt account is set up to which the bad debts are transferred at the year end. This bad debt account is then cleared to the statement of comprehensive income as it is an expense of trading.

Sometimes it is possible to find a situation where part of a debt will be paid and the remainder will be declared bad. This quite often occurs in bankruptcy situations where creditors receive a proportion of what they are owed. For example, it could have been the case that P. Rose was able to pay 50p in the pound in respect of his debts, in which case P. Rose's account would have been adjusted as follows:

P. ROSE ACCOUNT

31.12.X5 Balance		130	31.12.X5 Bad debts	65
			31.12.X5 Balance c/d	65
		130		130
1.1.X6 Balance b/d		65		

The balance of £65 will remain as a collectable debt on P. Rose's account as it is expected he will pay this amount in the future and will be shown under accounts receivable on the statement of financial position.

Provision for bad debts

In addition to adjusting for debts that you know are bad, a provision in respect of amounts owing that may turn out to be bad is also required. This **provision for bad debts** is to accord with prudence and ensure that assets are not overstated in the statement of financial position. The problem is, how does the business assess the amount of debts that may turn out to be bad; how much provision do they need to make? Or, to put this another way, how much is it probable that the debt will be impaired by?

Businesses generally assess the amount of debts that may turn out to be bad by looking at the length of time a debt has been outstanding and making an estimate based on past experience of the probability of a debt turning bad.

By doing this a trader could arrive at the conclusion that of the balance of debtors at the year end there is a probability that 2% could turn out bad. A provision will then be made for this amount of 2%, but the debtors' balances will not be reduced as the trader still hopes to recover the debts. He is just being prudent by making a provision for any bad debts that could occur.

Let's see how this works in the books.

Example 6.3

A. Flower has a total accounts receivable (debtors) balance of £11,600 at the year end after writing off the bad debts. From past experience he estimates that 2% of these debtors may be bad. He therefore needs to make a provision for bad debts of £232. Note that the provision is calculated after taking account of bad debts! To make this provision the accounting entries necessary are:

▶ Credit provision for bad debts account.

▶ Debit statement of comprehensive income.

PROVISION FOR BAD DEBTS ACCOUNT

31.12.X5 Balance c/d	232	31.12.X5	Statement of comprehensive income	232
	232			232
		1.1.X6	Balance b/d	232

You must note that this provision for bad debts account will have a balance on it at the year end and this must be shown, as all other balances, on the statement of financial position. It is customary to show this provision together with the accounts receivable (debtors) balance as follows:

A. FLOWER STATEMENT OF FINANCIAL POSITION EXTRACT AS AT 31.12.X5

Current assets		
Accounts receivable	11,600	
Less provision for bad debts	232	11,368

This treatment ensures that accounts receivable are shown at their estimated recoverable amount.

Provision for bad debts after the first year

This provision for bad debts of £232 will form part of the ledgers for the following year of A. Flower, and at the end of the next year a further estimate for bad debts will be made.

Suppose that at 31.12.X6 A. Flower has an accounts receivable (debtors) balance of £12,400 after writing off bad debts, and estimates that 2% of these debtors may not pay, i.e. £248.

In the ledgers there is already a provision for £232 from the previous year and therefore the only adjustment necessary at 31.12.X6 is to increase this provision to £248 by crediting the provision account and debiting the statement of comprehensive income with £16.

PROVISION FOR BAD DEBTS ACCOUNT

		1.1.X6	Balance b/d	232
31.12.X6	Balance c/d	248	31.12.X6	Statement of comprehensive income	16
		248			248
			1.1.X7	Balance b/d	248

Again there is a practice question for you with the answers below. This practice question incorporates adjustments in respect of bad debts and provision for bad debts

Activity 6.6

As at 30.6.X1 Mr Wong's accounts receivable balance was £7,900. Within this amount he notes that Lee, who owes £250, has recently been declared bankrupt as has Hue who owes £90. Wong currently estimates his provision for bad debts at 2% of debtors after writing off bad debts. The provision for bad debts in the books at 1.7.X0 was £145. Show the ledger accounts in relation to the above with the necessary year-end adjustments.

Answer

ACCOUNTS RECEIVABLE

30.6.X1	Balance b/d	7,900	30.6.X1	Bad debt	250
			30.6.X1	Bad debt	90
			30.6.X1	Balance c/d	7,560
		7,900			7,900
1.7.X1	Balance b/d	7,560			

PROVISION FOR BAD DEBTS

			1.7.X0	Balance b/d	145
30.6.X1	Balance c/d	151	30.6.X1	Statement of comprehensive income	6
		151			151
			1.7.X1	Balance b/d	151

BAD DEBTS

30.6.X1	Wong	250	30.6.X1	Statement of comprehensive income	340
30.6.X1	Hue	90			
		340			340

Activity 6.7

As at 31.12.X1 Mrs Martin's accounts receivable (debtor) balance was £43,900. Within this amount she notes that Orchard, who owes £2,500, has recently been declared bankrupt as has Lea who owes £900. Martin currently estimates her provision for bad debts at 3% of debtors after writing off bad debts. The provision for bad debts in the books at 1.1.X1 was £1,800. Show the ledger accounts in relation to the above with the necessary year-end adjustments.

Answer

ACCOUNTS RECEIVABLE

31.12.X1	Balance b/d	43,900	31.12.X1	Bad debt	2,500
			31.12.X1	Bad debt	900
			31.12.X1	Balance c/d	40,500
		43,900			43,900
1.7.X1	Balance b/d	40,500			

PROVISION FOR BAD DEBTS

31.12.X1	Statement of comprehensive income	585	1.1.X1	Balance b/d	1,800
31.12.X1	Balance c/d	1,215			
		1,800			1,800
			1.7.X1	Balance b/d	1,215

BAD DEBTS

31.12.X1 Orchard	2,500	31.12.X1	Statement of comprehensive income	3,400
31.12.X1 Lea	900			
	3,400			3,400

This activity was slightly different from Activity 6.6 as instead of the provision for bad debts being increased this year it is in fact reduced. This required a credit to the statement of comprehensive income for £585. Note that the statement of comprehensive income is also debited with the bad debts that have materialised of £3,400 so that the net charge to the statement of comprehensive income for the year is £2,815.

Depreciation

Another adjustment that is required at the year end is depreciation. But what is depreciation?

In Chapter 5, Mr Bean purchased a van for £5,000 for use in his business. This van was regarded as an asset of the business and was shown on the statement of financial position as a non-current asset at the amount it was purchased for. If this van is not sold by Mr Bean then, after several years, unless an adjustment is made in the accounts, it will still be shown on the statement of financial position as an asset of £5,000, but it may in fact be quite useless if it has come to the end of its useful life. In other words non-current assets generally have a finite life and are therefore used up in the business. An estimate of the amount of this use in each year must be made and charged to the statement of comprehensive income for the year in the same way as all other expenses that are used up are matched to the revenue they generate. This estimate of usage of fixed assets is known as **depreciation**.

Activity 6.8

Provide a definition for the term 'depreciation' as it is used in accounting.

Answer

Depreciation is an assessment of the amount of a non-current asset used up in a period by a business as it earns revenue.

Depreciation estimate

How is the estimate of depreciation arrived at?

Activity 6.9

Identify two factors that you think will influence the estimate of depreciation to be charged in a period.

Answer

There are several factors that you could have chosen from:

▶ *Original cost of asset* – the amount used up will obviously depend on the amount originally paid for the asset. The expense of depreciation will be greater for a more expensive van.

▶ *Life of the asset* – the longer the use of the asset in the business then the lower the depreciation charge in each period.

▶ *Residual value of asset at the end of its useful life* – the total amount of the asset used up in the business will be the original cost less any resale value at the end of its useful life.

▶ *Method of use of the asset* – the charge for each period will depend upon how the asset is used in each period. For example, the asset may be used up more in the first period than in the second. This will need reflecting in the depreciation charge.

The business has to combine all these factors in order to arrive at the depreciation charge. The method of combination may well be different for each business as each business will use the asset in a unique way. Thus there are no rules that state how each type of asset should be depreciated. Within accounting practice there are two methods of combining these factors that are quite popular: straight line and reducing balance (also known as diminishing balance method), but there are others.

Straight line method

The **straight line method** assumes that the asset is used evenly throughout its useful life and allocates cost less residual value over the useful life of the asset providing an estimate of depreciation that is the same for each period of use.

Activity 6.10

An asset was purchased for £10,000 on 1.1.X0 and has an estimated residual value of £1,500 at the end of its useful life of five years. Calculate the depreciation charge for each year assuming the straight line method.

Answer

$$\text{Depreciation} = £(10,000 - 1,500)/5$$
$$= £1,700 \text{ per annum}$$

Reducing balance method (diminishing balance)

The **reducing balance method** assumes that more of the asset is used up in the first period than the next and so on. It is calculated by applying a fixed percentage to the reducing balance of the asset. This is easiest to explain by the use of an example.

Example 6.4

An asset is purchased for £8,000 and is estimated to have a residual value of £2,000 at the end of its useful life of four years. The percentage charge for depreciation will be 30% applied to the reducing balance of the asset as follows:

Cost at beginning of Year 1	8,000
Depreciation charge Year 1, 30% × 8,000,	2,400
Reducing balance Year 2, 8,000 – 2,400,	5,600
Depreciation charge Year 2, 30% × 5,600,	1,680
Reducing balance Year 3	3,920
Depreciation charge Year 3, 30% × 3,920,	1,176
Reducing balance Year 4	2,744
Depreciation charge Year 4, 30% × 2,744,	823
Reducing balance end of Year 4	1,921

The reducing balance at the end of Year 4 should have equated to the residual value of £2,000. It didn't as the percentage depreciation figure used was rounded for ease of calculation. The percentage charge for reducing balance depreciation is calculated from the following formula:

$$r = 1 - \sqrt[n]{s/c}$$

where:

r = percentage;
n = useful life;
s = residual value;
c = original cost.

$r = 1 - \sqrt[4]{2,000/8,000}$
$r = 1 - \sqrt[4]{0.25}$
$r = 1 - 0.707107$
$r = 29.2893\%$

There are other methods of calculating depreciation but the two identified above will suffice for your studies at this stage.

Ledger entries for depreciation

Having identified a figure for depreciation this must now be entered in the ledger accounts as a period end adjustment so as to charge depreciation as an expense to the statement of comprehensive income for the period.

Activity 6.11

If the depreciation estimate is debited to the statement of comprehensive income in a period, identify where the equal and opposite credit entry will be made. Show the entries in the accounts for the period ending 31.12.X0 and 31.12.X1 for the straight line example used in Activity 6.10.

Answer

You need to identify another provision account here as you did for provision for bad debts. A provision for depreciation account is created and credited with the provision.

ASSET ACCOUNT

1.1.X0	Bank	10,000	31.12.X0	Balance c/d	10,000
1.1.X1	Balance b/d	10,000	31.12.X1	Balance c/d	10,000
1.1.X2	Balance b/d	10,000			

PROVISION FOR DEPRECIATION ACCOUNT

31.12.X0	Balance c/d	1,700	31.12.X0	Statement of comprehensive income	1,700
			1.1.X1	Balance b/d	1,700
31.12.X1	Balance c/d	3,400	31.12.X1	Statement of comprehensive income	1,700
		3,400			3,400
			1.1.X2	Balance b/d	3,400

Note how the asset account remains at its original amount in the ledgers and that the provision for depreciation account increases each period as further charges are made to the statement of comprehensive incomes.

These two accounts will be reflected in the statement of financial position as at 31.12.X0 and 31.12.X1 as follows:

STATEMENT OF FINANCIAL POSITION EXTRACT AS AT 31.12.X0

Asset	10,000
Depreciation	1,700
Net book value	8,300

STATEMENT OF FINANCIAL POSITION EXTRACT AS AT 31.12.X1

Asset	10,000
Depreciation	3,400
Net book value	6,600

The above is quite often written in columnar form as follows:

	Cost	Depreciation	Net book value
Non-current asset	10,000	3,400	6,600

Activity 6.12

C. Charm purchases assets at the commencement of her business as follows:

	Cost	Useful life	Residual value
	(£)	(years)	(£)
Premises	40,000	50	5,000
Equipment	10,000	10	400
Vehicles	12,000	7	800

Depreciation is to be charged on a straight line basis for all assets. Show the ledger accounts for all fixed assets and provision for depreciation together with the statement of financial position extracts in columnar form for the first two years of business.

Answer

PREMISES

Yr 1	Bank	40,000	Balance c/d	40,000
Yr 2	Balance b/d	40,000	Balance c/d	40,000
Yr 3	Balance b/d	40,000		

EQUIPMENT

Yr 1	Bank	10,000	Balance c/d	10,000
Yr 2	Balance b/d	10,000	Balance c/d	10,000
Yr 3	Balance b/d	10,000		

VEHICLES

Yr 1	Bank	12,000	Balance c/d	12,000
Yr 2	Balance b/d	12,000	Balance c/d	12,000
Yr 3	Balance b/d	12,000		

DEPRECIATION PREMISES

Yr 1	Balance c/d	700	Statement of comprehensive income	700
Yr 2	Balance c/d	1,400	Balance b/d	700
			Statement of comprehensive income	700
		1,400		1,400
			Balance b/d	1,400

DEPRECIATION EQUIPMENT

Yr 1	Balance c/d	960	Statement of comprehensive income	960
Yr 2	Balance c/d	1,920	Balance b/d	960
			Statement of comprehensive income	960
		1,920		1,920
			Balance b/d	1,920

DEPRECIATION VEHICLES

Yr 1	Balance c/d	1,600	Statement of comprehensive income		1,600
Yr 2	Balance c/d	3,200	Statement of comprehensive income		1,600
			Balance b/d		1,600
		3,200			3,200
			Balance b/d		3,200

STATEMENT OF FINANCIAL POSITION EXTRACT YEAR 1

	Cost	Depreciation	Net book value
Premises	40,000	700	39,300
Equipment	10,000	960	9,040
Vehicles	12,000	1,600	10,400
	62,000	3,260	58,740

STATEMENT OF FINANCIAL POSITION EXTRACT YEAR 2

	Cost	Depreciation	Net book value
Premises	40,000	1,400	38,600
Equipment	10,000	1,920	8,080
Vehicles	12,000	3,200	8,800
	62,000	6,520	55,480

Sale of non-current assets

The last adjustment to be considered in this chapter is that for the sale of a non-current asset.

When a **non-current asset** is sold the proceeds will, of course, be debited to the bank account as would all other income received. But where will the corresponding credit appear? The accounting answer is to credit a **sale of non-current asset account**. At this stage, though, the ledger accounts will still include the asset account showing the original cost of the asset and a provision for depreciation account which has been built up over the period of use of the asset before its sale. These accounts need deleting from the books otherwise an asset will be recorded in the statement of financial position which no longer belongs to nor is controlled by the business. These ledger accounts are deleted through the sale of asset account. We will return to this again in Chapter 13 when we look at the sale of revalued assets.

Activity 6.13   An asset is purchased for £12,000 on 1.1.X0 and is estimated to have a useful life of four years with a residual value at the end of its useful life of £2,000. Its method of use is assumed to be straight line. On 1.5.X2 the asset is sold for £5,400. Assume a charge for depreciation is made in the year of purchase but not in the year of sale. Show the ledger entries required for all three years and identify what the balance is on the sale of asset account at 31.12.X2.

Answer

ASSET ACCOUNT

1.1.X0	Bank	12,000	31.12.X0	Balance c/d	12,000
1.1.X1	Balance b/d	12,000	31.12.X1	Balance c/d	12,000
1.1.X2	Balance b/d	12,000	31.12.X2	Sale of asset	12,000

PROVISION FOR DEPRECIATION ACCOUNT

31.12.X0	Balance c/d	2,500	31.12.X0	Statement of comprehensive income	25,000
			1.1.X1	Balance b/d	2,500
31.12.X1	Balance c/d	5,000	31.12.X1	Statement of comprehensive income	2,500
		5,000			5,000
31.12.X2	Sale of asset	5,000	1.1.X2	Balance b/d	5,000

SALE OF ASSET ACCOUNT

31.12.X2	Asset	12,000	1.5.X2	Bank	5,400
			31.12.X2	Depreciation	5,000
			31.12.X2	Balance c/d	1,600
		12,000			12,000
31.12.X2	Balance b/d	1,600			

Note how the asset account and the depreciation account have been cleared to the sale of asset account. The balance on the sale account is the difference between what was paid for the asset, the amount of the asset estimated to have been used up in the business and the amount received on its sale. It is a loss on sale and will be charged to the income statement as are all other expenses of the business.

SALE OF ASSET ACCOUNT

31.12.X2	Bal b/d	1,600	31.12.X2	Statement of comprehensive income	1,600

The following activity tests if you can deal with depreciation and sale of assets without using ledger accounts.

Activity 6.14

An asset is purchased for £15,000 on 1.1.X0 and is estimated to have a useful life of four years with a residual value at the end of the useful life of £3,000. Its method of use is assumed to be straight line. On 1.4.X2 the asset is sold for £7,350. Another asset was purchased on 1.1.X1 for £20,000 and the depreciation method applied to it is 25% reducing balance per annum. This asset is also sold on 1.4.X2 but for £17,500. You may assume that a charge for depreciation is made in the year of purchase but not in the year of sale. Show the entries in the statement of comprehensive income and statement of financial position for the years ended 31.12.X0, X1 and X2 for both assets. You do not need to show the ledger accounts.

Answer

	Asset 1	Asset 2
Year ended 31.12.X0		
Depreciation charge for year	(15,000 – 3,000)/4 = 3,000	
Net book value	15,000 – 3,000 = 12,000	
Statement of comprehensive income charge for depreciation	3,000	
S of FP non-current asset	12,000	
Year ended 31.12.X1		
Depreciation charge for year	(15,000 – 3,000)/4 = 3,000	2,0000 × 25% = 5,000
Net book value	12,000 – 3,000 = 9,000	20,000 – 5,000 = 15,000
Statement of comprehensive income charge for year	3,000	5,000
S of FP non-current asset	9,000	15,000
Year ended 31.12.X2		
Profit/(loss) on sale	7,350 – 9,000 = (1,650)	17,500 – 15,000 = 2,500
Statement of comprehensive income profit/(loss) on sale	(1,650)	2,500
S of FP non-current asset	0	0

(S of FP = statement of financial position)

Summary

This chapter has:

▶ introduced you to several adjustments that have to be made to the ledger accounts at the end of a period in order to draw up the statement of comprehensive income and statement of financial position in accordance with accounting concepts and conventions

▶ identified for you that the concepts and conventions used were mainly accruals (matching) and prudence

▶ illustrated adjustments for accruals and prepayments, both for expense and revenue, bad debts and provision for bad debts and provision for depreciation

▶ identified that depreciation is perhaps the hardest adjustment to get to grips with as it is an attempt to measure the use of the asset within the business, not an attempt to reduce the asset to its realisable (sale) value at any point in time. You must ensure that you are very clear on this fact.

This chapter concludes with several exercises involving these adjustments.

Key terms

prepayment (p. 97)
accrual (p. 97)
ledger adjustments (p. 98)
bad debts (p. 103)
provision for bad debts (p. 105)
depreciation (p. 108)

straight line method (p. 109)
reducing balance method (p. 109)
non-current asset (p. 113)
sale of a non-current asset account
   (p. 113)

Self-assessment questions

Accruals and prepayments

1 The following adjustments are required to be made to the ledger accounts for Mr Cog for the year ended 31.12.X5:

▶ Stationery expenses paid in X5 £450, amount owing as at 31.12.X5 £50.

▶ Building insurance paid in X5 £600 for the period 1.7.X5 to 30.6.X6 – note: the building was purchased 1.7.X5.

▶ Motor expenses paid in X5 £550, amount owing 31.12.X4 £70, amount owing 31.12.X5 £90.

▶ Rents paid in X5 £1,500 for the period 1.7.X5 to 30.6.X6, £1,200 had been paid last year for the period 1.7.X4 to 30.6.X5.

▶ Rents receivable during the year should be £50 per month. Only £500 has been received as at 31.12.X5.

Show the ledger accounts for the above, the amounts transferred to the income statement and any balances carried down.

2 Answer TRUE or FALSE in respect of the following and fully explain your choice:

(a) If an accrued expense is ignored at the year end the profit will be understated.

(b) If an accrued expense from the previous period is not carried forward into the current year the profit for the current year will be understated.

(c) An accrued expense is an expense that has been paid but not used up in generating revenue.

(d) A prepayment is an expense that has been paid but not used up in generating revenue.

(e) When adjusting a ledger account for an accrued expense, you debit the account with the accrual before balancing and bring down a credit balance.

(f) An accrued expense is an asset.

(g) An accrued revenue item is an asset.

3 Complete the following:

Adjustments for accruals and prepayments are made in the accounts in accordance with the concept of ... .

4 The following adjustments are required to the ledger accounts for Mr Black for the year ended 31 December 20X5:

▶ office expenses paid in 20X5 £1,425, amount owing £75

▶ rents paid £4,800 relating to the period 1 April 20X5 to 31 March 20X6

▶ goods sold and delivered on credit no entry made in the books £2,500

▶ insurance paid £3,600 relating to the period 1 October 20X4 to 30 September 20X5, insurance is likely to increase by 10% per annum thereafter.

Identify all accruals and prepayments for the period in question and the amounts to be transferred to the income statement.

Bad debts and provision for bad debts

5 Creating a provision for bad debts uses which accounting concept? Explain your choice.

6 When bad debts are eliminated from accounts a provision for bad debts is no longer necessary. Discuss.

7 As at the year end 31.12.X5 the following debts out of a total debtors' figure of £54,500 are found to be bad:

A. Bloggs	£780
B. Swift	£320
P. Trent	£1,500 – 50p in the £ is payable.

The balance sheet as at 31.12.X4 showed a provision for bad debts for the business of £2,100. The provision for bad debts as at 31.12.X5 is estimated to be 5% of debtors' balances. Show the bad debts account, provision for bad debts account and the balance sheet as at 31.12.X5.

8 At the year end the following debts, out of a total debt figure of £45,680, are found to be bad:

▶ David £450

▶ Alex £650

▶ Sand £240 but 10p in the pound payable.

It is also estimated that a further provision for bad debts of 4% of debtors is required.
   Show the amount of bad debts to be written-off, the provision for bad debts and the balance for debtors to be shown in the balance sheet of the business.

Depreciation

9 Identify the factors involved in the calculation of depreciation for a non-current asset.

10 Are the following statements TRUE or FALSE? Explain your answer fully.

(a) Depreciation is the amount necessary to reduce the asset to its net realisable value at the year end.
(b) Depreciation is the assessment of the amount of an asset used up in generating revenue for a period.
(c) The amount of depreciation charged by two businesses using an identical asset will be the same.
(d) Motor vehicles are always depreciated using the reducing balance method and buildings using the straight line method.

▶

(e) The straight line method of depreciation allocates an equal charge for depreciation to each period of use.

(f) If depreciation is omitted from the accounts, profit for the year will be overstated.

11 The following non-current assets are bought by C. Brewer for use in her business on 1.1.X0.

	Cost	Estimated useful life	Estimated residual value at end of useful life
	(£)	(years)	(£)
Building	60,000	50	10,000
Vehicle	12,000	10	300
Equipment	9,000	10	800

Buildings and equipment are to be depreciated using the straight line method, vehicles reducing balance of 25%.

The vehicle is sold for £6,500 on 1.12.X2 and an item of equipment costing £1,500 for £1,200 on the same date. Assume that the residual value of the item of equipment sold was estimated to be £100 at its date of purchase. Assume a full year's depreciation in the year of purchase and none in the year of sale.

Show the asset accounts, provision for depreciation accounts, sale of asset accounts and extracts from the income statement and balance sheet in respect of these assets for the years ended 31.12.X0, 31.12.X1, 31.12.X2.

12 Currant commenced business on 1.10.X2 purchasing fixtures and fittings for £25,000 and a van for £16,000. The fixtures and fittings were estimated to have a useful life of eight years and a residual value of £1,800. Further fittings were purchased on 1.11.X5 for £15,200 with nil residual value.

During December 20X6 the van was involved in an accident and the insurance assessors considered it a write-off. A cheque for £3,200 was received in December from the insurers in full settlement. Another van was purchased on 5 January 20X7 at a cost of £18,500. Depreciation policy of Currant is to charge a full year in the year of purchase and none in the year of sale, and to depreciate fixtures and fittings on a straight line basis and vehicles by 25% reducing balance.

Prepare the ledger accounts for the two years ending 30.9.X6 and 30.9.X7 for each non-current asset together with related provision for depreciation and the sale of asset accounts. Show the balance sheet extract for fixed assets as at the two year ends.

13 Provide a definition of depreciation as it is used in accounting.

14 What information is needed in respect of an asset in order in order to make an assessment of depreciation for that asset.

15 The following non-current assets are owned by Black for use in his business:

	Cost	Estimated useful life	Estimated residual value at end of useful life
	(£)	(years)	(£)
Building	400,000	40	190,000
Vehicle	110,000	6	6,000
Equipment	80,000	8	1,000

All assets were bought on 1 January 20X0 and the depreciation policy of Black is as follows:

▶ Buildings 1% straight line.

▶ Equipment and vehicles 10% reducing balance.

Show the depreciation charges for the year ended 31 December 20X0 and 31 December 20X1 and comment on the depreciation policy of Black.

16 The income statement of Tosuso shows a profit of £10,870 for the period ended 31 December 200X. However, this income statement has been drawn up before adjustments have been made for the following:

▶ Non-current assets of £54,000 are to be depreciated on a straight line basis over ten years. Residual value is assumed to be £5,400.

▶ Bad debts of £6,700 have been identified for the period.

▶ The provision for bad debts, which is set at 5% of debtors balance, is shown in the balance sheet as £3,000. Debtors at the year end amount to £63,000 before the bad debt of £6,700 is written off.

▶ Accruals of £1,500 for electricity and prepayments of £4,500 for rent of office space.

Required
Show the adjustments to be made to the income statement to account for the above and recalculate the profit for the period.

Answers to these questions can be found at the back of this book.

7

Preparation of statement of comprehensive income and statement of financial position from trial balance and adjustments

Objectives

By the end of this chapter you should be able to:

▶ Prepare a statement of comprehensive income from a trial balance after taking account of several adjustments.

▶ Prepare a statement of financial position from a trial balance after several adjustments.

Introduction

This chapter aims to bring together your knowledge of Chapters 5 and 6 so that you can prepare statements of comprehensive income and statements of financial position at the period end of a business after taking account of all the period-end adjustments necessary to the ledger accounts. These period-end adjustments will ensure that the final statements prepared will be in accordance with concepts and conventions of accounting that were identified in Chapter 4. Use will be made of the extended trial balance technique in compiling these final statements. At this stage we are still only dealing with accounts of a sole trader business.

First, though, a recap of Chapters 5 and 6:

▶ Ledger accounts are required for all assets, liabilities, expenses and income within a business.

▶ These ledger accounts are written up using double entry – the duality concept.

▶ At a period end, ledger accounts are balanced.

▶ Expense and income accounts are transferred to the statement of comprehensive income which is a double entry account.

▶ Any other balances remaining in the ledgers are shown on a statement of financial position.

▶ To prepare accounts in accordance with accounting concepts and conventions several adjustments need to be made to the ledger accounts before transfers are made to the statement of comprehensive income.

▶ These adjustments take account of accruals and prepayments so that expenses used up are matched to the revenue they generate.

▶ Adjustments are required for bad debts and provision for bad debts to comply with prudence and accepted accounting practice.

▶ A depreciation adjustment for non-current assets that are used up in generating revenue is also required.

This chapter will consist of two examples that will demonstrate adjustments required to the ledgers at the period end, the extraction of a trial balance at this stage, and the preparation of a statement of comprehensive income and statement of financial position for the period. Work through these examples carefully as you will then be expected to complete a similar activity yourself. Our examples will conclude with a technique called an extended trial balance, which is a working paper from which the adjustments to the double entry accounts will be made. This speeds up the process of producing a statement of comprehensive income and a statement of financial position without having to wait for all the ledger accounts to be adjusted. This can be a useful technique for students in examinations. Remember that in Chapter 6, Activity 6.14, we asked you to prepare non-current asset adjustments without using ledger accounts. Note that the ledgers will eventually have to be amended for the period-end adjustments whether or not we use an extended trial balance.

Extended example

Example 7.1

The following trial balance was extracted from the ledgers of a sole trader, Mai Wong, as at 31.12.X5:

	Dr	Cr
Sales		45,000
Purchases	15,000	
Inventory 1.1.X5	2,300	
Wages	5,200	
Office expenses	900	
Heating and lighting	850	
Telephone	450	
Rent	2,200	
Fixtures and fittings	7,550	
Vehicles	8,500	
Provision for depreciation 1.1.X5:		
Fixtures and fittings		755

Example 7.1
continued

Capital		8,805
Accounts receivable	1,300	
Accounts payable		1,150
Insurance	650	
Motor expenses	210	
Drawings	10,400	
Bank and cash	200	
	55,710	55,710

The following **period-end adjustments** are required:

▶ Office expenses to be accrued, £50.

▶ Heating and lighting to be accrued, £150.

▶ Rent paid in advance, £200.

▶ Insurance paid in advance, £80.

▶ Fixtures and fittings to be depreciated at 10% of cost and vehicles 20% of cost.

▶ An item of fixtures was sold during the year for £90. The item had been bought on 1.1.X3 for £120. The sale proceeds were credited to the sales account.

▶ Closing inventory is valued at £1,950.

▶ £90 of the motor expenses relates to items for Mai Wong's own use.

Show the adjustments necessary to the ledger accounts to account for the above and the transfers to the statement of comprehensive income for the year.

OFFICE EXPENSES ACCOUNT

31.12.X5	Balance b/d	900			
31.12.X5	Balance c/d (1)	50	31.12.X5	Statement of (2)	950
				comprehensive	
		950		income	950
			1.1.X6	Balance b/d (1)	50

Entry 1 is the accrual of £50 for the year and the corresponding carry-down of the balance to the following year.

Entry 2 shows the charge to the statement of comprehensive income for the year, which is the £900 cash paid plus £50 accrual. This accrual is to ensure matching of expenses used up to the revenue generated.

HEATING AND LIGHTING ACCOUNT

31.12.X5	Balance b/d	850			
31.12.X5	Balance c/d (1)	150	31.12.X5	Statement of	1,000
				comprehensive	
				income	
		1,000			1,000
			11.X6	Balance b/d	150

Example 7.1
continued

RENT ACCOUNT

31.12.X5	Balance b/d	2,200	31.12.X5	Statement of comprehensive income	2,000
			31.12.X5	Balance c/d	200
		2,200			2,200
1.1.X6	Balance b/d	200			

INSURANCE ACCOUNT

31.12.X5	Balance b/d	650	31.12.X5	Statement of comprehensive income	570
			31.12.X5	Balance c/d	80
		650			650
1.1.X6	Balance b/d	80			

The above three accounts show similar entries to those for office expenses.

FIXTURES AND FITTINGS ACCOUNT

31.12.X5	Balance b/d	7,550	31.12.X5	Sale	120
			31.12.X5	Balance c/d	7,430
		7,550			7,550
1.1.X6	Balance b/d	7,430			

Here we have shown the 'write-out' from the asset account of the fixtures sold. The corresponding debit entry will be shown in the sale of fixtures account. A similar write-out needs to be made in the provision for depreciation account for fixtures and fittings. The depreciation previously provided on the fixtures sold will have been £120 × 10% for two years, that is, £24.

PROVISION FOR DEPRECIATION OF FIXTURES ACCOUNT

31.12.X5	Sale	24	31.12.X5	Balance c/d	755
31.12.X5	Balance c/d	1,474	31.12.X5	Statement of comprehensive income (1)	743
		1,498			1,498
			1.1.X6	Balance b/d	1,474

Entry 1 is the depreciation for the current year calculated on the remaining assets of £7,430 after the sale of £120. A corresponding entry will be made in the statement of comprehensive income.

Example 7.1
continued

The sale of fixtures account will appear as follows:

SALE OF FIXTURES ACCOUNT

31.12.X5	Fixtures	120	31.12.X5	Depreciation	24
			31.12.X5	Sales (1)	90
			31.12.X5	Statement of	6
				comprehensive	
				income	
		120			120

Entry 1 is the transfer of the sale proceeds of the fixtures which had been included in the sales account. The transfer of £6 to the statement of comprehensive income represents a loss on sale of the asset. The sales account will need amending as follows:

SALES ACCOUNT

31.12.X5	Sale of fixtures	90	31.12.X5	Balance b/d	45,000
31.12.X5	Statement of	44,910			
	comprehensive				
	income	45,000			45,000

The charge for depreciation on the vehicles also needs calculating and entering into the accounts: depreciation for the year 20% × £8,500 = £1,700.

PROVISION FOR DEPRECIATION OF VEHICLES ACCOUNT

31.12.X5	Balance c/d	1,700	31.12.X5	Statement of	1,700
				comprehensive	
				income	
			1.1.X6	Balance b/d	1,700

The motor expenses account also needs amending as £90 of these expenses related to Mai Wong's own use. This £90 is treated as drawings of Mai Wong.

MOTOR EXPENSES ACCOUNT

31.12.X5	Balance b/d	210	31.12.X5	Drawings	90
			31.12.X5	Statement of	120
				comprehensive	
				income	
		210			210

The accounts for purchases, inventory 1.1.X5, wages and telephone will all be transferred to the income statement and an account for closing inventory opened as follows:

Example 7.1
continued

CLOSING INVENTORY ACCOUNT

31.12.X5 Statement of comprehensive income	1,950	

The income statement will now appear as follows:

STATEMENT OF COMPREHENSIVE INCOME FOR THE YEAR ENDED 31.12.X5

Sales		44,910
Opening inventory	2,300	
Add purchases	15,000	
	17,300	
Less closing inventory	1,950	15,350
Gross profit		29,560
Wages	5,200	
Office expenses	950	
Heating and lighting	1,000	
Rent	2,000	
Insurance	570	
Depreciation: Fixtures	743	
Vehicles	1,700	
Telephone	450	
Motor expenses	120	
Loss on sale	6	12,739
Net profit		16,821

All balances now remaining in the ledgers are entered in the balance sheet as follows:

STATEMENT OF FINANCIAL POSITION AS AT 31.12.X5

	Cost	Depreciation	Net book value
ASSETS			
Non-current assets			
Fixtures and fittings	7,430	1,474	5,956
Vehicles	8,500	1,700	6,800
	15,930	3,174	12,756
Current assets			
Inventory		1,950	
Accounts receivable		1,300	
Rent prepaid		200	
Insurance prepaid		80	
Bank and cash		200	3,730
TOTAL ASSETS			16,486
EQUITY AND			
LIABILITIES			

Example 7.1
continued

Equity		8,805
Add profit	16,821	
Less drawings	10,490	6,331
		15,136
Current liabilities		
Accounts payable	1,150	
Office expenses accrued	50	
Heat and light accrued	150	1,350
TOTAL EQUITY AND LIABILITIES		16,486

Adjusting the ledger accounts as shown above is very time consuming but has to be done by a business if it keeps double entry records. Many businesses will use computerised ledgers. We will look at these in Chapter 15. The process of adjusting the ledgers for both computerised and manual systems can be controlled by the use of an extended trial balance – a worksheet. The worksheet for the example above would appear as follows:

	Trial balance		Adjustments		Statement of comprehensive income		Balance sheet	
	Dr	Cr	Dr	Cr	Dr	Cr	Dr	Cr
Sales		45,000	90			44,910		
Purchases	15,000				15,000			
Inventory	2,300				2,300			
Wages	5,200				5,200			
Office	900		50		950			
Heating and lighting	850		150		1,000			
Telephone	450				450			
Rent	2,200			200	2,000			
Fixtures and fittings	7,550			120			7.430	
Vehicles	8,500						8,500	
Depreciation, furniture and fittings		755	24	743				1,474
Capital		8,805						8,805
Accounts receivable	1,300						1,300	
Accounts payable		1,150						1,150
Insurance	650			80		570		
Motor	210			90		120		
Drawings	10,400		90				10,490	
Bank	200						200	
	55,710	55,710						
Accruals				200				200
Prepayments			280				280	
Depreciation, furniture and fittings			743		743			

Example 7.1 continued

Depreciation, vehicle	1,700		1,700			
Profit on sale	6		6			
Provision for depreciation, vehicle				1,700		1,700
Closing inventory	1,950				1,950	
Statement of comprehensive income		1,950		1,950		
Net profit			16,821			16,821
	5,083	5,083	46,860	46,860	30,150	30,150

This worksheet has been constructed as follows:

▶ The first two columns, headed trial balance, are simply a listing of the income, expenses, assets and liabilities from the question trial balance.

▶ The third and fourth columns, headed adjustments, take account of all the period end adjustments:

  ▶ Office expenses – debit 50, credit accruals 50.

  ▶ Heating and lighting – debit 150, credit accruals 150; accruals balance is now 200.

  ▶ Rent – credit rent 200, debit prepayments 200.

  ▶ Insurance – credit insurance 80, debit prepayments 80; prepayments balance now 280.

  ▶ Fixtures and fittings sale – debit sales 90, credit sales account 90. Write out the cost of the fixtures sold by crediting fixtures asset account 120, debiting sale account 120. Write out depreciation accrued on the item sold by debiting provision for depreciation 24 (two years depreciation at 12 per year), crediting sale account 24. Now balance the sale account and you are left with a debit balance b/d of 6 which is profit on sale.

  ▶ Depreciation on fixtures and fittings – the extended trial balance now shows a debit of 7,550 and a credit of 120. The overall debit is 7,430. Depreciation is provided on this at 10% by crediting provision for depreciation 743 and debiting depreciation charge 743.

  ▶ Vehicles only has a debit balance showing in the extended trial balance so far of 8,500, so the depreciation charge is 20% × 8,500 = 1,700 which is credited to provision for depreciation and debited to provision charge.

  ▶ Closing inventory needs entering, so debit closing inventory account, 1,950. Credit statement of comprehensive income.

  ▶ The last adjustment is to account for the personal drawings of Mai Wong by crediting motor expenses 90, then crediting drawings 90.

▶ Columns five and six show the transfers of balances on income and expense ledgers after the adjustments have been made to the statement of comprehensive income.

▶ Columns seven and eight show the assets and liabilities and capital and reserves tranferred to the statement of financial position.

Example 7.1
continued

▶ As each pair of columns is completed we check the extended worksheet by totalling the columns and the pairs should be equal. If they are not, then a mistake will have been made somewhere in the worksheet and this must be corrected.

Look at this extended trial balance carefully and follow all the adjustments made and the entries into the statement of comprehensive income and statement of financial position. You may find this method of drawing up the final accounts useful for examinations. The extended trial balance technique lends itself to computer spreadsheet applications.

The following activity is similar to Example 7.1 but only uses the extended trial balance technique not the ledgers.

Activity 7.1

The following trial balance was extracted from the ledgers of a sole trader Sue Chong as at 31.12.X8.

	Dr	Cr
Sales		95,500
Purchases	42,500	
Sales returns	4,500	
Inventory 1.1.X7	13,700	
Salaries	9,700	
General expenses	1,700	
Rent and rates	6,200	
Insurance	1,700	
Heating and lighting	4,300	
Plant and equipment	15,000	
Vehicles	12,000	
Vehicle expenses	1,700	
Capital		15,500
Drawings	13,200	
Accounts receivable	3,200	
Accounts payable		3,750
Bank		5,000
Cash	670	
Provision for depreciation:		
Plant and equipment		6,000
Vehicles		4,320
	130,070	130,070

The following period-end adjustments are required:

1 General expenses to be accrued, £90.

2 Heating and lighting to be accrued, £250.

3 Rent paid in advance, £400.

4 Rates paid in advance, £70.

5 Plant and equipment to be depreciated on a straight line basis assuming a useful life of four years and a residual value at the end of the useful life of £3,000.

6 Vehicles to be depreciated 20% reducing balance method.

7 An item of plant was purchased by the use of a loan for £15,000 on 1.1.X8. The loan carries interest at 5% per annum and the plant has a useful life of five years, no residual value and a straight line method of use. The loan is repayable 31.12.Y2. No entries have been made in the ledgers or the trial balance of Sue Chong for this purchase or any aspect of the loan.

8 Closing inventory is valued at £12,500.

Prepare the extended trial balance and the statement of comprehensive income for the period ended 31.12.X8 and the statement of financial position as at that date.

Answer

Extended trial balance for Sue Chong for the period ended 31.12.X8

	Trial balance		Adjustments		Statement of income		Statement of financial position	
	Dr	Cr	Dr	Cr	Dr	Cr	Dr	Cr
Sales		95,500				95,500		
Purchases	42,500				42,500			
Sales returns	4,500				4,500			
Inventory	13,700				13,700			
Salaries	9,700				9,700			
General expenses	1,700		90		1,790			
Rent and rates	6,200			400 +70	5,730			
Insurance	1,700				1,700			
Vehicle expense	1,700				1,700			
Heating and lighting	4,300			250	4,550			
Plant and equipment	15,000		15,000				30,000	
Vehicles	12,000						12,000	
Capital	15,500		15,500					
Drawings	13,200						13,200	
Accounts receivable	3,200						3,200	
Accounts payable		3,750						3,750
Bank		5,000						5,000
Cash	670						670	
Prov dep P and E		6,000		6,000				12,000
Prov dep veh		4,320		1,536				5,856
Accruals				340				340
Prepayments			470				470	
Closing inventory			12,500				12,500	
Statement of comprehensive income				12,500		12,500		
Loan				15,000				15,000

Dep P and E		6,000		6,000			
Dep veh		1,536		1,536			
Loan interest accrual			750				750
Loan interest expense		750		750			
Net profit				13,844			13,844
	130,070	130,070	36,596	36,596	108,000	108,000	72,040	72,040

STATEMENT OF COMPREHENSIVE INCOME FOR THE PERIOD ENDED 31.12.X8

Sales		95,500
Less sales returns		4,500
		91,000
Opening inventory	13,700	
Purchases	42,500	
	56,200	
Closing inventory	12,500	43,700
Gross profit		47,300
Salaries	9,700	
General expenses 1,700+90	1,790	
Rent and rates 6,200 – 400 – 70	5,730	
Insurance	1,700	
Heating and lighting 4,300+250	4,550	
Vehicle expenses	1,700	
Depreciation plant and equipment (15,000 – 3,000)/4 + 15,000/5	6,000	
Depreciation vehicles (12,000 – 4,320)×20%	1,536	
Loan interest 15,000×5%	750	33,456
Net profit		13,844

STATEMENT OF FINANCIAL POSITION AS AT 31.12.X8

	Cost	Depreciation	NBV
ASSETS			
Non-current assets			
Plant and equipment	30,000	12,000	18,000
Vehicles	12,000	5,856	6,144
	42,000	17,856	24,144
Current assets			
Inventory		12,500	
Accounts receivable		3,200	
Prepayments		470	

Cash	670	16,840
TOTAL ASSETS		40,984
EQUITY AND LIABILITIES		
Equity		
Capital	15,500	
Less drawings	13,200	2,300
Profit		13,844
		16,144
Non-current liabilities		
Loan		15,000
Current liabilities		
Accounts payable	3,750	
Accruals 90+250+750	1,090	
Bank	5,000	9,840
TOTAL EQUITY AND LIABILITIES		40,984

So far we have dealt with year-end account preparation for a sole trader, but the same process applies when preparing a statement of comprehensive income and statement of financial position from a trial balance and making adjustments for any type of business or organisation. Try the following activity which deals with the transactions of a club.

Activity 7.2

From the following trial balance relating to the position of a tennis club as at 31 March 200X, draw up the income and expenditure account (similar to the statement of comprehensive income) and the statement of financial position as at that date.

	Debit	Credit
Clubhouse at cost	54,700	
Accounts payable		3,300
Accounts receivable	2,200	
Inventory 31 March 200X	1,080	
Gross profit on bars, etc.		1,240
Furniture and fittings	7,600	
Bank and cash	5,600	
General expenses	760	
Insurance	1,200	
Heating and lighting	780	
Subscriptions to the club		10,100
Accumulated fund 1 April 200W		
(similar to capital)		19,470
Provision for depreciation:		
Clubhouse		38,290
Furniture and fittings		1,520

	73,920	73,920

The following information is also available:

▶ The insurance paid for the year only relates to the first six months of the period.

▶ Heating and lighting of £230 needs to be accrued.

▶ Clubhouse is depreciated 10% on cost and furniture and fittings 20% on cost.

Answer

INCOME AND EXPENDITURE ACCOUNT FOR THE PERIOD ENDED 31 MARCH 200X

Subscriptions		10,100
Gross profit		1,240
		11,340
Insurance (1,200 + 1,200)	2,400	
Heating and lighting (780 + 230)	1,010	
General expenses	760	
Depreciation: Clubhouse	5,470	
Furniture and fittings	1,520	11,160
Surplus		180

STATEMENT OF FINANCIAL POSITION AS AT 31 MARCH 200X

ASSETS

Non-current assets		
Clubhouse (54,700 – 5,470 – 38,290)	10,940	
Furniture and fittings (7,600 – 1,520 – 1,520)	4,560	15,500
Current assets		
Inventory	1,080	
Accounts receivable	2,200	
Bank and cash	5,600	8,880
TOTAL ASSETS		**£24,380**

EQUITY AND LIABILITIES

Equity		
Accumulated fund 1 April 200X		19,470
Surplus		180
		19,650
Current liabilities		
Accounts payable	3,300	
Accurals (1,200 + 230)	1,430	4,730
TOTAL EQUITY AND LIABILITIES		24,380

Summary

This chapter has combined your learning from Chapters 5 and 6. You should now be able to:

▶ prepare an income statement and balance sheet from a trial balance after making several adjustments at the period end to this trial balance for a business and a club.

We also illustrated the technique of an extended trial balance which is, in fact, a worksheet to control the adjustments within the ledger accounts. It can, however, be a useful tool to use in an examination.

We have only provided four self-assessment questions in this chapter as you will find plenty of practice in preparing statements of comprehensive income and statements of financial position in Chapter 8. You may like to attempt to do the exercises at the end of the chapter using an extended trial balance but note that we have not provided the answers in that way.

Key terms

extended trial balance (p. 121)   period-end adjustments (p. 122)

Self-assessment questions

1 The following trial balance was extracted from the books of Rodney, a sole trader, as at 31.12.X5:

	Dr	Cr
Capital 1.1.X5		15,500
Drawings	4,660	
Accounts receivable and payable	6,530	5,210
Sales		71,230
Purchases	29,760	
Inventory 1.1.X5	4,340	
Rates	800	
Heat and light	2,650	
Wages	8,250	
Bad debts	230	
Provision for bad debts		280
General expenses	2,340	
Motor expenses	3,240	
Premises at cost	30,000	
Fixtures and fittings	8,000	
Vehicles	12,000	

▶

Provision for depreciation 1.1.X5:		
Premises		2,400
Fixtures and fittings		1,600
Vehicles		5,400
Bank	820	
Loan		12,000
	113,620	113,620

The following matters have not been taken into account in the preparation of the above trial balance:

▶ Inventory 31.12.X5 £4,870.

▶ Light and heat due 31.12.X5 £120, general expenses due £80.

▶ Depreciation is to be provided for the year as follows:

  Premises – 2% on cost

  Fixtures and fittings – 10% on cost

  Vehicles – 20% reducing balance.

▶ A further bad debt of £130 is to be written off and the bad debts provision is to be at 5% of debtors after the write-off.

▶ The loan interest of £600 has not been paid for the year.

You are required to prepare a statement of comprehensive income for the year ended 31.12.X5 and a statement of financial position as at that date.

2 The following trial balance was extracted from the books of ATEC as at 31.12.X9:

	Dr	Cr
Sales		53,500
Purchases	29,200	
Inventory 1.1.X9	5,400	
Office expenses	· 150	
Electricity	700	
Salaries and wages	12,100	
Rates	600	
Telephone	280	
Other expenses	120	
Premises	30,000	
Rents received		550
Equipment	12,000	
Vehicles	12,000	
Provisions for depreciation:		
Premises		4,200
Equipment		8,400
Vehicles		3,000
Drawings	16,000	

Accounts receivable and payable	4,800	5,200
Provision for bad debts		90
Capital 1.1.X9		46,500
Bank		2,000
Cash	90	
	123,440	123,440

The following matters have not been taken into account in the preparation of the above trial balance:

▶ inventory as at 31.12.X9 £6,200

▶ accruals required as at 31.12.X9

- electricity   £230

- salaries and wages   £230

- telephone   £90

▶ rents receivable are £50 per month as from 1.1.X9

▶ the business commenced 1.1.X2 and depreciation has been provided on a straight line basis for premises and equipment since that date except for the current year for which no depreciation charge has yet been made

▶ vehicles are depreciated at 25% reducing balance and were purchased 1.1.X8

▶ no sales of non-current assets have been made prior to 1.1.X9. On 1.7.X9 part of the premises, cost £15,000, was sold for £25,000. These sale proceeds have been credited to the capital account

▶ drawings includes the purchase of a second–hand van for £5,000 on 1.2.X9. This van is used solely for business purposes

▶ bad debts to be written off as at 31.12.X9 amount to £120 and bad debts provision is to be set at 2% of accounts receivable after writing off bad debts

▶ depreciation is to be provided on the basis of a full year's charge in the year of purchase of the asset but none in the year of sale of the asset.

You are required to prepare a statement of comprehensive income for the year ended 31.12.X9 and a statement of financial position as at that date.

3 The following balances have been extracted from the accounting records of Celia, a sole trader, as at 31 March 20X8.

Sales	295,500
Sales returns	1,800
Purchases	154,500
Purchase returns	750
Accounts receivable	49,250
Accounts payable	32,180
Provision for bad debts	1,970
Plant and equipment	92,000
Plant and equipment depreciation provision 1.4.20X7	36,800
Vehicles	15,000

Vehicles depreciation provision 1.4.20X7	6,000
Drawings	19,750
General expenses	16,750
Wages	32,500
Rent and rates	12,000
Loan repayable 2015 carrying 8% interest per annum	25,000
Bank	12,175
Inventory 1.4.20X7	18,000
Capital	10,000
Retained profits 1.4.20X7	15,525

The following information is also available:

▶ The provision for doubtful debts is to be adjusted to 2% of accounts receivable

▶ Depreciation is to be provided for the year to 31.3.2008 at the following rates:

 – Plant and equipment 20% on cost

 – Vehicles 25% reducing balance

▶ Wages of £700 are to be accrued at 31.3.20X8

▶ Rent of £400 has been prepaid as at 31.3. 20X8

▶ The interest on the loan needs to be accrued for the year

▶ The inventory at 31.3.20X8 has been valued at £18,750. This includes damaged inventory items of £2,000 that are expected to be sold for £600.

Prepare the statement of comprehensive income for the year ended 31.3.20X8 and a statement of financial position as at that date for Celia.

4 From the following balances relating to the accounts of a small football club as at 31 March 20X8 draw up the income and expenditure account and the statement of financial position as at that date.

Club house at cost	25,000
Accounts receivable	1,200
Accounts payable	990
Inventory 31 March 20X8	550
Gross profit on bars, etc.	5,600
Gross profit on events	8,200
Furniture and fittings at cost	3,400
General expenses	2,300
Insurance	500
Heat and light	2,200
Subscriptions to the club	12,300
Accumulated fund 1 April 20X7	8,400
Provision for depreciation as at 1 April 20X7:	
Clubhouse	1,000
Furniture and fittings	340
Bank and cash	1,680

The following information is also available:

► The insurance paid only amounts to that for the first nine months of the year.

► Subscriptions due totaling £2,300 have not been paid to the club.

► Heating and lighting of £450 needs to be accrued.

► The local DJ, who provided the entertainment at several of the events run by the football club, has recently submitted his invoice for £2,800. This amount has not been included in the accounts payable.

► It is estimated that 1% of the accounts receivable as at 31 March 20X8 may not be paid.

► Depreciation for the year is to be provided as follows: premises straight line useful life 25 years with no residual value, furniture and fittings straight line useful life 10 years with no residual value.

Answers to these questions can be found at the back of this book.

8

Accounts of limited companies and other organisations

Objectives

By the end of this chapter you should be able to:

- ▶ Explain what is meant by corporate entity.
- ▶ Identify the nature of capital invested in companies and the returns available on this capital.
- ▶ Identify the main changes to company law from the company law review.
- ▶ Describe the term 'reserves'.
- ▶ Identify and account for the taxation charge within company accounts.
- ▶ Prepare the statement of comprehensive income and statement of financial position for companies.
- ▶ Prepare accounts for clubs and societies.
- ▶ Identify the differences between the preparation of accounts for companies and charities/public sector.
- ▶ Explain the difference between a company and a partnership.
- ▶ Prepare statements of comprehensive income and statements of financial position for a partnership.

The need for companies

In previous chapters we have assumed that the business is that of a sole trader. This is where an individual invests his/her capital in a business and trades with the intention of earning profit that will belong to him/her to do with as he/she chooses. However, this type of business has several drawbacks.

Activity 8.1   Identify two drawbacks of sole trader businesses.

Answer   You should have chosen two from the following list. However, this list is not exhaustive and you may have come up with drawbacks that we have not mentioned. You should be able to explain whether your drawbacks are reasonable.

▶ A sole trader has limited resources available – the capital he/she is able to invest in the business – and limited specialist and management skills.

▶ For a business to grow, more resources are required in terms of capital and expertise.

▶ The sole trader is personally liable for all debts of the business – creditors can claim on the personal assets of the sole trader.

▶ The sole trader business is dependent upon the owner.

Establishing the business as a limited company can overcome all the above drawbacks. Capital resources are available from more than one person, and the company also has easier access to loan funds. Specialist and management skills can be brought into the business by widening the number of owners. A company provides what is known as limited liability to the owners. Ownership can change without there being any effect on the business.

The company

A company has two notions as its basis:

▶ corporate entity

▶ limited liability.

The notion of corporate entity means that several people can band together as owners of a business by investing capital. The business will be a legal entity separate from the owners. It also means that the owners, the investors of capital, can change without the need to change the legal entity of the company.

The notion of limited liability limits the claim on the owners of the business from any of its creditors to the capital these owners invested. It also means that a creditor has to sue the company, not the owners, for payment of any debts due, and these creditors could indeed force the winding up, or liquidation, of the company. There are several hundred thousand companies in the United Kingdom and mainland Europe, many of them large conglomerates such as British Telecom, Guinness, Shell and ICI.

The law in relation to companies in the UK was established by the first Companies Act of 1844, which fused these two notions of corporate entity and limited liability. Any confusion in respect of the two notions was put to rest by the judgment in the case of *Salomon* v *Salomon & Co. Ltd* (1897). The judgment handed down by the House of Lords stated that the company was a separate legal entity distinct from the owners and that creditors could not claim on the personal assets of the owners, only on the assets of the company. Creditors trade with a limited company at their own risk. It is advisable for creditors to investigate the financial stability of a company before they trade with it.

Formation of a company

Further detail in respect of the formation of a company will be found in a company law course, but it is worthwhile identifying the main points here:

▶ All companies must be registered with the Registrar of Companies by the submission of a number of legal documents. This marks the legal birth of a company.

▶ The two most important documents to be filed are the **Memorandum of Association** and the **Articles of Association**.

▶ The Memorandum of Association defines the relationship between the company and any external parties. It also identifies the maximum capital to be invested in the company by the owners, known as the Share Capital. All companies must have at least two shareholders whose names and addresses appear in the memorandum.

▶ The Articles of Association define the rights of shareholders, the rules of operation of the company, and the rights and duties of owners and employees of the company.

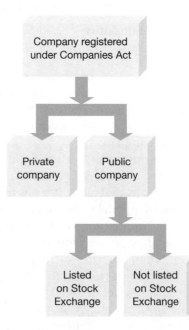

▶ Companies are registered as either public limited companies (plcs) or private companies. Essentially the distinction is that plcs can, if they wish, raise capital by selling shares to the general public. They must have a minimum allotted (i.e. issued to shareholders) share capital of £50,000. Many plcs are quoted on the London Stock Exchange, thus anyone who wants to can become an owner of the company as long as they have the necessary capital to invest. Private companies have restricted ownership. The diagram on the previous page illustrates the type of companies in general that exist.

▶ There must be at least two shareholders in any company but there is no maximum number.

▶ The day-to-day business of the company is generally not carried out by the owners but by directors who are appointed by the owners. The directors report to the owners through the facility of an Annual General Meeting and an **Annual Report** that incorporates the financial statements.

Company law review in the UK

A review of company law was undertaken during 2001/2 and resulted in a new Companies Act in 2006. This was the most extensive reform of Company Law for nearly 150 years in the UK. As a result of Enron and other corporate scandals across the world, there has been a significant push to require companies to report clearly about their business actions through new legislation. Much of the detail of the review was produced in a steering group report in July 2001 and then in a Government White Paper, *Modernising Company Law*, in July 2002. The objective of the review was to streamline procedures for all companies, especially smaller companies, to make the law clearer, more accessible and responsive to developments. According to the Department of Trade and Industry website on modernising company law, the Company Law Review will:

▶ enable better shareholder engagement,

▶ modernise and de-regulate the law,

▶ give greater clarity to directors on their duties and responsibilities, so that they do not inadvertently fall foul of the law,

▶ facilitate better communications with shareholders,

▶ help speed up decision making, and

▶ deregulate aspects of current law.

All of this should help maintain the UK's position as the best place to set up and run a business.

Company capital

The capital of a company is divided into **shares**. Investors purchase as many of these as they are able, and want, to buy. For example, a company could be registered with a maximum share capital of 100,000 £1 shares.

The maximum capital of the company would therefore be £100,000 and this would be termed its authorised share capital. A company, not the same one, could also be registered with a share capital of say 50,000 £3 shares – a maximum capital of £150,000. The pound value attached to a share is known as its nominal (or par) value and a company can decide on the nominal value and total number of shares it wishes to issue. The decision will depend on how much capital the company needs to commence its operations. Note that the company does not have to issue all its authorised share capital.

Once a company has made the initial issue of the shares, further trading in these shares can take place in what is known as the share market – for many plcs this is the Stock Exchange. Company shares may well be bought and sold every day on the Stock Exchange, but the company will make no reference to this in the ledger accounts as it is not a transaction between the corporate entity and the buyer, but between the separate shareholder and the buyer. Thus we are differentiating again between the entity of a company and the individual. The company will need to keep a list of who owns shares in it so that it can pay over any return from the trading of the company due to the shareholders. This return paid over to shareholders is known as the **dividend**.

Companies are also able to vary the rights of shareholders within a company by issuing different types of shares. The following activity is concerned with share issues and share transactions.

Activity 8.2   Obtain a set of company financial statements. This can be done by accessing library facilities, using company websites or by using the Annual Reports Service offered in the *Financial Times* – read the small print at the end of the daily stock exchange listings to see how this is done. Identify the types of shares in issue for your chosen company from the financial statements and notes.

Answer   Your company almost certainly has in issue ordinary shares. These are the most important type of share and are those most commonly traded on the stock exchange. They generally carry voting rights in proportion to the number of shares held. These voting rights give control over the operations of the company to the shareholders through the right to appoint the directors. You should also have been able to identify the dividends paid to ordinary shareholders.

Preference shares may also have been issued by the company. The main feature of preference shares is that they usually carry a specific rate of return to the holder from the company's profits. For example, 5% £1 preference shares would require a payment to the shareholders every year of 5p for every share held. A holder of £10,000 of these preference shares would receive £500.

Preference shares can also be termed cumulative. This means that if the company does not make enough profit in any one year to pay out the amount due to the preference shareholders, it carries over to the next year and accumulates until the company does have enough profit to pay out the amount due – the dividend.

The preference shares may also be *redeemable*, giving the company the right to repay the capital to the preference shareholders at a determined future date.

Shares can also be issued by a company at a value above the nominal value declared in the Memorandum of Association. This is known as issuing shares at a premium.

Activity 8.3   Explain why a company may wish to issue shares at a premium.

Answer   A company may wish to raise additional capital. To issue £1 ordinary shares at a price of £1 to new investors would be unfair to the initial investors in the company. The following example illustrates this point.

A company was initially formed by the issue of 100 £1 ordinary shares. The statement of financial position of the company at its formation can be summarised as follows:

Bank	100
Capital 100 £1 ordinary shares	100

The company trades for a number of years, earning profits of £250 in total. Its statement of financial position will then appear as follows:

Assets	350
Capital 100 £1 ordinary shares	100
Profit	250
	350

From this statement of financial position we can conclude that each share now has a book value of £3.50. It is also feasible that if these ordinary shares were traded on the stock exchange they would probably sell at a price in excess of £1. The company at this stage now wishes to raise more capital, £140, so that it can expand by the purchase of further assets. If it issues more £1 ordinary shares at their nominal value then this will be unfair to the original shareholders as the statement of financial position would now be:

Assets	490
Capital 240 £1 ordinary shares	240
Profit	250
	490

Now each share has a book value of £2.04. The original shareholders have lost £1.46 on each share!

To ensure equity (fairness) between old and new shareholders the new shares will be issued at a premium. In this case the shares of £1 nominal value will be issued at £3.50 and the number issued will be 40.

The statement of financial position will now be:

Assets	490
Capital 140 £1 ordinary shares	140
Share premium	100
Profit	250
	490

Now each share has a book value of £3.50.

Note that the premium paid on the shares is entered in a separate ledger account known as share premium.

Activity 8.4

A company is formed with a total authorised (authorised by its inclusion in the Memorandum of Association) share capital of £500,000, consisting of 300,000 £1 ordinary shares and 100,000 5% £2 preference shares. The company wishes to raise £400,000 in capital to start the business. Identify the number of shares of each type it should issue to minimise the preference dividend payment in each of the following circumstances:

1 All shares are to be issued at par.
2 Ordinary shares are to be issued at a premium of 25p and preference shares at a premium of 50p.

Answer

1 300,000 £1 ordinary shares and 50,000 £2 5% preference shares. Preference dividend payment £5,000.
2 300,000 £1 ordinary shares at £1.25 raises £375,000, the further £25,000 required is raised by issuing 10,000 £2 5% preference shares at £2.50. Preference dividend payment £1,000. Issuing the minimum number of preference shares in each case ensures that the preference dividend payment will be minimised. Note that the preference dividend is only calculated on the nominal value of shares issued not the premium.

Rights issues and bonus issues

Companies often make what is termed a rights issue of shares. This is an offer of shares to the existing shareholders that they have a right to purchase at a price below the current market value of the shares. The amount the existing shareholders are allowed to purchase is pro-rata to their existing share holding.

Example 8.1

Alpha plc has in issue one million £1 (nominal value) shares. The current market value of the shares is £3.50. The company proposes a rights issue of one share for every four held at a price of £2.

If all of this rights issue is taken up by the shareholders then the company will issue a further 250,000 shares and will receive £500,000 from the shareholders. The company has benefited in this transaction, as it is a very inexpensive way to raise further

Example 8.1
continued

capital. It does not have to go through all the formalities associated with a full share issue to the public, such as producing what is known as a prospectus. The shareholders benefit, as they are able to buy more shares in the company at a beneficial price and, of course, control of the company remains in their hands. Under a normal issue of shares the existing shareholders could have their control diluted if they did not buy all of the shares issued.

A company can also make a 'bonus issue' of shares to its existing shareholders. As is the case with a sole trader, a company will build up its retained profits over the years and these will appear as a reserve on the statement of financial position. We will talk further about reserves after Activity 8.8.

Example 8.2

Alpha plc's statement of financial position as at 31 March 20X5 shows the following:

Share capital – £1 ordinary shares	500
Retained profits	1,000
	1,500

The company makes a bonus issue of two shares for every one held by the existing shareholders. This means every shareholder receives two free shares for every one held. Note no money changes hands and the cash of the company will not be increased. The statement of financial position after the bonus issue will appear as follows:

Share capital – £1 ordinary shares	1,500
Retained profits	0
	1,500

Once a bonus issue of shares is made, the market value of the shares will fall to reflect the extra number of shares in issue.

Other forms of capital

When considering the business of a sole trader you saw that the owner could increase the funds available in the business not only by investing more money him/herself, but also perhaps by acquiring a loan from a bank. Companies can also raise extra finance in a similar way. However, they are also able to raise loan capital by the issue of **debentures** that can be traded in the market in the same way as a share.

The debenture document sets out the capital value, the interest rate payable, the date the loan is redeemable and any security for the loan. The capital value of the debenture is expressed in nominal value terms, usually in multiples of £100. The interest rate payable on the debenture is set at a fixed percentage of this nominal value. It is important to remember that debentures are loans to the company, not part of its share capital. Because of this, debenture interest is shown as a charge against profits within the statement of comprehensive income, rather than an appropriation of profits. The only difficulty with debentures is that they are often issued at a value above or below nominal value. Thus a £100 debenture could be issued at £99. This means that on issue the cash received by the company will only be £99; that is, the debenture has been issued at a discount of £1. Note, though, that the amount payable by the company on redemption, repayment, of the loan will be £100. In the same way that shares are entered into the company's ledger accounts at nominal value so are the debentures. The question to answer is 'How do we account for the £1 discount on issue?'

Activity 8.5

A company makes an issue of £10,000 6% debentures at £99. Show the entries in the ledger accounts, including cash, to account for this issue.

Answer

The debentures account is used to record the nominal value of the debentures issued as for share capital.

6% DEBENTURES ACCOUNT

		Issue	10,000

CASH ACCOUNT

Debentures	9,900		

The above entries do not maintain duality. A debit of £100 is required to be made somewhere in the ledgers.

This £100 discount on issue can be considered as an expense of making the debenture issue. Therefore we have:

DEBENTURE DISCOUNT ACCOUNT

Issue	100		

Like all other expenses this debenture discount should be written off to the income statement by debiting the income statement.

DEBENTURE DISCOUNT ACCOUNT

Issue	100	Statement of comprehensive income	100

There is also another possibility for the write-off of this discount on issue which is permitted by the Companies Act in the UK and that is to charge it against the share premium account if there is one.

Return on shares and debentures

Any investment is made with the expectation of some form of return. For the sole trader this return was in the form of profits that he/she was free to withdraw from the business. In the same way, the profits of a company belong to the shareholders and they will expect some return on their capital invested. This return is made in the form of a dividend payment. These dividend payments are usually made in two instalments, the interim dividend and the final dividend.

Activity 8.6

From your set of company accounts (see Activity 8.2) identify the interim and final dividend payments made.

Answer

The dividends identified were probably expressed as so many pence per share. For example, if the dividend was declared as 6p per share and there were 100,000 £1 shares in issue, then the total dividend payment made would be £6,000. Note that the dividend is calculated by reference to the nominal value of shares issued.

The interim dividend is generally paid halfway through the financial period and the final dividend, an additional payment, is proposed at the year end. This means that the shareholders will vote at the annual general meeting on the payment of this final dividend as proposed by the directors and, after a vote in favour, the dividend will be paid. Note that this means that all final, proposed, dividends are unpaid at the year end. It has long been UK accounting practice to include this proposed dividend as a current liability in the statement of financial position. However, International Accounting Standards now explicitly state that dividends declared after the statement of financial position date, i.e. proposed dividends, should not be recognised as a liability at the statement of financial position date. This will be a change of accounting practice for all UK companies who report under IASs.

The return made to the debenture holder is in the form of interest at the rate specified on the debenture. In the example at Activity 8.5, the interest payable was 6% on a nominal debenture value of £10,000. Thus the company will be required to pay £600 in interest.

Activity 8.7

Is the interest payable on the debenture an expense of trading for the company?
Is the dividend payable to the shareholders an expense of trading for the company?

Answer

For the debenture interest the answer is yes. This interest is treated in exactly the same way as the interest on a loan for a sole trader, as an expense of trading.

The dividend payable, though, is not an expense. Remember the drawings of a sole trader are not an expense but an extraction of capital invested.

For a company, the dividend payment is shown as a change in equity (which we dealt with in Chapter 2), as the following example demonstrates.

Alpha Ltd made a net profit before the payment of interest and dividends of £35,000 in year X. There were £10,000 6% debentures in issue and 100,000 £1 ordinary shares in issue at the beginning of year X and retained profits were £20,000. No further issues of shares or debentures were made during the year. The interim dividend declared was 3p per share and the final dividend 4p per share. The interest and dividend payments are shown in the statement of comprehensive income, as follows.

STATEMENT OF COMPREHENSIVE INCOME FOR ALPHA LTD

Profit	35,000
Interest on debentures 6%	600
Net profit	34,400

Statement of changes in equity

	Share capital	Retained profits	Total
Balance at beginning of year	100,000	20,000	120,000
Net profit for the year		34,400	34,400
Interim dividend 3p = 3,000			
Final dividend 4p = 4,000		(7,000)	(7,000)
Balance at end of year	100,000	47,400	147,400

Financing a company

This chapter has shown us so far that a company can raise capital by issuing ordinary shares, preference shares and debentures. There are many different forms of these instruments, e.g. options, warrants, deep discounted bonds, interest rate swaps, but we leave these to later, more detailed, studies of finance and financial management. However, in addition to companies using these various instruments to raise finance they also use bank overdraft facilities and their own earnings, in the form of non-distributed profit, to provide finance. We look at the non-distributed profit in the section on reserves (p. 150)

Pump Ltd, a newly forming company, estimates it will need capital of £1m so that it can remain in business. It estimates its profits per annum before interest payments and dividends as £100,000 in the first year with an estimated 2% increase year on year. It proposes to issue 500,000 50p ordinary shares at a premium of 40p, 220,000 4% £2 preference shares, and to raise the remaining capital it needs from an issue of 3% debentures. Show the capital section of the statement of financial position and the non-current liabilities assuming estimated profit is realised, the statement of changes in equity and the statement of comprehensive income as far as the information provided permits for the first two years of trading. The interim and final dividends for Year 1 are expected to be 2p and 3p, and for Year 2 4p and 5p. Assume the final dividend is paid before the year end.

Answer

STATEMENT OF COMPREHENSIVE INCOME FOR PUMP LTD

	Year 1	Year 2
Profit	100,000	102,000
Interest on debentures 3%	3,300	3,300
Net profit	96,700	98,700

Statement of changes in equity

		Share capital	Share premium	Accounting profits	Total
Balance as at 1.1.Year 1		690,000	200,000		890,000
Profit for Year 1				96,700	96,700
Preference dividend				(17,600)	
Interim dividend	2p			(10,000)	
Final dividend	3p			(15,000)	(42,600)
Balance as at 31.12. Year 1		690,000	200,000	54,100	944,100
Profit for Year 2				98,700	98,700
Preference dividend				(17,600)	
Interim dividend	4p			(20,000)	
Final dividend	5p			(25,000)	(62,600)
Balance as at 31.12. Year 2		690,000	200,000	90,200	980,200

CAPITAL BALANCE SHEET SECTION PUMP LTD

	Year 1	Year 2
Capital 500,000 50p ordinary shares	250,000	250,000
220,000 £2 4% preference shares	440,000	440,000
Share premium account	200,000	200,000
Profit	54,100	90,200
	944,100	980,200
Non-current liabilities		
3% debentures	110,000	110,000

There are several issues to note in the above activity. First, you needed to calculate the amount of debentures issued. Ordinary share raised £450,000 (including the share premium remember, thus 500,000 × 90p), preference shares raised £440,000 (220,000 × £2) and therefore the remaining amount (£1m − 890,000 = £110,000) was required from the debenture issue.

In Year 2, the profit after dividends of £36,100 is in addition to that already accumulated at Year 1, £54,100.

The percentage payable on the preference shares and debentures is applied to the monetary amount whereas the dividend payable is calculated by reference to the number of shares.

Taxation in company accounts

If you look at the statement of comprehensive income (income statement) in your set of company accounts you will notice that there is another item that did not appear in the statement of comprehensive income of a sole trader, and that is taxation.

Companies are separate legal taxable entities, unlike a sole trader's business, and are subject to taxation, corporation tax, which will be shown in the statement of comprehensive income. A sole trader does not show taxation in his/her accounts as the taxation authorities view the earnings of the business of the sole trader as personal income and tax accordingly. The calculation of corporation tax is complicated and based on taxable profits, which are not the same as accounting profits. At this level of study you will be given a figure to use as the taxation charge for the year. This tax will not be payable until nine months after the end of the accounting year, so it will be shown as a liability in the statement of financial position (balance sheet), and an expense in the statement of comprehensive income.

Reserves

If you look at the statement of financial position (balance sheet) in your set of company accounts you will notice that the share capital is entered under the heading, Capital and Reserves. Reserves that you have met so far consist of accumulated profits of the business, that is, profits that have not been extracted from the business by the shareholders but have been left as further investment, and share premium that was an initial investment by shareholders. These reserves are further classified into capital or revenue reserves. Share premium is an example of a capital reserve, initial capital invested by shareholders. Accumulated profit is an example of a revenue reserve, capital earned from the trading of the business. Another distinction between capital and revenue reserves is that revenue reserves can be distributed in the form of dividends; capital reserves must be retained within the business and cannot be distributed in the form of dividends. This is to protect creditors. Share capital and capital reserves are sometimes known as the creditors' buffer, i.e. the base capital of the company that must not be repaid to shareholders except in very exceptional circumstances.

Another reserve that you might see in your set of accounts is a revaluation reserve. When we considered the non-current assets of a business in our double entry system we tended to record them at historical cost or what the purchaser had paid for them. Look back to Chapter 5 and the details in the Mr Bean examples to revise this. However, there might be circumstances when recording the historical cost or purchase price of the non-current asset does not provide very relevant information to the user of the accounts, as we discussed in Chapter 2.

Activity 8.9   Identify a circumstance when recording a non-current asset at historical cost might not be the most relevant to the user.

Answer

When the asset has increased in value as the owner has held it due to circumstances outside his/her control. For example, business assets such as land and buildings tend to increase in value in the same way as your house price does. Providing the information on this increase in value is highly relevant, as the owner could if he/she wished sell the asset and increase the business worth. Knowledge of this unrealised, until actual sale, worth is useful both to owners and those who wish to invest in the business as well as other users of accounts.

Common practice has arisen and company law permits us to carry assets at their revalued amount, but we need to know how to account for this increase in value.

Activity 8.10

Company A purchased land in 20X1 for £10,000 for cash. As at 31.12.X5 the company estimates that the land could be sold for £50,000. Identify how this increase in value could be recorded in the company's books (ledgers).

Answer

The land would have been originally recorded in the books at its original purchase price of £10,000. The increase in value the company wishes to reflect is £40,000. This is the amount of the revaluation. Quite simply the fixed asset account of land is shown at £50,000 and the uplift in value, the revaluation, is credited to a revaluation reserve as follows:

LAND ACCOUNT

1.1.X5	Balance b/d	10,000			
31.12.X5	Revaluation reserve	40,000	31.12.X5	Balance c/d	50,000
		50,000			50,000
1.1.X6	Balance b/d	50,000			

REVALUATION ACCOUNT

31.12.X5	Balance c/d	40,000	31.12.X5	Land	40,000
		40,000			40,000
			1.1.X6	Balance b/d	40,000

The revaluation reserve, the £40,000 in the activity above, is shown in the statement of financial position under the capital and reserves section and is a capital un-realised reserve. We will consider revaluation reserves again in Chapter 13.

The following activity brings together various issues that you have come across in your studies so far.

Activity 8.11   The trial balance of Beta Ltd as at 31.12.X5, before adjustment for any of the items listed in the notes, is as follows:

	Dr	Cr
Issued £1 ordinary shares		50,000
Share premium		5,000
Buildings (cost)	55,000	
Fixtures and fittings (cost)	27,000	
Vehicles (cost)	15,000	
Depreciation as at 1.1 X5		
Buildings		3,300
Fixtures and fittings		6,750
Vehicles		5,400
Sales		111,000
Purchases	75,000	
Wages and salaries	12,000	
Other expenses	8,000	
Inventory 1.1.X5	2,500	
6% debentures		30,000
Debenture interest paid	900	
Interim dividend paid	2,000	
Trade receivables and trade payables	28,000	15,000
Accumulated profits 1.1.X5		9,500
Cash	10,550	
	235,950	235,950

The following notes are to be taken into account:

1 Inventory as at 31.12.X5 is £3,400 valued at cost.

2 Depreciation is to be provided for as follows:

- Buildings 2% per annum straight line
- Fixtures and fittings 25% straight line
- Vehicles 20% reducing balance.

3 Corporation tax for the year is estimated at £3,500.

4 Fittings originally costing £2,400 on which depreciation of £1,200 had been provided were sold on 31.12.X5 for £950. No entries have been made in the accounts for the sale nor has any cash been received.

Prepare the statement of comprehensive income, statement of changes in equity and statement of financial position for Beta Ltd for the year ended 31.12.X5.

Answer

BETA LTD
INCOME STATEMENT FOR THE YEAR ENDED 31.12.X5

Sales		111,000
Opening inventory	2,500	
Purchases	75,000	
	77,500	
Closing stock	3,400	74,100
Gross profit		36,900
Wages and salaries	12,000	
Other expenses	8,000	
Debenture interest	1,800	
Depreciation:		
Buildings	1,100	
Fixtures and fittings	6,150	
Vehicles	1,920	9,170
Loss on sale	250	31,220
Profit before tax		5,680
Taxation		3,500
Profit after tax		2,180

BETA LTD
STATEMENT OF CHANGES IN EQUITY

	Share capital	Share premium	Accumulated profits	Total
Balance as at 1.1.X5	50,000	5,000	9,500	64,500
Profit for the year			2,180	2,180
Dividends			(2,000)	(2,000)
Balance as at 31.12.X5	50,000	5,000	9,680	64,680

BETA LTD
BALANCE SHEET AS AT 31.12.X5

	Cost	Depreciation	Net book value
Non-current assets			
Buildings	55,000	4,400	50,600
Fixtures and fittings	24,600	11,700	12,900
Vehicles	15,000	7,320	7,680
	94,600	23,420	71,180
Current assets			
Inventory		3,400	
Trade receivables		28,000	
Trade receivables (fixtures)		950	
Cash		10,550	
		42,900	

Current liabilities

Trade payables	15,000		
Taxation	3,500		
Debenture interest	900	19,400	23,500
			94,680

Non-current liabilities

6% debentures	30,000
	64,680

Capital and reserves

Ordinary shares of £1	50,000
Share premium	5,000
Accumulated profits	9,680
	64,680

Note that we have used the format non-current assets + (current assets – current liabilities) – non-current liabilities = equity for the statement of financial position in this example.

Format presentation

As you have been looking at your set of company accounts you may have noticed that the presentation of the statement of comprehensive income and statement of financial position are slightly different from the ones we have used so far. The Companies Act UK and the EU Fourth Directive actually specify four types of **format presentation** that can be used for the statement of comprehensive income of a company and two for the statement of financial position. However, the IASs are not as specific as UK law or the EU directives on the format for the statement of comprehensive income and statement of financial position. We will use for our purposes at this level of study simplified versions of the Fourth Directive formats, which also take account of the IAS regulations.

STATEMENT OF COMPREHENSIVE INCOME FOR THE YEAR ENDED 20YZ

Turnover/Revenue		X
Cost of sales		(X)
Gross profit		X
Distribution costs	(X)	
Administration costs	(X)	(X)
Operating profit		X
Income from investments		X
Interest paid and similar charges		(X)
Profit on ordinary activities before tax		X
Tax on ordinary activities		(X)
Profit on ordinary activities after tax		X

Extraordinary charges	X	
Tax	(X)	(X)
Profit for year		X

This presentation of the statement of comprehensive income requires the analysis of expenses under three headings: cost of sales, distribution and administration. Wages and salaries will have to be analysed across these three headings, as will depreciation.

STATEMENT OF FINANCIAL POSITION AS AT 20YZ

ASSETS

Non-current assets

Intangible assets		X
Property, plant and equipment		X
Investments		X
		X

Current assets

Inventory	X	
Trade receivables	X	
Cash at bank and in hand	X	
		X
TOTAL ASSETS		X

EQUITY

Capital and reserves

Called up share capital	X	
Share premium account	X	
Revalution reserve	X	
Other reserves	X	
Retained earnings	X	X

Non-current liabilities

Loans		X

Current liabilities

Trade payables	X	
Other	X	X
TOTAL EQUITY AND LIABILITIES		X

This format is therefore:

Non-current assets + current assets = equity + non-current liabilities + current liabilities.

This is the format for the statement of financial position recommended by IAS 1 'Presentation of Financial Statements', but remember it is *not required* by IAS 1. You will find that the company accounts you look at will not all be presented in the same format but you should be able to clearly identify the totals for non-current assets, current assets, equity, non-current liabilities and current liabilities and put these together in the various formats of the accounting equation.

You might also have noticed two more statements in your set of accounts in addition to the statement of comprehensive income and statement of financial position: the statement of cash flows (cash flow statement) and the statement of changes in equity. The statement of cash flows we will deal with in Chapter 10 and we will look further at the statement of changes in equity in Chapter 13 (see Chapter 2 also).

Exemplar accounts

We include here for you an exemplar of the presentation of the financial statements. The company we have chosen is Tesco plc and we have summarised the accounts for you.

STATEMENT OF COMPREHENSIVE INCOME YEAR ENDED 23 FEBRUARY 2008

	2008 (£m)	2007 (£m)
Revenue	47,298	42,641
Cost of sales	(43,668)	(39,401)
Pensions adjustment		258
Impairment of the Gerrards Cross site		(35)
Gross profit	3,630	3,463
Administrative expenses	(1,027)	(907)
Profit arising on property related items	188	92
Operating profit	2,791	2,648
Share of post-tax profits of joint ventures and associates	75	106
Profit on sale of investments in associates		25
Finance income	187	90
Finance costs	(250)	(216)
Profit before tax	2,803	2,653
Taxation	(673)	(772)
Profit for the year from continuing operations	2,130	1,881
Profit for the year from discontinued operations		18
Profit for the year	2,130	1.899

STATEMENT OF FINANCIAL POSITION AS AT 23 FEBRUARY 2008

	2008 (£m)	2007 (£m)
Non-current assets		
Goodwill and other intangible assets	2,336	2,045

Property, plant and equipment	19,787	16,976
Investment property	1,112	856
Investments in joint ventures and associates	305	314
Other investments	4	8
Other	320	32
	23,864	20,231
Current assets		
Inventories	2,430	1,931
Trade and other receivables	1,311	1,079
Derivative financial instruments	97	108
Current tax assets	6	8
Short term investments	360	
Cash and cash equivalents	1,788	1,042
	5,992	4,168
Non-current assets classified as held for sale	308	408
	6,300	4,576
Current liabilities		
Trade and other payables	(7,277)	(6,046)
Financial liabilities	(2,527)	(1,640)
Current tax liabilities	(455)	(461)
Provisions	(4)	(4)
	(10,263)	(8,152)
Net current liabilities	(3,963)	(3,576)
Non-current liabilities		
Financial liabilities	(6,294)	(4,545)
Post-employment benefit obligations	(838)	(950)
Other non-current payables	(42)	(29)
Deferred tax liabilities	(802)	(535)
Provisions	(23)	(25)
	(7,999)	(6,084)
NET ASSETS	11,902	10,571
EQUITY		
Share capital	393	397
Share premium	4,511	4,376
Other reserves	40	40
Retained earnings	6,871	5,693
Equity attributable to equity holders	11,815	10,506
Minority interests	87	65
TOTAL EQUITY	11,902	10,571

For the statement of financial position Tesco has used the format:

Non-current assets + (Current assets – Current liabilities) – non-current liabilities = Equity

23,864 + (6,300 – 10,263) – 7,999 = 11,902.

They could just have easily set this out as:

Non-current assets + Current assets = Equity + Non-current liabilities + Current liabilities

23,864 + 6,300 = 11,902 + 7,999 + 10,263

You also should have noted that the previous year's figures are shown on the financial statements to aid comparison between the years. We will return to this comparison in Chapter 12 when we deal with interpretation of financial statements.

We would recommend that you look at several sets of financial statements on the internet. Our suggestions would be:

Adidas at **www.adidas-group.corporate-publications.com**

Shell at **www.annualreview.shell/investor.com**

McDonald's at **www.computershare.com/mcdonalds**

Vodafone at **www.vodafone.com/static/annual_report**

Activity 8.12   Identify the presentational statement of financial position format used by Adidas, Shell, McDonald's and Vodafone in their published financial statements.

Answer   Adidas in its statements for 31 December 2007 uses:

Current assets + Non-current assets = Current liabilities + Non-current liabilities + Equity

This is the format recommended in IAS 1.
  Shell in its financial statements for 2007 uses:

Non-current assets +Current assets = Non-current liabilities + Current liabilities + Equity

McDonald's in its financial statements for 31 December 2007 uses:

Current assets + Non-current assets = Current liabilities + Non-current liabilities + Equity

Vodafone in its financial statements for 31 March 2008 uses:

Non-current assets + Current assets = Equity + Non-current liabilities + Current liabilities

---

All of these four are using the format we would recommend to you of Assets = Equity + Liabilities, but you must be able to read financial statements that use any format.

You might also note when you look at the financial statements of real entities that both the company and the group are referred to and often you will have the financial statements for both presented. We will explain the issue of group accounts in Chapter 9.

Other entities

Introduction

We have looked in some detail in this chapter at accounts for companies. There are many other types of organisations/entities that have a need to keep records and prepare information similar to that of companies. We have referred to clubs and societies in Chapter 7, but charities and public sector organisations also need similar information. Statements of comprehensive income and statements of financial position for these types of organisations are prepared using the same principles and concepts as for companies, but of course the Companies Act does not apply to them. Charity accounts have to be prepared in accordance with the Charities Acts and national governments provide detailed requirements for the public sector. We will also look at partnerships and preparation of accounts for them in this section. All these other entities generally use the format of Assets – Liabilities = Capital for their statement of financial position, as this is more useful to them as it gives the figure of working capital.

Clubs and societies

Below, we provide a fully worked example for the preparation of a set of accounts for a club. We advise you to work through this example diligently before you try to answer the question on clubs at the end of the chapter. You will remember that we initially looked at these in Chapter 3.

Example 8.4

The following information is extracted from the records of Mudby Rugby Club for the year ended 31.12.X5:

	1.1.X5	31.12.X5
Bar inventory	16,200	17,860
Creditors for bar purchases	8,600	8,100
Creditors for other expenses	230	1,240

Summary of bank account for the year ended 31.12.X5:

Balance 1.1.X5	16,290	Bar purchases	120,650
Subscriptions received	24,530	Bar wages	15,230
Bar sales	146,320	Other salaries and wages	5,340
Interest on investments	1,230	Rent and rates of club premises	5,670
		General expenses	8,760
		Cost of fittings and furniture	7,680
		Balance 31.12.X5	25,040
	188,370		188,370

Example 8.4
continued

Other information available at the year end is as follows:

▶ Rent and rates have only been paid for three-quarters of the year.

▶ Investments held by the club at 1.1.X5 had several years ago cost £30,750.

▶ Fixtures and fittings held at 1.1.X5 had cost £42,500 on 1.1.X2 and all fixtures and fittings are to be depreciated at 10% on original cost.

Prepare a bar trading account and an income and expenditure account for year ended 31.12.X5 and a statement of financial position as at that date in good form.

A bar trading account simply groups together all the income and expenditure relating to the bar to see if it has been operating at a profit.

BAR TRADING ACCOUNT FOR MUDBY RUGBY CLUB FOR THE YEAR ENDED 31.12.X5

Bar sales		146,320
Opening inventory	16,200	
Bar purchases (120,650 – 8,600 + 8,100)	120,150	
	136,350	
Closing inventory	17,860	118,490
Gross profit on bar		27,830
Bar wages		15,230
Net profit on bar		12,600

INCOME AND EXPENDITURE ACCOUNT FOR THE YEAR ENDED 3.12.X5

Subscriptions		24,530
Bar net profit		12,600
Interest on investments		1,230
		38,360
Other salaries and wages	5,340	
Rent and rates (5,670 + 1,890 for last quarter)	7,560	
General expenses (8,760 – 230 + 1,240)	9,770	
Depreciation of fixtures and fittings		
(10% × 42,500 + 7,680)	5,018	27,688
		10,672

STATEMENT OF FINANCIAL POSITION AS AT 31.12.X5

	Cost	Depreciation	Net book value
Non-current assets			
Fixtures and fittings	50,180	17,768 (W1)	32,412
Investments			30,750
			63,162
Current assets – inventory bar	17,860		
Cash at bank	25,040	42,900	
Current liabilities – rent and rates	1,890		
Creditors other expenses	1,240		

Example 8.4
continued

Bar purchases	8,100	11,230	31,670
			94,832

Accumulated fund 1.1.X5	84,160 (W2)
Surplus	10,672
	94,832

W1 total cost value of fixtures and fittings £42,500 + £7,680 = £50,180
Depreciation 10% on £50,180 = £5,018 for Year 31.12.X5
Depreciation at 10% for 3 years on £42,500 = £12,750
Total depreciation £12,750 + £5,018 = £17,768
W2 Net book value 1.1.X5 fixtures and fittings

(£42,500 − £12,750 depreciation)	29,750
Investments	30,750
Inventory	16,200
Bank	16,290
Creditors (£8,600 + £230)	(8,830)
	84,160

Charities

As we stated earlier **charity accounts** have to be prepared in accordance with the charities acts. In this text we do not intend to provide full instruction on the preparation of charity accounts but we have included an exemplar set of financial statements for Oxfam.

STATEMENT OF FINANCIAL POSITION AT 30 APRIL 2007 OXFAM

	2007 (£m)	2006 (£m)
Fixed assets		
Tangible assets	16.6	17.1
Investments	4.4	4.4
	21	21.5
Current assets		
Stocks	1.5	1.6
Trade receivables	20.4	25.5
Cash at bank and in hand	75.6	73.8
	97.5	100.9
Trade payable amounts falling due within one year	(18)	(14)
Net current assets	79.5	86.9
Total assets less current liabilities	100.5	108.4
Trade payable amounts falling due after one year	(1.3)	(2)

Provisions for liabilities and charges	(8.5)	(7.9)
Net assets before pension scheme liabilities	90.7	98.5
Pension scheme liability	(20.1)	(23.3)
Net assets	70.6	75.2
Funds		
General reserve	48.6	47.4
Charitable unrestricted funds	15	19.3
Pension reserves	(20.1)	(23.3)
Endowment funds	2.6	2.6
Restricted funds	24.5	29.2
Total funds	70.6	75.2

SUMMARY INCOME AND EXPENDITURE ACCOUNT 30 APRIL 2007 OXFAM

	2007 (£m)	2006 (£m)
Income	290.7	310.5
Expenditure	297.2	298
(Deficit)/Surplus of income over expenditure before realised losses and gains	(6.5)	12.5
Realised loss on disposal of investment		(0.1)
(Deficit)/surplus of income over expenditure	(6.5)	12.4
Transfers (to)/from other funds		
Transfer from endowment funds		0.2
Transfer (to)/from restricted funds	4.6	(3.5)
Transfer (to)/from unrestricted funds	4.3	0.4
Transfer (to)/from pension funds	(1.2)	(1.4)
General reserves at 30 April 2006	47.4	39.3
General reserves at 30 April 2007	48.6	47.4

Activity 8.13   Identify the differences in the financial statements of Oxfam, the charity, and Tesco, the company.

Answer   Several of the differences are due to the fact that a charity is not set up to make a profit, whereas a company is. Thus the charity uses an income and expenditure account in place of a statement of comprehensive income (profit and loss account). The income and expenditure account of the charity is still prepared using accruals accounting. The (deficit)/surplus on the income and expenditure account is then transferred to the funds of the charity, which are similar to the reserves of a company.

The charity statement of financial position does not show any shares, as of course a charity does not have shareholders. All funds donated to the charity are identified as restricted or unrestricted funds.

The statement of financial position format for the charity is similar to that of a company except the terminology is not in international form, e.g debtors is used not trade receivables, and fixed assets is used not non-current assets.

Public sector

The preparation of accounts for the public sector will depend upon national government legislation and some (although now a minority) will still be prepared using cash accounting instead of accruals accounting. We do not intend to provide further detail on public sector accounting in this text but you will find it useful to look at the final accounts of a public sector organisation in your own country and compare them with the financial statements of a company, charity or club.

Partnerships

Introduction

In Chapters 5, 6 and 7 we dealt primarily with the accounts of a sole trader. However, it is extremely difficult for a sole trader business to grow beyond a certain size. One method of growing a business is to form a **partnership**, whereby two or more individuals run the business.

Benefits of a partnership

This type of business arrangement has several benefits:

► Capital within the business can be increased as it is injected by each partner.

► Each partner brings their own, often complimentary, skills to the business. For example, one partner may have marketing skills, another financial, and another may be the producer of the items sold.

► Decisions and responsibilities within the business are shared.

► Lenders may be more inclined to provide resources to the business given the increased skills and expertise available from the partners as compared with that of a sole trader.

Like a sole trader, partners are liable to the full extent of their personal assets for the debts of the business unless they form a limited partnership, which rarely occurs.

Partnership Act 1890 UK

Within the UK the law relating to partnerships is still defined by the Partnership Act of 1890, which was only partly updated in 2002. In law there is no maximum to the number of partners permitted within a business. The Act is invoked when no partnership agreement is in place for a business. A partnership agreement is required to identify how the partnership will operate and, in particular, to set down the financial arrangements between partners.

Activity 8.14   Identify financial factors that should be specified within a partnership agreement.

Answer   You should have identified the need for the following financial arrangements:

1 How much capital is to be introduced by each partner.
2 How profits are to be shared between the partners. This will include:

▶ Any remuneration payable to a partner for the specific work done
▶ The rate at which interest will be paid on capital, if any
▶ If drawings are to be permitted and what interest rate will be applied to them, if any
▶ How the remaining profit after deductions for partner salaries and interest on capital and addition for interest on drawings have been applied will be divided between the partners.

3 How goodwill should be valued
4 Arrangements covering the retirement or death of a partner
5 Arrangements for the introduction of a new partner.

You may not have identified all of the items that we did in our answer but we hope you at least identified (1) and (2).

Goodwill in partnerships

You probably did not identify this item in Activity 8.14 as we have not dealt with this issue so far. The value of a business, or what it could be sold for, is often greater than the addition of the individual net assets of the business. The difference between the value of a business' separable net assets and what the business could be sold for is known as goodwill in partnerships. Goodwill occurs in all businesses, not just partnerships. The sole trader will expect to build up goodwill in his/her business as he/she trades. It is an intangible asset as, unlike other assets such as a building, it cannot be touched. It is also very difficult to value and the only time we can place a reliable measure on it is when a business is sold.

Activity 8.15   Identify means by which a trader could build up goodwill in his/her business

Answer

Basically we need to identify those reasons why a customer would trade with a business. These could be as follows:

▶ Good location of the business
▶ Established customer base resulting in sales
▶ Established reputation or brand (e.g. Virgin or Coca Cola)
▶ Licences for sale of particular goods
▶ Experienced and customer-focused workforce
▶ Existing contracts
▶ Trademarks or patents developed.

You may well have identified other issues.

Why do we need to value goodwill in a partnership?

If a partner wishes to retire from a business or a new partner wishes to join then effectively the business is changing in ownership. The retiring partner will wish to ensure that he/she takes from the business his/her share of it, i.e. his/her share of what the business could be sold for. A new partner joining cannot simply be given the net assets of the business, he/she must pay for his/her share, including a share of the goodwill, or the other partners will have given the new partner something for nothing.

Partnership accounts

Partners will contribute capital to start up a business in the same way that a sole trader does. The profit made in the business will belong to the partners and they will share in these profits in a specific ratio. As the partners may well have contributed different amounts of capital and wish to withdraw different amounts then it would be equitable to give and charge interest on these before the remaining profits are allocated. As partners generally work in the business, to maintain equity between partners they will agree appropriate salaries to be paid, but these will be allocated from the profits made. All transactions between the business and the partners, except for the introduction of capital and goodwill transactions, are dealt with through the partners' current accounts. This is to ensure that we maintain a record of the capital contributed by each partner.

The following activity illustrates **partners' capital accounts** and **partners' current accounts**.

Activity 8.16

Bill and Ben form a partnership on 1 October 20X8. Bill contributes £50,000 in capital and Ben £40,000 in capital to the partnership. They have a partnership agreement that states that profits will be shared in the ratio Bill 60% and Ben 40% after providing for:

▶ An annual salary to Ben of £10,000
▶ Interest of 4% payable on capital balances at the beginning of the accounting year
▶ Interest charged on total drawings for the year at 5%.

▶

Drawings for the accounting year ended 30 September 20X9 were Bill £15,000 and Ben £8,000. Profits for the year before any of the above transactions were £95,000.

Required

Show the transactions in the partners' capital and current accounts for the year ended 30 September 20X9.

Answer

CAPITAL ACCOUNTS

	Bill	Ben		Bill	Ben
30.9.09 Balance c/d	50,000	40,000	1.10.X8 Capital introduced	50,000	40,000
	50,000	40,000		50,000	40,000
			1.10.X9 Balance b/d	50,000	40,000

CURRENT ACCOUNTS

	Bill	Ben		Bill	Ben
Interest on drawings	750	400	Salary		10,000
Drawings	15,000	8,000	Interest on capital	2,000	1,600
30.9.x9 Balance c/d	35,780	36,220	Share of profits (see note below)	49,530	33,020
	51,530	44,620		51,530	44,620
			1.10.09 Balance b/d	35,780	36,220

Note

Profits for the year			95,000
Interest on drawings	Bill	750	
	Ben	400	1,150
			96,150
Salary	Ben		10,000
Interest on capital	Bill	2,000	
	Ben	1,600	3,600
Profit available to share			82,550
60%	Bill	49,530	
40%	Ben	33,020	82,550

This note is usually shown as the profit appropriation account.

Note in the example for Bill and Ben that transactions relating to drawings, salary and interest are dealt with in the current accounts not the capital accounts of the partners.

Activity 8.17

Anne and Sally form a partnership on 1 October 20X8. Anne contributes £80,000 in capital and Sally £60,000 in capital to the partnership. They have a partnership agreement that states that profits will be shared in the ratio Anne 75% and Sally 25% after providing for:

▶ An annual salary to Anne of £10,000 and Sally £20,000
▶ Interest of 4% payable on capital balances at the beginning of the accounting year
▶ Interest charged on total drawings for the year at 5%.

Drawings for the accounting year ended 30 September 20X9 were Anne £15,000 and Sally £5,000. Profits for the year before any of the above transactions were £35,000.

Required
Show the transactions in the partners' capital and current accounts for the year ended 30 September 20X9.

Answer

CAPITAL ACCOUNTS

	Anne	Sally		Anne	Sally
30.9.X9 Balance c/d	80,000	60,000	1.10.X8 Capital introduced	80,000	60,000
	80,000	60,000		80,000	60,000
			1.10.X9 Balance b/d	80,000	60,000

CURRENT ACCOUNTS

	Anne	Sally		Anne	Sally
Interest on drawings	750	250	Salary	10,000	20,000
Drawings	15,000	5,000	Interest on capital	3,200	2,400
Share of loss (see note below)	1,200	400	30.9.X9 Balance c/d	3,750	
30.9.X9 Balance c/d		16,750			
	16,950	22,400		16,950	22,400
1.10.X9 Balance b/d	3,750		1.10.X9 Balance b/d		16,750

Note

Profits for the year			35,000
Interest on drawings:	Anne	750	
	Sally	250	1,000
			34,000
Salary:	Anne	10,000	
	Sally	20,000	
Interest on capital:	Anne	3,200	
	Sally	2,400	35,600
Loss to share:			(1,600)
75% Anne		(1,200)	
25% Sally		(400)	(1,600)

In this partnership, after the transactions for interest on drawings, interest on capital, and salaries there is a loss. This must be shared between the partners in the same ratio that a profit would be. Also in this partnership, because Anne has drawn out more than the total of her salary and net interest then she is overdrawn on her current account.

Retirement of a partner

As we have stated, when a partner retires from a partnership then we must value the goodwill in the partnership and ensure that this is allocated between the partners (in their capital accounts) before the retirement. This is to ensure that the retiring partner extracts his/her correct share from the partnership, i.e. his/her share of what it is 'worth'.

Activity 8.18

A, B and C are in partnership sharing profits in the ratio 5:3:2. As at 30 September 20X8 the balances on the partners' accounts are as follows:

Capital accounts	A	40,000
	B	30,000
	C	38,000
Current accounts	A	12,500
	B	9,600
	C	17,100

A wishes to retire on 30 September 20X8 and at this date the goodwill of the business is valued at £120,000.

Required

Show the partners' accounts immediately after the retirement of A identifying the amount transferred to A's loan account on retirement. After A's retirement profits are to be shared evenly between B and C. Goodwill is to be removed from the books of the partnership after the retirement.

Answer

CAPITAL ACCOUNTS

	A	B	C		A	B	C
Goodwill removed		60,000	60,000	30.9.X8 Balance	40,000	30,000	38,000
Loan account A	100,000			Goodwill	60,000	36,000	24,000
Balance c/d		6,000	2,000				
	100,000	66,000	62,000		100,000	66,000	62,000
				1.10.X8 balance b/d		6,000	2,000

CURRENT ACCOUNTS

	A	B	C		A	B	C
Loan account A	12,500			30.9.X8 Balance	12,500	9,600	17,100
30.9.X8 balance c/d		9,600	17,100				
	12,500	9,600	17,100		12,500	9,600	17,100
				1.10.X8 Balance b/d		9,600	17,100

In total A has left £112,500 on loan to the partnership.

Note in the above accounts that goodwill was brought in, in the old profit share ratios, and removed in the new profit share ratios.

Year-end accounts for a partnership

A partnership will prepare year-end accounts in the same way that a sole trader does. The only difference is that in the partnership there will be an appropriation of profit section in the statement of comprehensive income and/both capital and current accounts to record in the statement of financial position. The following activity involves the preparation of year-end accounts for a partnership and the retirement of a partner.

Activity 8.19

Rod, Harry and James are in partnership sharing profits in the ratio 2:2:1. Interest on drawings is charged at 6% on total drawings for the year and interest on capital is payable on the opening capital balances for the year at 5%. Salaries payable to the partners for a year are Rod £20,000, Harry £15,000 and James £25,000. At the year end 31.12.20X9 Rod wishes to retire. At that date goodwill in the partnership is valued at £100,000 but is not to remain in the books after the retirement of Rod. Rod agrees to leave half of the amount due to him on loan to the partnership. At 31 December 20X9 a loan is taken out with the bank for £65,000. After Rod's retirement Harry and James agree to share profits in the ratio 5:3. The trial balance for the partnership as at 31.12.20X9, before any of the above is accounted for, is as follows:

Trial balance as at 31.12.20X9 for Rod, Harry and James

	Dr	Cr
Sales		517,554
Purchases	256,700	
Stock as at 1 January 20X9	22,300	
Wages	94,000	
Rates and insurance	18,600	
Electricity and gas	9,450	
Vehicle expenses	5,700	

Capital accounts: Rod		60,000
Harry		35,000
James		30,000
Current accounts: Rod		1,240
Harry		1,540
James	650	
Drawings: Rod	18,600	
Harry	12,000	
James	19,000	
Premises	180,000	
Furniture and fittings at cost	12,400	
Vehicles at cost	15,600	
Depreciation premises		
1 January 20X9		9,000
Depreciation furniture and fittings		
1 January 20x9		6,200
Depreciation vehicles		
1 January 20x9		5,616
Trade receivables	1,350	
Trade payables		2,300
Cash at bank	2,100	
	668,450	668,450

Depreciation is to be charged at 10% straight line on fixtures and fittings, 1% straight line on premises and 20% reducing balance on vehicles. There are no accruals and prepayments to take account of. Closing stock at 31 December is valued at £23,400.

Required

Prepare the statement of comprehensive income and statement of financial position of the partnership immediately after the retirement of Rod, clearly showing all transactions in the partners' capital and current accounts.

Answer

The statement of comprehensive income for Rod, Harry and James for the year ended 31 December 20X9 is as follows:

Sales		517,554
Opening stock	22,300	
Purchases	256,700	
	279,000	
Closing stock	23,400	255,600
		261,954
Wages	94,000	
Rates and insurance	18,600	
Electricity and gas	9,450	
Vehicle expenses	5,700	
Depreciation: Premises		
Furniture and fittings		
Vehicles	1,800	
	1,240	
	2,496	
		133,286
		128668
Salaries: Rod	20,000	
Harry	15,000	
James	25,000	
Interest on capital accounts: Rod	3,000	
Harry	1,750	
James	1,500	
Interest charged on drawings: Rod	(1,116)	
Harry	(720)	
James	(1,140)	
Profit share: Rod	26,158	
Harry	26,158	
James	13,078	
		128,668

CAPITAL ACCOUNTS

		Rod	Harry	James			Rod	Harry	James
31.12.X9	Eliminate goodwill		62,500	37,500	1.1.X9	Balance.b/d	60,000	35,000	30,000
31.12.X9	Cash	50,000			31.12.X9	Goodwill introduced	40,000	40,000	20,000
	Loan	50,000							
31.12.X9	Balance c/d		12,500	12,500					
		100,000	75,000	50000			100,000	75,000	50,000
					1.1.X0	Balance/ b/d		12,500	12,500

CAPITAL ACCOUNTS

		Rod	Harry	James			Rod	Harry	James
1.1.X9	Balance b/d			650	1.1.X9	Balance b/d	1,240	1,540	
31.12.X9	Interest on drawings	1,116	720	1,140	31.12.X9	Salaries	20,000	15,000	25,000
31.12.X9	Drawings	18,600	12,000	19,000	31.12.X9	Interest on capital accounts	3,000	1,750	1,500
31.12.09	Rod cash loan	15,341 15,341							
31.12.09	Balance c/d		31,728	18,788	31.12.X9	Share of profits	26,158	26,158	13,078
		50,398	44,448	39,578			50,398	44,448	39,578
					1.1.X0	Balance b/d		31,728	18,788

CASH ACCOUNT

31.12.X9	Balance b/d	2,100	31.12.X9	Cash to Rod	65,341
31.12.X9	Loan from bank	65,000	31.12.X9	Balance c/d	1,759
		67,100			67,100
1.1.X0	Balance b/d	1,759			

STATEMENT OF FINANCIAL POSITION FOR ROD, HARRY AND JAMES AS AT 31 DECEMBER 20X9

	Cost	Depreciation	NBV
Premises	180,000	10,800	169,200
Furniture and fittings	12,400	7,440	4.960
Vehicles	15,600	8,112	7,488
	208,000	26,352	181,648
Stock		23,400	
Trade receivables		1,350	
Cash		1,759	26,509
			208,157
Capital accounts: Harry		12,500	25,000
James		12,500	

Current accounts: Harry	31,728	50,516
James	18,788	
Loan Rod		65,341
Loan bank		65,000
Trade payables		2,300
		208,157

Summary

This chapter has:

▶ introduced you to the accounts of a limited company

▶ identified the concept of legal entity of a company and the differences between a company and a sole trader

▶ noted that the capital of a company is issued in the form of shares

▶ noted that companies are subject to taxation, which is accounted for as a deduction from the profit of the company

▶ identified that companies are required to publish their final accounts, but that the format is only recommended, not specified. However, the preparation of the statement of comprehensive income and statement of financial position of the company require the same techniques as those used for a sole trader

▶ considered the preparation of accounts for clubs and societies, charities and the public sector

▶ introduced you to the concept of partnerships and the preparation of accounts for partnerships.

At the end of this chapter there are several exercises for you that will test your knowledge and understanding of accounting for companies and also the preparation of final accounts in accordance with the specified formats.

Chapter 9 looks at the concept of a group and the preparation of simple group accounts and in Chapter 14 we will look at the preparation of financial statements from incomplete records.

Key terms

limited company (p. 139)
limited liability (p. 139)
corporate entity (p. 139)
Memorandum of Association (p. 140)
Articles of Association (p. 140)
annual report (p. 141)
shares (share capital) (p. 141)
dividend (p. 142)
premium (p. 143)

debentures (p. 145)
taxation (p. 150)
reserves (p. 150)
format presentation (p. 154)
charity accounts (p. 161)
partnerships (p. 163)
goodwill in partnerships (p. 164)
partners' capital accounts (p. 165)
partners' current accounts (p. 165)

*S*elf-assessment questions

1 Answer the following questions for both sole traders and companies:

   (a) Is there any statutory regulation governing them?
   (b) Who owns the business?
   (c) Who manages the business?
   (d) Is the business a separate legal entity?
   (e) Does the business end when its owners change?
   (f)   Is taxation an expense of the business?
   (g) How do owners extract profits from the business for their own use?
   (h) Is the business quoted on the stock exchange?

2 The directors of Britton plc wish to raise additional capital. They currently have in issue one million £1 ordinary shares and no long-term loans. What options do they have available to raise extra capital and which would you advise them to choose?

3 The following is an extract from the statement of financial position of Comp plc as at 31.3.X6:

	£m
Ordinary shares £1	20
Share premium account	5
Accumulated profits	12
5% debentures £1	8

   (a) What is the par value of each share?
   (b) What is the book value of each share?
   (c) What is the interest payable per annum on the debentures?
   (d) If the interest rate in the market for debentures similar to those of Comp plc was higher than 5% would the market price of Comp's debentures in the market place be higher or lower than £1?

4 The following trial balance was extracted from the books of Cuddly Toy Ltd as at 31.12.X5.

	Dr (£000)	Cr (£000)
Sales		1,562
Inventory 1.1.X5	660	
Purchases	885	
Land	1,010	
Buildings	980	
Equipment	55	
Vehicles	72	
Depreciation: Premises		390
Equipment		18
Vehicles		25

Trade receivables and payables	180	235
Bank	121	
£1 ordinary shares		900
Share premium		350
Distribution expenses	98	
Administration expenses	24	
Accumulated profits 1.1.X5		185
5% debentures		420
	4,085	4,085

The following information has not yet been accounted for:

▶ Closing inventory 31.12.X5 is valued at £560,000.

▶ Depreciation is to be charged as follows:

 – 2% straight line on buildings

 – 20% straight line on equipment

 – 25% reducing balance on vehicles.

▶ Assets are used as follows:

 – buildings: 50% cost of sales, 25% distribution and 25% administration

 – equipment: all cost of sales

 – vehicles: all distribution.

▶ Taxation to be charged for the year is estimated at £200,000.

▶ An interim dividend has been declared but not yet paid of 6p per share.

Prepare the published income statement, statement of changes in equity and balance sheet for the company as at 31.12.X5.

5 You are required to prepare the statement of comprehensive income for the year ended 31.3.X6 and the statement of financial position as at that date for internal purposes for the following company:

TRIAL BALANCE OF GERRY LTD AS AT 31.3.X6

	Dr	Cr
Ordinary shares £1		100,000
6% preference shares £1		20,000
8% debentures		30,000
Share premium		9,500
Revaluation reserve		10,000
General reserve		12,000
Accumulated profit b/f 1.4.X5		976
Non-current assets (cost £210,000)	191,000	
Inventory 1.4.X5	14,167	
Trade receivables and payables	11,000	7,500
Provision for doubtful debts		324
Bank	9,731	
Purchases and sales	186,000	271,700

Wages and salaries	31,862	
General expenses	15,840	
Debenture interest	1,200	
Preference dividend	1,200	
	462,000	462,000

You are also given the following information:

▶ Inventory 31.3.X6 £23,483.

▶ Depreciation of non-current assets is to be provided at the rate of 10% per annum on cost.

▶ The provision for doubtful debts is to be at 5% of debtors.

▶ £1,200 of debenture interest and £1,437 of general expenses are to be accrued.

▶ £925 of general expenses have been paid in advance.

▶ Provision is to be made for taxation on this year's profits of £9,700.

▶ The directors have decided to increase the general reserve by a further £3,000.

6 The trial balance of Hobo Ltd as at 30.9.X6 was as follows:

	Dr	Cr
Audit fee	1,200	
Bad debts	5,320	
Trade receivables and trade payables	92,360	111,450
Delivery expenses	22,060	
Productive wages	32,300	
Warehouse wages	30,200	
Administrative salaries	15,200	
Purchases and sales	426,500	623,300
Administration expenses	5,600	
Rents administration	12,600	
Inventory 1.10.X5	18,950	
Ordinary 50p shares		100,000
Share premium account		50,000
Accumulated profits 1.10.X5		26,000
Premises	275,000	
Vehicles	18,500	
Equipment	12,000	
Depreciation as at 1.10.X5		
Premises		3,750
Equipment		3,600
Vehicles		6,500
7% debentures		95,000
Bank	51,810	
	1,019,600	1,019,600

The following additional information is available:

▶ Inventory as at 30.9.X6 was valued at £20,650.

▶ Premises and equipment are used at 50% production and 50% distribution, and are to be depreciated at the rate of 1% and 10% straight line respectively.

▶ Vehicles are only used for distribution, and are depreciated at 20% reducing balance.

▶ A provision for bad debts of 5% is to be allowed for.

▶ £500 was prepaid for rent and £600 is owing for production wages as at 30.9.X6.

▶ Taxation for the year is estimated at £22,680.

Prepare the statement of comprehensive income and the statement of financial position for Hobo Ltd as at 30.9.X6 in a form suitable for publication.

7 The trial balance of Burn Ltd. as at 31.12.X9 was as follows:

	Dr	Cr
Purchases and sales	15,260	83,460
Inventory 1.1.X9	6,230	
Trader receivables and payables	8,240	7,210
Production salaries and wages	12,320	
Production expenses	7,210	
Warehouse expenses	950	
Warehouse wages	10,100	
Administration salaries	14,200	
Administration expenses	950	
Ordinary £1 shares		100,000
Share premium account		20,000
Accumulated profits 1.1.X9		62,000
Premises	200,000	
Equipment	50,000	
Vehicles	15,000	
Provision for depreciation: Premises		20,000
Equipment		15,000
Vehicles		6,560
6% Debentures		50,000
Bank	103,520	
Cash	250	
New capital		80,000
	444,230	444,230

The following additional information is available, none of which has been accounted for in the trial balance:

▶ Inventory 31.12.X9 £4,560.

▶ Premises and equipment are used 50% production, 25% distribution and 25% administration and are depreciated at the rate of 2% and 10% respectively.

▶ Vehicles are only used by distribution and are depreciated at 25% reducing balance.

▶ A provision for bad debts of 5% is to be made.

▶

▶ The new capital consists of the issue on 1.12.X9 of 40,000 £1 shares; the ledger clerk did not know how to treat this item in the ledgers.

▶ Tax for the year is estimated at £1,200.

▶ A vehicle, purchased 1.1.X7 for £7,000 was sold on 1.8.X9 for £3,750. The proceeds had been credited to sales.

▶ 5% Debentures were issued on 1.1.X9, par value £10,000, for £9,500. The £9,500 has been credited to accumulated profits 1.1.X9 account.

Prepare the statement of comprehensive income and the statement of financial position for Burn Ltd. as at 31.12.X9 in a form suitable for publication.

8 The trial balance of Black Ltd as at 31 December 20X5 was as follows:

	Dr	Cr
Trade receivables and trade payables	46,800	34,200
Returns inwards	2,450	
Productive wages	74,000	
Distribution expenses	32,870	
Administrative salaries	61,230	
Purchases and sales	321,700	552,600
Office expenses	5,630	
Returns outwards		4,670
Inventory 1.1.X5	22,300	
Ordinary £1 shares		150,000
Debentures 6%		50,000
Accumulated profits 1.1.X5		9,870
Premises	150,000	
Vehicles	85,000	
Equipment	70,000	
Depreciation as at 1.1.X5		
Premises		11,600
Equipment		27,500
Vehicles		29,250
Bank		2,290
	871,980	871,980

The following information is available, none of which has been taken account of in the preparation of the trial balance above:

▶ Inventory as at 31 December 20X5 is valued at £22,000.

▶ Vehicles are primarily used for distribution, buildings equally between production, distribution and administration and equipment equally between production and administration.

▶ Buildings are to be depreciated 1% straight line, equipment 20% straight line and vehicles 25% reducing balance.

▶ Equipment was sold on the 31 December 20X5 for £15,000. This had been credited to sales. The original cost was £20,000 and it had been purchased on 31 December 20X2. No further entries than cash and sales had been made in the books.

► Bad debts of £2,600 need writing off and a provision for bad debts at the rate of 5% is to be introduced.

► Taxation for the year is estimated at £9,860.

► Accruals of £3,500 for administration expense are required and prepayments of £5,600 have been identified within distribution expenses.

► The interest on the debentures has not yet been paid.

Prepare the statement of comprehensive income for the year ended 31 December 20X5 and the statement of financial position as at that date in a form suitable for publication.

9 Explain the terms rights issue and bonus issue of shares.

10 Gamma plc has issued share capital of £1,000,000, nominal value of ordinary shares is £2 and accumulated profits of £456,000 as at 31.12.X6. The company proposes to make a rights issue of 2 for 5 existing shares held at a price of £4.25 and a bonus issue of 200,000 ordinary shares. The market value of the shares as at 31.12.X5 is £6.70. Show the capital section of the balance sheet after the two share issues and also identify how many shares a holder of 1,000 shares before the issues will have afterwards.

11 The trial balance of Ria Enterprise for the year ended 31 December 20X0 is as follows:

	Debits £000	Credits £000
Cost of sales	191,700	
Revenue		285,100
Trade receivables (debtors)	18,000	
Trade payables (creditors)		15,700
Operating expenses	39,500	
Rental income from investment properties		1,600
Closing Inventory 31 December 20X0 (note i)	14,000	
Bank interest	1,030	
Preference dividend (full year)	1,330	
Ordinary dividend paid 1 July 20X0	5,340	
Investment property at valuation (note ii)	21,300	
Land and property at valuation (note iii)	84,000	
Plant and equipment at cost (note iv)	48,000	
Plant and equipment accumulated depreciation as at 1 January 20X0		22,400
Revaluation reserve		28,000
Retained earnings as at 1 January 20X0		23,300
Ordinary share capital 25p shares		26,700
10% redeemable preference shares £1		13,300
Bank		8,100
	424,200	424,200

►

The following notes are applicable:

(i) The inventory (stock) valuation as at 31 December 20X0 included damaged goods valued at £1,070,000. These damaged goods, it is estimated, could be sold for £1,270,000 if £600,000 of remedial work on them were carried out.

(ii) On 31 December 20X0 the investment property was valued at £18m.

(iii) Land and property were revalued to £20m and £64m respectively on 1 January 20X0. The revaluation reserve of £28m represents this revaluation. No further change in valuation has occurred since 1 January 20X0. As at 1 January 20X0 the remaining life of the property was 16 years and property is depreciated on a straight-line basis.

(iv) Plant and equipment is depreciated at 12.5% reducing balance basis.

(v) Depreciation on all non-current assets is charged 50% cost of sales and 50% operating expenses.

(vi) The taxation charge for the year is estimated at £12m.

Prepare the statement of comprehensive income (profit and loss account) for the year ended 31 December 20X0 and the statement of financial position as at that date for Ria.

12 Jacob, Henry and Isaac are in partnership sharing profits in the ratio 3:3:4. Interest on drawings is charged at 5% on total drawings for the year and interest on capital is payable on the opening capital balances for the year at 4%. Salaries payable to the partners for a year are Jacob £30,000, Henry £25,000 and Isaac £33,000. At the year end 31.12.20X0 Jacob wishes to retire. At that date goodwill in the partnership is valued at £250,000 but is not to remain in the books after the retirement of Jacob. Jacob agrees to leave 40% of the amount due to him on loan to the partnership. At 31 December 20X0 a loan is taken out with the bank for £185,000. No entries in respect of this loan have yet been made in the accounts of the partnership. After Jacob's retirement Henry and Isaac agree to share profits in the ratio 2:3. The trial balance for the partnership as at 31.12.20X0, before any of the above is accounted for is as follows:

Trial balance as at 31.12.20X0 Jacob, Henry and Isaac

		Dr	Cr
Sales			623,430
Purchases		323,700	
Stock as at 1 January 20X0		32,300	
Wages		114,000	
Rates and insurance		22,300	
Electricity and gas		19,450	
Vehicle expenses		8,450	
Capital accounts:	Jacob		80,000
	Henry		65,000
	Isaac		60,000
Current accounts:	Jacob	980	
	Henry		2,880
	Isaac	1,450	

Drawings: Jacob	9,600	
Henry	22,000	
Isaac	13,500	
Premises	220,000	
Furniture and fittings at cost	16,400	
Vehicles at cost	32,600	
Depreciation premises 1 January 20X0		28,600
Depreciation furniture and fittings 1 January 20X0		6,560
Depreciation vehicles 1 January 20X0		6,520
Trade receivables	11,870	
Trade payables		12,480
Cash at bank	36,870	
	885,470	885,470

Depreciation is to be charged at 10% straight line on fixtures and fittings, 1% straight line on premises and 20% reducing balance on vehicles. There are no accruals and prepayments to take account of. Closing inventory at 31 December is valued at £34,250.

Prepare the statement of comprehensive income and statement of financial position of the partnership immediately after the retirement of Jacob clearly showing all transaction in the partners' capital and current accounts.

Answers to these questions can be found at the back of this book.

9

Group accounting

Objectives

By the end of this chapter you should be able to:
- ▶ Explain the principles of group accounting.
- ▶ Prepare simple group accounts.

Introduction

So far in this book we've only looked at the accounting for a single business, be that a sole trader or a company. As companies, in particular, grow, they could expand gradually, or by buying another entire company, rather than by buying individual assets. In other words, what we do is buy the legal framework of a company, by buying its shares, and thus controll it. It is arguably then easier to take over the reputation of the business, and the existing workforce. In this case, ownership of the underlying net assets remains with the company acquired, but as we own that company, we also control its net assets.

For example, if company A buys all the shares of company B, this means that company A is now owned by its shareholders, as usual, and company B is owned by company A. When it comes to appointing the directors of company B, company A will presumably appoint people who will act in accordance with the wishes of the directors of company A. Indeed, they may even appoint themselves, so that the same people are now the directors of both companies. This means that both companies are under a single point of control.

Legally, of course, we still have two separate entities. However, remember from Chapter 4 that we don't go by the legal form but by the economic substance of a transaction, so the legal position isn't as important as the substance of the position we now have. The standard view in accounting is that the substance is that we don't have two entities, but actually only one, because there's only one point of control.

After all, back in Chapter 4 we saw that one of the key characteristics of financial statements is the provision of relevant information. As far as group accounts are concerned, information on both companies is required by the users, but the shareholders of company A will not receive by right any information on company B as they are not the direct shareholders. Accordingly, we need to provide information on the two companies to the shareholders of A in some sort of combined form.

What this means is that the two companies constitute a single entity for accounting purposes. Accordingly, we prepare a single set of financial statements to cover both companies. The challenge is thus to bolt together the statements of financial position of each individual company to create a single one covering the group of two. We call this single statement the 'group' or 'consolidated' statement of financial position. We can, of course, also prepare a group (or consolidated) statement of comprehensive income, and so on. Note that we therefore prepare financial statements for the individual companies as normal, and then also prepare a single set of consolidated, or group, financial statements to report on the group as a whole.

The company which owns shares in others is known as the 'holding company', because it holds shares in others. Companies which are owned are known as subsidiary companies.

This chapter now goes on to explore how to consolidate two statements of financial position and two statements of comprehensive income. Other consolidated statements, such as cash flow, will also be prepared but are beyond the scope of this book. In practice, of course, company A could also buy the shares of company C, and so on, so a group of companies can become very large. However, all that needs be done is to consolidate the additional companies in the same way as the first, so once we've learned to deal with one company we can deal with groups of any size.

We start by looking at the simplest situation, that is, where the holding company buys all the shares in another. In all the examples we will use a layout for the individual statements of financial position that shows assets as debits, and liabilities and equity as credits, so that you can follow the underpinning double entry.

Acquisition of whole subsidiary

H Ltd buys all the share capital of S Ltd for £8,000, and this investment is, of course, shown in H's own statement of financial position as an asset.

H LTD

Non-current assets	2,000	Share capital	10,000
Investment in S	8,000		
	10,000		10,000

S LTD

Non-current assets	3,000	Share capital	6,000
Bank	3,000		
	6,000		6,000

Remember what we're aiming to do, which is to add together these two statements. For many of the items in the two statements this will be easy. For example, the total non-current assets for the group will be 2,000 + 3,000 = 5,000, and the bank balance for the group will be nil + 3,000 = 3,000. It's good practice to tick these items off as you use them, to keep track of your accounts preparation.

You might reasonably think that we would also add together the two share capitals. However, we need to bear in mind that the share capital of S is what H bought for the £8,000. In other words, the share capital in S's statement and the 'Investment in S' in H's statement are the same thing. Hence, on consolidation these two items will be set one against the other, since one is a debit and the other a credit, leaving a net debit of £2,000. This debit represents the amount that H has paid over the apparent book value of S to acquire the subsidiary.

Activity 9.1

Why would a company pay more for a company than the statement of financial position says it is worth? What does the extra amount represent?

Answer

Given that H has paid £8,000 for S, H presumably believes this is what the new subsidiary is actually worth. Consequently, there must be something, worth the extra £2,000, that is not shown on S's statement of financial position.

You will remember from Chapters 2 and 4 that a statement of financial position shows the assets and liabilities of an entity, but only where these can be objectively measured. The implication must be that there's some asset of S which is not shown on the statement, and that this must be because it's not deemed to be objectively measurable. This could be a number of things, such as reputation, skilled management, a committed and skilled workforce, etc. These things are all assets but are inherently difficult, if not impossible, to measure objectively. Nevertheless, in acquiring S, H is recognising that such things do exist and are worth paying £2,000 for. For accounting purposes, we lump these things together and call them 'goodwill'. Hence, in our example, the debit of £2,000 represents the asset of goodwill.

If you check back now to see which items in the statements of H and S have not yet been ticked off, you should find that we've just the share capital of H left. This becomes the share capital in the group statement of financial position.

H LTD

CONSOLIDATED STATEMENT OF FINANCIAL POSITION

Non-current assets	5,000	Share capital	10,000
Goodwill	2,000		
Bank	3,000		
	10,000		10,000

Non-controlling interests

Remember that we are preparing consolidated, or group, statements because we control the other company. We can usually acquire control by buying most of the subsidiary's shares, so we don't need to buy 100%, as we did in the example above. If we don't buy all the company, there will be a '**non-controlling interest**', previously known as a 'minority interest'. We can show this as a diagram:

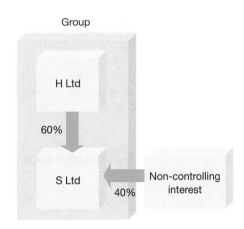

As far as the accounting is concerned, however, we will still control all the net assets, so we will add 100% of each to the equivalent figure in our accounts, even if we only own, say, 60%. In other words, what we're going to do is add 100% and then subtract the 40% non-controlling interest, to recognise that some of the funding of the total net assets has come from outside the group. This may become clearer if we look at an example.

H Ltd buys 60% of the shares in S Ltd for £8,000. Again we have the statements of financial position for the two companies immediately after accounting for the purchase of the shares.

H LTD

Non-current assets	3,000	Share capital	15,000
Investment in S	8,000		
Inventory	4,000		
	15,000		15,000

S LTD

Non-current assets	4,000	Share capital	10,000
Inventory	1,000		
Bank	5,000		
	10,000		10,000

We will adopt the same basic approach as before and add together similar items, for non-current assets, inventory and bank. Again, the share capital for the group statement is going to be simply the share capital of H. That leaves just the share capital of S and the 'investment in S' from H's statement.

As before, we will set these off, but with the key difference that the investment of £8,000 only bought us 60% of S's share capital. The calculation of goodwill is therefore:

Investment in S	8,000
Shares acquired (60% × 10,000)	6,000
Goodwill	2,000

Using these figures means that we can tick off the debit of 8,000 from H's statement, but can only tick off 6,000 of the 10,000 share capital from S's statement. The missing credit of 4,000 is, of course, the non-controlling interest. When we put all this together in the group statement of financial position we produce:

H LTD
CONSOLIDATED STATEMENT OF FINANCIAL POSITION

Non-current assets	7,000	Share capital	15,000
Goodwill	2,000	Non-controlling interest	4,000
Inventory	5,000		
Bank	5,000		
	19,000		19,000

Subsidiary with reserves

So far we've always dealt with companies which have share capital but no reserves. This is obviously unrealistic so our next step is to explore how to cope when both the holding company and the subsidiary have reserves at the date of acquisition. As before, we'll use an example to show how this works.

H bought 80% of the share capital in S for £11,000 some time ago when reserves in S were £2,000. The individual statements of financial position are now as follows:

H LTD

Investment in S	11,000	Share capital	12,000
Inventory	2,000	Reserves	2,000
Bank	1,000		
	14,000		14,000

S LTD

Non-current assets	5,000	Share capital	10,000
Inventory	5,000	Reserves: Pre-acquisition	2,000
Bank	3,000	Post-acquisition	1,000
	13,000		13,000

The only new elements in this example are the reserves. The reserves of H Ltd are easy to deal with – we simply show them as reserves in the group statement. The difficult bit is dealing with the reserves of the subsidiary. Bear in mind that we acquired the subsidiary a while ago, when the reserves were £2,000. Together with the share capital (which we assume hasn't changed), that's a total net worth for S Ltd of £12,000 at the date of acquisition. In other words, when we bought our shares in S, the book value of S was £12,000, so that's what we will use to calculate goodwill.

The other £1,000 in reserves is what has arisen from trading profits since the date of acquisition, i.e. 'post acquisition'. By definition, this can't form part of any calculation of goodwill on acquisition since it didn't exist at the date of acquisition. So who does this post-acquisition reserve belong to? The answer is the holding company and the non-controlling interest. Consequently, the accounting treatment of this is simple: we add our group share to the group reserves, and the non-controlling interest's share to the non-controlling interest.

This all might seem complex enough, but there's a further complication we need to be aware of before we start the accounting. There's not only the reserves, some pre-acquisition and some post-acquisition, to be dealt with, but there's also a non-controlling interest to be accounted for, as in the previous example. This all means that accounting for the reserves of the subsidiary is going to require divisions not only between the group share and the non-controlling interest share, but also between pre- and post-acquisition reserves. It might help if we summarise this:

	Group's share	*Non-controlling share*
Share capital	Goodwill calculation	Non-controlling interest
Pre-acquisition reserve(s)	Goodwill calculation	Non-controlling interest
Post-acquisition reserve(s)	Group revenue reserve	Non-controlling interest

When we put all this together, the group statement of financial position will look like this:

H LTD

CONSOLIDATED STATEMENT OF FINANCIAL POSITION

Non-current assets	5,000	Share capital	12,000
Goodwill	1,400	Reserves (2,000 +	
		80% × 1,000)	2,800
Inventory	7,000	Non-controlling interest	2,600
Bank	4,000		
	17,400		17,400

GOODWILL CALCULATION

Investment in S	11,000
Shares acquired (10,000 × 80%)	(8,000)
Pre-acquisition reserves	
(2,000 × 80%)	(1,600)
Goodwill	1,400

NON-CONTROLLING INTEREST CALCULATION

Shares acquired (10,000 × 20%)	2,000
Pre-acquisition reserves (2,000 × 20%)	400
Post-acquisition reserves (1,000 × 20%)	200
	2,600

Note that you could, of course, calculate the non-controlling interest in the reserves as simply 20% of the total £3,000. However, you might find the above technique of dealing with the pre- and post-acquisition bits separately to be more understandable, since that's what we do with the group's share.

Revaluation on acquisition

Our final complication in this introduction to group accounting is the question of whether the books of the subsidiary are actually a fair reflection of the worth of the company at the date it is acquired. We have already noted that there will be assets that are not included in the normal statement of financial position, such as reputation, skilled workforce, etc. We then accounted for these things as goodwill in the group statement of financial position by comparing the total we paid with the book value of the subsidiary's net assets. What we didn't consider, however, was the possibility that the book value could be significantly wrong.

Consequently, what we need to do is review the valuation of the net assets of the subsidiary at the date we acquire it to ensure that it's reasonably up to date and accurate. After all, if it isn't then the valuation of the goodwill will be wrong. Once more, we'll explore how to account for this using an example.

Example 9.1

H Ltd buys 80% of the share capital in S for £13,000, some time ago when reserves in S were £2,000. At acquisition the non-current assets of S were actually worth £8,000, and the inventory was worth £4,000. Initially, then, we have the statements of financial position for the two companies, before the adjustments to the 'fair values' of S's non-current assets and inventory have been dealt with.

H LTD

Investment in S	13,000	Share capital	14,000
Inventory	2,000	Reserves	2,000
Bank	1,000		
	16,000		16,000

S LTD

Non-current assets	5,000	Share capital	10,000
Inventory	5,000	Reserves: Pre-acquisition	2,000
Bank	3,000	Post-acquisition	1,000
	13,000		13,000

Our first step in the consolidation process needs to be to bring the statement of S up to date and adjust it so that it reflects the fair values rather than the existing book values. The method is to put the revaluation through the accounts of S just before the consolidation itself. This is done only as a consolidation working adjustment, i.e. we don't actually change the books of S Ltd. The values of non-current assets and inventory will change, and will be balanced by the creation of a revaluation reserve in S. We'll look in more detail at revaluations in Chapter 13, but for the moment we only need to know that any change in the value of an asset will be reflected in the equity as a 'revaluation reserve'.

Consequently, we amend the existing statement of financial position of S for the three changes, non-current assets, inventory and the balancing revaluation reserve, resulting in a new statement as follows:

S LTD

Non-current assets	8,000	Share capital	10,000
Inventory	4,000	Revaluation reserve	2,000
Bank	3,000	Reserves: Pre-acquisition	2,000
		Post-acquisition	1,000
	15,000		15,000

Example 9.1
continued

Having got an up-to-date statement for S Ltd which reflects the fair values, we can now continue with the consolidation as before, using the new statement. One thing to note here is that the new revaluation reserve reflects the increase in net assets prior to the consolidation, so we need to deal with that in the same way as the other pre-acquisition reserve. That means that we credit the group's 80% share to the goodwill calculation and the non-controlling interest's 20% share to their account.

H LTD
CONSOLIDATED STATEMENT OF FINANCIAL POSITION

Non-current assets	8,000	Share capital	14,000
Goodwill	1,800	Reserves (2,000 + 80%	
		× 1,000)	2,800
Inventory	6,000	Non-controlling interest	3,000
Bank	4,000		
	19,800		19,800

GOODWILL CALCULATION

Investment in S	13,000
Shares acquired (10,000 × 80%)	(8,000)
Revaluation reserve (2,000 × 80%)	(1,600)
Pre-acquisition reserves (2,000 × 80%)	(1,600)
Goodwill	1,800

NON-CONTROLLING INTEREST

Shares acquired (10,000 × 20%)	2,000
Revaluation reserve (2,000 × 20%)	400
Pre-acquisition reserves (2,000 × 20%)	400
Post-acquisition reserves (1,000 × 20%)	200
	3,000

This exploration of **revaluation on acquisition** concludes our introduction to consolidated statements of financial position. Holding companies, will, of course, also produce a consolidated statement of comprehensive income, so the final section of this chapter is an introduction to such accounting.

Consolidated statements of comprehensive income

The consolidation of statements of comprehensive income follows the same principles as for statements of financial position, that is:

1 Add together equivalent items, including all of S's revenue, etc. The logic for adding all, even where there is a non-controlling interest, is the same as for the statement of financial position, i.e. all the subsidiary is controlled.

2 **Inter-company transactions** should be eliminated, for example interest paid by the subsidiary will cancel against interest received by the hold-

ing company. Sales made by one company to the other will cancel against the cost of sales in that other, since they are not sales in the context of the group, i.e. they haven't been sold to a third party and so aren't realised. (Note that where some of the goods are still held at the end of the year by the company which bought them, then we will have to make an allowance for the profit element inherent in those goods, since we want the inventory to be valued at the original cost to the group as a whole. This unrealised profit on inventory is, however, not something that we'll deal with any further in this book.)

3 The non-controlling interest in the net profit should be subtracted to leave the profit attributable to the holding company. The non-controlling interest's share will be credited to the non-controlling interest in the statement of financial position and the group's share will be credited to group retained profits.

As before, this should become clearer if we follow through an example.

Example 9.2

H Ltd owns 75% of the shares of S Ltd. During the year H sold goods worth 200 to S. These goods have since been sold by S and the sales are included in the sales figure for S below:

INDIVIDUAL STATEMENTS OF COMPREHENSIVE INCOME

	H Ltd	S Ltd
Revenue	2,090	800
Expenses	1,400	560
Profit before tax	690	240
Tax	260	60
Retained profits	430	180

A useful approach is to set out the calculations as a table, showing how the individual items are added together, and how the inter-company sale is cancelled out in the consolidation.

	H	S	Inter-company adjustment	Total
Revenue	2,090	800	(200)	2,690
Expenses	(1,400)	(560)	200	(1,760)
	690	240		930
Tax	(260)	(60)		(320)
Profit	430	180		610

The non-controlling interest will be 25% of the profit after tax of S Ltd, hence 25% of 180, so 45. Using this figure and the total column in the table above, we can now prepare the consolidated statement of comprehensive income:

Example 9.2
continued

H LTD

CONSOLIDATED STATEMENT OF COMPREHENSIVE INCOME

Revenue	2,690
Expenses	1,760
Profit before tax	930
Tax	320
Profit after tax	610
Attributable to non-controlling interest	45
Attributable to shareholders of H	565

Summary

This chapter has introduced accounting for groups. As you may have guessed, group accounting is a complex topic and this chapter has only dealt with the basic principles and the more straightforward accounting. Nevertheless, you should now have a sound understanding of the basics. Specifically, we've covered:

▶ the rationale for group accounting

▶ the preparation of a consolidated statement of financial position including goodwill, non-controlling interest and revaluations on acquisition

▶ the preparation of a consolidated statement of comprehensive income.

Key terms

consolidated statement of financial position (p. 183)
goodwill (p. 184)
non-controlling interest (p. 185)
group accounting (p. 188)

revaluation on acquisition (p. 190)
consolidated statement of comprehensive income (p. 190)
inter-company transactions (p. 190)

*S*elf-assessment questions

1   'If we only buy 75% of a company, surely we should only add 75% of that company into our consolidated statement of financial position?' What is the argument against this statement?

2   Harper Ltd bought 60% of the share capital in Sharpe for £220,000, two years ago when reserves in Sharpe Ltd were £40,000. At 31 December 20X9, the individual statements of financial position are as follows:

HARPER LTD

Investment in S	220,000	Share capital	240,000
Inventory	40,000	Reserves	40,000
Bank	20,000		
	280,000		280,000

SHARPE LTD

Non-current assets	100,000	Share capital	200,000
Inventory	100,000	Reserves	60,000
Bank	60,000		
	260,000		260,000

Prepare Harper's consolidated statement of financial position at 31 December 20X9. The information above is presented in the double-entry format that we've used throughout this chapter, but you could use this to calculate the figures and then draft a consolidated statement of financial position using the normal layout that we've seen earlier in this book.

3 O'Malley Ltd bought 90% of the share capital in Tamworth Ltd for £390,000 one year ago when reserves in S were £60,000. At acquisition the non-current assets of Tamworth were actually worth £200,000. The statements of financial position for the two companies are as follows. (Note that these are presented in the standard vertical format rather than in the side-by-side format that has been used so far in this chapter, but the same approach can be applied.)

Prepare the consolidated statement of financial position for O'Malley Ltd.

O'MALLEY LTD
STATEMENT OF FINANCIAL POSITION

Investment in S	390,000
Inventory	60,000
Bank	30,000
	480,000
Share capital	420,000
Reserves	60,000
	480,000

TAMWORTH LTD
STATEMENT OF FINANCIAL POSITION

Non-current assets	150,000
Inventory	150,000
Bank	90,000
	390,000
Share capital	300,000
Reserves	90,000
	390,000

4 Hammonds Ltd owns 60% of the shares of Seaway Ltd. During the year to 30th June 20X9 Hammonds sold goods worth 300 to Seaway, and this transaction is fully reflected in the statements below.

INDIVIDUAL STATEMENTS OF COMPREHENSIVE INCOME

	Hammonds Ltd	Seaway Ltd
Revenue	3,000	1,200
Expenses	2,150	860
Profit before tax	850	340
Tax	60	90
Retained profits	790	250

Prepare the consolidated statement of comprehensive income for Hammonds Ltd for the year ended 30 June 20X9.

Answers to these questions can be found at the end of the book.

10

Statement of cash flows

Objectives

By the end of this chapter you should be able to:

► Explain the importance of cash flow within the business.

► Identify cash flows within a business.

► Prepare a statement of cash flows.

► Explain the relationship between the statement of cash flows, statement of comprehensive income and statement of financial position within a business.

► Identify the difference between the indirect and direct methods of preparing a statement of cash flows.

► Identify and calculate a simple cash flow ratio.

► Explain the word 'fund' as used in accounting.

Introduction

In previous chapters we have concentrated on preparing financial information for a business based on the concept of profit. You should have already realised that profit does not equal cash and therefore it is quite possible for a business to be making reasonable profits but have very little cash. However, cash is vital to a business. Without it the business cannot purchase inventory, pay trade payables, wages or any other expenses. Cash is quite often referred to as the 'lifeblood' of a business – without it it will not survive!

A business therefore must pay attention to both its profit and cash position.

Cash flows within a business

At this point in your studies you should be able to complete the following activity quite quickly. If you do have problems return to Chapter 5 and consider the cash transactions that Mr Bean made.

Activity 10.1   Identify as many cash flows as you can for a business. Enter them in the table below. Two are already entered for you.

CASH FLOWS

Into the business	*Out of the business*
▶ Capital contributed in the form of cash	▶ Wages paid in cash

Answer   **CASH FLOWS**

Into the business	*Out of the business*
▶ Capital contributed in the form of cash	▶ Wages paid in cash
▶ Cash sales	▶ Cash purchases
▶ Receipts from trade receivables	▶ Payments to trade payables
▶ Cash loans and debentures	▶ Purchase of non-current assets
▶ Sale of fixed assets	▶ Cash paid for rent, heat, etc.
▶ Rents or other income received	▶ Dividends paid
▶ Interest and dividends received	▶ Interest paid
	▶ Taxation paid

You have, in fact, just constructed a cash account and this is essentially what a **statement of cash flows** is about.

Remember what we said in Chapter 1 about a statement of cash flows, which was that:

▶ Many accountants regard it as more objective and reliable than a statement of comprehensive income.

▶ Cash flows are generally hard fact, whereas assessment of profit requires estimation and subjective judgement.

▶ It is much easier to manipulate profit figures than cash figures.

The above factors are demonstrated in the following activity.

Activity 10.2   Alex Ltd has drawn up the following statement of comprehensive income for the first year of trading:

Sales	60,000
Cost of sales	(35,000)
Gross profit	25,000
Depreciation	(5,000)
Expenses	(10,000)
Net profit	10,000

The following information is also available:

▶ The company started the year with £20,000 cash in the bank.

▶ Sales for cash throughout the year were £58,000 and cost of sales for cash £38,000. No trade receivables or trade payables existed at the beginning of the year.

▶ Of the expenses figure of £10,000, £1,500 has not yet been paid.

▶ The company acquired £15,000 of non–current assets during the year paying in cash.

Identify:

▶ The cash figure at the end of the year and explain why this is different from the profit figure.

▶ Cash inflows and outflows during the year.

▶ Any figures in the statement of comprehensive income that could be manipulated.

Answer

Opening cash	20,000
Add cash sales	58,000
	78,000
Deduct: Cash cost of sales	(38,000)
Cash expenses	(8,500)
Non-current assets paid for	(15,000)
Closing cash	16,500

Cash inflows were sales of £58,000.

Cash outflows were cost of sales of £38,000, expenses of £8,500 and purchase of assets of £15,000, a total of £61,500.

A net outflow of £3,500 has occurred. This is mainly due to the purchase of non-current assets, which, remember, is not recorded in the statement of comprehensive income in the year of acquisition, but is spread over the useful life of the asset by means of a depreciation charge. The profit figure above of £10,000 can be changed if different assumptions are made about the depreciation charge.

In the above activity Alex Ltd is profitable but if, to remain in business, it had to purchase £50,000 of non-current assets, or if it had to repay a loan of £50,000 immediately after the end of the year, then it would not have enough cash to do this and would need to organise an overdraft facility. The future of the business depends, to a large extent, on its cash position and its ability to generate cash to pay off the overdraft. As cash is so important to businesses they are required to prepare a statement of cash flows, which identifies the cash position of the business at a point in time and the inflows and outflows of cash for the users of the financial statements.

Using the above activity we can also calculate a very simple cash flow ratio. You will learn more about ratios and ratio analysis in Chapter 12, but it is useful to deal with this one ratio at this stage. Ratios can help us to interpret/analyse the information in a set of financial statements. From the above activity we can calculate a ratio of total cash inflows divided by total cash outflows: 58,000/61,500 = 0.94. This is close to 1, indicating that our inflows have almost matched our outflows and we have been able to purchase some non-current assets.

Statement of cash flows

Accountants prepare a statement of cash flows to a given format prescribed by the International Accounting Standards Board in IAS 7. This format incorporates all the items you have listed in Activity 10.1 above, but identifies cash flows under specific headings as follows:

STATEMENT OF CASH FLOWS FOR THE YEAR ENDED XX

Net cash inflow/outflow from operating activities	X	
Interest paid	(X)	
Taxation paid	(X)	X
Net cash used in investing activities		
Acquisition of subsidiary less cash acquired	X	
Purchase of non-current assets	X	
Proceeds from sale of non-current assets	X	
Interest received	X	
Dividends received	X	X
Net cash used in financing activities		
Proceeds from issuing shares	X	
Proceeds from long-term borrowing	X	
Dividends paid	(X)	X
Increase/Decrease in cash and cash equivalents		X

One item on this statement of cash flows, the net cash inflow/outflow from operating activities, does not equate directly to an item on the cash account. We will explain how this figure is derived later in this chapter. To familiarise yourself with the cash flow format, work through the following activity.

Activity 10.3

The following information is available in respect of White Rose Ltd for the year end 31.12.X5:

▶ Net cash inflow from operating activities was £120,000.

▶ The company received dividends during the year of £45,000, paid an interim dividend of £30,000 and proposed a dividend of £20,000 at the year end. Last year's proposed dividend was £25,000.

▶ The taxation charge for the year was estimated at £55,000 which was £3,000 less than that estimated for the year ended 31.12.X4.

▶ Interest was payable during the year on £200,000 of 5% debentures. All interest due had been paid at the year end.

▶ White Rose Ltd had purchased £120,000 of fixed assets during the year to 31.12.X5 and fixed assets sold had produced a profit on sale of £10,000. The net book value of fixed assets sold was £50,000.

▶ White Rose Ltd had also issued 50,000 £1 ordinary shares at a premium of 50p. All shares were fully paid at the year end. A loan of £40,000 had also been raised by the company at the same time as redeeming loans of £20,000 at par.

Prepare the statement of cash flows for the year ended 31.12.X5. NB: There were no acquisitions or disposals of subsidiaries.

Answer

STATEMENT OF CASH FLOWS FOR THE YEAR ENDED 31.12.X5

Net cash inflow/outflow from operating activities	120	
Interest paid	(10)	
Taxation paid	(58)	52
Net cash used in investing activities		
Acquisition of subsidiary		
less cash acquired		
Purchase of non-current assets	(120)	
Proceeds from sale of non-current assets	60	
Interest received		
Dividends received	45	(15)
Net cash used in financing activities		
Proceeds from issuing shares	75	
Proceeds from long-term borrowing	40	
Repayment of debentures	(20)	
Dividends paid	(55)	40
Increase/Decrease in cash and cash equivalents		£77

In completing this activity care was required when dealing with the following items to ensure that the cash flow was identified:

▶ Dividends proposed at the year end 31.12.X5 were not paid but the proposed dividend from the previous year was.

▶ Tax is not due until nine months after the end of the year so the tax paid is last year's liability.

▶ The actual receipt from the sale of assets was the cash flow not the profit on sale which is the figure included in the statement of comprehensive income.

▶ The cash flow from the issue of shares included the share premium.

Net cash flow from operating activities

This item refers to cash flows in respect of buying and selling goods and expenses incurred. It can, of course, be derived from the cash book by identifying all cash receipts from trading and all cash payments such as payments to trade payables, payments for wages, rent, rates, electricity and so on. This would be the **direct method** of arriving at the **net cash flow from operating activities**. However, it can also be derived from the statement of comprehensive income for the year.

Activity 10.4   Identify as many items as you can that appear in the statement of comprehensive income before interest, taxation and dividends that do not involve a flow of cash.

Answer

▶ Depreciation – a book entry not a flow of cash.

▶ Profit or loss on sale of assets – the cash receipt of sale price is the cash flow.

▶ Accruals and prepayments – income and expense within the statement of comprehensive income is recognised in accordance with accounting concepts. It is not the cash receipt and payment.

▶ Sales (cash sales and sales on credit) – the cash flow is cash sales and receipts from trade receivables.

▶ Cost of sales (cash and credit purchases adjusted for opening and closing inventory) – the cash flow is the cash spent during the year on purchases and payments to trade payables.

Another method, in contrast to the direct method, of arriving at the net cash flow from operating activities would be to adjust the operating profit before taxation, interest and dividends for all the items listed in the answer to Activity 10.4. This is known as the **indirect method**. IAS 7 actually prefers the direct method as it provides information which may be useful in estimating future cash flows which is not available under the indirect method. It does, however, permit the use of the indirect method as it can be easily derived from the statement of comprehensive income.

The reconciliation of operating profit and net cash flows from operating activities is required as a note to the statement of cash flows. The note is formatted as follows:

Reconciliation of operating profit and net cash flows from operating activities:		
Operating profit (as per statement of comprehensive income)		X
Adjustment for items not involving the movement of funds		
Depreciation	X	
(Profit)/loss on sale of assets	(X)	
Amortisation	X	X

(Increase)/decrease in inventory	X
(Increase)/decrease in trade receivables	X
(Decrease)/increase in trade payables	X
Net cash inflows from operating activities	X

Note in the above that:

▶ Depreciation and amortisation charges are added back to the operating profit as these were deducted in arriving at the profit figure. Amortisation is the term used to describe the depreciation of leases.

▶ Profit on sale is deducted.

▶ Decrease in inventory and trade receivables from last year to this is added to the operating profit as this means less cash has been tied up in inventories and trade receivables. Conversely an increase would mean more cash had been tied up.

▶ An increase in trade payables is also added back to the profit figure as this means cash has been kept in the business not paid out to reduce the liability to trade payables.

The direct method of arriving at net cash flows from operating activities is formatted as follows:

Cash received from customers	X
Cash paid to suppliers	(X)
Cash paid to and on behalf of employees	(X)
Other cash payments	(X)
Net cash inflow from operating activities	X

Activity 10.5

The following information is available in respect of Red Rose Ltd for the year ended 31.12.X5.

STATEMENT OF COMPREHENSIVE INCOME EXTRACT FOR THE YEAR ENDED 31.12.X5

Net profit	120
Net interest charges	(30)
Net profit before taxation	90
Taxation	(15)
Net profit after taxation	75
Dividends paid and proposed	(40)
Retained profit	35

Net profit of £120 is after charging depreciation of £25 and including loss on sale of assets of £15.

▶

STATEMENT OF FINANCIAL POSITION EXTRACTS

	31.12.X4	31.12.X5
	£	£
Inventory	8	6
Trade receivables	5	4
Cash	2	3
	15	13
Trade payables	7	8

Prepare the reconciliation of operating profit to net cash flow from operating activities.

Answer

Net profit before interest and taxation		120
Adjustments for items not involving the movements of funds		
Depreciation	25	
Loss on sale	15	40
		160
Decrease in inventory	2	
Decrease in trade receivables	1	
Increase in trade payables	1	4
		164

Purpose of statement of cash flows

The statement of cash flows provides information in addition to that provided by a statement of comprehensive income and the statement of financial position. It identifies the cash flows in a business which are not apparent from the other two statements. It also identifies whether cash has increased or decreased from one year to the next. It does, however, have several drawbacks, some of which it shares with the other statements.

Activity 10.6   Identify two drawbacks of a statement of cash flows.

Answer

Several clues have already been given to you to answer this question. You should have identified two from the following:

▶ Cash is the 'lifeblood' of an organisation but the statement of cash flows is historical. If we are concerned over the liquidity of a business, the ability to pay its debts, then a cash flow forecast would be more useful.

▶ Cash flow from operating activities is derived by either the direct or indirect method. The indirect method uses information from the accruals-based accounting system. If cash flow is what we are interested in then there should only be one alternative –

the direct method. This would also avoid confusion for users who may have difficulty in understanding the reconciliation between operating profit and cash flow.

▶ What is cash? Is it cash in the shop till, cash in the bank, short-term investments? Just what do we mean by cash?

Funds flow

This section will provide you with an answer to the last question raised in the answer to Activity 10.6.

We have already looked at the idea of funds in Chapter 2, which identified the concept of funds coming into and out of the business – sources and applications. Sources of funds were such items as profit from trading, capital invested and loans taken out. Applications were the purchase of non-current assets and investments. Funds were not necessarily cash funds.

In Chapter 12 you will meet the phrase 'return on shareholders' funds'. These funds are the total of share capital and reserves, which are certainly not represented solely by cash. Shareholder funds are represented by the business's net assets, that is, non-current assets and current assets less current liabilities.

In general, in accounting the word 'funds' is used in connection with the accruals-based accounting system. It is possible to prepare a statement of sources and applications of funds for every business. In fact, prior to the introduction of the statement of cash flows requirement businesses did prepare such a statement. The statement, instead of arriving at a figure showing the increase/decrease in cash balances, showed the change in working capital – the funds flow. Working capital is the difference between current assets and current liabilities including accruals and prepayments. It is quite feasible for a business to have a net inflow of funds, as defined in terms of working capital, but an actual net outflow of cash. This is demonstrated by the following example.

STATEMENT OF FINANCIAL POSITION EXTRACTS

	31.12.X4	31.12.X5
Inventory	12	14
Trade receivables	8	9
Cash	6	5
	26	28
Trade payables	(12)	(9)
	14	19
Increase in working capital (19 – 14)	5	
Decrease in cash (6 – 5)	1	

The move away from preparing source and application of funds statements to that of preparing a statement of cash flows is regarded by many as being an important step forward in the provision of useful information.

Activity 10.7

Identify two reasons why a statement of cash flows may be regarded as more useful than funds flow (working capital) statements.

Answer

You should have identified two of the following:

▶ Cash is more objective and verifiable. It is not blurred by estimates of accruals and prepayments.

▶ Cash is more easily understood by users.

▶ Cash flow is a better guide to a business's ability to pay its liabilities than a funds flow.

▶ Working capital is not an indication of the solvency of a business.

Cash and cash equivalents, for our cash flow, still needs to be defined. In general, cash is determined as cash on hand and all deposits payable on demand. Deposits payable on demand are defined as those that are easily convertible into cash and can be withdrawn at any time without notice and without penalty. Don't forget that overdrafts repayable on demand will also have to be taken into account. Cash equivalents refers to short-term investments. Investments are viewed as short term if the maturity date is within three months or less from the date of acquisition.

Activity 10.8

Determine whether the following items are cash, cash equivalents, investing activities or financing activities:

1 An account held with a bank where a withdrawal requires 80 days' notice.

2 An account held with a bank where a withdrawal requires 150 days' notice.

3 An overdraft with the bank which is seen as short term and part of the everyday cash flows of the business.

4 A loan from a bank for 75 days for a specific purpose.

5 An investment with the bank which has 60 days to maturity but its final value payable fluctuates in accordance with stock market values.

Answer

1 This can be viewed as short term and therefore cash equivalent.

2 This is really a long-term investment as far as cash flows are concerned and therefore part of investing activities.

3 This is cash.

4 This is financing activities as a loan for a specific purpose cannot be viewed as everyday cash management.

5 There is a significant risk with this investment and therefore it should be viewed as part of investing activities.

Relationship between the statement of cash flows, statement of comprehensive income and statement of financial position

In the preparation of a statement of cash flows so far, in this chapter, you have been given the information required. However, some of this information can be deduced from the statement of comprehensive income and the opening and closing statement of financial positions. For example, you should be able to identify the increase in share capital from the opening and closing statement of financial positions. The following example illustrates the connections between the three statements and demonstrates the preparation of a statement of cash flows by using information from the other two plus additional information.

Example 10.1

The following information is available in respect of Yellow Rose Ltd.

STATEMENT OF COMPREHENSIVE INCOME FOR THE YEAR ENDED 31.12.X5

Gross profit		140
Depreciation		30
Interest receivable	(5)	
Interest payable	8	3
Profit on sale of asset		(8)
Amortisation of intangibles	20	45
Net profit before taxation		95
Taxation		(40)
Net profit after taxation		55
Dividends paid and proposed		(40)
Retained profit after dividends		15

STATEMENT OF FINANCIAL POSITIONS AS AT

	31.12.X4	31.12.X5
Non-current assets		
Intangibles	120	140
Property, plant and equipment	320	389
	440	529
Current assets		
Inventory	30	34
Trade receivables	24	22
Cash and bank	64	72
	118	128
Current liabilities		
Trade payables	32	36
Dividends	15	20
Taxation	45	40
	92	96

Example 10.1
continued

Net current assets	26	32
	466	561
non-current liabilities	100	120
	366	441
Ordinary share capital	250	280
Share premium	20	30
Retained profits	96	111
	366	441

The sale proceeds from the sale of non-current assets was £36. All interest due has been received and the interest payable has been paid. The first task to carry out in preparing the statement of cash flows is to identify all changes from last year's statement of financial position to this year's. Note that in the above example the current year's figures are on the right. It is advisable when you are given several columns in a table referring to different years to take great care in identifying the appropriate year's figures.

Intangible fixed assets have increased by £20. Amortisation of intangibles for the year was £20, therefore cash of £40 must have been spent.

Property, plant and equipment has changed according to the statement of financial positions from £320 to £389. However, assets have been bought, sold and depreciated throughout the year. If assets sold produced a profit of £8 and proceeds of £36 then the net book value of assets sold was £28. We can now identify how the assets have changed:

1.1.X4 balance	320
Sale of assets	28
	292
Depreciation year 31.12.X5	(30)
	262
31.12.X5 balance	389
Therefore purchase	127

However, a revaluation reserve of £20 has been created during the year. If we assume this is in respect of non-current assets, then the figure for the purchase of assets reduces to £107. Current asset changes are easy to identify as inventory increases £4, trade receivables decrease £2 and cash increase £8. Similarly, trade payables increase £4.

We need to be more careful when identifying the changes in respect of taxation and dividends. The statement of financial position as at 31.12.X5 shows the liability remaining in respect of these items, the statement of comprehensive income shows the matched charge for the year.

Thus dividends paid during the year will be:

Balance 1.1.X5	15
Charge for year	40
	55
Balance 31.12.X5	(20)
Paid	35
and taxation:	

Example 10.1
continued

Balance 1.1.X5	45
Charge for year	40
	85
Balance 31.12.X5	(40)
Paid	45

The change in non-current liabilities indicates a further loan of £20 raised and the changes in respect of ordinary share capital and share premium, issue of shares for cash of £40.

We can now prepare the reconciliation of operating profit to net cash flow from operating.

Profit before interest and taxation (95 + 3)		98
Depreciation	30	
Amortisation	20	
Profit on sale	(8)	42
		140
Increase in inventory	(4)	
Decrease in trade receivables	2	
Increase in trade payables	4	2
Net cash inflow from operating activities		142

STATEMENT OF CASH FLOWS FOR THE YEAR ENDED 31.12.X5

Net cash inflow from operating activities	142	
Taxation paid	(45)	
Interest paid	(8)	89
Net cash used in investing activities		
Payments to acquire intangible non-current assets	(40)	
Payments to acquire property, plant and equipment	(107)	
Sale of non-current assets	36	
Dividends received		
Interest received	5	(106)
Net cash used in financing activities		
Dividends paid	(35)	
Issue of shares	40	
Loans raised	20	25
Increase in cash balances		8

Note: The figure derived from the statement of cash flows for the increase in cash equates to the increase we identified from the statement of financial position 1.1.X5 to 31.12.X5.

Interpretation of a statement of cash flows

It is possible to gain an insight into the activities of a business by reviewing the statement of cash flows. For example, the cash flow in respect of Yellow Rose Ltd identifies the following facts:

▶ Interest, dividend and taxation payments are more than covered by the cash generated from operating activities.

▶ Acquisition of non-current assets has been financed partly from internal resources and partly from new capital raised in the form of shares and loans.

▶ Working capital displays no significant changes during the year, the small increase in inventory being matched by an increase in trade payables.

▶ The company could either be expanding or just replacing worn out assets.

*A*ctivity 10.9   Review the cash flow for White Rose Ltd, and identify any facts you can about the business from it.

Answer

▶ Interest, dividend and taxation payments are slightly more than the cash generated from operating activities. The business has gained a benefit from its investments in the form of dividends received.

▶ Acquisition of non-current assets has been partly financed by sale of old assets and partly from issue of new capital in the form of shares and loans.

▶ New debentures were issued in part to finance the redemption of older debenture stock.

▶ The remainder of the cash raised from the issue of shares and loans still remains in the cash balances.

▶ It is possible that from these cash balances the business intends to purchase more non-current assets.

Summary

This chapter has:

▶ introduced you to the statement of cash flows

▶ reiterated the fact that profit does not equal cash and that for a business to survive it must have cash – it is its 'lifeblood'. A statement of cash flows is historical in nature but identifies cash inflows and outflows within a business

▶ presented statement of cash flows in a prescribed format which also includes a reconciliation of operating profit to net cash inflow

▶ derived cash flows from operating activities by using either the direct or indirect method. The direct method is more appropriate and is the method preferred by the IASB as this identifies cash from customers and cash paid to customers and others, whereas the indirect method arrives at the cash flow by adjusting profit for movements in working capital and items not involving the movement of funds. The majority of businesses, though, prepare their cash flow using the indirect method as it demonstrates the link between the three required financial statements and does not require the business to adapt their information systems to extract additional information

▶ continued the discussion in respect of the definition of funds, which we began in Chapter 2.

The self-assessment exercises at the end of this chapter provide you with practice in preparing a statement of cash flows.

Key terms		
	cash flows (p. 196) statement of cash flows (p. 196) direct method (p. 200)	net cash flow from operating activities (p. 200) indirect method (p. 200) funds flow (p. 203)

*S*elf-assessment questions

1 Identify information provided by a statement of cash flows to users that is not provided by a statement of comprehensive income and the statement of financial position.

2 From the following information in respect of Sparrow Ltd prepare the statement of cash flows for the year ended 31.12.X5.

STATEMENT OF FINANCIAL POSITIONS AS AT

	31.12.X4 £000	31.12.X5 £000
Non-current assets		
Intangible	237	222
Property, plant and equipment	637	738
Investments	100	120
	974	1,080

▶

Current assets		
Inventory	230	256
Trade receivables	136	194
Bank	–	26
	366	476
Current liabilities		
Trade payables	97	103
Taxation	64	61
Dividends	60	66
Bank overdraft	24	–
	245	230
Net current assets	121	246
Total assets less current liabilities	£1,095	£1,326
Ordinary shares of £2	500	520
Share premium	–	130
Retained profits	545	576
Debentures	50	100
	£1,095	£1,326

STATEMENT OF COMPREHENSIVE INCOME FOR THE YEARS ENDED

	31.12.X4	31.12.X5
	£000	£000
Net profit for the year before tax	151	158
Taxation	64	61
Net profit after tax	87	97
Dividends	60	66
Retained profit for the year	27	31
Retained profit b/f	518	545
	545	576

Depreciation charged during the year was £187,000 and assets sold during the year produced a profit of £45,000. The net book value of the assets sold was £88,000. No intangible non-current assets have been acquired or sold during the year. Interest charged in the statement of comprehensive income for the year was £12,000 and all of this was paid.

3 Review the statement of cash flows prepared in answer to question 2 and summarise any conclusions which may be drawn from it in respect of the financial operations and position of Sparrow Ltd for the year ended 31.12.X5.

4   On 1 September 200Y CIP Ltd issues 21 million £1 ordinary shares at a premium of 100%. The financial statements for the year to 30 September 200Y were as follows:

STATEMENT OF COMPREHENSIVE INCOME FOR THE YEAR ENDED 30 SEPTEMBER 200Y

	£m	£m
Turnover		587
Cost of sales		(260)
Gross profit		327
Distribution costs	(51)	
Administration costs	(38)	(89)
Operating profit		238
Interest payable	(12)	
Interest receivable	5	(7)
Profit before tax		231
Taxation		(53)
Profit after tax		178
Dividends		(33)
Retained profit for the year		145

STATEMENT OF FINANCIAL POSITIONS AS AT

	30.9.0Y		30.9.0X	
	£m	£m	£m	£m
Property plant and equipment		587		331
Current assets:				
Inventory	232		256	
Debtors	215		182	
Interest receivable	2		3	
Investments	25		0	
Cash	18		35	
	492		476	
Current liabilities falling due within one year:	382		292	
Net current assets		110		184
Total assets less current liabilities		697		515
Non-current liabilities due after one year:				
Debentures		124		141
Net assets		573		374
Capital reserves				
Ordinary shares		170		149
10% £1 preference shares		35		35
Share premium account		79		58
Revaluation reserve		12		0
Retained profits		277		132
		573		374

Additional information:

▶ The current assets investment is a 30–day government bond.

▶ Property, plant and equipment include certain properties which were revalued in the year.

▶ Depreciation charged in the year is £38 million.

▶ Debentures were redeemed at par on 30 September 200Y.

▶ Assets with a net book value of £31 million were disposed of during the year for £35 million.

▶ Trade payables falling due within one year are further analysed as follows:

	30.9.0Y (£m)	30.9.0X (£m)
Bank overdraft	13	33
Trade payables	309	210
Taxation	48	33
Dividends	7	13
Interest payable	5	3
	382	292

Prepare a statement of cash flows for the year ended 30.9.0Y in accordance with IAS 7 showing clearly the reconciliation of operating profit to net cash flows from operating activities.

5 Prepare a statement of cash flows in acceptable form for Peak Ltd for the year ended 31 December 20X5.

STATEMENT OF FINANCIAL POSITIONS AS AT

	31.12.X4		31.12.X5	
Property, plant and equipment nbv				
Buildings	543,100		624,500	
Other	93,450		102,300	
Investments	56,000	692,550	142,000	868,800
Current assets:				
Inventory	82,400		83,400	
Trade receivables	54,300		48,750	
Bank	1,100			
	137,800		132,150	
Current liabilities falling due within one year:				
Trade payables	63,470		35,480	
Taxation	10,500		12,500	
Dividends	35,000		38,000	
Bank			10,500	
	108,970		96,480	

Net current assets	28,830	35,670
Total assets less current liabilities	721,380	904,470
Non-current liabilities due after one year:		
5% Debentures	45,000	150,000
Net assets	676,380	754,470
Capital reserves		
Ordinary £1 shares	600,000	620,000
Share premium account		40,000
Revaluation reserve	50,000	70,000
Retained profits	26,380	24,470
	676,380	754,470

STATEMENT OF COMPREHENSIVE INCOME FOR THE YEAR ENDED 31 DECEMBER

	20X4	20X5
Profit before tax	65,600	48,590
Taxation	10,500	12,500
Profit after tax	55,100	36,090
Dividends	35,000	38,000
Retained profit for the year	20,100	(1,910)
Retained profit b/f 1 January	6,280	26,380
Retained profit at 31 December	26,380	24,470

The following additional information is available:

▶ A market issue of shares was made on 1 January 20X5.

▶ During 20X5 equipment originally purchased at £65,200 was sold for £17,900, accumulated depreciation being £37,700. The difference on disposal had been taken to the statement of comprehensive income.

▶ Buildings costing £100,000 had been purchased during 20X5 and the depreciation charged for the year 20X5 on other assets was £25,000. The only assets revalued during the year were the buildings.

▶ Dividends received amounted to £7,500 and interest received £15,000 during 20X5 both of which had been credited to the statement of comprehensive income.

▶ The debentures were issued on 1 January 20X5 and all interest due had been paid.

Required
(a) Prepare the statement of cash flows for the year ended 31 December 20X5 in a form suitable for publication.
(b) Summarise the main conclusions arising from the cash flow produced for Peak Ltd.
(c) Comment on the usefulness of the statement of cash flows to users of financial statements.

6 Prepare a statement of cash flows in acceptable form for Campus Ltd for the year ended 31 December 20X5.

STATEMENT OF FINANCIAL POSITION AS AT

	31.12.X4		31.12.X5	
Property, plant and equipment nbv				
Buildings	324,100		624,500	
Other	76,450		102,300	
Investments	36,000	436,550	142,000	868,800
Current assets:				
Inventory	72,400		83,400	
Trade receivables	64,300		48,750	
Bank	100		–	
	136,800		132,150	
Current liabilities:				
Trade payables	42,470		35,480	
Taxation	18,500		12,500	
Dividends	25,000		38,000	
Bank	–		16,500	
	85,970		102,480	
Net current assets		50,830		29,670
Total assets less current liabilities		487,380		898,470
Non-current liabilities:				
5% Debentures		45,000		150,000
Net assets		442,380		748,470
Capital reserves				
Ordinary £1 shares		350,000		614,000
Share premium account				40,000
Revaluation reserve		50,000		70,000
Retained profits		42,380		24,470
		442,380		748,470

STATEMENT OF COMPREHENSIVE INCOME FOR THE YEAR ENDED 31 DECEMBER

	20X4	20X5
Profit before tax	83,600	32,590
Taxation	18,500	12,500
Profit after tax	65,100	20,090
Dividends	25,000	38,000
Retained profit for the year	40,100	(17,910)
Retained profit b/f 1 January	2,280	42,380
Retained profit at 31 December	42,380	24,470

The following additional information is available:

▶ A market issue of shares was made on 1 January 20X5.

▶ During 20X5 equipment originally purchased at £55,200 was sold for £21,900, accumulated depreciation being £27,700. The difference on disposal had been taken to the statement of comprehensive income.

▶ Buildings costing £400,000 had been purchased during 20X5 and the depreciation charged for the year 20X5 on other assets was £25,000. The only assets revalued during the year were the buildings.

▶ Dividends received amounted to £8,500 and interest received £12,000 during 20X5 both of which had been credited to the statement of comprehensive income.

▶ The debentures were issued on 1 January 20X5 and all interest due had been paid.

Required

(a) Prepare the statement of cash flows for the year ended 31 December 20X5 in a form suitable for publication.

(b) Summarise the main conclusions arising from the cash flow produced for Campus Ltd.

(c) Comment on the usefulness of the statement of cash flows to users of financial statements

7 The following information is available in respect of B entity.

STATEMENT OF COMPREHENSIVE INCOME FOR THE YEAR ENDED 30 SEPTEMBER 20X7

	£m	£m	£m
Gross profit			
			280
Depreciation		60	
Interest receivable	(10)		
Interest payable	16	6	
Profit on sale of assets		(16)	
Impairment of intangibles		40	90
Net profit before tax			190
Tax			80
Net profit after tax			110
Dividends paid and proposed			80
Retained earnings			30

▶

STATEMENT OF FINANCIAL POSITIONS AS AT

	30.9.06	30.9.07
Assets	(£m)	(£m)
Non-current assets		
Intangibles	240	280
Property, plant and equipment	640	778
	880	1058
Current assets		
Inventory	60	68
Trade receivables	48	44
Cash and bank	128	144
	236	256
Total assets	1,116	1,314
Equity and liabilities		
Equity		
Ordinary share capital	500	600
Share premium	40	60
Retained earnings	192	222
	732	882
Non-current liabilities	200	240
Current liabilities		
Trade payables	64	72
Dividends	30	40
Tax	90	80
	184	192
Total equity and liabilities	1,116	1,314

The sale proceeds from the sale of non-current assets was £72m. All interest due has been received and the interest payable has been paid.

Required

(a) Prepare the statement of cash flows for B entity for the year ended 30 September 20X7 in accordance with IAS, 7– 'Cash Flow Statements'. (Notes to the cash flow statement are not required.)

(b) Identify two limitations of a cash flow statement.

8 The following information is available in respect of T entity.

**STATEMENT OF COMPREHENSIVE INCOME FOR THE YEAR
ENDED 31 DECEMBER 20X7**

	£m	£m	£m
Gross profit			420
Depreciation		90	
Interest receivable	(15)		
Interest payable	24	9	
Profit on sale of assets		(24)	
Impairment of intangibles		60	135
Net profit before tax			285
Tax			120
Net profit after tax			165
Dividends paid and proposed			120
Retained earnings			45

STATEMENT OF FINANCIAL POSITIONS AS AT

	31.12.X6 £m	31.12.X7 £m
Assets		
Non-current assets		
Intangibles	360	420
Property, plant and equipment	960	1,167
	1,320	1,587
Current assets		
Inventory	90	102
Trade receivables	72	66
Cash and bank	192	216
	354	384
Total assets	1,674	1,971
Equity and liabilities		
Equity		
Ordinary share capital	750	900
Share premium	60	90
Retained earnings	288	333
	1,098	1,323
Non-current liabilities	300	360
Current liabilities		
Trade payables	96	108
Dividends	45	60
Tax	135	120
	276	288
Total equity and liabilities	1,674	1,971

The sale proceeds from the sale of non-current assets was £108m. All interest due has been received and the interest payable has been paid.

Required

(a) Prepare the statement of cash flows for T entity for the year ended 31 December 20X7 in accordance with IAS 7, 'Cash Flow Statements'. (Notes to the cash flow statement are not required.)

(b) Identify information that is provided by a cash flow statement to users that is not provided by a statement of comprehensive income and statement of financial position.

Answers to these questions can be found at the back of this book.

11

Regulatory framework, corporate social responsibility and corporate governance

Objectives

By the end of this chapter you should be able to:

▶ Describe the regulatory framework of accounting in the UK.

▶ Describe the regulatory framework of accounting in other European countries.

▶ Describe the international regulatory framework of accounting.

▶ Compare and contrast the regulatory framework of accounting in the UK with those of other European countries, the United States of America and the international framework.

▶ Explain the need for corporate social responsibility (CSR).

▶ Describe, briefly, the regulation relating to corporate governance.

Introduction

The regulatory framework of accounting in the UK has been shaped by various factors, many of which are historical. The same is true of other European countries and the United States of America. Several countries have a framework similar to that of the UK due to the influence of the UK in these countries at some point in history. Others have a very different framework. Attempts have been made to harmonise accounting across the EU, the initial steps in this being taken by the issue of EU Directives. The Fourth Directive issued by the EU requires all EU members to prepare their financial statements in accordance with a true and fair view. In fact, the Fourth Directive can be said to have exported the true and fair view from the UK to the rest of Europe and imported formatted presentation of accounts to the UK.

In addition we also look at the framework identified by the International Accounting Standards Board (IASB) and note that all listed companies in Europe are required to prepare their accounts in accordance with International Accounting Standards (ISAs) as from January 2005. Remember that small and medium-sized companies will still be able to use the national standards of the country they operate in. This means you will find companies from the same country using two different sets of standards in their reporting:

▶ National standards for unlisted companies.

▶ International standards for listed companies.

This chapter is intended to provide you with a brief introduction to, and flavour of, European accounting and US accounting, as well as identifying the framework of accounting within the UK and that of the IASB. The chapter concludes with a brief look at corporate social responsibility (CSR) and corporate governance, both of which are very topical internationally as well as nationally.

We hope this chapter will encourage you to develop your studies in the area of European accounting at a later stage. Remember, the world is getting ever smaller due to the improvements in communication networks, and it is essential to know something about how the rest of the world operates, particularly mainland Europe.

UK legal framework

In Chapter 8 we referred to the legal framework in respect of limited companies. This legal framework consists of case law and the Companies Act.

Activity 11.1　Identify the case law that is at the base of corporate organisations in the UK.

Answer　A simple bit of revision here for you.

The case law was *Salomon* v *Salomon* & Co. Ltd (1897). This case, after a ruling handed down by the House of Lords, clearly identified the fact that a limited company is a separate legal entity from its shareholders.

The Companies Act details numerous requirements for the preparation of published accounts. We have touched on the main requirements at various points within this text. A summary of these is provided below:

▶ Directors must prepare a statement of financial position and statement of comprehensive income for each financial year.

▶ Notes, as prescribed, to the accounts must also be provided.

▶ The statement of financial position and statement of comprehensive income must be prepared to a prescribed format.

▶ The statement of financial position and statement of comprehensive income must give a true and fair view of the state of affairs of the company.

▶ Accounting rules and principles are identified. These are consistent with those identified in Chapters 1 and 4.

This, then, identifies the legal framework within which accountants must work in the UK. However, there was and is a need for more than just a legal framework.

The need for a regulatory framework

The accounting concepts and conventions were identified in Chapter 4. The five principal accounting concepts used in the preparation of financial statements before the advent of the Framework were:

▶ Going concern.

▶ Consistency.

▶ Prudence.

▶ Accruals/matching.

▶ Separate valuation of asset and liability.

These five principles were also contained within company law in the UK but they have now been removed from the Companies Act and we are now required to prepare financial statements in accordance with a true and fair view and the IASs.

The faithful application of these five principles resulted in different judgements being made, which led to different statement of comprehensive income and statement of financial position figures. For example:

▶ Does the prudence concept require us to account for all possible liabilities, even those we believe have only a remote chance of occurring?

▶ Does the matching concept require us to delay charging advertising and research expenditure within the statement of comprehensive income until we account for the income it has generated, if any?

Activity 11.2

Boss Ltd identifies a profit of £110,000 for the year before accounting for the following items:

▶ There is a law suit pending against Boss Ltd for which the amount of damages could be £200,000 if the case is lost.

▶ Expenditure on research for the year was £150,000. This was in respect of the development of new products. It is probable that a half of this expenditure will lead to a viable product in two years.

Identify two different accounting treatments for each of the above items, both of which are in accordance with accounting concepts and conventions.

Answer

▶ The concept of prudence would suggest that we should take account of this potential liability for damages of £200,000. If a provision is made for all of the liability then the profit for the year will be reduced to a £90,000 loss!

Does prudence require us to provide for this liability no matter how remote the possibility of the damages becoming payable? Prudence should be about making judgements with a degree of caution, not about the deliberate overstatement of liabilities, which may not result in a true and fair view being presented. Perhaps a more reliable view to take would be to obtain an assessment of the likelihood of the damages becoming a liability. Therefore the profit for the company could be declared as anywhere from a £90,000 loss to a £110,000 profit.

▶ Accounting concepts require us to charge all expenses in the year of payment – prudence – unless they can be matched with the generation of future revenue. Note that we use this idea of prudence and matching in accounting for prepayments and depreciation. The research expenditure of £75,000 will be charged against the profit for the year as there is no possibility of future matching – the profit is therefore £35,000. The other £75,000 could either be written off in the year under prudence or carried forward to be matched with future income which looks very probable as it is stated there is a viable product. Therefore the profit is either £35,000 or a loss of £40,000.

Accounting for these two transactions together gives a profit figure of either £240,000 loss or a profit of £35,000, or indeed any figure in between.

The above activity clearly demonstrates the effects on profits of applying different judgements permitted within the faithful application of the five accounting principles as identified within the previous UK Companies Acts. These differences were highlighted in the 1960s and led to the introduction of a **regulatory framework** for accounting, as well as a legal framework.

One publicised case in the 1960s, demonstrating the above, was that of the takeover of Associated Electrical Industries Ltd (AEI) by General Electric Company Ltd (GEC). Before the takeover AEI published forecast profits of £10 million for 1967; after the bid the actual results showed a loss of £4.5 million. The majority of this difference of nearly £15 million was attributed to the difference in application of accounting concepts and conventions by the two companies.

UK regulatory framework

The regulatory framework in the UK has its roots in the 1940s, when the Institute of Chartered Accountants in England and Wales (ICAEW) issued a series of Recommendations on Accounting Principles. These were little more than general summaries of existing practice and by the late 1960s, as we have seen above, something more was required. In 1971 the Accounting Standards Steering Committee was established by the ICAEW. In 1976 this became the Accounting Standards Committee (ASC), which was responsible for preparing standards of accounting under the auspices of the Consultative Committee of Accounting Bodies (CCAB). The CCAB comprises the six accounting bodies ICAEW, ICAS, ICAI, ACCA, CIMA and CIPFA.

The aims of the ASC were to narrow the areas of difference in accounting practice and to require full disclosure of all accounting bases. It attempted to achieve these aims by issuing Statements of Standard Accounting Practice (SSAPs), for example SSAP 12 Accounting for Depreciation.

By the middle of the 1980s the ASC was facing a barrage of criticism because:

▶ it had no legal power to force companies to follow the standards

▶ the standards issued by the ASC allowed alternative treatments and were essentially of a general, rather than detailed nature

▶ the time taken to issue a standard was often several years.

Activity 11.3   Why did the ASC have no legal power to enforce standards?

Answer   The ASC was a function of the professional accounting bodies. Directors are responsible for accounts and may or may not be accountants. The ASC had no power to force directors to follow SSAPs, which were not legal requirements. It was possible to view them as an interpretation of the true and fair view, though.

As a result of the criticism of the ASC another committee was established in 1987 – the Dearing Committee – with the task of reviewing the accounting standard-setting process within the UK. Dearing reported in 1988, proposing several radical changes to the process which resulted in the current regulatory framework.

Current regulatory framework UK

This is now a two-tier structure. First, the Financial Reporting Council (FRC) was established as the body responsible for overseeing accounting policy and direction.

Second, the Accounting Standards Board (ASB) was established under the auspices of the FRC with the power to issue accounting standards without the prior approval of the CCAB. To date, the ASB has issued 29 Financial Reporting Standards (FRSs), covering issues such as cash flow, FRS1, reporting financial performance, FRS3, and has also adopted all of the statements issued by the ASC. It has also issued in its lifetime 41 Financial Reporting Exposure Drafts (FREDs), the latest of which is concerned with Related Party Transactions. These FREDs are issued by the ASB for consultation prior to the issue of the definitive FRS.

Activity 11.4   Find a copy of any FRS. These should be available in your library in a text of accounting standards, or may even be available on your computer network. Identify the main sections of an accounting standard.

Answer

Summary of the main requirements of the standard:

▶ Objectives of the standard.

▶ Definitions of terms used.

▶ Statement of standard accounting practice covering scope, detailed requirements and the date from which it is effective.

▶ Reference to compliance with International Accounting Standards.

▶ Explanation of why the standard was needed.

▶ Illustrative examples.

▶ History of the development of the standard.

As you can see from the above activity the FRSs are detailed and comprehensive, covering, in addition to the actual accounting practice required, the logic and reasoning behind the issue of the standard. You can also access the full text of the UK standards on **www.frc.org.uk/asb/publications**.

In addition to this two-tier structure the Financial Reporting Review Panel (FRRP) was formed under the FRC with the remit to review compliance with accounting standards by individual companies. The panel advises companies when their accounts do not appear to be in accordance with standards and/or a true and fair view, and can request the company to re-draft its accounts. In addition the panel has the facility to apply to the law courts for a declaration that the annual accounts do not comply with standards, and if this is given the company will be legally required to change its accounts. The FRRP reviews on average about 50 plcs each year. This then provides some legal backing for accounting standards, although just applying to the courts does not guarantee a judgment in the panel's favour. A QC has issued a statement to the effect that compliance with accounting standards would constitute a true and fair view. Court cases are also a very expensive activity and for this reason the FRRP is provided with a 'fighting fund'. To date, no court cases have occurred so the FRRP seems to have been successful in persuading companies to alter their accounts where they did not agree with standards.

Activity 11.5

Identify any other reasons that you can think of why no court cases have occurred.

Answer

▶ Companies may be preparing accounts in accordance with accounting concepts and conventions. However, this may still lead to the possibility of different profit figures being declared from the same set of information.

▶ Differences in profit figures may be allowed/permitted by the ASB. This is actually the case. The ASB was only established in 1990, has only issued 29 FRSs and has not completed the review of all other standards that it took over from the old ASC.

The ASB has another body to assist it in meeting its objectives, the Urgent Issues Task Force (UITF). The UITF deals very quickly with emerging issues that require an immediate method of treatment. For example, the UITF has issued advice on revenue recognition.

Activity 11.6   Draw a diagram to show the relationships between the bodies governing the regulatory framework.

Answer

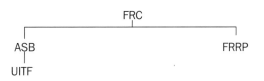

The ASB has issued FRS 18 Accounting Policies which updates our Activity 11.2. FRS 18 sets out the principles to be followed in selecting accounting policies, which are defined as 'those principles, bases, conventions, rules and practices applied by an entity'. The standard states that two concepts are pervasive, going concern and accruals, and that accounting policies should be judged against the following objectives: relevance, reliability, comparability and understandability. Note that the objective of relevance can lead us to provide information on a different cost base to historical cost. In other words, we can revalue assets if that would provide more relevant information to users provided we balanced the information with objectivity. Interestingly, prudence is only referred to in FRS 18 where conditions of uncertainty exist. Prudence is not a pervasive accounting concept.

International regulatory framework

Like the UK, several countries have their own regulatory framework for accounting and the preparation of annual accounts such as statement of comprehensive income account, statement of financial position, etc. However, there is also an international regulatory framework. This international framework is gaining in importance as investors seek to invest in global markets and therefore require more comparable information between companies.

International regulation first began in 1973 with the creation of the International Accounting Standards Committee which was an independent private sector body and therefore had no formal authority. Many countries adopted international accounting standards (IASs) to avoid developing their own or amended IASs to suit their needs. The IASs were, because the committee had no formal authority, fairly flexible and in many cases allowed alternative treatments. During the 1980s the IASC moved to minimise this flexible approach by clearly stating its preference for a particular method but its formal authority was not increased.

In 1995 the IASC achieved a breakthrough in terms of authority when it entered into an agreement with the International Organisation of Securities

Commissions (IOSCO) to complete a core set of standards by 1999. These core standards would then be endorsed by IOSCO as an appropriate reporting regime for business entities in the global marketplace for the raising of finance, i.e. worldwide stock exchanges. This deal was to give the IASC its authority but in order to achieve the deal the IASC had to agree to a restructuring which occurred in 2000, becoming the **International Accounting Standards Board (IASB)**, and the core standards were accepted by IOSCO in May 2000. To date IASs are accepted in over 100 countries and almost all are working towards converging their own national standards with those of the IASB. The US is moving at a pace to accept IASs with a '**Roadmap for convergence**' of US standards and IASs being currently approved. If all goes to plan US companies listed on the US stock exchange will be required to use international standards by 2014.

European regulation

The European Union has also entered the arena of international regulation in terms of the Directives on company law that it has issued, **Fourth and Seventh Directives**, and also in terms of its latest statement requiring all listed companies in the EU to prepare their accounts in accordance with international standards.

Structure of IASB

The IASB is governed by a group of 19 individual trustees with diverse geographical and functional backgrounds. The trustees form the IASC Foundation and are responsible for governance, fundraising and public awareness of the IASB. The IASB is solely responsible for setting International Financial Reporting Standards and has 12 full-time members and two part-time. Its members are chosen for their technical expertise and experience and its Chair is Sir David Tweedie who was the Chair of the UK ASB. It's also interesting to note that the IASC Foundation and the IASB are based in London.

The structure also includes a Standards Interpretation Committee (SIC) and a Standards Advisory Council, both of which sit alongside the IASB.

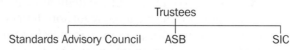

Trustees

Standards Advisory Council   ASB   SIC

The IASB is at the forefront of harmonisation as it pushes for acceptance of its accounting standards around the world. In addition the requirement that all listed companies prepare their financial statements in accordance with IASs will increase the pressure for national standards to harmonise with those of the IASB. This process has already begun in the UK as the UK ASB issues new standards that converge with those of the IASB. The UK convergence programme takes as its starting point the principle that there can be no case in the medium term for two sets of different accounting standards in the UK. The UK ASB publishes a convergence handbook and it would be useful for you to look at this on the website.

Activity 11.7 Visit the UK ASB website at www.asb.co.uk and review the progress on the convergence programme with international accounting standards.

Answer We provide no answer for you here as it will depend upon what date you visit the site.

As you can see, the IASB is a key mover in establishing global harmonisation of accounting but whether this can be achieved perhaps depends on what determines accounting practices in any country.

Determinants of the accounting framework

Many factors have determined the legal and regulatory framework of accounting in the UK. Accounts are prepared ostensibly for their usefulness to users, therefore the first of the **determinants** of the accounting framework should be users' needs. Looking back over the history of accounting in the UK we can see that providers of finance, shareholders, have influenced the framework, notably the establishment of the ASC and then the ASB. Looking further back in history we can see that as companies were established, and owners passed the running of the company to directors, owners required information on stewardship (i.e. the management of the company's assets), which led to the establishment of the legal framework. The accounting profession is a determinant of the framework: the ICAEW was successful in promoting the idea of the true and fair view in the 1940s. The economic environment also has an effect on the framework. For example, the high levels of inflation suffered in the UK in the 1970s led to a consideration of alternatives to historical cost accounts, to reflect changing values.

The tradition of law within a country also has an effect on the framework. The UK has a common law system, that is, our laws are about broad principles, for example Companies Acts, with the detail being left to case law or other forms of regulation, for example FRSs. Countries with a tradition of Roman law, that is, detailed rules and regulations, will probably have a more codified set of rules for accounting regulation.

The framework of accounting in one country can also be influenced by another country. For example, many British Commonwealth countries have a system of regulation derived from the UK.

Activity 11.8 List five possible determinants of a country's regulatory framework of accounting.

Answer
▶ Providers of finance.
▶ Accounting profession.
▶ Economic environment.
▶ System of law.
▶ Other country influences.

These are not the only determinants, but they are the main ones and will help in understanding why the framework of accounting in other European countries is different from that of the UK. We cannot look at all countries in Europe so we have chosen three: Germany, France and the Netherlands. We will also very briefly look at China. The consideration of these four countries will be brief but we hope it stimulates your interest to study international accounting further.

Accounting framework in Germany – the determinants

The providers of finance in Germany were traditionally not so much individual shareholders but large banks. These banks were able to force companies to provide financial information to their requirements, thus there was no pressure for full public disclosure. Germany has a tradition of Roman law and a strong tradition of central authority imposed by the government. One interesting element within German law is in relation to taxation; benefits given under tax law can only be claimed if reflected in the accounts. This is known in Germany as *Massgeblichkeitsprinzip* – principle of bindingness – it binds tax and accounting rules together. In the UK tax laws are, by and large, separate from accounting legislation. The strength of Germany as a world power has enabled it to resist influences from other countries so far.

*A*ctivity 11.9

Given the information above, suggest in one sentence what type of accounting framework Germany may have.

Answer

Law and government prescription are prevalent in Germany, therefore one might expect a system of detailed instruction dominated by tax law.

Germany's accounting framework is indeed dominated by legislation. Companies Acts and tax law identify the legal framework and a uniform chart of accounts is also prescribed. There is no official institution for the setting of binding accounting standards as they are all prescribed by law, particularly tax law. There is a strong accounting profession but it is one geared towards carrying out the letter of the law, not developing Generally Accepted Accounting Principles (GAAP). The majority of accounting decisions are formulated by the Supreme Tax Court.

However, Germany as a member of the EU is subject to EU Directives and has had to introduce into its law the concept of a true and fair view, but this is not treated as an override as in the UK. Accounts are still prepared in accordance with law, which according to German law will provide a true and fair view. An interesting way of interpreting true and fair!

German law also identifies the concepts of going concern, consistency, accruals, prudence and individual determination (separate valuation of assets).

Accounting framework in France – the determinants

Providers of finance in France have traditionally been the government or banks. The accounting profession is government controlled as is the economic environment. The law is Roman law and one of the main influences on accounting in modern times has come from Germany. During the occupation of France in the Second World War, Germany introduced a General Accounting Plan, which was an accounting guide detailing valuation and measurement rules, definitions of accounting terms and structured financial statements. This plan was retained by France after the liberation as it provided the government with a means of control when rebuilding French industry. This plan – *plan comptable* – was referred to in Chapter 4.

Activity 11.10   Suggest in one sentence what type of accounting framework France may have.

Answer

Government control is at the centre of these determinants, therefore the accounting framework will be one of detailed prescription by law.

The accounting framework is dominated by legislation. Accounting regulations and Charts of Accounts are drawn up by the *Conseil National de la Comptabilité* (CNC), a body closely linked to the Finance Ministry.

The legal framework is dominated by the General Accounting Plan, which identifies the accounting concepts of accruals, consistency, individual determination, prudence and going concern. The EU Fourth Directive also introduced the principle of *Image Fidèle* – true and fair view – to French accounting.

Accounting framework in the Netherlands – the determinants

Providers of finance are traditionally shareholders and the Netherlands is also home to some of the world's major multinational enterprises. There is a strong independent accounting profession founded in 1895, which focused attention on the development of accounting theory, particularly replacement value theory.

Economic environment is one dominated by the concept of economic value, that is, businesses must ensure availability of resources to replace used inputs. Law is Roman but a distinction is made between accounting and tax law.

Activity 11.11   Suggest in one sentence what type of accounting the Netherlands may have.

Answer

The Netherlands law is Roman but not dominant and as providers of finance are shareholders and there is a strong accounting profession, then the accounting framework could well be similar to that in the UK.

The Netherlands, system is basically similar to that of the UK but there are notable differences. One is that the Netherlands places emphasis on economic value not historical cost. Legal provisions tend to identify the general rules of accounting and the concept of true and fair was incorporated into Dutch law in 1970 prior to the EU Fourth Directive. Generally Accepted Accounting Principles (GAAP) is in the hands of the accounting profession, the Council for Annual Reporting, which has representatives from employers, employees and professional accountants. Standards produced by the council tend to be flexible and are not legally binding although they would provide evidence as to the true and fair view. In 1970 a law was enacted to establish an Enterprise Chamber – a court of law – to consider cases where companies failed to comply with accounting standards. This chamber can order the issue of revised accounts. The general concepts of accounting are going concern, consistency, accruals and prudence.

Accounting framework in China

China is becoming a major economic force globally and its economic growth is being controlled quite carefully to ensure it does not overheat. By 2020 it is expected that China will be the largest economy in the world. International trade with China is increasing and investment in the country is undergoing massive change. However, all of this investment and growth is still subject to substantial control from the government. The Chinese accounting system is also undergoing massive change and new accounting laws substantially based on IASs are being introduced. When considering accounting in China you must however always keep in mind the size of the country and the size of its population – around 1.3 billion. Remember, some of its smaller cities have a population greater than that of London.

China has a long history of communism and as it moves forward with economic reform this history will have an impact. Market-orientated principles are being taken on board but a socialist theme is still maintained. Many institutions will still remain under state control. The legal system in China can be regarded as unique. It has only recently developed contract and commercial law, but this is still tightly controlled by the government and the whole process is quite bureaucratic. Tax is collected from all enterprises, including state enterprises, but the accounting rules and tax rules are decoupled as in the UK. Stock markets operate in China but they only started in the early 1990s. The accounting profession prior to 1980 was almost non-existent, as recording of economic information was simply a case of following prescribed systems rather than providing information which would be useful to users. The accounting profession in a modern form was only set up in 1980 and although the government is now issuing standards similar to those of the IASB, they are simpler and more rigid allowing less choice and judgement.

A*ctivity 11.12*   Suggest in one sentence what type of accounting China has.

Answer   •   Government control is still dominant in China and thus the accounting system will display characteristics of uniformity and rigidity

Activity 11.13   Complete the following table – the UK entries have already been made for you.

	UK	Germany	France	Netherlands	China
Type of law	Common				
Role of profession	Forceful				
Providers of finance	Shareholders				
Source of accounting regulation	Companies Acts, professional standards				

Answer

	UK	Germany	France	Netherlands	China
Type of law	Common	Roman	Roman	Roman	Roman state controlled
Role of profession	Forceful	Compliance	Minor	Forceful	Minor
Providers of finance	Shareholders	Banks	Banks Government	Shareholders	Government limited shareholder and foreign investment
Source of accounting regulation	Companies Acts, professional standards	Legal Tax Binding	Legal plans	Companies Acts and standards	Government

Accounting standards in the United States of America

The US has a very similar system of law, providers of finance and accounting profession to that of the UK. It also has a market economy. One would therefore imagine that the system of accounting in the US would be the same as that in the UK. To some extent it is but there is one major difference: the US system is 'rules based' not 'principles based'. This is due to the use of the legal system to solve issues in the US and thus the accounting profession there has tried to protect itself by producing rules for all situations. The accounting standards in the US are issued by the **Financial Accounting Standards Board (FASB)** which to date has issued more than 150 standards and over 50 interpretations of standards. These rules form a text nine inches high and comprise three volumes.

The FASB was established 75 years ago and is a group of seven accounting professionals independent of government. The standards it issues are adopted by the Securities Exchange Commission (SEC) and all companies listed on the SEC are required to prepare their financial statements in accordance with them. The collection of standards is referred to as US GAAP. US GAAP has four basic assumptions:

▶ business entity
▶ going concern
▶ monetary unit
▶ time period

four basic principles:

▶ historic (acquisition) cost
▶ accruals accounting
▶ matching
▶ disclosure

and four basic constraints:

▶ objectivity
▶ materiality
▶ consistency
▶ prudence.

This is all very similar to the UK principles/concepts we covered in Chapter 4. This rules based system operated in the US did not stop trillions of dollars in financial assets and liabilities being kept off the statements of financial position of US companies, and thereby contributing to the credit crunch of 2008 and the demise of several financial institutions. International standards,which focus on the underlying economics of transactions and principles, may have shown these items on the statements of financial position.

In 2002 the convergence between US GAAP and IASs commenced with the Norwalk Agreement whereby the FASB and IASB agreed to work together to achieve convergence. In 2008 SEC announced a proposed 'Roadmap' for the adoption of IFRSs by US listed companies, which will see mandatory adoption of IFRS in the US in 2014. It is widely expected that the largest companies will switch to IFRS in 2009.

Corporate social responsibility (CSR) accounting

Corporate social responsibility (CSR) is a topic that is growing in importance. It is not part of the regulatory framework of financial reporting but its importance is growing. CSR is about entities taking account of the social and environmental impact of their decisions when making business decisions. Entities who voluntarily do this will be seen as 'good corporate citizens'.

As long ago as 1975 CSR accounting was suggested in the UK via the corporate report. Through legislation, both country and EU based, society is imposing duties on entities to comply with anti-pollution, safety and health, and other socially beneficial requirements. Legislation of this type will continue to increase in the future. Such legislation imposes costs on entities that were previously borne by the community at large and there is therefore good reason to require such expenditure, both compulsory and voluntary, to be reported. If entities do disclose information on their impact on society and the environment then we will, of course, need generally agreed measurement and recognition criteria for such impacts.

The last 15 years or so have seen an extensive growth in environmental reporting and legislation, which has forced entities to begin to assess their environmental liabilities and risks. Shell plc discovered the pressure that environmental groups can assert when they were forced to abandon their attempts to dump the Brent Spar oil platform at sea. Users of Shell's financial statements may now demand a great deal more information in respect of Shell's environmental risks and liabilities.

Activity 11.14   Traditionally, accounting was based around the concepts of money measurement, going concern, and accruals. Identify whether CSR issues are taken into account in the application of these concepts to a business and, if not, why not.

Answer   Money measurement requires that only those facts that can be recorded in monetary terms with some objectivity are taken into account even if other facts are extremely relevant. CSR factors are very difficult to measure in monetary terms. How, for example, do you place a monetary measure on the damage being done to the environment through the car exhaust emissions of employees travelling to work?

The going concern convention requires that in the absence of evidence to the contrary it is assumed that the entity will continue into the future. This concept is principally concerned with solvency and financial performance, not with the impact of CSR factors. For example, in assessing going concern for Shell, little regard was had as to whether pressure groups could ever force them out of business.

Accruals require a matching of expenses used up in generating revenues. However, entities make no assessment of the expense of CSR factors, such as their contribution to global warming through the emission of carbon dioxide or to acid rain from the emission of sulphur and nitrogen oxides.

The EU also urged greater corporate social responsibility in Europe through a green paper promoting a European framework for CSR (Commission of the European Community, 2001). The aim of the paper was to trigger debate on all aspects of CSR and views on it were requested by 31 December 2001. When the paper was launched, two commissioners, Diamantopouilou and Liikanen, stated: 'more and more firms are realising the link between profitability and best ethical and environmental practice. Conscientious firms not only attract and retain best workers, they can also get ahead in the technology game, vital for that all-important competitive edge.'

The debate on CSR was also influenced by the Commission's proposals for a European strategy on sustainable development endorsed at the Gothenburg Summit in June 2001.

Exemplars of CSR

Shell in its 2000 annual report made the following statement:

> Sustainable development underlies our strategy and is being integrated into everything Shell companies do – in oil and gas as much as renewables. We have to do business in the real world, with all its complexities. We look to governments to create conditions that foster social and economic development but some lack the means. We believe responsible business promotes development. We support Kofi Annan's Global Compact and the Global Sullivan Principles.
>
> (Shell, 2000)

Since 2000, Shell has produced comprehensive Sustainability reports providing an overview of its efforts to live up to its commitment to contribute to sustainability development. In the 2007 report it states, 'our commitment means helping meet the world's growing energy needs in economically, environmentally and socially responsible ways. This includes both running our operations responsibly today and helping build a responsible energy system for tomorrow.'

Bayer's sustainability report for 2007 runs to 112 pages and for the first time includes a Performance Report. This performance report includes financial data as well as quantitative and qualitative data in the subject areas of economics, employees, human rights, social responsibility, and ecology and product stewardship. This is very extensive information but will users read it and gain any benefit from it?

Activity 11.15   Identify key criteria for CSR in order for it to be useful to users.

Answer

▶ Continuity – in that the same methods and metrics are used year after year.
▶ Comparability – to allow for benchmarking and assessing progress.
▶ Credibility – to ensure that the information provides a 'true and fair' picture of the company's environmental performance.

You could, of course, have listed understandability, comparability, relevance and reliability just as easily.

Several worldwide companies produce CSR reports and make these freely available on their websites.

Nokia in its CSR report for 2005 makes the following statements:

> At Nokia reporting is an integral part of our corporate responsibility work. We see clear and consistent communications on our progress as fundamental to building trust and reputation that goes far beyond the financial community. We produced

our first CR report in 2002. Since then, we've worked steadily to increase the quality and scope of our reporting content as well as raise the level of awareness on ethical and environmental issues internally and with our stakeholders.

(Nokia, 2005)

McDonald's publish a Europe Corporate Responsibility Report within which it makes the following statement:

Corporate responsibility in McDonald's Europe is not an 'add-on' programme: it is an intrinsic part of our decision making. One of the best ways to ensure that CR is fully embedded within our organisation is to present management at regular intervals with the expectations of stakeholders. Our three priority focus areas for CR are nutrition, food quality and safety, and employment practices.'

(McDonald's, 2007)

McDonald's also provide a table outlining its responsibilities.

You can find lots of examples of CSRs on company websites and, in addition to those reports referenced previously, we would also refer you to **http://starbucks.com/csr** to gain an insight into the type of information that entities are producing.

Corporate governance

Corporate governance is another 'hot topic' in the world of accounting today.

Corporate governance, according to the Organization for Economic Cooperation and Development (OECD), is 'the system by which business corporations are directed and controlled. The corporate governance structure specifies the distribution of rights and responsibilities among different participants in the corporation, such as, the board, managers, shareholders and other stakeholders, and spells out the rules and procedures for making decisions on corporate affairs. By doing this, it also provides the structure through which the company objectives are set, and the means of attaining those objectives and monitoring performance' (OECD, 1999).

Corporate governance is therefore multi-faceted, covering processes, systems, culture, etc., from the viewpoint of multiple stakeholders. Corporate scandals such as Enron, WorldCom and Parmalat have focused attention on governance, accountability and disclosure. Indeed the 2008 credit crunch and the turmoil within financial markets in September 2008 have placed even more emphasis on corporate governance.

The OECD sees corporate governance as one key element in improving economic efficiency and growth as well as enhancing investor confidence. Good corporate governance should provide proper incentives for the board and management to pursue objectives that are in the interests of the company and its shareholders and should facilitate effective monitoring. The presence of an effective corporate governance system, within an individual company and across an economy as a whole, helps to provide a degree of confidence that is necessary for the proper functioning of a market economy. As a result, the cost of capital is lower and firms are encouraged to use resources more efficiently, thereby underpinning growth.

Activity 11.16   Identify the role of financial reporting within corporate governance.

Answer   Financial reporting is about providing useful information to users to enable them to make informed decisions regarding stewardship and the future, and therefore must be key to corporate governance.

History of corporate governance

Corporate governance is not new, as it has been around for as long as corporate entities have existed, but the study of corporate governance is relatively new. Governance issues arise as soon as ownership is separated from management, as occurred with the invention of the limited liability company.

In the 1970s, emphasis on independent outside directors, audit committees and the establishment of two-tier boards in companies drew attention to the governance issue. The EEC, in the draft of its Fifth Directive in 1972, advocated two-tier board governance as seen in Germany and Holland. Increasing litigation in the US, where shareholders of failed companies sought recompense from directors, etc., again emphasised the need for appropriate governance.

The 1970s also saw the growth of the idea that public companies, in addition to their duty to shareholders (owners), also had responsibilities to other stakeholders such as employees, customers, suppliers, lenders, community and government. This list is very similar to those we identified as the users of financial reports in Chapter 1, Activity 1.8.

In the UK the collapse of several companies in the 1970s, for example Pergamon Press, Rolls Royce, Lohnro, also enhanced the interest in corporate governance.

During the 1980s, action on corporate governance was minimal and more company collapses and questionable practices were seen throughout the world, which were attributed by many to the power of executive directors who had no checks or balances upon them. In particular, the combination of the chief executive officer (CEO) and chair roles was questioned, as was the lack of power of the non-executive directors.

The 1990s saw the growth in power of major institutional investors, who also began to focus on corporate governance.

In the UK the issue was brought to the fore by the Cadbury Report in 1992 and the establishment of the Cadbury Code that focused on the financial aspects of corporate governance, corporate behaviour and ethics and led to improved boardroom practice. In 1995 the Greenbury Report added Principles on the Remuneration of Executive Directors in an attempt to curb CEO salaries. These two reports were brought together by the Hampel Report of 1998 and formed the first Combined Code. The Hampel Report had three main themes:

▶ Good corporate governance needs broad principles not prescriptive rules. This sounds like a familiar theme from financial reporting, where the IASB wish to adopt a principles based approach rather than the rules based approach practised in the US.

▶ A unitary board is acceptable, thus rejecting the proposal of two-tier boards.

▶ The board is accountable to shareholders, thus down-grading the need for responsibility to other stakeholders.

In 1999 the Turnbull Report was published, which concentrated on risk management and internal controls. All of these reports were as a result of shareholder disquiet as regards corporate performance and to avoid the threat of UK government legislation if such codes were not developed voluntarily by the business sector.

The Cadbury Report had great influence around the world and several other countries published their own corporate governance reports in the 1990s. All of these reports were concerned with the abuse of corporate power and recommended wider use of audit committees, outside non-executive directors, remuneration, committees composed of independent outside directors to advise on director remuneration, and separation of the roles of chair and CEO. In 1998 the OECD proposed the development of global guidelines for corporate governance and emphasised the difference between the strong external investment culture of the US and UK and the firm corporate governance practices of Japan, France and Germany, where employees had more influence and investors seemed to take a longer-term view.

Another report on corporate governance was the Higgs Report, which was published in the UK in 2003. It built on all the previous reports to produce a single combined code, and made the following recommendations:

▶ Define 'independence' and the proportion of independent non-executive directors on the board and its committees.

▶ Expand the role of the senior independent director to provide an alternative channel for shareholders and to lead evaluations on the chair's performance.

▶ Enhance the process of nominations to the board through a transparent and rigorous process and evaluation of the performance of the board, its committees and individual directors.

The FRC in the UK published its Combined Code of Corporate Governance in July 2003. This was further revised by the Turnbull Review Group and a revised code was issued by the FRC in 2005. Around the same time the European Commission also issued its Corporate Governance and Company Law Action Plan, which covered disclosure requirements, exercise of voting rights, cross-border voting, disclosure by institutional investors and the responsibilities of board members. You can access the code on the FRC website **www.frc.org.uk**.

OECD principles of corporate governance

The OECD originally issued their principles of corporate governance in 1999 and published a revised version in 2004. In the preamble to the code they state:

> The principles are intended to assist OECD and non-OECD governments in their efforts to evaluate and improve the legal, institutional and regulatory framework for corporate governance in their countries, and to provide guidance and suggestions for stock exchanges, investors, corporations, and other parties that have a role in the process of developing good corporate governance. The Principles focus on publicly traded companies both financial and non-financial. Increasingly, the OECD and its member governments have recognized the synergy between macroeconomic and structural policies in achieving fundamental policy goals. Corporate governance is one key element in improving economic efficiency and growth as well as enhancing investor confidence. (OECD, 2004)

You can of course access the full principles on the OECD website **www.oecd.org**.

The future for corporate governance

We would expect to see further emphasis on corporate governance in light of the events in the financial markets of September 2008. As the OECD 2004 state in their preamble:

> The Principles are evolutionary in nature and should be reviewed in light of significant changes in circumstances. Governments have an important responsibility for shaping an effective regulatory framework that provides for sufficient flexibility to allow markets to function effectively and to respond to expectations of shareholders and other stakeholders.

Indeed the OECD Secretary-general Angel Gurria called on 25 September 2008 for a new drive in corporate governance to raise standards and performance in this area, stating that

> Rebuilding investor confidence will be vital to helping the economy get back on track. Strengthening the rules, regulations and codes of corporate governance will be central to this. I call on member countries to work urgently with us to address major corporate governance failures. This will be a vital step to reinforcing market integrity.

A statement on the way forward is expected from the OECD in the near future.

Summary

This chapter has:

▶ identified the accounting framework within the UK, both legally and regulatory

▶ given you a flavour of accounting in three other European countries, the US and also China, and compared and contrasted those with that of the UK

▶ introduced you to the international work on financial accounting/ reporting driven by the IASB

▶ introduced you to the topic of CSR

▶ described, briefly, the issue of corporate governance.

The work of the IASB is very important as we move towards more global markets for both products and financial instruments. Investors now need to be able to compare companies in terms of their financial position and performance from all countries and without an **harmonised reporting framework** this will not be easy. The EU has declared that it requires all companies listed on an EU stock exchange to report under IAS regulation as from 2005. This means that large British plcs will need to convert their reporting from UK GAAP to IAS GAAP. This will not be easy as the standards issued by the UK Board and International Board are not always directly comparable. The UK ASB is currently working on a convergence programme between UK and IAS GAAP.

The study of accounting in the international arena is, we believe, both interesting and essential as we move into the twenty-first century. Indeed the international expansion of the UK accounting profession during the twentieth century saw the development of what are now among the world's largest accounting, auditing and management consultancy firms, including PriceWaterhouseCoopers and KPMG. We hope this chapter has stimulated your interest in this area.

We have also introduced you to two 'hot topics' in the international arena, CSR and corporate governance. We have only given you a flavour of these topics but we hope your interest has been stimulated so that you study them further. It is quite possible that there will be further regulation in both these areas from international bodies.

Key terms

regulatory framework (p. 222)

Dearing Committee (p. 223)

Financial Reporting Council (FRC) (p. 223)

Accounting Standards Board (ASB) (p. 223)

Fourth and Seventh Directives (p. 226)

International Accounting Standards Board (IASB) (p. 226)

Roadmap for convergence (p. 226)

determinants (p. 227)

Financial Accounting Standards Board (FASB) (p. 231)

rules based (p. 232)

corporate social responsibility (CSR) (p. 232)

environmental reporting (p. 232)

corporate governance (p. 233)

Harmonised reporting framework (p. 239)

References

Commission of the European Community (2001) Green paper promoting a European framework for corporate social responsibility, Brussels 18/7/2001, 366 final.

Hicks, J.R (1946) *Value and Capital*, 2nd edn. Oxford University Press, Oxford.

McDonald's (2007) McDonald's Worldwide Corporate Responsibility report, **www.mcdonalds.ca/en/community/social.aspx**.

Nokia (2005) Annual report, **www.nokia.com/crr/index.html**.

OECD (1999) *Principles of Corporate Governance*. Organization for Economic Cooperation and Development, Paris.

OECD (2004) *Principles of Coorporate Governance*. Organization for Economic Cooperation and Development, Paris. Available at **www.occd.org**.

Shell (2000) Annual report, **www.shell.com/annualreport**.

*S*elf-assessment questions

1 Identify the reasons for differences in financial accounting practices within Europe.

2 Do all European countries adopt the principle of the true and fair view?

3 The IASB can establish worldwide influence over financial reports even if China does not adopt the IASs. Discuss.

4 Identify reasons why European enterprises should take CSR accounting seriously.

5 It has been stated that:

The purpose of income calculations in practical affairs is to give people an indication of the amount which they can consume without impoverishing themselves (Hicks, 1946 – capital maintenance theory).
Can this statement be applied to CSR?

Answers to these questions can be found at the back of this book.

No further questions are provided in respect of this chapter as we feel students will benefit more from open discussion in seminars on the following topics:

(a) 'The regulatory framework in the UK and other European countries is identical.' Discuss.

(b) 'The only influences on the regulatory framework of a country are the legal system and the language of a country.' Discuss with particular reference to China.

(c) 'Any moves towards European harmonisation of regulatory frameworks are doomed to failure.' Discuss.

(d) 'The convergence of US GAAP to International GAAP is doomed to failure'. Discuss.

(e) 'Strong corporate governance regulation is essential in the twenty-first century.' Discuss

(f) 'Corprorate social responsibility reporting is an essential ingredient of any financial reporting framework.' Discuss.

We would suggest that students are given the discussion topics before the seminar and asked to present information to support their arguments. Such information can be obtained by library and CD-ROM search and will aid students in the development of their information search skills. These discussion topics can also be given as summative assessment.

12

Interpretation, including ratio analysis and consideration of additional information required

Objectives

By the end of this chapter you should be able to:

▶ Identify the needs and objectives of users of accounting information.

▶ Explain the standards by which a particular set of accounts can be judged.

▶ Understand the technique of ratio analysis and calculate ratios.

▶ Explain what the ratios mean and their limitations.

▶ Identify additional information that users may require.

Accounting information and users

Throughout the previous chapters you have learnt how to collect information about a company and how that culminates in its published financial statements. For a sole trader you have also seen that the production of a statement of comprehensive income and the statement of financial position in respect of his/her business is very important even though it is not required to be published.

These financial statements therefore provide valuable information for both the owners of the business and for any potential owners/investors. It is therefore important that we learn how to analyse the information provided and make informed decisions by interpreting this analysis.

In Chapter 1 you identified the users of accounting information.

Activity 12.1 Identify the users of accounting information. Note that your list could be wider than that identified in Chapter 1 if you refer to your studies in other areas such as economics.

Answer

You should have included the following in your list:

► Trade receivables/debtors – customers.

► Trade payables/creditors – suppliers.

► Employees and their representatives.

► Taxation authorities.

► Financial analysts and stockbrokers.

► Other government departments – those concerned with the economy and environment.

► Those considering investing in the business – potential investors or purchasers of the business.

► The public, particularly environmental pressure groups and those who live close to the location of the business.

The above is not an exhaustive list and you may have thought of others. A list of users is also provided in the IASB's 'Framework for Preparation and Presentation of Financial Statements' and you will find our list is similar.

Needs and objectives of users

Each of the users we have listed may well want to know different things about the business; they will have different **needs and objectives**. We must identify these needs and objectives so that the correct information is abstracted for them.

Activity 12.2

Complete the following table:

User	Needs/objectives
Investors/owners	
Suppliers	
Customers	
Lenders	
Employees	

Answer

► Investors/owners – could their resources earn more if invested elsewhere, should they invest even more money in the business? Is the business likely to become insolvent, i.e. bankrupt, and thus the owners may not receive their investment back?

► Suppliers – is the business able to pay for the goods bought on credit? Will the business wish to purchase more goods from the supplier?

► Customers – do the customers receive the goods they want when they want them? Will the business continue in operation so that guarantees on goods purchased will be met?

▶ Lenders – is there adequate security for the loan made? Is the business able to make the interest payments on the loan when they fall due? Can the business redeem the loan on its due date?

▶ Employees – does the business make sufficient profit and have enough cash available to make the necessary payments to employees? Will the business continue in operation at its current level so that employees have secure employment?

From the above answer to Activity 12.2 you should be able to identify three general areas of interest in which users' needs and objectives may lie.

Activity 12.3

Identify the three general areas of interest for users of financial statements.

Answer

1 Performance – how successful is the business? Is it making a reasonable profit? Is it utilising its assets to the fullest? Is it, in fact, profitable and efficient?
2 Investment – is the business a suitable investment for shareholders or would returns be greater if they invested elsewhere? Is it a *good investment*?
3 Financial status – can the business pay its way? Is it in fact *liquid*?

Standards

The three questions posed above are subjective not objective. For instance, how do we define a 'reasonable profit'? We have to do so by comparing current profit to profit made in previous years and to profit made by other businesses. We need benchmarks against which we can compare current performance, financial status and investment potential. However, we need to take care with this comparison against benchmarks otherwise our comparison will not be valid.

Consider, for example, your opinion of a movie you recently watched. You may think it was the best movie you have seen; your friend may think it was the worst movie he or she has seen. This is because the experiences/benchmarks you each have are different and you are making a subjective judgement on how the movie compares with those you have previously seen. Thus, in setting benchmarks against which we can compare a company, we must be aware of the subjectivity that could be involved in these benchmarks.

First we need to identify benchmarks/indicators we can use, and then we can consider their limitations.

Four possible benchmarks are:

▶ Past period achievements.

▶ Budgeted achievements.

▶ Other businesses' achievements.

▶ Averages of business achievements in the same area.

Activity 12.4   Complete the following table:

Indicator	Uses of indicator	Limitations of indicator
Past periods		
Budgets		
Other business		
Industry averages		

Answer

Indicator	Uses of indicator	Limitations of indicator
Past periods	Is current activity better or worse than previous periods?	External factors may have influenced activity levels, e.g. public awareness of environmental issues may have necessitated a change in manufacturing process leading to increased costs
Budgets	Has current activity matched that planned?	The budget may not have been a valid standard of performance, e.g. underlying assumptions may have been unrealistic or set at too high a level
Other business	Is our business performing as well as another?	Businesses may not be truly comparable with regard to size and type, e.g. grocer sole trader compared to hairdresser, grocer sole trader compared to supermarket. External factors may affect one business, e.g. a lengthy strike. Accounting policies, bases on which accounting information is prepared, may be different, e.g. inventory valuations, depreciation
Industry averages	As other business	As other business

Technique of ratio analysis

From the study of previous chapters you now have enough knowledge to be able to pick out certain figures such as profit before tax, gross profit, total of non-current assets, net current assets, etc. from a set of financial statements. But what do these figures mean? For example, the financial statements for a record company may show profit before tax is £8m but is this a good profit? It may, for example, be more than a computer company's profit, but does it mean the record company is performing better? Consider the following example:

Example 12.1

You have £5,600 to invest, and discover that Type 1 investment will provide interest of £315 per annum and Type 2 investment, £1,500 after five years. Which investment would you choose assuming no compound interest and no change in the value of the pound?

The return on Type 1 investment is 315/5,600 = 5.625% per annum. The return on Type 2 investment is 300/5,600 = 5.36% per annum. Thus Type 1 investment provides the highest return. To reach this conclusion we compared the return with the amount invested and expressed the figures in the same units – interest per annum.

In evaluating the financial status, performance, and investment potential of a business we first need to identify which figures in a set of financial statements we need to have regard to and which other figures to compare these with. We will use the financial statements of Rodann Ltd, which are reproduced below to demonstrate this process.

RODANN LTD STATEMENT OF COMPREHENSIVE INCOME

Year ended (£000s)	31.12.20X4		31.12.20X5	
Sales		150		250
Opening Inventory	8		12	
Purchases	104		180	
	112		192	
Closing inventory	12		16	
		100		176
Gross profit		50		74
Wages and salaries	20		26	
Depreciation	4		8	
Debenture interest	–		2	
Other expenses	14		16	
		38		52
Net profit before tax		12		22
Taxation		4		10
Net profit after tax		8		12
Proposed dividend		4		6
Retained profit for year		4		6

RODANN LTD STATEMENT OF FINANCIAL POSITION AS AT

(£000s)	31.12.20X4		31.12.20X5	
Non-current assets		72		110
Current assets				
Inventory	12		16	
Trade receivables	18		40	
Bank	10		4	
	40		60	
Current liabilities *due for payment within one year*				
Trade payables	10		28	
Taxation	4		10	
Proposed dividends	4		6	
	18		44	
Net current assets		22		16
		94		126
Non-current liabilities *due for payment after more than one year*				
10% debentures		–		20
		94		106
Share capital and reserves				
Ordinary share capital		70		76
Retained profits		24		30
		94		106

Note that the statement of financial position for Rodann is in the format Assets – Liabilities = Equity.

Activity 12.5

Compare and contrast each item on the statement of financial position and statement of comprehensive income of Rodann with the figure for the previous year. Note seven points of interest from this comparison.

Answer

The points of interest are as follows:

▶ Sales increased in 20X5.

▶ Cost of sales has increased.

▶ Expenses have increased.

▶ Profit after tax has increased by 50%.

▶ Non-current assets have increased by 50%.

▶ Net current assets have reduced.

▶ Shares and debentures have increased in 20X5.

Having gained a 'pen picture' of what has occurred in the company from one year to the next we can now carry out a ratio analysis which will help us to 'fill in' this pen picture with more detail.

Performance

Performance is generally assessed by the **return on capital employed (ROCE)** ratio:

$$\text{ROCE} = \frac{\text{Profit before taxation and long-term loan interest}}{\text{Net assets (capital employed including long-term loans)}}$$

This ratio identifies how much profit the business has made from the capital invested in it. It will also identify whether the owners would be better off placing their money in a bank deposit account rather than leaving it invested in the company.

Activity 12.6   Calculate the ROCE for Rodann Ltd for 20X4 and 20X5.

Answer

ROCE	20X4	20X5
	12/94 = 12.77%	24/126 = 19.05%

This ratio has increased from 20X4 to 20X5 indicating an increase in profitability of the business from the increased investment. But where has this increased profitability come? Is it because the business has increased sale prices or reduced expenses, that is, increased **net profit margins (NPM)**, or is it because the business has increased the **volume of trade (VofT)** compared to the capital employed?

These two questions can be expressed as ratios as follows:

$$\text{Net profit margin} = \frac{\text{Profit before tax and long-term interest}}{\text{Sales}}$$

$$\text{Volume of trade} = \frac{\text{Sales}}{\text{Capital employed}}$$

Calculating these two ratios for Rodann Ltd:

Net profit margin	20X4	20X5
	12/150 = 8%	24/250 = 9.6%

The net profit margin has increased indicating benefit gained from control of expenses or increased sale prices:

Volume of trade	20X4	20X5
	150/94 = 1.6 times	250/126 = 1.98 times

indicating that Rodann Ltd is earning more sales per £ of net assets or capital employed in 20X5 than 20X4.

These three ratios have the following relationship:

$$\text{ROCE} = \text{Margin} \times \text{Volume}$$
$$\text{NP/CE} = \text{NP/S} \times \text{S/CE}$$

where NP = profit before interest and tax, CE = capital employed, and S = sales.

This relationship can be shown as a family tree as follows:

```
                        ROCE
          ┌───────────────┴───────────────┐
        NP/S                             S/CE
```

This family tree can be expanded and will provide a framework for ratio analysis. For example:

$$\text{NP/S} = \text{GP/S} - \text{E/S}$$

where GP = gross profit and E = expenses.

If we invert S/CE first to CE/S, this can then be expanded as:

$$\text{FA/S} + \text{NCA/S}$$

where FA = non-current assets and NCA = net current assets.

We invert again and calculate S/FA and S/NCA.

Activity 12.7

Calculate these four ratios for Rodann Ltd and interpret them.

Answer

Gross profit margin	20X4	20X5
	50/150 = 33.3%	74/250 = 29.6%

This shows a reduction in gross profit probably due to a decrease in sale prices which has generated more sales or an increase in the cost of goods sold.

Expenses/sales	20X4	20X5
	38/150 = 25.3%	50/250 = 20%

This has decreased from 20X4 to 20X5 indicating a better control of expenses.

	20X4	20X5
S/FA	50/72 = 2.08	250/110 = 2.27

Non-current assets have generated 2.08 times their value in sales in 20X4 and 2.27 times their value in sales in 20X5. Non-current assets are earning more sales in 20X5 than 20X4.

	20X4	20X5
S/NCA	50/22 = 6.82	250/16 = 15.6

Net current assets are also earning more sales in 20X5 than 20X4.

The family tree of ratios now looks like this:

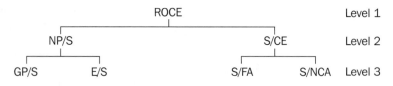

The pyramid can be extended to a fourth level by comparing individual expenses to sales and breaking down the non-current assets and net current assets into their constituent parts:

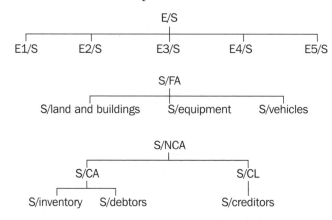

However, as inventory is recorded at cost not selling price then a more appropriate ratio than sales/inventory would be, cost of goods sold/inventory, and as creditors relates to goods purchased on credit, credit purchases/creditors. Lastly S/debtors would be more appropriate as credit sales/debtors. Example 12.2 demonstrates the calculation and interpretation of these Level 4 ratios.

Example 12.2

The following information is provided for Anne Ltd as at 31.12.20X4:

	£000
Cost of goods sold	110
Average inventory	25
Trade creditors	43
Credit purchases	108
Trade debtors	48
Credit sales	142

Cost of goods sold/inventory = 110/25 = 4.4, that is 4.4 times the average inventory level has been used in the cost of goods for the year. This could be written much simpler as inventory is turned over every 83 days, i.e. 365/4.4 = 83 days.

The ratio is therefore:

$$\frac{\textbf{Average inventory}}{\textbf{Cost of goods sold}} \times \textbf{365}$$

Example 12.2 continued

The debtors and creditors ratio is written as:

$$\frac{\text{Trade debtors}}{\text{Credit sales}} \times 365$$

which will tell us on average how long it takes debtors to pay:

$$\frac{\text{Trade creditors}}{\text{Credit purchases}} \times 365$$

which will tell us how long on average it takes the business to pay its creditors.

Total sales and total purchases will have to be used in lieu of credit sales and credit purchases in this example.

$$\text{Debtors period} = 48 \times 365/142 = 123 \text{ days}$$
$$\text{Creditors period} = 43 \times 365/108 = 145 \text{ days}$$

Whether or not these Level 4 ratios should be calculated when carrying out a ratio analysis will depend upon the information produced at previous levels. For example, when considering Rodann Ltd we noted a marked improvement in the efficiency of net current assets, therefore calculating the Level 4 ratios may tell us where this improvement came from.

Activity 12.8

Calculate inventory, debtor and creditor turnover periods for Rodann Ltd and interpret them.

Answer

	20X4	20X5
Inventory turnover =	$(8 + 12)/2 \times 365/100$	$(16 + 12)/2 \times 365/176$
	= 36.5 days	29 days

Thus inventory is being turned over quicker in 20X5, demonstrating greater efficiency.

	20X4	20X5
Debtors turnover period	$18/150 \times 365$	$40/250 \times 365$
	= 44 days	= 58 days

Thus debtors have been allowed 14 more days in 20X5 than 20X4 in which to pay their debts to the business. This could possibly indicate that Rodann Ltd is losing control of its debtor collection or that it has purposely allowed debtors more time to pay so as to encourage more sales.

	20X4	20X5
Creditors turnover period	$10/104 \times 365$	$28/180 \times 365$
	= 35 days	= 57 days

(Note that cost of goods sold could be used as a substitute for purchases if the financial statements do not provide a figure for purchases.) This indicates Rodann Ltd is taking longer to pay its suppliers – 22 days longer. This may damage relations with suppliers if Rodann does not take care, but also shows how Rodann is using creditors to finance its business operations. A balance has to be struck within this dichotomy.

Within the analysis of Rodann Ltd at Level 3 there was also a benefit gained from control of expenses. Therefore Level 4 analysis is required here.

Activity 12.9

Calculate ratios of wages, depreciation and other expenses to sales and interpret them for Rodann Ltd.

Answer

	20X4	20X5
Wages/sales	20/150 = 13.3%	26/250 = 10.4%

indicating that the amount of wages expended to generate one £ of sales has been reduced.

	20X4	20X5
Depreciation/sales	4/150 = 2.7%	8/250 = 3.2%

Depreciation has marginally increased as a proportion of sales, which may be due to an increase in assets.

	20X4	20X5
Other expenses/sales	14/150 = 9.3%	16/250 = 6.4%

Other expenses have also been controlled as a percentage of sales.

These three ratios, as we saw earlier, when combined gave an increase in profit margin – increased *profitability*. The pyramid also demonstrates that the ratios on the left-hand side show profitability and those on the right efficiency in the use of assets.

Let us look again at the first ratio on the pyramid – ROCE. Capital employed consists of shareholder funds, that is, share capital and reserves, and long-term debt, for example debentures. In the example of Rodann Ltd ROCE was:

20X4	12.77%
20X5	19.05%

The debentures in 20X5 only required a return to be paid to the holders of 10% even though the capital invested, £10,000, earned 19.05%. The earnings over and above the 10% will therefore accrue to the shareholders and their return will be increased beyond the 19.05% that the total capital earned. If we calculate another ratio, **return on shareholders' funds (ROSHF)**, we can demonstrate the above quite easily. Return on shareholders' funds or **owners' equity (ROOE)** =

$$\frac{\text{Profit before tax but after long-term debt interest}}{\text{Shareholders' capital}}$$

20X4	20X5
12/94 = 12.77%	22/106 = 20.75%

The shareholders have increased their earnings in the business partly due to the benefit gained by borrowing at a lower rate of return than the business is earning. However, the converse can also occur! Note that ROCE and ROSHF were exactly the same in 20X4 as there was no long-term debt.

Activity 12.10   Given the following information relating to Rickmar Ltd, calculate ROCE and ROOE for Ricmar Ltd for 20X4 and 20X5:

	20X4	20X5
Profit before tax	80	85
Interest charged	10	10
Capital employed	1,250	1,280
Long-term debt	100	100

Answer

20X4	20X5
ROCE 90/1250 = 7.2%	95/1280 = 7.4%

20X4	20X5
ROOE 80/1150 = 7%	85/1180 = 7.2%

The return made in each year is 7.2% and 7.4% but the return payable to the long-term debt holders is 10% in both years, therefore the return available to the shareholders reduces to 7% and 7.2%.

Investment potential

Before looking in detail at investment ratios it is useful to carry out some practical research.

Activity 12.11   Obtain a fairly recent copy of the *Financial Times* or access the website at **www.ft.com/home/uk**. Look up the London share information service found in the *FT* and make a note of the data provided for each company. Also read the 'UK company news' either in the *FT* or any other quality newspaper and note down any ratios or indicators used to evaluate the companies.

Answer   Your list possibly included the following:

▶ Book value per share compared with market value per share.
▶ Net dividend.
▶ Dividend cover.
▶ Earnings per share.
▶ Gross dividend yield.
▶ Price/earnings ratio.

We will look at each of these ratios in turn.

Book value per share

This is:

$$\frac{\text{Ordinary shareholders' funds}}{\text{Number of shares}}$$

This book value is the value each share would have if the company's assets and liabilities were sold at their balance sheet (book) value. The market value is the price a potential shareholder is willing to pay to acquire a share in the company. Comparing these two values identifies whether the market values the company at more or less than its book value.

Net dividend

This is the amount of dividend declared in any one year per share:

$$\frac{\text{Paid and proposed dividends}}{\text{Number of shares}}$$

People invest in shares either:

▶ to earn dividends or

▶ to gain capital growth in the value of the share, or both.

The level of dividend and its comparison with previous years is generally regarded as an important indicator of future expectations. However, one danger with this comparison is that dividends are not necessarily just paid out of the current year's earnings but can be paid out of retained earnings. It is therefore important to look at dividend cover in any one year.

Dividend cover

$$\frac{\text{Net profit available to ordinary shareholders}}{\text{Total ordinary dividend}}$$

---

*A*ctivity *12.12* The following information is available in respect of Shamar Ltd.

	20X4	20X5
Ordinary shares issued £1	2,500,000	2,500,000
8% preference shares £1	500,000	500,000
Dividend ordinary shares	300,000	250,000
Net profit after tax	287,500	271,900

Calculate dividend per share in pence for both preference and ordinary shares, and dividend cover.

Answer		20X4	20X5
	Dividend per share in pence preference	8p	8p
	Dividend per share ordinary	12p	10p
	Dividend cover	287,500/340,000 = 0.85	271,900/290,000 = 0.94

The dividend has reduced per share from 20X4 to 20X5 but the dividend cover has improved. However, this dividend cover is less than one, which indicates that the company is not earning enough in either year to pay the dividend and is therefore using past earnings retained to fund the dividend payment. This may be a danger sign for potential investors.

Earnings per share

This is another indicator used widely by the investment community. It represents the amount of profit, in pence, the company has earned during the year for each ordinary share.

For the example of Shamar above the **earnings per share (EPS)** in 20X4 is:

$$247,500/2,500,000 = 9.9p$$

and 20X5 is:

$$231,900/2,500,000 = 9.3p$$

Earnings per share is:

$$\frac{\text{Net profit available to ordinary shareholders}}{\text{Number of ordinary shares in issue}}$$

Gross dividend yield

This is calculated from the formula:

$$\frac{\text{Gross dividend}}{\text{Market price of ordinary share}}$$

Shareholders may be willing to accept a low gross dividend yield if there is a greater than average capital growth in share value expected or if the company is a safe investment. Gross dividend is calculated by grossing up the dividend declared in the accounts for basic rate taxation as dividends are always declared and paid net of basic income tax at least in the UK.

For example, in the case of Shamar Ltd if the basic rate of tax is 20% then the gross dividend is:

	20X4	20X5
	300,000/80%	250,000/80%
	375,000	312,500
or per share	15p	12.5p

If the market value per share for Shamar was £1.75 in 20X4 and £1.82 in 20X5 then the gross dividend yield is:

20X4	20X5
15/175	12.5/182
= 8.6%	= 6.9%

Price/earnings ratio (P/E ratio)

The formula for the price/earnings (P/E) ratio is:

$$\frac{\text{Market price per share}}{\text{Earnings per share}}$$

For Shamar this is:

20X4	20X5
175/9.9	182/9.3
= 17.7	= 19.6

Like the dividend yield the P/E ratio will change as the market price per share changes. It represents the market's view of the growth potential of the company, its dividend policy and the degree of risk involved in the investment. In general a high P/E indicates the market has a high/good opinion of these factors, a low P/E a low/poor opinion of these factors. Another way of looking at the P/E is that it represents the number of years' earnings it is necessary to have at the current rate to recover the price paid for the share. For Shamar this was 19.6 years at the 20X5 rate of earnings.

Financial status

It is vital for a business to be able to pay its debts as and when they fall due, otherwise its chances of remaining in operation become remote. There is a need to analyse the assets available to meet liabilities. This can be done in the short, medium and long term.

For the short term we use the quick assets ratio or acid test:

$$\frac{\text{Current assets less inventory}}{\text{Current liabilities}}$$

Inventory is excluded from current assets as it is regarded as less liquid than other assets within that category.

For the medium term the current ratio is:

$$\frac{\text{Current assets}}{\text{Current liabilities}}$$

If current liabilities exceed current assets this is not necessarily a sign of weakness. For example, major supermarket chains usually have a negative ratio as they have few debtors and yet take as much credit as possible from suppliers. Their strong cash flow ensures that creditors will be paid when due.

For the long term the gearing ratio is:

$$\frac{\text{Long-term debt}}{\text{Shareholders' funds}}$$

Another ratio, interest cover, can also be used:

$$\frac{\text{Net profit before interest and tax}}{\text{Total interest charges}}$$

Activity 12.13 Calculate the four liquidity ratios for Rodann Ltd and explain what the figures calculated mean.

Answer

	20X4	20X5
Acid test	$\dfrac{40 - 12}{18} = \dfrac{28}{18}$	$\dfrac{60 - 16}{44} = \dfrac{44}{44}$
expressed as	1.6:1	1:1

The ratio has decreased from 20X4 to 20X5 quite considerably but there are still plenty of liquid assets. The ratio will need careful monitoring to control this downward trend.

	20X4	20X5
Current ratio	40/18 = 2.2:1	60/44 = 1.4:1

Again this ratio has been substantially reduced but still appears adequate. Monitoring of this downward trend is again required.

	20X4	20X5
Gearing ratio	not relevant	20/106 = 18.9%

This is low and we would consider this company low geared. If a company is high geared then it may have difficulty meeting the required interest payments.

	20X4	20X5
Interest cover	not relevant	(22 + 2)/2 = 12

In 20X5 the profit covered the required interest payment 12 times indicating no immediate problem for Rodann Ltd.

Notice how consideration of all four ratios helped to build up a picture of the financial status of Rodann Ltd.

Limitations of ratio analysis

There are seven principal limitations of ratio analysis:

▶ Differences in accounting policies.
▶ The historical nature of accounts.
▶ Absence of suitable comparable data.
▶ Differences in the environments of periods compared.

▶ Hidden short-term fluctuations.

▶ Changes in the value of money.

▶ Other non-monetary factors.

Three of these were examined in Activity 12.4: accounting policies, absence of suitable comparable data and changes in environment. Non-monetary factors relates to the fact that nowhere in the analysis is the quality of the product or service considered, whether labour relations are good or bad. In fact, no regard is had to the goodwill of the business. Let's look in a little more depth at the effect fair valuation of non-current assets could have on interpretation using ratio analysis. (Valuation is dealt with in more detail in Chapter 13.)

Example 12.3

The following information is available in respect of Colmar Ltd for the years ended 31 December 20X7 and 31 December 20X8:

	31 December 20X7	31 December 20X8
	(£000s)	(£000s)
Profit before tax	268	356
Non-current assets net book value	1,235	1,750
Equity (share capital + reserves)	980	1,240
Interest charged	25	35
Long-term debt	100	120

The following information is also relevant:

(a) At 1 January 20X8 Colmar revalued its non-current assets upwards by £200,000.

(b) This revaluation gave rise to additional depreciation charge for the year ended 31 December 20X8 of £30,000

(c) Both (a) and (b) have been incorporated in the data given for 31 December 2008.

Calculate ROCE, ROOE and ratio of sales to non-current assets for Colmar:

1 Before adjusting for the revaluation
2 After adjusting for the revaluation.

1 Before adjusting for the revaluation

ROCE =	268+25/ 980+100	356 + 35/ 1240 + 120
	27.13%	28.75%
ROOE =	268/980	356/1240
	27.34%	28.71%
Sales/NCA =	1750/1235	1850/1750
	1.42	1.06

These calculations imply that Colmar has only slightly increased its performance in 20X8 and that the increased debt taken on has led to a gearing down in return (28.75% compared with 28.71%) to the equity holders. 20X7 showed a gearing up in return. In addition, non-current assets generated more sales in 20X7 than 20X8.

Example 12.3
continued

2 After adjusting for the revaluation

The information provided on Colmar is not strictly comparable as in 20X7 the non-current assets were recorded at historic cost but in 20X8 they were recorded at fair value. We must adjust the 20X8 figures so as to disregard the revaluation.

Profit before tax will become 356 + 30 additional depreciation charged = 386

Non-current assets net book value will become 1750 – (200 – 30) = 1580

Equity will become 1240 – 200 = 1040

ROCE	27.13%	386 + 35/1040 + 120
		36.3%
ROOE	27.34%	386/1040
		37.12%
Sales/NCA	1.42	1850/1580
		1.17

This now shows a much better picture for Colmar in 20X8. They have greatly increased the ROCE and ROOE compared with 20X7 and the increase in long-term debt has been beneficial in terms of return to the equity holders – a gearing up on performance ratio. The NCA have still not generated as much sales as in 20X7 but the performance is slightly better after adjustment for the revaluation.

It is very important before you carry out a ratio analysis, either year to year or company to company, to ensure that the figures you are comparing have been derived using the same accounting policies, otherwise your findings will be distorted, as Example 12.3 shows.

The historical nature of accounts must always be borne in mind as our interpretation of the business is based on this historical information. However, it may not be the best guide as to the future performance, financial status and investment potential.

Short-term fluctuations are also hidden in ratio analysis as our appraisal is based on a statement of financial position that provides values of assets and liabilities as at a point in time. For example, consider the following information relating to a company whose year end is 31 December:

	September	October	November	December
	£	£	£	£
Debtors	2,000	2,100	2,500	5,000
Other current assets	4,000	4,000	3,950	3,900
Current liabilities	5,500	5,600	5,550	5,500
The current ratio for each month is	1.09:1	1.09:1	1.16:1	1.62:1

However, calculating the current ratio by reference to the statement of financial position would show a figure of 1.6:1 in December which represents a better view of liquidity than has been the case over the past four months. It is important to remember that the statement of financial position only provides a 'snap-shot' of a company at a particular point in time and that considerable changes can occur to that picture in a short period of time. Shamar may well have increased its debtors, and therefore its liquidity position, due to an increased level of sales for the Christmas period or other festival period.

Changes in the value of money

We all know how inflation affects the value of the pound in our pocket and this is no different for a business. In fact the effects of inflation on our ratio analysis could make the whole analysis invalid. To demonstrate this, consider a company with sales last year of £350,000 and sales this year of £400,000. Would you interpret this as an increase in volume of trade of 14%?

If you were informed that the price of the goods sold had been subject to an increase of 10% (inflation) then the increase in volume would only be approximately 4%.

Additional information

From the work you have already completed in this chapter you should be able to identify additional information that may help you in assessing the performance, financial status and investment potential of a business.

Activity 12.14   Make a list of additional information that you would like when undertaking a ratio analysis of a company.

Answer   You should have identified several of the following:

▶ Inflation effects on the company.

▶ Does the statement of financial position represent the position of the business throughout the year or just at the year end?

▶ Cash flow throughout the year.

▶ Forecast business plans in the form of budgets and cash flows.

▶ Information in respect of the quality of goods and services and other factors affecting the assessment of goodwill in the business.

▶ Industrial averages of ratios.

▶ Differences in accounting policies between businesses.

However, you must be aware that several items in this list may not be available to you as a potential investor as they will not be public information in respect of the business. For example, it would be very difficult, probably impossible, for a potential investor to obtain detailed information in respect of future plans of the business apart from that disclosed in the Chairman's Report in the financial statements.

Cash flow and ratio analysis

In Chapter 10 we showed you how to construct a cash flow statement and we also made reference to using this in analysing the performance and financial position of a business. The following activity consists of interpretation using ratios and information derived from the statement of comprehensive income, statement of financial position and cash flow.

Activity 12.15 From the following information assess, as far as the information permits, the financial position and performance of the business.

STATEMENT OF COMPREHENSIVE INCOME FOR THE YEARS ENDED

	31.12.X6	31.12.X5
	(£m)	(£m)
Turnover	2,516	2,203
Cost of sales	1,762	1,548
Gross profit	754	655
Distribution costs	159	145
Administration costs	226	211
Operating profit	369	299
Net interest payable	16	(2)
Profit before tax	353	301
Taxation	108	91
Profit after tax	245	210

STATEMENT OF FINANCIAL POSITION AS AT

	31.12.X6	31.12.X5
Non-current assets	1,392	1,354
Investments	67	47
	1,459	1,401
Current assets		
Inventory	270	244
Trade receivables/Debtors	379	318
Bank and cash	62	33
	711	595
Current liabilities		
Trade payables/Creditors	577	665
	134	(70)
Non-current liabilities		
Debentures 5%	160	56
Net assets	1,433	1,275
Share capital	1,027	1,029
Revaluation reserve	15	15
Retained profits	391	231
	1,433	1,275

▶

STATEMENT OF CASH FLOWS FOR THE YEAR ENDED

	31.12.X6	31.12.X5
Net cash inflow from operating activities	402	315
Interest paid	(10)	(1)
Taxation paid	(96)	(90)
Net cash used in investing activities	(120)	(126)
Net cash used in financing activities	(12)	(182)
Dividends paid	(132)	(88)
Increase/decrease in cash and cash equivalents	32	(172)

Answer

The first task in this activity is to review the statements you are given and identify the changes that have taken place from one year to the next.

From the statement of comprehensive income we can see that:

▶ gross profit has increased by 15%

▶ expenses have also increased but only by 8.1%

▶ profit after tax has increased by 16.7%.

From the statement of financial position we can see that:

▶ investment has been made in non-current assets – a net increase of £38m so the actual investment will have been much higher that this to offset any sales and the depreciation/amortisation of the year

▶ more funds are tied up in current assets particularly stock but current liabilities have been greatly reduced

▶ further loans in the forms of debentures have been acquired during the year.

From the cash flow it is evident that the operating activities for the year have financed interest, taxation, dividends, purchase of non-current assets and that dividends have increased by 50% from last year to this.

We can then calculate several ratios for the information:

ROCE   20X6   20X5
369/1433 +160 = 23.2%   299/1275+56 = 22.5%

Slightly more return has been made this year:

ROSHE   20X6   20X5
353/1433 = 24.6%   301/1275 = 23.6%

A gearing up has occurred in both years and the increase in ROCE is also shown in ROSHE from last year to this:

GP/S   20X6   20X5
754/2516 = 30%   655/2203 = 29.7%

The company has made a slight increase here:

NP/S	20X6	20X5
	369/2516 = 14.7%	299/2203 = 13.6%

This shows a bigger increase than at gross profit level so the company has controlled its expenses during the year which is also demonstrated by looking at:

Expenses/sales	20X6	20X5
	385/2516 = 15.3%	356/2203 = 16.2%

The volume of trade is demonstrated by:

S/CE	20X6	20X5
	2516/1593 = 1.58	2203/1331 = 1.66

Thus volume has fallen but margins have increased resulting in a greater return on capital employed. However, the company must ensure capital employed continues to generate a good volume of trade. We can extend the volume indicator by looking at volume generated by non-current assets and current assets as follows:

S/NCA	20X6	20X5
	2516/1392 = 1.81	2203/1354 = 1.63

This shows that the volume of trade generated from NCA is much higher than last year so the problem must lie with net current assets:

S/net current assets	20X6	20X5
	2516/134 = 18.78	2203/(70) and thus the reduction in current liabilities from £665m to £577m coupled with an increase in current assets from £595m to £711m is the problem for the company

The liquidity ratios further demonstrate this:

CA/CL	20X6	20X5
	711/577 = 1.23	595/665 = 0.89

The company is much more liquid and therefore could be keeping excess funds tied up in working capital; but remember the statement of financial position is a snapshot at a point in time so this will require further investigation within the company.

	20X6	20X5
CA-inventory /CL	441/577 = 0.76	351/665 = 0.53
Inventory turnover	270×365/1762 = 56 days	244×365/1548 = 57.5 days
Debtors turnover	379×365/2516 = 55 days	318×365/2203 = 52.7 days
Creditors turnover	577×365/1762 = 119.5 days	665×365/1548 = 156.8 days

Thus the company has made a great change in the time it takes them to pay creditors. This has been speeded up considerably.

We noticed earlier that the dividend had been increased and this can be further demonstrated by calculating the net dividend if we assume £1 shares:

Dividends/number of share	20X6	20X5
	132/1027 = 12.8p	88/1029 = 8.55p

Earnings per share can also be calculated:

E/Number of shares	20X6	20X5
	245/1027 = 23.86p	210/1029 = 20.4p

Overall

The company has increased its return by controlling expenses and has had a slight drop in volume of trade. It has also increased the dividend payment to the shareholders but this is greatly in excess of the increased earnings. Creditors' period has been reduced and the company is much more liquid. This liquidity and the increased dividend payment must be kept under review.

The following activity involves a ratio analysis using real information from the accounts of Royal Dutch Shell plc for the year ended 31 December 2007.

Activity 12.16 **ROYAL DUTCH SHELL SUMMARISED STATEMENT OF COMPREHENSIVE INCOME**

	2007 ($million)	2006 ($million)
Revenue	355,782	318,845
Cost of sales	(296,697)	(262,989)
Gross profit	59,085	55,856
Selling, distribution and administration costs	(16,621)	(16,616)
Exploration costs	(1,712)	(1,562)
Share of profit from associated companies	8,234	6,671
Interest and other income	2,698	1,428
Interest expense	(1,108)	(1,149)
Income before taxation	50,576	44,628
Taxation	(18,650)	(18,317)
Income for period	31,926	26,311

ROYAL DUTCH SHELL CONSOLIDATED STATEMENT OF FINANCIAL POSITION

	2007 ($million)	2006 ($million)
Non-current assets	15,4073	143,391
Current assets	11,5387	91,885
	269,397	235,276
Non-current liabilities	49,118	43,583
Current liabilities	94,384	76,748
Equity	125,968	114,945
	269,470	235,276

Calculate relevant ratios for Royal Dutch Shell plc and comment on the company performance as far as the information permits.

Answer

Ratios that can be calculated are:

Return on capital employed 51,684/175,086 = 29.5% 45,777/158,528 = 28.9%

This shows that Shell slightly improved its performance in 2007 compared with 2006.

Return on owners' equity 50,576/125,968 = 40% 44,628/114,945 = 38.8%

The return on owners' equity has also improved but slightly more than the return on capital employed so presumably shareholders are benefiting from the gearing.

Gearing 49,118/125,968 = 39% 43,583/114,945 = 38%

Gearing has remained similar from 2006 to 2007 and it is relatively low geared.

Gross profit /sales 59,085/355,782 = 16.6% 55,856/318,845 = 17.5%

Shell appears to have suffered a slight downturn on its gross profit to sales indicating that cost of sales has increased as a percentage of sales.

Net profit /sales 50,576/355,782 = 14.2% 44,628/318,845 = 14%

Shell has been able to control costs to improve net profit to sales ratio. The next ratio demonstrates this control on costs as selling, distribution and administration costs have decreased from 5.2% to 4.7%, thus the lower gross profit return has been turned into a higher net profit return.

Selling, distribution and admin/sales
16,621/355,782 = 4.7% 16,616/318,845 = 5.2%

Sales/capital employed
355,782/175,086 = 2.03 times 318,845/158,528 = 2.01 times

Shell has also increased its return on capital employed by slightly improving their volume indicator. Thus the capital employed has been working harder during 2007. This is demonstrated in the next ratio, as non-current assets compared to sales has increased by 0.09:

Sales/non-current assets

355,782/154,073 = 2.31 times   318,845/143,391 = 2.22 times

Overall, Shell has improved its performance from 2006 to 2007.

Summary

This chapter has:

▶ introduced you to the technique of ratio analysis

▶ demonstrated the calculation of such ratios

▶ identified ratio analysis as a tool that users of accounts can make use of in order to meet their needs and objectives

▶ noted that there were several limitations in the use of ratio analysis and that these must be borne in mind when making an assessment as to the performance, financial status and investment potential of a business; and

▶ shown you how to calculate and interpret the ratios referred to in this chapter.

The interpretation is the most difficult part of ratio analysis and requires a great deal of practice and use of common sense! This interpretation is also not definitive – there is no right or wrong answer – as much of the analysis requires subjective judgements to be made by the analyst. The chapter concludes with a few exercises for you to complete in this area.

Key terms

needs and objectives (p. 243)
benchmarks/indicators (p. 244)
return on capital employed (ROCE) (p. 248)
net profit margins (NPM) (p. 248)
volume of trade (VofT) (p. 248)

return on shareholders' funds (ROSHF) (or return on owners' equity (ROOE)) (p. 252)
earnings per share (EPS) (p. 255)
price/earnings (P/E) ratio (p. 256)
gearing ratio(p. 257)

Self-assessment questions

1 Obtain a set of accounts for a supermarket and a manufacturer. You can do this by accessing your university library or using the service provided by the *Financial Times* (www.ft.com).

Compare and contrast the nature of the current assets and liabilities of your two companies.

2 You are given the following information in relation to Olivet Ltd:

STATEMENT OF COMPREHENSIVE INCOME FOR 20X4 AND 20X5

	20X4	20X5
Sales	100,000	100,000
Cost of sales	50,000	60,000
	50,000	40,000
Expenses	30,000	30,000
	20,000	10,000
Dividends	10,000	10,000
	10,000	
Retained profits b/f	2,500	12,500
	£12,500	£12,500

STATEMENT OF FINANCIAL POSITIONS AS AT 20X4 AND 20X5

	20X4	20X5
Land	21,500	31,500
Buildings	20,000	39,500
Equipment	3,000	3,000
	44,500	74,000
Investments at cost	25,000	40,000
Inventory	27,500	32,500
Trade receivable/Debtors	20,000	25,000
Bank	1,500	
	118,500	171,500
Ordinary £1 shares	20,000	25,000
Share premium	6,000	7,000
Revaluation reserve		10,000
Retained profits	12,500	12,500
Debentures 10%	50,000	75,000
Trade payables/Creditors	20,000	30,000
Proposed dividend	10,000	10,000
Bank		2,000
	118,500	171,500

You are required to comment on the financial position of Olivet Ltd as at 20X5. Calculate any ratios you feel necessary.

3 A Ltd and B Ltd, two separate companies, manufacture IT equipment. Their financial statements at 31.12.X9 are as follows:

STATEMENTS OF COMPREHENSIVE INCOME FOR THE YEAR ENDED 31.12.X9

	A Ltd (£000)	B Ltd (£000)
Sales	2,150	1,512
Cost of sales	1,430	1,148
Gross profit	720	364
Other expenses	250	190
Operating profit	470	174
Interest on debentures	20	60
Net profit before tax	450	114
Taxation	100	30
Net profit after tax	350	84
Dividends	200	80
Retained profit	150	4

STATEMENTS OF FINANCIAL POSITION AS AT 31.12.X9

	A Ltd (£000)		B Ltd (£000)	
Property, plant and equipment cost		2,750		3,420
Depreciation		980		2,524
		1,770		896
Current assets				
Inventory	420		340	
Trade receivable/Debtors	900		680	
Cash	40			
	1,360		1,020	
Current liabilities				
Trade payable/Creditors	360		400	
Dividends	200		80	
Overdraft	200		560	
	760		1,040	
Net current assets		600		(20)
		2,370		876
Debentures 10%		200		600
		2,170		276
Capital and reserves				
Ordinary share capital		1,200		200
Retained profits		970		76
		2,170		276

Comment on the profitability, liquidity and risk of the above companies. Calculation of relevant ratios for the above two companies is essential in answering this question.

4 From the financial statements of Ocean Ltd, a retailer, identify:

(a) Five points of interest from comparing this year's results with those of the previous year.

(b) Calculate relevant ratios for Ocean Ltd to enable you to assess the performance of the company in the current year.

(c) Identify any further information you might find useful.

STATEMENTS OF COMPREHENSIVE INCOME FOR THE YEARS ENDED

	31.12.20X0 (£000)	31.12.20X1 (£000)
Sales	1,168	1,944
Cost of sales	778	1,370
Gross profit	390	574
Wages and salaries	156	202
Depreciation	32	62
Other expenses	108	124
Operating profit	94	186
Interest on debentures		16
Net profit before tax	94	170
Taxation	32	78
Net profit after tax	62	92
Dividends	32	46
Retained profit	30	46

STATEMENT OF FINANCIAL POSITIONS AS AT

	31.12.20 X0 (£000)	31.12.20 X0 (£000)	31.12.20 X1 (£000)	31.12.20 X1 (£000)
Property, plant and equipment cost		560		856
Current assets				
Inventory	94		124	
Trade receivables/Debtors	140		312	
Cash	78		32	
	312		468	
Current liabilities				
Trade creditors/Creditors	78		218	
Taxation	32		78	
Dividends	32		46	
	142		342	
Net current assets		170		126

Non-current liabilities		
Debentures 10%		160
	730	822

Capital and reserves		
Ordinary share capital	544	590
Retained profits	186	232
	730	822

Note inventory, debtors and creditors figures at 1.1.20X0 were £102,000, £100,000 and £60,000 respectively.

5 Many plc financial reports now include information on ratios or these can be found on such systems as Extel or Datastream. A useful exercise for you would be to obtain a set of financial statements of a plc, and to calculate some ratios and compare them with any published information available. You could also attempt an analysis of the company in simplistic terms or using a published analysis (e.g. from the *Financial Times* or elsewhere) comment on it. These sorts of exercises lend themselves to group work by students and group presentations so if you are studying with others try doing this exercise as a group.

6 Spiral is hoping to raise a bank loan to help fund the company's expansion plans. It has supplied accounts for the years ended 30 September 20X7 and 30 September 20X6:

SPIRAL STATEMENT OF FINANCIAL POSITION AS AT

	30/09/X7 (£000)	30/09/X6 (£000)
Non-current assets		
Plant and equipment – Net book value	524	318
Current assets		
Inventory	46	51
Trade receivables	104	88
Cash at bank	2	12
	152	151
Current liabilities		
Trade payables	97	80
Tax liabilities	26	19
	123	99
Non-current liabilities		
Debentures 10%	53	40
Net assets	500	330

Represented by:		
Share capital	180	140
Share premium account	18	6
Retained profits	302	184
	500	330

SPIRAL STATEMENT OF COMPREHENSIVE INCOME FOR THE YEAR ENDED

	30/09/X7	30/09/X6
	(£000)	(£000)
Sales	1,644	1,495
Cost of sales	1,365	1,270
Gross profit	279	225
Distribution costs	25	14
Administrative expenses	81	60
Operating profit	173	151
Interest paid	6	4
Profit before tax	167	147
Tax	33	28
Profit after tax	134	119
Dividends paid	16	28
Retained profit for the year	118	91

Additional information relating to the year ended 30 September 20X7:
▶ The depreciation charge for the year, included in administrative expenses was £20,000.

Required

(a) Calculate the following ratios for 30 September 200X and 30 September 20X6, to two decimal places:
   (i)   Gross profit percentage
   (ii) Net (operating) profit percentage
   (iii) Current ratio
   (iv) Acid test ratio (quick ratio).
(b) Explain why the bank will be interested in the profitability and liquidity ratios of Spiral as it assesses whether or not to lend the company money.
(c) Identify two *other* users of financial information and explain why they may use ratios to assess the performance of Spiral.
(d) Prepare the reconciliation of operating profit to net cash flow from operating activities for the year ended 30.0.x7.

▶

7 Camber is considering investing in one of two companies. It has supplied the following financial information:

FINANCIAL INFORMATION AT 31 MARCH 20X8

	United (£000)	Prince (£000)
Inventory	1,800	2,640
Trade receivables	1,740	2,200
Cash at bank	500	268
Trade payables	2,140	3,528
Long-term loans	1,000	3,000
Share capital	2,000	4,000
Retained profits (after addition of current year operating profit)	4,720	3,340
Sales (for the year to 31.03.X8)	18,600	22,000
Purchases (for the year to 31.03.X8)	10,400	13,800
Cost of sales (for the year to 31.03.X8)	10,230	14,300
Operating profit (for the year to 31.03.X8)	2,720	1,640

Required

(a) Calculate the following ratios for United and Prince at 31 March 20X8, to two decimal places:
   (i)   Gross profit percentage
   (ii) Current ratio
   (iii) Acid test ratio (quick ratio)
   (iv) Debtors collection period
   (v)   Creditors payment period
   (vi) Return on capital employed (ROCE).

(b) Recommend which company Camber should invest in, if either. Give reasons to support your recommendation, referring to your calculations in part (a) above.

(c) Identify five ways, other than ratio analysis, that Camber could use to analyse the financial position of companies that it is considering investing in.

Answers to these questions can be found at the back of this book.

13

Valuation and performance measurement

Objectives

By the end of this chapter you should be able to:

▶ Describe valuation theory, including economic value.

▶ Explain why constant purchasing power and current cost accounting failed.

▶ Account for revaluations.

▶ Prepare a statement of changes in equity.

Introduction

You have now reached a point in your studies where you should be reasonably confident in your ability to account for fairly complex economic events, and to present the outcomes using a statement of comprehensive income, statement of financial position and cash flow statement. You may remember from Chapter 4 that there is a fourth statement required by IAS 1, and that is the statement of changes in equity. We will deal with that in some detail towards the end of this chapter. Before doing so, however, we should take a more rigorous look at some of the implicit assumptions we have made in preparing all these statements.

Specifically, we need to reconsider the validity of the historical cost concept. There are two aspects to this. First, historical cost may be the simplest and most objective basis for valuing our assets, but it may not be the most relevant and reliable, especially if prices are changing significantly. What, after all, is the use of quantifying a building at what it cost 20 years ago, if, during that time, prices have doubled or trebled? Is it still a relevant and reliable figure to help users make decisions about the entity?

Second, we will take a brief look at attempts that have been made to explicitly allow for the effects of changing prices, and at why they have so far failed. It could be argued that restating our assets at a more current valuation than historical cost is one way of making at least some such allowance, so we will also study the accounting for this process.

Alternatives to historical cost

In Chapter 2 we considered replacement cost, net realisable value (NRV), and touched on economic value, as alternatives to historical cost. To recap, replacement cost is what an asset would cost if we were to replace it today. Strictly, this should be the cost of a similarly part-worn asset. In times of rising prices this will usually be higher than the historical cost. Note, however, that, even when prices generally are rising, the prices of some assets may be rising at a different rate, or even falling. Think, for example, about what has happened to the prices of computers in recent years. Net realisable value is what we could sell the asset for, after allowing for any direct selling costs.

In this chapter we concentrate on the conceptually most difficult of the three alternatives, that is, economic value. Having done that, we can consider all the alternatives, together with historical cost, and arrive at a single coherent approach to asset valuation.

Economic value rests on the definition of an asset given in the Framework for the Preparation and Presentation of Financial Statements, that is, 'a resource controlled by the entity as a result of past events and from which future economic benefits are expected to flow to the entity'. The essence of an asset is thus the stream of benefits that will flow in to us in the future, because we control that asset. It therefore seems reasonable to value the asset by adding up all those future economic benefits. This is sometimes called the **value in use** of the asset.

If, for example, an asset is expected to last three years, the products we make using it can be sold for £25,000 per year, and the direct costs of making those products are £10,000 per year, then the net economic benefit is £15,000 for each of three years. We could then simply add up the benefits, i.e. £45,000, and use that as the valuation of the asset. We would then show the asset in our statement of financial position at £45,000, rather than at its historical cost.

---

*A*ctivity 13.1

Comparing economic value with historical cost, what are its advantages and disadvantages?

Complete this table by making at least one entry in each box.

Advantages	Disadvantages

Answer

In the advantages box, you should have noted such points as its consistency with the formal definition of an asset, and the fact that it is an up-to-date valuation. The disadvantages include its uncertainty, in that the method assumes that we can predict future incomes and costs with reasonable certainty. This is unlikely. More subtly, the method in its crude form above simply adds together net inflows from different years. This is highly questionable, because of the time value of money.

The time value of money

The **time value of money** is a concept that states which money has a value, not just in terms of its absolute amount, but also in terms of when that amount is received. If you are offered £100 today, or £100 in a year's time, which would you take? The answer is almost certainly that you would want the money now, perhaps because there is something you urgently want to spend it on, and perhaps because you have realised that, given inflation, that same amount will be worth less in real terms in a year from now. Even without these two reasons, however, you may have realised that if you get the money now, you could invest it for a year, so that the total sum would be £110, if we assume a 10% rate of interest.

Looking at this situation from a slightly different angle, there must be some sum of money which you could receive now, instead of getting £100 a year from now, and be indifferent about which one you got. If we again assume interest at 10%, this amount would be £90.91. It is the amount which you could invest now, at 10%, and expect to receive £100 a year from now (£90.91 + £9.09 = £100.00). The £90.91 is called the Present Value of £100 received in one year, at a 10% discount rate.

Returning to our example of the machine that will yield a net £15,000 for three years, we should now note that simply adding the three lots of £15,000 is not actually adding like to like, because it is expressed in £s at different points in time, and the time value of money concept tells us that these three amounts are therefore not expressed in the same terms. In a theoretically pure world, we should add the present value of each of the three inflows, since they would then, by definition, all be expressed in £s at the same point in time – the present.

The key to this technique is applying the correct discount factor to each inflow. Fortunately, there is a fairly simple formula for working out what this factor should be:

$$\frac{1}{(1 + r)^n}$$

where r is the rate of interest applicable to the entity – often, slightly inaccurately, called the cost of capital, and n is the number of years before we receive the inflow. The cost of capital is the rate of interest that the organisation or individual would have to pay if they wanted to borrow money. In the case of an individual, it is often called their 'personal cost of capital'.

Note that we will be making a simplifying assumption, namely that the net inflow associated with each year is actually received at the end of that year. If we assume a cost of capital of 10%, then we are finally in a position to work out the economic value of our asset, as follows:

End of year	Inflow	Discount factor	Present value
1	15,000	0.90909	13,636
2	15,000	0.82645	12,397
3	15,000	0.75131	11,270
			37,303

The base value of this asset that should go in our statement of financial position is therefore £37,303. Note that what we paid for the asset, its historical cost, has not figured anywhere in the calculation.

Activity 13.2

Ms Lee's entire wealth consists of one investment which cost her £30,000, and which will yield £20,000 for each of the next two years, with no further returns. If her personal cost of capital is 10%, calculate the present value of the inflows today, and hence value her asset.

Answer

Your calculation should look like this:

Year	Inflow	Discount factor	Present value
1	20,000	0.90909	18,182
2	20,000	0.82645	16,529
			34,711

Putting the valuations together

We now have three alternatives to historical cost as bases for asset valuation. These are:

▶ Replacement cost.

▶ Net realisable value.

▶ Economic value.

In terms of practical accounting, this is not a satisfactory position, because we are faced with trying to determine which is the most relevant, reliable, comparable and understandable basis for any given entity. Not only may opinions vary, but the answer may change as circumstances in the real world change. There are two ways out of this problem. First, we could decide on one as being the most appropriate most of the time, although this would inevitably be a rather arbitrary decision. Second, we could use the more rigorous approach known as the **deprival value** model. It is usually summarised by the following diagram:

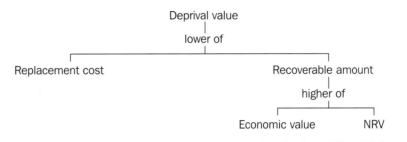

This approach rests on asking two questions, which we then use to work upwards through the model. In other words we start at the bottom of the diagram and compare economic value and net realisable value. Once we've chosen one of these as the 'recoverable amount' we then continue to work upwards to compare this recoverable amount with the replacement to arrive at the deprival value. The two questions are:

1 *Assuming we have an asset, what should we do with it – keep it and use it, or sell it?*

The answer to this question will depend on what would result in the most money for the entity. If we keep it and use it, the benefit is best measured by the economic value method, since this measures the value in use. If we sell, the most appropriate valuation will be the NRV. The higher of these two represents the greatest benefit we could derive from the asset, and is called the recoverable amount.

2 *Assuming we were deprived of the asset, would we replace it?*

The answer to this second question depends on whether the cost of replacement is more or less than the recoverable amount. If it is less, then it is economically logical to replace the asset, since we can recover more from either using it or selling it than it costs to acquire in the first place. In this case, the most appropriate valuation will be replacement cost. Otherwise, the best valuation will be the recoverable amount, because the consequent non-replacement leaves us with recoverable amount as the best we can do with the asset we are attempting to value.

Activity 13.3

A property company owns two plots of land, in Leeds and Bradford, with the following values. It is aware that property prices bear little resemblance to historical costs and therefore wishes to value its property on a deprival value basis.

	Leeds	Bradford
Original cost	£730,000	£185,000
Replacement cost	£815,000	£170,000
Net realisable value	£775,000	£165,000
Estimated economic value (value in use)	£800,000	£180,000

Select the best answer from the list below of respective deprival values for the plots in Leeds and Bradford:

1 £730,000 and £180,000.

2 £800,000 and £170,000.

3 £815,000 and £170,000.

4 £775,000 and £185,000.

5 None of the above.

Answer

Deprival value is the lower of replacement cost and recoverable amount, where the recoverable amount is the higher of net realisable value and economic value. For Leeds, recoverable amount is therefore the higher of £775,000 and £800,000, i.e. £800,000, and this is lower than the replacement cost of £815,000. The deprival value for Leeds is therefore £800,000. For Bradford, the recoverable amount is the higher of £165,000 and £180,000, i.e. £180,000. Deprival value is then the lower of this and the replacement cost of £170,000, i.e. £170,000. The correct answer is therefore (2) '£800,000 and £170,000'.

Finally, note that, in nearly all cases, the economic value will be greater than the NRV – if it were not then few enterprises would be using any asset, since they could derive more from it by selling it second-hand, and this is obviously not the case. In other words, the recoverable amount will usually be economic value. Furthermore, when this economic value is then compared with the replacement cost, the outcome will usually be that the replacement cost is lower. If this were not so, then no entity would be buying any asset, and this is again patently not so. In the great majority of cases, therefore, deprival value can be equated with replacement cost.

We therefore have a single, logically coherent alternative to historical cost. This alternative has so far been used in accounting for two things. First, it has been used to help clarify general thinking on asset valuation. Second, and more practically, it has been applied to help address the distortions caused to historical cost accounting by changing prices. The next section of this chapter is thus concerned with a brief look at inflation accounting.

Inflation accounting

Inflation accounting is accounting that makes specific allowances for the effects of inflation. As we will see, it actually includes allowances for changes in prices which are specific to a particular entity. To be pedantic, such accounting is not strictly 'inflation accounting' because inflation is defined as a persistent and *general* rise in prices. Nevertheless, any accounting that makes some explicit allowance for changes in prices, whether general or not, is commonly referred to as inflation accounting.

The need for inflation accounting arises out of the distortions caused within historical cost accounting. Specifically, there are two accounting effects. First, if we buy an asset and record it at historical cost, then its reported value will be increasingly out of date, and often materially lower than a current valuation such as deprival value. Similarly, a liability such as a loan will be recorded in our accounts at its original historical value. A loan of £20,000, for example, is the amount we will show in our statement of financial position and it is also the amount we will repay, despite the fact that each of the £s we repay will, in real terms, be worth less than each of the £s that we borrowed.

Second, inflation will also have an effect on our real profits. Revenues will be in current terms, i.e. we will sell at today's prices, but the cost of sales will be based on historical cost, i.e. at the date, a little while ago, when we bought the goods we're now selling. We are therefore not comparing like with like, and the effect will be to relatively understate the cost of sales, and so to overstate reported profit. Further, the depreciation charge will be based on a historical asset cost, and thus understated in current terms. Again, the net effect will be to overstate the reported profit. To understand these points more fully, try the next two activities one after the other.

Activity 13.4

Realia Ltd recorded sales of £480,000, and purchases of £360,000. Its opening inventory cost £30,000 and its closing inventory was valued at £35,000. Depreciation was to be provided at 10% straight line on assets which cost £160,000, and other expenses totalled £72,000. Use these figures to prepare a historical cost statement of comprehensive income for the year.

Answer

This should have been a fairly easy exercise, and your answer should be the same as ours, that is:

REALIA LTD
HISTORICAL COST STATEMENT OF COMPREHENSIVE INCOME FOR THE YEAR

Sales		480,000
Cost of sales:		
Opening inventory	30,000	
Purchases	360,000	
	390,000	
Closing inventory	35,000	
		355,000
Gross profit		125,000
Depreciation (10% × 160,000)	16,000	
Other expenses	72,000	
		88,000
Historical cost net profit		37,000

Now we take some account of inflation. It seems reasonable to assume that sales, purchases and other expenses took place fairly steadily through the year. Some sales, purchases and expenses will then have taken place early in the year, when prices were relatively low, and some towards the end of the year, when prices were high. Assuming that prices rose fairly steadily through-out the year, and given our first assumption, we can then also assume that the typical transaction took place half-way through the year, at an average price level. In other words, the sales, purchases and other expenses shown in our statement of comprehensive income are stated at average prices.

However, the opening inventory would be stated at its cost when bought, some time before the beginning of the year, and the closing inventory at a cost that reflects the price level towards the end of the year, when the closing inventory was probably bought. Furthermore, the underlying price level for the depreciation would be that when the non-current assets were bought, which could well have been many years ago. The traditional historical cost statement of comprehensive income ignores these differences in price levels, and so does not actually compare like with like.

If we want a more meaningful statement of comprehensive income, then one answer would be to restate the opening and closing inventory and the depreciation so that they reflect average, mid-year prices, in the same way that the sales, purchases and other expenses implicitly do.

*A*ctivity 13.5

Realia Ltd knows that if it had bought its opening inventory at mid-year prices, it would have cost £33,000, and the closing inventory at mid-year prices would have cost £32,000. Finally, it also knows that the cost of its non-current assets at mid-year prices would have been £250,000. Use these figures to redraft the statement of comprehensive income for Realia Ltd. When you have done that, compare it with the original historical cost statement. Which gives the more true and fair view?

Answer

REALIA LTD

PRICE ADJUSTED STATEMENT OF COMPREHENSIVE INCOME FOR THE YEAR

Sales		480,000
Cost of sales:		
Opening inventory	33,000	
Purchases	360,000	
	393,000	
Closing inventory	32,000	
		361,000
Gross profit		119,000
Depreciation (10% × 250,000)	25,000	
Other expenses	72,000	
		97,000
Price adjusted net profit		22,000

It is our view that the price-adjusted statement presents a more true and fair view, simply because it makes at least some allowance for the fact that the accountant's unit of measurement, the £, changes in size from year to year, because of inflation. The historical cost statement of comprehensive income is presented for all UK companies, and most other entities, but it is distorted whenever inflation is material.

Accountants in the UK have had two major attempts to address this distortion. The first was an approach known as current purchasing power (CPP). If the root problem is that the real value of a £ falls with inflation, then an obvious way to counteract the effects of this would seem to be to develop a system of accounting that uses a unit of currency that is, by definition, current. Monetary items, that is, items whose values are expressed and fixed in nominal money terms, such as the £20,000 loan we considered above, always have the same nominal and real value, so need no adjustment. By contrast, non-monetary items, such as non-current assets and inventory whose value is not given by the number of £s attached to them, should be index-linked using a general index of inflation. This index linking then compensates for the fall in the value of each £ by attaching a correspondingly greater number of them to each non-monetary item.

The following example provides a further illustration of the points we have been covering in the last two activities. In particular, it provides a good overview of the alternative approaches that have been taken to accounting under changing prices.

A company begins the year with share capital of £100 and £100 worth of newly purchased inventory. Inflation during the year is 5%. The company sells the inventory at the end of the year for £200. Replacement cost of the inventory is £150.

OPENING STATEMENT OF FINANCIAL POSITION

Newly purchased inventory	100
Share capital	100

Traditional historical cost accounting

STATEMENT OF COMPREHENSIVE INCOME

Sales	200
Less: cost of sales	100
Nominal money profit	100

Current purchasing power

STATEMENT OF COMPREHENSIVE INCOME

Sales	200
Less: cost of sales	105
Current purchasing power profit	95

What the CPP method thus does is uplift the cost of sales by the rate of inflation, so that it is expressed in something like current terms, i.e. the same terms as the sales. Notice that the effect, when compared with the traditional historical cost accounting approach is to reduce the reported profit by £5. The policy prescription here is that this company should pay a maximum dividend of only £95, not £100. Paying out all the historical cost profit of £100 would, in fact, amount to a distribution of capital. In other words, £5 of the profit would not be a return on capital but a return of capital.

Notice that paying out a dividend of £100 would leave the statement of financial position total at £100, which is what we started the business with, and it would seem that we have therefore maintained capital. In a historical cost world this is true. However, CPP takes the view that true capital maintenance should maintain the original £100 adjusted by 5% inflation, i.e. £105. The CPP profit calculated above is therefore the most we should distribute if we are to maintain CPP capital.

CPP formed the basis of Statement of Standard Accounting Practice 7 (SSAP 7) but was short lived. The main reasons for its lack of acceptance by accounts preparers and users were:

▶ The use of a general index, such as the retail price index (RPI), is strictly only relevant to a mythical average entity. No business or individual actually experiences average inflation – it always depends on what you buy in a particular period. SSAP 7, however, explicitly required the use of the RPI.

▶ It is not directly relevant to the needs of the specific business, since CPP does not aim to maintain the capital of each particular business, but only of the mythical average business. Organisations in the information technology market tend to experience falling prices, even when inflation is positive. CPP accounting would require even these organisations to account for rising prices.

▶ The process is not easy to understand, takes time to implement, and is therefore expensive.

The issue of the non-specific nature of CPP was addressed by the second attempt at inflation accounting, namely **current cost accounting (CCA)**. This was implemented by SSAP 16 in 1980, and was longer lasting. The essential difference between CPP and CCA is that the latter has a very different view of the capital it is trying to maintain. CCA assumes that the issue is less to maintain the purchasing power of the entity (and hence of its owners), than to maintain the ability of the entity to physically do the same things this year as it could last year. If our physical infrastructure allowed us to produce 10,000 tables last year, then the point is to ensure that we can produce the same number again this year, and the money capital needed to do that is incidental.

This 'operating capability' approach implies a basis of valuation which rests on 'value to the business', i.e. what an asset can do, rather than what it cost. SSAP 16 took the view that this means deprival value. We saw earlier in this chapter that deprival value tends, in practice, to equate with replacement cost. CCA therefore uses replacement cost as a basis for valuing both assets and expenses. Using the same example as before, we can again calculate the reported profit, this time using CCA.

Physical capital maintenance

STATEMENT OF COMPREHENSIVE INCOME

Sales	200
Less: cost of sales	150
Current cost operating profit	50

The policy prescription in this case is even more stark. The entity should only distribute a maximum dividend of £50 if it is to maintain the real value of its net assets. SSAP 16 set out a number of adjustments to profit to ensure that funds are retained to allow for:

▶ replacing inventory despite the fact that its price has risen – as above

▶ replacing non-current assets, despite the fact that their prices have risen

▶ funding working capital, despite the fact that the absolute amount will have risen in terms of nominal £s.

It also uplifted the value of non-current assets and inventory in the statement of financial position to ensure that they are fairly represented at something close to their current values, rather than their historical values. All these adjustments will, in principle, make the inflation-adjusted accounts more reliable, and perhaps more relevant. However, the increased complexity does also make them less understandable. This was not the only problem with CCA accounting as implemented by SSAP 16. In summary the problems were:

▶ Complexity and hence lower understandability, as above.

▶ The provision of both the traditional, historical cost profit and an inflation-adjusted profit, as above. The provision of two profits in the same set of accounts did not improve either the credibility or the understandability of those accounts.

▶ The fact that tax continued to be levied on the historical cost profit.

▶ The conceptual difficulty of much of the process.

▶ The consequent time and expense involved in the production of inflation-adjusted accounts.

As a result of these problems, many companies stopped producing inflation-adjusted accounts around 1983 and 1984. The fact that inflation began to fall probably helped their decision. They were, of course, still producing historical cost accounts, so users had what they were used to. Finally, the Accounting Standards Committee accepted the demise of the standard, and it was formally withdrawn in 1988. Nevertheless, that was not the end of inflation accounting. IAS 29 'Financial Accounting in Hyperinflationary

Economies' requires companies to use what is essentially CPP accounting where inflation is significant. 'Significant' is primarily defined as a rate of inflation of more than 100% over three years. In other words, inflation and inflation accounting are continuing issues.

This section on inflation accounting has only scratched the surface of an extensive and difficult topic. Nevertheless, you may have had trouble following the arguments. If so, you are not alone, but a broad understanding of the issues that were tackled will help you in any further studies of accounting. As a final brief check on your understanding, try the following activity.

Activity 13.6

Choose the most appropriate response from those listed below. The method of asset valuation which best measures the operating capability of a business is:

1 Net realisable value.

2 Replacement cost.

3 Deprival value.

4 Recoverable amount.

5 None of the above.

Answer

SSAP 16 'Current Cost Accounting' was based on the idea of maintaining the operating capability, and suggested that assets should be valued at their value to the business. This is then defined as net current replacement cost, or, if lower, recoverable amount. In other words, value to the business is based on the deprival value model, and answer (3) is therefore correct. Deprival value will usually turn out to be replacement cost, so choice (2) is reasonable but not strictly correct.

Current thinking on the future of inflation accounting appears to be that a return to something like SSAP 7 or 16 is unlikely, because of the complexity and widespread scepticism among accountants over the value of the consequent financial statements. Nevertheless, as we saw above, when inflation again becomes significant there will be a need to allow in some form for the distortions that we have seen occur under historical cost accounting. One possible, albeit partial, answer would be to regularly revalue all non-current assets to some current value, probably replacement cost.

The rationale for this is that non-current assets tend to cost a lot in the first place, and then inflation impacts on them for their relatively long lives. Allowing for the effects of inflation on non-current assets would therefore address a large part of the distortion. It would ensure that the non-current assets are presented at an up-to-date figure in the statement of financial position, and that the depreciation charge reflects this more current amount. The next part of this chapter deals with the accounting for such revaluations.

Accounting for revaluations

When we revalue an asset our aim is primarily to restate the asset in the statement of financial position at a current value. In times of rising prices, this will mean an adjustment upwards. An incidental issue is that the same depreciation policy will then be applied to the higher amount and will itself be a larger charge in the statement of comprehensive income, so resulting in a smaller reported profit. The best way to see all this is to follow an example.

Asif owns a building which cost £400,000 on 1 January 20X0. The depreciation policy has always been to write off the building over 40 years on a straight-line basis. In the ledger accounts for the year ended 31 December 20X6, the following amounts will therefore appear, before any year-end adjustments.

BUILDING AT COST

1.1.X0	Cost	400,000		

PROVISION FOR DEPRECIATION

			1.1.X6 Balance b/f (*)	60,000

* Six years' depreciation at £10,000 per year (400,000/40)

As part of the year-end accounting, Asif values the building at £540,000, and considers that the remaining useful life is another 30 years including 20X6. The first matter is to revalue the buildings in the books. The key to doing this is to open a revaluation account, which will hold the uplift in value from the present net book value (NBV) to the new valuation. Note that this uplift is therefore not £140,000 (540,000 – 400,000), but £200,000 (540,000 – 340,000 (NBV)). The necessary entries will be:

BUILDING AT VALUATION

1.1.X0	Cost	400,000	
31.12.X6	Revaluation account	140,000	
		540,000	

PROVISION FOR DEPRECIATION

31.12.X6	Revaluation account	60,000	1.1.X6 Balance b/f	60,000
			31.12.X6 Statement of comprehensive income	18,000

REVALUATION ACCOUNT

		31.12.X6 Buildings	140,000
		31.12.X6 Depreciation	60,000
			200,000

You should be able to follow what is going on here. The building account is uplifted to the value we want, with the corresponding credit going to the revaluation account. Notice also, however, that the provision for depreciation account is cleared out, with another credit going to the revaluation account, giving the total uplift on that account of £200,000. Finally, since we have benefited from the building during 20X6, we must match some charge against that benefit. In other words, we must make a depreciation charge for 20X6.

You may object that we have only just got the value up to where we wanted it and this seems to be immediately reducing it. True, but remember that the purpose of depreciation is not to get the right value in the statement of financial position, but to match a cost in the statement of comprehensive income to reflect the using up of the asset in earning the benefits that appear in the statement of comprehensive income. This depreciation charge will be based on the revised estimate of a 30-year life, and will therefore be £18,000, i.e. 540,000/30. This is shown in the provision for depreciation account above.

Incidentally, note that the increase in the revaluation reserve of £200,000 is a non-trading result of the year, so will be reported in the 'other comprehensive income' part of the statement of comprehensive income.

It may be that we subsequently sell the building. The way to deal with this is to open one final account, namely the sale of assets account. Assuming Asif sells the building on 1 September 20X7 for £500,000, the accounting will be:

BUILDING AT VALUATION

1.1.X0	Cost	400,000			
31.12.X6	Revaluation account	140,000			
		540,000	1.9.X7	Sale of assets	540,000

PROVISION FOR DEPRECIATION

31.12.X6	Revaluation account	60,000	1.1.X6	Balance b/f	60,000
1.9.X7	Sale of assets	18,000	31.12.X6	Statement of comprehensive income	18,000

REVALUATION ACCOUNT

1.9.X7	Revenue reserve	200,000	31.12.X6	Buildings	140,000
			31.12.X6	Depreciation	60,000
		200,000			200,000

SALE OF ASSETS

1.9.X7	Building	540,000	1.9.X7	Bank	500,000
			1.9.X7	Depreciation	18,000
			1.9.X7	Loss to Statement of comprehensive income	22,000
		540,000			540,000

The additional entries are mostly straightforward. The balances on the building account and on the provision for depreciation account are transferred to the sale of assets account. The proceeds are debited in the bank account and credited in the sale of assets account. In common with generally accepted practice, no depreciation is charged in the year of disposal. The resulting balance on the sale of assets account then represents the profit or loss on the sale of the building, and is shown in the statement of comprehensive income for the year. In this case it is a loss of £22,000.

The treatment of the balance of £200,000 on the revaluation account is contentious. There are two possibilities:

1 Clear it by transfer to the sale of assets account. Note that this would make the balance on the sale of assets account a credit of £178,000, so that we would report a profit of this amount in the statement of comprehensive income for the year. This is the difference between the cost of £400,000, less the total depreciation charged over the years of £78,000 (60,000 + 18,000), i.e. £322,000, and the proceeds of £500,000. You might think there is some logic to this.

2 Clear it by transfer direct to the revenue reserve. In this way it will not be reported as part of the profit for the year. This is what we have done above. The logic of this approach is that the building is now considered to be worth £540,000 (less depreciation) to Asif, and it is this amount that should be compared with the proceeds. The £540,000, less depreciation, is known as the 'carrying value'.

The treatment of the balance on the revaluation reserve obviously makes a material difference to the profit for the year, and most businesses would probably want to use method 1 above. However, the IASB prefers the logic of method 2, and IAS 16 'Property, Plant and Equipment' requires that approach. Nevertheless, in order to disclose what the situation would have been if we had used historical cost, good practice requires that the historical cost figures should be shown as a note to the accounts. In Asif's case, this would allow for showing a loss of £22,000 in the statement of comprehensive income and a profit of £178,000 as a note of historical cost profit. Notice that the difference between the two results is, of course, the balance of the revaluation account.

Activity 13.7

Faraday Ltd has always prepared its final accounts to 31 March. The company bought a building on 1 April 20X3 for £72,000. Its depreciation policy on buildings has always been to depreciate at 10% p.a. on a reducing balance basis, but no depreciation is ever charged in the year of a disposal.

When preparing the final accounts for the year ended 31 March 20X6, before any depreciation had been charged for that year, it was decided to revalue the building to £100,000. On 1 September 20X6, the company sold the building for £95,000.

▶

Write up the ledger accounts for all years up to and including the year ended 31 March 20X7, including all opening and closing balances, for:

▶ Building account.

▶ Provision for depreciation account.

▶ Revaluation account.

▶ Sale of asset account.

Indicate how the balances would be dealt with in the final accounts at 31 March 20X6.

Answer

You will learn more easily and more effectively if you try this activity before you look at the answer. It's your choice!

BUILDING

1.4.X3	Cost	72,000			
31.3.X6	Revaluation account	28,000	1.9.X6	Sale of asset	100,000
		100,000			100,000

PROVISION FOR DEPRECIATION

			31.3.X4	Statement of comprehensive income	7,200
31.3.X6	Revaluation account	13,680	31.3.X5	Statement of comprehensive income	6,480
		13,680			13,680
1.9.X6	Sale of asset	10,000	31.3.X6	Statement of comprehensive income	10,000

REVALUATION

			31.3.X6	Cost	28,000
1.9.X6	Revenue reserve	41,680	31.3.X6	Depreciation	13,680
		41,680			41,680

SALE OF ASSET

1.9.X6	Building	100,000	1.9.X6	Depreciation	10,000
1.9.X6	Profit – Statement of comprehensive income	5,000	1.9.X6	Bank	95,000
		105,000			105,000

You should be able to follow our answer, since the logic is the same as in the Asif example. Remember that reducing balance depreciation takes a fixed percentage of the net book value every year.

In the statement of financial position at 31 March 20X6, the building and depreciation will be shown under non-current assets as usual, except that it will be described as being 'at valuation', rather than as 'at cost'. The revaluation account is a capital reserve (i.e. not available for dividend payments), and will be shown with shareholders' funds.

There is just one matter remaining to be dealt with in this chapter, and that is the further reporting of revaluation gains, and similar gains and losses. We saw above that a revaluation gain recognised in the year should not only appear as a reserve in the statement of financial position, but should also be reported in the 'other comprehensive income' part of the statement of comprehensive income. This gain will, of course, increase the total shareholders' funds, since it will finish up in the revaluation reserve, and will complement the increase in shareholders' funds that arises from the trading profit being added to the revenue reserve. Bearing in mind that shareholders' funds, also known as equity, will also change as a result of any changes in share capital, then this is all getting a bit complex. Specifically, it can be difficult to keep track of what's happened to equity during the year. Consequently, we prepare a summary of such changes, known as the statement of changes in equity.

Statement of changes in equity

You may recall from Chapter 4 that this statement is identified as one of the four primary statements in IAS 1, along with the statement of financial position, statement of comprehensive income and statement of cash flows. It complements the statement of comprehensive income by including not just the realised and unrealised gains and losses for the year but also reconciles these changes to the opening and closing balances of equity.

If, continuing the same example as above, Asif had:

▶ recognised a revaluation gain of £200,000, as above
▶ reported a realised trading profit of £145,000 for the year ended 31 December 20X6
▶ an opening balance on the revenue reserve of £550,000
▶ opening share capital of £40,000, but no share premium reserve
▶ issued 20,000 new £1 shares for £2.40 each

then the statement of changes in equity for the year ended 31 December 20X6 would be:

	Share capital	Share premium	Revaluation reserve	Revenue reserve	Total
Opening balance	40,000			550,000	590,000
Trading profit				145,000	145,000
Revaluation gain			200,000		200,000
Share issue	20,000	28,000 (20,000 × £1.40)			48,000
Closing balance	60,000	28,000	200,000	695,000	983,000

Such a short and simple statement will often be all that is needed. Indeed, if there are no unrealised gains or losses, the company will simply report this fact, instead of producing the statement. In more complex enterprises, you may come across gains and losses on foreign exchange, which we looked at briefly back in Chapter 3.

Summary

This has been a wide-ranging chapter, covering some difficult ideas. We have followed a train of argument covering:

▶ an introduction to the theory of valuation and concentrated on the new ideas of economic value and deprival value

▶ a major application of these ideas, namely inflation accounting

▶ the need for some allowance for changing prices in our accounting, and the main efforts that have so far been made to tackle the problems

▶ a look at the uses and mechanics of revaluations needed if our assets and profits are to reflect at least some changing values

▶ the statement of changes in equity.

In Chapter 14 we shift the emphasis of study, and consider the need for and techniques of control in accounting.

Key terms

economic value (p. 274)
value in use (p. 274)
time value of money (p. 275)
deprival value (p. 276)

current purchasing power (CPP) (p. 281)
current cost accounting (CCA) (p. 282)
statement of changes in equity (p. 289)

Self-assessment questions

1 It is conceivable that UK accounting and reporting for non-current assets could be changed to a system based on one of the valuation methods dealt with in this chapter, perhaps deprival value. List three reasons for such a change, and three reasons for retaining historical cost as the base method of valuation.

2 Jerome plc bought a large plot of freehold land for £3,600,000 on which Jerome intends to build a storage depot. The land was bought just before news was released of a new road link, and the neighbouring plot, which is very similar, is now on the market at £4,700,000. Indeed, Jerome has been offered £4,200,000 for its own plot. However, Jerome intends to build on the new plot because it is believed that the present value of future inflows just from the land will amount to at least £5,000,000.

   Jerome's only other major asset at the moment is a fleet of delivery lorries, for which a total of £1,300,000 was paid at various times over the past year. Prices of new lorries have not moved significantly since then, but the transport manager estimates that the second-hand value of the existing fleet is only about £800,000. More positively, she has estimated the net benefit of the fleet at £1,100,000 in present value terms. The lorries have a useful life of about four years.

   (a) Draft the historical cost and deprival value statement of financial positions for Jerome, including depreciation where appropriate.

   (b) Assuming Jerome originally recorded all assets on a historical cost basis, but, after preparing the statement of financial position, wishes to revalue them on an undepreciated deprival value basis, show the Revaluation Account.

3 Holderness Ltd prepares its final accounts to 31 December. The company bought a building on 1 January 20X7 for £520,000. Its depreciation policy on buildings has always been to depreciate at 5% p.a. on a straight-line basis, but no depreciation is charged in the year of a disposal.

   When preparing the Final Accounts for the year ended 31 December 20X8, before any depreciation had been charged for that year, it was decided to revalue the building to its estimated replacement cost of £800,000. On 1 September 20X9, the company sold the building for £750,000.

   Required

   (a) Write up the ledger accounts for the years ended 31 December 20X7 to 20X9, including all opening and closing balances, for:

   ▶ asset cost account

   ▶ provision for depreciation account

   ▶ revaluation account

   ▶ sale of asset account.

   (b) Indicate how the balances would be dealt with in the Final Accounts at 31 December 20X9.

   (c) Briefly outline the alternative bases of valuation that Holderness could have used at 31 December 20X8, instead of replacement cost.

4 **(a)** Outline the problems with historical cost accounting. (You may find it helpful to refer back to Chapter 4 as well as Chapter 13.)

(b) Mystron Products has prepared its Trading Account for its first year of trading in traditional historical cost terms, and this is set out below:

Sales		400,000
Purchases	340,000	
Closing inventory	80,000	
		260,000
Gross profit		140,000

Sales and purchases were made steadily throughout the year. General inflation ran at 10% through the year. The closing inventory could have been bought for about £65,000 in average price terms.

Restate the Trading account on a current cost accounting (CCA) basis.

(c) Which of the profits, the historical cost figure of £140,000 or the CCA figure you have calculated, gives the most true and fair view of Mystron Products' trading activities for the year? Justify your decision.

Answers to these questions can be found at the back of this book.

14

Control of accounting systems

Objectives

By the end of this chapter you should be able to:

▶ Outline the main features of control in a financial accounting system.

▶ Explain the function of internal and external audit.

▶ Prepare a bank reconciliation statement.

▶ Prepare control accounts.

▶ Calculate a statement of affairs and profit from incomplete records.

Introduction

So far in this book we have tended to assume that bookkeeping procedures and the preparation of final accounts will be carried out by competent people of integrity, who never make mistakes. This is obviously unlikely. This chapter therefore deals with the issue of the controls in accounting systems, which enable us to address the effects of any failings.

Many of the techniques that we examine in this chapter have their roots in traditional manual accounting systems. Such systems are becoming increasingly rare, in any but the smallest organisations, because of the growing cost-effectiveness of computer-based systems. Nevertheless, the principles of control remain, although they may be implemented very differently in a computer system. This chapter looks at the basic principles and at how they have traditionally been applied, and Chapter 15 explores the impact on such controls of the introduction of computers to accounting.

The need for controls

We identified above three requirements of those involved in the accounting function if financial statements are to show a true and fair view. These are requirements in terms of:

▶ avoidance of mistakes

▶ competence

▶ integrity.

It is worth considering a response to each of these requirements in turn. First, it is as common for accountants to make mistakes as for anyone else. Arithmetic errors are probably less common since the advent of computers, but errors of principle are still possible. Errors of principle include, for example, entering a transaction twice, or omitting it entirely, or making an entry in the wrong account. It would be quite possible, for instance, to record a purchase invoice from J. Smith as a purchase invoice from a supplier called L. Smith.

Some errors, such as a one-legged entry, i.e. entering only the debit or only the credit, will be shown up by a trial balance that does not balance. The trial balance is thus a basic, but very effective, control on the accuracy of bookkeeping. If you are unsure exactly what a trial balance looks like and how it is constructed, you can, and should, revise it now from Chapter 5. There are two other widely used controls, the bank reconciliation and control accounts, which we study later in this chapter. We noted back in Chapter 3 that information technology can help us to reduce such errors, and we will look at this topic in more detail in Chapter 15.

Second, financial statements can fail to show a true and fair view because of a lack of technical ability on the part of those involved in their preparation. Mistakes can be made even if you know what you are supposed to be doing, but they are more likely if you are unsure about appropriate techniques of accounting and the rules concerning the presentation of financial information. Third, those involved in the preparation of financial statements may be tempted to bend those rules in order to present a more favourable picture of the entity. If your annual bonus is linked to the reported profit of your organisation, you may occasionally be tempted to adopt an accounting treatment that results in a higher profit, rather than one that you objectively believe to show a more true and fair view. Both of these possibilities are, in principle, addressed by the existence of audit. However, not only do company employees occasionally bend the rules, but auditors have also been known to do so. Furthermore, as we'll see, not all businesses, and not even all companies, are required to have an audit. Accordingly, it is worth being clear about what audit is supposed to achieve.

Audit

There are two types of **audit**, external and internal. External audit is carried out by persons from outside the organisation, who should be both expert and independent. They investigate the accounting systems and transactions and then ensure that the financial statements have been prepared in accordance with the underlying books, and with the law and accounting standards. The purpose of an external audit is for the auditor to be in a position to express an opinion on whether the financial statements being reported on show a true and fair view or not. A satisfactory 'clean' audit report provides considerable reassurance to the users of the accounts that those accounts are reliable. This is so obviously fundamental to the purpose of financial statements that an external audit is required by the Companies Act. This Act requires all limited companies, except those with turnover below £6.5m and a statement of financial position total of less than £3.26m, to have, and to pay for, an external audit. The Act then requires the auditors to report to the shareholders of the company on whether, in their opinion, the financial statements do actually show a true and fair view.

The above is the position as it currently operates in the UK. However, this should be seen in the context of auditing world-wide. For example, if we audit a company in the UK which has a subsidiary in Australia, the group accounts will combine the UK company's accounts with those of the Australian company and we will want to audit both so that the combined group accounts have credibility. We could fly out to Australia to do this or we could use Australian auditors to do the work on our behalf. This means that we need to be sure that audit practices in Australia, and in any other country where we may be involved, are consistent with UK auditing practices. To this end, just as international accounting standards set rules for international accounting, so International Standards of Auditing, published by the International Auditing and Assurance Standards Board, set rules for international auditing.

Notice what the purpose of an external audit is not. It is not an attempt to find fraud, and it is not a management control. Fraud may be discovered during an audit, and the auditor will usually be well placed to give advice to management about potential improvements in the internal control systems, but these benefits are incidental. The auditor's report is addressed, not to the management, but to the members (shareholders). Nevertheless, the reassurance as to the truth and fairness of the statements will usually also be of value to all the other users of those statements, that is, all the users we considered back in Chapter 1.

However, as you may know, such reassurance is not always given by an audit. Recent failures of the audit process to detect and report poor accounting have damaged users' confidence in the validity of financial statements. Failures at Enron and WorldCom in the US, for example, have led many to question whether such failures could happen in the UK.

Internal audit is a management tool, which aims to verify that accounting procedures are being carried out as they should be. It often has the incidental benefit of recommending improvements to those systems. Internal auditors tend to be found only in larger organisations, where the cost is justified by the benefits of monitoring relatively complex accounting systems. Standards and procedures in internal audit are thus a matter for the management of individual organisations to determine, whereas external audit is governed by extensive regulation. A detailed exposition of audit regulation would fill this book, and would probably not thrill you. What follows is a brief summary of the major issues that you should appreciate in relation to external audit, arranged under three headings: Who are external auditors?; Procedures of external audit; and Reporting of external audit.

Who are external auditors?

The essential point is that external auditors should be both expert and independent. The Companies Act empowers the Secretary of State to nominate 'recognised supervisory bodies', whose members can audit UK companies, provided they are registered as auditors with those bodies. The relevant bodies at the moment are:

▶ Institute of Chartered Accountants in England and Wales (ICAEW).

▶ Institute of Chartered Accountants of Scotland (ICAS).

▶ Institute of Chartered Accountants in Ireland (ICAI).

▶ Association of Chartered Certified Accountants (ACCA).

Independence should be ensured by the requirement in the Companies Act that an 'officer or servant' (i.e. an employee) of the company, or their partner or employee, is ineligible for appointment as auditor of a company. Furthermore, they should not normally be reliant on the one company for more than 15% of their total income.

It has been proposed by the EU that preparing the accounting records of audit clients should be prohibited, although it is currently permitted by the professional bodies. The objective of the proposal is to prevent accountants from suppressing information, or failing to notice their own errors, by insisting that audits should be carried out by someone independent of the preparer of the accounts. It is supported by many other EU countries.

Auditors are notionally appointed by, and report to, the shareholders of the company. A simple majority vote at the company's annual general meeting (AGM) is sufficient to appoint, or remove, them. In practice, the choice of auditors is often delegated to the directors. Indeed, the Companies Act allows directors to appoint auditors if a vacancy occurs between general meetings. Such vacancies usually occur because the auditor has resigned. They may do this at any time, provided they confirm to the shareholders that there are no matters connected with the resignation that the shareholders should be aware of. This language can be interpreted to mean that auditors should tell the shareholders if the directors are pressurising the auditors to resign, perhaps because they are finding evidence of a lack of total integrity.

Procedures of external audit

The Auditing Practices Board is to auditing what the Accounting Standards Board is to accounting. It has published mandatory 'Auditing Standards', on a wide range of audit topics and practices. From December 2004 it has been working with 'International Standards on Auditing' (ISAs), which are more in line with international practice on auditing, albeit contextualised for the UK and Ireland. The detail of these standards is beyond the scope of this book, but note that the practice of auditing is increasingly becoming as tightly regulated as the practice of accounting. Of particular importance is ISA 700 'The Auditor's Report on Financial Statements', which details the procedures for the audit report.

Reporting of external audit

The audit report is the auditor's opinion, addressed to the shareholders, on whether the financial statements show a true and fair view. According to ISA 700, the audit report should state:

▶ which financial statements have been audited

▶ an emphasis that it is the management's responsibility to prepare the financial statements and the auditors' purely to audit them

▶ the fact of compliance with auditing standards in doing the audit

▶ a brief overview of the work done to provide the auditor with the evidence for the opinion

▶ the audit opinion

▶ the identity of the auditor, and the date of the report.

Where an issue arises during the audit which does not affect the opinion but the auditor believes that it needs to be brought to the attention of readers, then the audit report will include an 'emphasis of matter', which outlines the issue. A typical example might be uncertainty over future loans from the bank; if such loans can be raised the company will be a going concern, but any significant uncertainty arguably needs to be emphasised.

More seriously, a modified audit report is one in which the auditor has reservations that have a material effect on the financial statements. The circumstances giving rise to a qualification will typically be where:

▶ there is a limitation on the scope of the audit, and hence an unresolvable uncertainty, which prevents the auditor from forming an opinion, or

▶ where the auditor is able to form an opinion but, even after negotiation with the directors, disagrees with the financial statements.

In such cases the audit report will be modified in one of the following ways:

▶ where the issue is so serious as to affect the audit opinion then the audit report should be modified to say 'except for' the issue the financial statements provide a true and fair view,

▶ where the auditor believes that the issue is so fundamental that its misstatement invalidates the whole financial statements, then the opinion should say that the financial statements do not give a true and fair view,

▶ where there were significant restrictions on the scope of the audit the report should say that the auditor was unable to form an opinion.

A*ctivity 14.1*

For each of the following situations, decide which audit report you, as auditor, would give. Following on from the explanation above, your choices are:

▶ a clean report

▶ an 'except for' report

▶ a 'the accounts do not show a true and fair view' report.

1 The inclusion of a material debt from a company that is known to be in liquidation.

2 A fraud involving £1,800 is discovered in a large public company.

3 Controls over the cash accounting system were found to be non-existent, and records incompletely kept, so that there was no way of verifying the amount of cash sales included in the accounts.

4 In a supermarket chain, inventory has been valued at selling price, which is very much higher than cost.

Answer

First, we should say that making a judgement about the correct form of audit report is a highly skilled activity, requiring extensive knowledge and experience. In particular, any judgement needs to be made in the light of the overall impact on the accounts, and particularly of the materiality of each issue. In the absence of such fuller information, our answers can be no more than good indications of what an auditor would probably decide. Furthermore, we have only attempted to cover the main features of an audit report, and you should be aware that more complex audit opinions are possible. These, however, would be the subject of a specialist book or course in auditing.

Nevertheless, we would write an 'except for' opinion for situations 1 and 3. The inclusion of what is almost certainly a bad debt will result in materially incorrect trade receivables and profit figures, and the accounts are therefore unlikely to show a true and fair view. However, the rest of the accounts will be unaffected, and it should not be necessary to give an adverse opinion. In situation 3, the cash sales figure may well be right, but we have been unable to determine this, so our report should explain this problem of a limitation on the scope of our audit, and again report that 'except for' this issue, the accounts show a true and fair view.

Situation 2 is easier, in that a mis-statement of £1,800 will almost certainly not have a material effect on the truth and fairness of the accounts of a large public company. In this case, the audit report should make no mention of the issue, and a clean report can be given.

Finally, situation 4 is an example of a fundamental mis-statement. Inventory will be a very large item in the accounts of a supermarket, and a treatment that conflicts with IAS 2 'Inventories' will almost certainly have such a pervasive impact on the accounts as to mean that they do not show a true and fair view. The report should therefore be adverse, i.e. 'the accounts do not give a true and fair view'.

A qualified audit report is usually regarded as a serious matter, because it significantly reduces the reliability of the financial statements. This may then mean, for example, that a potential lender will not lend.

Finally, you should be aware that there is a continuing debate over whether an audit is of real benefit to very small companies. The shareholders, to whom the audit report is nominally addressed, tend to also be the directors, managers and much of the workforce. What then is the benefit of using the traditional financial statements to tell them about their business? They already know. If the financial statements are of little value, so must the related audit report be. The counter-argument is that outsiders, such as lenders and the Revenue, are also interested in the business and would benefit from the financial statements, and hence from an audit report that enabled them to rely on the truth and fairness of those statements.

Before we move on from this introduction to auditing, use the following activity to test your basic knowledge

Activity 14.2

Select the best answer or answers in each of the following cases.

1 Which of the following cannot be appointed as a company auditor?

(a) A director.

(b) An employee.

(c) An ex-employee.

(d) A member of the Chartered Institute of Management Accountants.

2 Which of the following circumstances would probably result in a qualified audit report?

(a) The loss of the cash book.

(b) Gross inaccuracies in the register of shareholders.

(c) The omission of a statement of cash flow.

(d) Discovery of the theft of £200 petty cash.

Answer

The correct answers are (a), (b) and (d) for question 1, and (a) and (c) for question 2. If this doesn't make sense, go back and re-read the material above on the audit.

Audit, particularly external audit, can thus have a valuable function in ensuring that financial statements are prepared competently and objectively. As we noted earlier, control to guard against mistakes feeding through the accounting system undetected in the first place can be improved through the use of bank reconciliations and control accounts.

Bank reconciliations

Activity 14.2 demonstrated the fundamental importance of the bank records, that is, our own record of amounts in and out of our bank account. It is possible that deliberate or accidental mistakes will be made in writing it up, but fortunately there is an independent record of exactly the same transactions. That independent record is, of course, the bank statement.

The balance in our bank ledger account should be the same as the balance on the bank statement. This independent record can therefore provide an excellent check on the accuracy and completeness of our bank records. In practice, however, the two balances may not be the same. There may, for example, be amounts we have received and paid into our bank, and which we have therefore entered in the ledger account, but which have not yet cleared through the banking system. The two balances will therefore differ by the amount of the 'uncredited lodgement'. However, if we can identify all such items in transit, we can allow for them and so still reconcile the two balances. Such a summary of items in transit, which reconciles the bank statement balance with our balance, is called a **bank reconciliation** statement. Its purpose is to verify the bank balance in our own books and, by inference, all entries in that account.

Note that our own records of bank transactions were traditionally recorded in a separate 'cash book' and this term is still used to refer to the bank ledger account in our books. In what follows we'll use this term.

Activity 14.3

List four items which might cause the cash book balance not to immediately agree with the balance per the bank statement.

Answer

The items we have identified are as follows:

1 A very common transit item is an unpresented cheque. This is a cheque that you have entered in the cash book but which has not yet been presented to the bank.
2 The opposite item is the uncredited lodgement that we have already seen. This is an amount you have paid in to the bank, and entered in your cash book, but which has not yet been received by the bank and entered on the bank statement.
3 The bank may have charged interest or bank charges, or have given you interest on your account, but you will usually only find out about these when you receive the bank statement. Until you then enter them in the cash book they will also be sources of difference.
4 You may have made a mistake in writing up your cash book, or the bank statement may be wrong.

There are two broad reasons why these differences occur, and the distinction is crucial. First, there are legitimate reasons, such as items 1, 2 and 3 above. Second, there are mistakes, either by you or by the bank. The purpose of a bank reconciliation statement is to allow for all such legitimate differences. Any residual difference must then have been caused by an error.

Items 1 and 2 in the list above are items that we have entered in our cash book but which the bank has not yet entered on the bank statement. All we can do is list them as part of the reason why the two balances disagree, i.e. they will form part of the bank reconciliation statement. Conversely, item 3 is an item that the bank has entered up but we haven't. We can therefore eliminate this source of difference before we prepare the bank reconciliation statement. In other words, we should complete the writing up of the cash book to take account of items that are so far only on the bank statement. Such items will then no longer be a source of difference.

Activity 14.4

Gloria started business with £200 in her account at the bank. During June she issued the following cheques:

1st	£86 to Garside Books
4th	£480 to Fletcher Cars
13th	£300 to Harker Ltd
27th	£430 to Fletcher Cars
30th	£182 to Plant Supplies

She also recorded the following amounts paid into the bank:

4th	£490 from Darley Building
15th	£38 from a cash sale
20th	£780 from Darley Building
30th	£75 from a cash sale

Write up the cash book, i.e. our own bank ledger account, for the above transactions, remembering to include the opening £200, and to show the closing balance. You should be able to do this by thinking back to what you learnt about the writing up of ledger accounts earlier in this book. Write up the cash book as simply another ledger account.

Answer

CASH BOOK

1st Balance b/f	200	1st Garside Books	86
4th Darley Building	490	4th Fletcher Cars	480
15th Cash sale	38	13th Harker Ltd	300
20th Darley Building	780	27th Fletcher Cars	430
30th Cash sale	75	30th Plant Supplies	182
		30th Balance c/f	105
	1,583		1,583

Activity 14.5

At the end of the month, Gloria receives the following bank statement. Note that it is in overdraft (O/D) at some points during the month, i.e. there is a negative balance. Check each item against the cash book and identify which items are not common.

BANK STATEMENT

Date	Detail	Payments	Receipts	Balance	
1	Balance b/f			200	
4	Cheque	86		114	
6	Cheque	480		366	O/D
8	Counter credit		490	124	
16	Cheque	300		176	O/D
17	Counter credit		38	138	O/D
22	Counter credit		780	642	
30	Cheque	430		212	
30	Charges for June	20		192	

Answer

The items you should have identified are:

▶ The cheque paid out on 30 June to Plant Supplies for £182 is not on the bank statement.
▶ The cash sale of £75 on 30 June similarly does not appear on the bank statement.
▶ The bank statement shows charges of £20, which have not been entered in the cash book, because Gloria did not know about them until she received the bank statement.

Activity 14.6

Recalculate the cash book balance after the bank charges have been entered, i.e. complete the writing up of the cash book.

Answer

The revised balance will be the existing balance of £105, less the bank charges of £20, i.e. the cash book balance, written up as far as Gloria is able, will be £85. It is this amount which we must reconcile to the balance per the bank statement of £192.

Hopefully, we know the reasons for the whole of the difference. It should be attributable to the cheque paid on 30 June and the cash sale paid in on the same date. All that remains is to set these items out formally to prove that this is the case. In order to do so, you need to be aware of how the bank balance is affected by the items in transit. A cheque drawn on our bank account will be deducted from our account balance by our bank. In other words, the balance will go down. Conversely, an uncredited lodgement will increase the bank balance when it reaches the bank. Providing we start with the balance per the bank statement, unpresented cheques should therefore be deducted, and uncredited lodgements should be added.

Activity 14.7

Bearing the above in mind, about the direction of adjustments, draft a bank reconciliation statement for Gloria at 30 June. It should start with the balance per the bank statement, then adjust for the unpresented cheque, and the uncredited lodgement, and so arrive at the balance per the cash book.

Answer

As always, you will learn faster and more easily if you discipline yourself to trying the activity before you look at the answer.

GLORIA
BALANCE RECONCILIATION STATEMENT AT 30 JUNE

Balance per bank statement	192
Less: Unpresented cheque; 30 June, Plant Supplies	182
	10
Add: Uncredited lodgement; 30 June, cash sale	75
Balance per cash book, as adjusted	85

Activity 14.8   Consolidate your knowledge now by outlining the purposes of a bank reconciliation statement. You may find it most helpful to do this by creating a list of the purposes.

Answer   Our suggested list would include these points:

- ▶ The bank reconciliation statement constitutes a comparison between the cash book and the independent bank statement, allowing for items in transit.
- ▶ It thus provides a check on the completeness and accuracy of the cash book.
- ▶ Agreement of the two adjusted balances provides a high level of assurance of the accuracy and completeness of the cash book.
- ▶ Non-agreement of the two adjusted balances indicates an error, probably in the cash book, since errors on bank statements are less frequent.
- ▶ A trial balance difference may have indicated an error somewhere in the accounting system; the same amount showing up as a bank reconciliation difference indicates that any search for an error can be restricted to the bank accounting system.

We thus have a way of verifying the bank account in our books. However, it is still possible that we will make mistakes in the writing up of our other accounts. Fortunately, control accounts provide a way of checking the accuracy of our sales and purchase ledgers.

Control accounts

Think back to your earlier studies about how sales and purchase ledgers are written up. Back in Chapter 5 we saw that the sales ledger is the collecting together of the ledger accounts for our customers, the purchase ledger is the set of ledger accounts for our suppliers, and the nominal ledger is made up of all the remaining accounts.

You should recall that individual accounts in the sales ledger are written up by posting sales invoices and cash receipts from customers. In practice, the sales invoices would not be entered up one by one directly in the sales account and individual customer accounts, but would usually first be listed and summarised. This listing is called a 'sales journal' or 'sales day book'. It does not form part of the double entry system, and so was not covered in the earlier chapters on double entry bookkeeping. Nevertheless, it becomes significant once we turn our attention to control accounts.

This sales journal is no more than a listing of sales invoices as they are sent out, but it does offer the opportunity to total all the invoices, usually monthly, and to post just the total to the sales account, instead of having to post the sales one by one from the individual invoices. Entries into individual customers' accounts would, however, still have to be posted individually, in order to record sales to each customer. Receipts from each customer would, of course, be entered from the cash book, but note that such receipts could also be totalled in the cash book for the month.

In a computer-based system, of course, we would not have to prepare such a separate listing of invoices and cash movements, since the act of entering them into the ledgers would be tracked by the accounting software and such listings would implicitly be created. Control in a computer-based system is something we will explore further in Chapter 15.

Now imagine that, as well as doing all that, for the same month we also posted the total amount of sales invoices from the sales journal and the total amount of receipts from customers in the cash book. In other words, we would make just one total entry from the sales journal, and one total entry from the cash book, to a new account, created for the purpose. This new account is called either a total account or a control account. In this case it would be the sales control account, but you could create a purchases control account using exactly the same principles. The total postings would be from the purchases journal (a listing of purchase invoices) and from the total of payments to suppliers in the cash book.

Notice that we now have two sales ledgers (and two purchase ledgers), one made up of individual accounts, and one made up of the control account. Both of these sales ledgers should record the same transactions, one customer by customer, and one in total, but both for the same month. The implication is that the total of the balances on the individual ledger accounts should add up to the same as the balance on the single control account. This is the point of the control account. What we have created is a check on the accuracy of the individual sales ledger accounts. If the total of the balances on the individual accounts is the same as the balance on the control account, then we can be reasonably confident that the individual accounts have been written up correctly.

This can be invaluable if the trial balance does not agree, and we are therefore faced with looking for one or more mistakes somewhere in the accounting system. If, however, we prepare a sales control account and the balance agrees with the total of individual sales ledger balances, then we can be reasonably confident that the mistakes are not in the sales ledger. This dramatically reduces the search we have to undertake. If we prepare a purchase control and that also agrees with the total of the individual purchase ledger accounts, then we can also eliminate the purchases sub-system as a source of error. We now know the trial balance difference must be somewhere in the nominal ledger, and we can focus our search there. What we have achieved is a way of checking the accuracy of the sales and purchases ledgers in isolation.

It is, of course, always possible that we make the same mistake in preparing the control account as we did in writing up the individual accounts. In this case the control account would agree with the total of the individual accounts, and we would have failed to detect the error. Control accounts are not as effective as bank reconciliations because they check against an internally produced source, rather than against an independent source, such as a bank statement.

You may have wondered what happens to the integrity of the double entry system if there are two sales ledgers in existence. The answer is that *either* the total of the individual accounts *or* the control account forms part of the double entry. There is no absolute rule about which forms part of the double entry system, although it is obviously easier to list a control account in a trial balance, rather than hundreds of individual accounts. Understanding that only one of the control account or the individual accounts goes into the double entry system is fundamental to understanding control accounts.

If the individual accounts are put into the trial balance then the control account is known as a memorandum account. On the other hand, if the control account balance is included in the trial balance, then the individual ledger accounts form the memorandum. A memorandum is just that, a working note of detail which is outside the double entry system.

Activity 14.9   Identify which of these errors can affect the agreement of the sales control account:

Error		Affects agreement?
A	Posting the total of the sales journal to the purchase ledger control account	
B	Omission of entry from control account only	
C	Making the same mistake in the individual account as in the control account	
D	Posting the correct amount to the wrong account in the individual accounts	
E	Omission of entry from individual and control account	

Answer   You should have answered yes in the boxes against errors A and B, and no against the others. Error A will result in the same difference in the sales control and in the purchases control – a good indication of what has happened. It is worth noting that three errors will not be shown up by the control account technique. Nevertheless, it is a fairly easy and cheap technique, and typically found in all but the most basic accounting systems.

Activity 14.10   The following information has been taken from the records of Garside Books. Prepare the sales ledger account for the year to 31 December 20X6. It can be written up in exactly the same way as an individual sales ledger account.

Debtor balances at 1 January 20X6, per control account and per list of balances	14,890
Sales for the year to 31 December 20X6, per sales journal	203,680
Cash received from debtors, per cash book	205,905
Bad debts written off	400

Answer

SALES LEDGER CONTROL

1.1.X6	Balance b/f	14,890	31.12.X6	Cash book	205,905
31.12.X6	Sales journal	203,680	31.12.X6	Bad debt	400
			31.12.X6	Balance c/f	12,265
		218,570			218,570

*A*ctivity 14.11

A list of the balances on the individual customers' accounts in Garside Books' sales ledger at 31 December 20X5 totalled £11,771. Investigation reveals:

1 An invoice for £263 to Sandringham was entered twice in the sales journal and subsequently posted twice to the customer's account.

2 An invoice for £485 to S. Patel was correctly entered in the sales journal but was subsequently posted to I. Patel's account in the purchase ledger.

3 A receipt of £78 from Foster was correctly entered in the control account, but entered as £87 in the individual trade receivables account.

Correct the control account and/or the list of individual trade receivable balances as necessary and so reconcile the total with the balance on the sales control account. You may find it helpful to deal with each item in both the control account and the individual account, before considering the next.

Answer

Our approach is to consider whether Item 1 will result in a control difference. It appears to have been entered twice both in the individual account and in the control account. It will be included twice in the control account because that is, of course, written up from the sales journal, where it has been entered twice. While this is a mistake which needs correction, it will not help us to agree the control account to the total of individual balances.

We then consider Item 2. The sales journal treatment, and hence the control account, is correct. However, the individual account for S. Patel will be understated by the omission of the invoice for £485. This must therefore be added to the total of the individual balances. Note that it will also need to be corrected in I. Patel's account in the purchase ledger, but that is not our immediate concern.

Item 3 is also correct in the control account, but the individual account for Foster will have been credited with £9 too much. This therefore needs to be added back, so increasing the balance on Foster's individual account.

The net effect of all this can be summarised as follows:

Existing total of individual balances	11,771
Add: Omission of sales invoice to S. Patel	485
Correction of over credit to Foster	9
Balance per sales control account	12,265

If we now make correcting entries in the accounts of S. Patel and Foster, the total of the individual accounts will then agree with the balance on the control account. Notice what the construction and use of the control account has done for us. It has enabled us to detect a problem with two accounts in our sales ledger, which it is quite possible we would not otherwise have found until the mistakes had damaged our relationship with those customers.

The final section of this chapter now deals with the situation where our accounting is so poor, perhaps despite the type of controls we've explored so far, that the accounting system effectively breaks down. This means that we have little or no accounting system – in the jargon we have 'incomplete records'.

Incomplete records

The term 'incomplete records' is applied to any situation where a double entry system of bookkeeping has not been followed. This could mean that an organisation has used a 'single-entry' approach, perhaps recording cash and bank transactions but not completing the double entry in the corresponding ledger account. This is obviously not ideal, but small businesses and other organisations, perhaps with little accounting knowledge, do use such an approach. However, as we will see in Chapter 15, the almost universal use of computers for accounting has meant that such a partial approach is less and less common. Accordingly, this is not something we will explore any further in this book.

At the other extreme, the business may keep no written accounting records at all. In this situation it would seem impossible to prepare any financial statements at all. However, we may be able to salvage something. Before we explore how we might do this, however, we should have a quick look at the legal position, at least as it exists in the UK.

Legal requirements

For limited companies, the Companies Act contains specific requirements. Section 386 states that:

Every company shall keep accounting records ... sufficient ...

(a) to show and explain the company's transactions,
(b) to disclose with reasonable accuracy, at any time, the financial position of the company at that time.

This requirement will, of course, not be met if we keep no accounting records, or very partial records, so companies will usually keep good double-entry records along the lines of those we've seen earlier in this book.

On the other hand, there is no explicit legal obligation for a sole trader business to keep accounting records or to produce annual financial statements, although VAT registered businesses must keep appropriate accounting records. This means that we can occasionally be faced with a small sole trader business which keeps very poor, or no, records. In this case, we need to adopt an alternative way of constructing financial statements.

Constructing financial statements from very incomplete records

Even where no proper records have been maintained, it is still necessary to establish the financial position and profits earned by such businesses to establish any tax liability, or to obtain loans, or for many other purposes. The key to doing this is to construct a statement of financial position. In these circumstances, we often refer to this statement as 'a statement of affairs', but it's essentially a statement of financial position as we've already seen it. The best way to follow the approach is to work step by step through an example.

Example 14.1

John, a market trader, has not maintained proper accounting records for his business, so will prepare a minimal set of financial statements using the statement of affairs approach.

Even where we can't take the figures from a proper set of books, we can usually work out a list of assets and liabilities. For example, we'll obviously know if we have property, and we should be able to estimate what it's worth, and the same will apply to other assets. Similarly, we should know if we owe anything to suppliers so we should be able to estimate the trade payables, and so on. On this basis, we reckon that John had the following assets and liabilities at 31 December 20X9:

Property	100,000
Van	12,000
Bank loan	60,000
Equipment	4,000
Inventory	5,000
Trade payables	10,700
Bank balance (in hand)	150

The first step is to prepare a statement of affairs for John at 31 December 20X9. All we do is list the assets and liabilities, netting one off against the other. Since this isn't a proper statement of financial position, we don't need to worry about the layout. We can then rely on the balance sheet equation to give us the equity.

Property	100,000
Van	12,000
Equipment	4,000
Inventory	5,000
Bank balance (in hand)	150
	121,150
Bank loan	(60,000)
Trade payables	(10,700)
Net assets	50,450
Equity, i.e. the same as the net assets	50,450

So, John's statement of affairs tells us that his net assets are £50,450. Alternatively, this amount could be said to represent the 'net worth' or 'capital' of the business entity as at 31 December 20X9. This figure can only represent an estimate, however, since it is based on the estimated values of the assets and liabilities. Nevertheless, we've been able to calculate something close to a statement of financial position without proper accounting records.

What we don't have, of course is a statement of comprehensive income, or even a profit figure. However, step two allows us to address this.

In earlier chapters we've seen how the profit (or loss) for a period results in an equivalent increase (or decrease) in the capital of the business from one year end to the next. This principle can also be used to calculate the profits of a business when accounting records are not available. Specifically, when profits are earned by a business there will be a corresponding increase in the capital (and the net assets) of a business between one year end and the next. Consequently, it is possible to calculate the profit or loss for an accounting period by comparing the statements of affairs at the beginning and end of the period.

To continue our example, John traded throughout the next year, i.e. 20Y0. John had the following assets and liabilities as at 31 December 20Y0, the amounts being estimated as before:

Bank loan	54,000
Property	100,000
Van	9,600
Equipment	3,600
Trade payables	12,370
Inventory	8,000
Bank balance (in hand)	1,730

Activity 14.12   Prepare a statement of affairs for John, showing the net asset position of the business as at 31 December 20Y0. When you have done this, try to calculate the profit which has been earned during 20Y0.

Answer   Our statement of affairs looks like this – remember that the exact layout isn't critical, provided you include the correct assets and liabilities at their correct figures, any layout will do:

Property	100,000
Van	9,600
Equipment	3,600
Inventory	8,000
Bank balance (in hand)	1,730
	122,930
Bank loan	(54,000)
Trade payables	(12,370)
Net assets	56,560
Equity	56,560

If you have completed your calculations correctly, you will note that John's statement of affairs indicates that his net assets figure, that is to say his equity, is now £56,560 compared to only £50,450 at the start of the year. This implies that the increase of £6,110 is a reflection of the profit for the 20Y0 which has been retained in the business.

Two further points should be made here. First, since the statements of affairs includes estimates of the values of assets and liabilities, the calculated figure for retained profit will only be as accurate as those estimates. Second, the calculation only indicates the value of profits retained in the business. Adjustments may need to be made for cash or other assets introduced or withdrawn by the proprietor during the period.

Our estimate of John's profit for 20Y0 at £6,110 is fine as far as it goes, but it doesn't take account of the possibility that John has taken money out of the business to live on during the year. After all, if there have been such 'drawings' then the increase of £6,110 is what's left of the total profit after such drawings.

To extend our example one last step, assume that John now informs you that he has taken a regular salary from the business of £300 each week. Now we try to calculate the profit actually earned by the business during 20Y0.

This is fairly straightforward. John's drawings were £300 per week for 52 weeks, i.e. £15,600. Whatever the total profit was, there was £6,110 left after taking out £15,600. So, the total profit must have been £21,710. In other words, all we do is add the drawings to the residual profit.

Finally, note that any extra money John put into his business would be subtracted. For example, if John had received a legacy of £5,000 during the year and put that into the business, then the profit calculation would be:

Residual profit, i.e. increase in equity over the year	6,110
Add: Drawings	15,600
Less: New money introduced	(5,000)
Total profit for 20Y0	16,710

Summary

This chapter has introduced a key issue in accounting – that of control. We have seen:

▶ how a lack of control can open up an entity to both mistakes and deliberate fraud

▶ how the achievement of a true and fair view may be consequently compromised

▶ the use of audit, both internal and external

▶ the use of bookkeeping controls, notably the bank reconciliation and the control account

▶ the construction of financial information from incomplete records.

None of these controls will ensure the integrity of our accounting records and financial statements, either individually or together. However, what they will do is significantly increase the likelihood of achieving something close to such integrity. In the case of external audit, we have seen that the benefits of the control are considered so important that an audit is required by the Companies Act.

Chapter 15 examines the role of the computer in accounting systems, and includes a look at the control features involved in such systems.

Key terms

audit (p. 294)
external audit (p. 295)
bank reconciliation (p. 300)

control accounts (p. 303)
incomplete records (p. 307)

Self-assessment questions

For each of the following issues, select the single most appropriate answer. Our answers are at the end of this book. If you get any wrong, then re-read the relevant part of this chapter.

1 Which of the following is an error of principle?

   (a) Entering a sales invoice for £89 as £98 in the customer's account.
   (b) Not using a control account.
   (c) Entering a sales invoice twice.
   (d) Adding up the cash book incorrectly.

2 A main purpose of an external audit is:

   (a) To enable the auditors to detect fraud.
   (b) To enable the directors to use correct accounting policies.
   (c) To enable auditors to report on the truth and fairness of the accounts.
   (d) To enable the shareholders to monitor the managers.

3 A clean audit report implies that:

   (a) The auditors believe that the accounts show a true and fair view.
   (b) The directors believe that the accounts show a true and fair view.
   (c) The shareholders believe that the accounts are reliable.
   (d) The auditors have not detected any fraud or error.

▶

4 Which of the following are required by law to have an external audit?

(a) Small limited companies.
(b) Sole traders.
(c) All limited companies.
(d) Larger limited companies.

5 The purpose of a bank reconciliation statement is to:

(a) Detect cash book errors.
(b) Make sure the cash book includes all bank interest and charges.
(c) Highlight items in transit within the banking system.
(d) None of the above.

6 If a bank reconciliation statement starts with the balance per the bank statement, and that balance is in overdraft, then, in the reconciliation statement, any unpresented cheques should be:

(a) Added to the balance per the bank statement.
(b) Subtracted from the balance per the bank statement.
(c) Omitted from the statement.
(d) Added back and then subtracted once the bank balance is positive.

7 The balance on a sales control account should agree with:

(a) The total of both individual sales ledger and individual purchase ledger balances.
(b) The total of individual sales ledger balances.
(c) The trial balance total.
(d) The balance on the purchase ledger control account.

8 The purpose of a purchase ledger control account is to ensure that:

(a) All errors in the writing up of the purchases system are detected.
(b) Most errors in the writing up of the purchases system are detected.
(c) The purchases figure in the financial statements is correct.
(d) The trade payables figure in the financial statements is correct.

9 **(a)** Julia has written up her cash book in double entry form for September as follows:

CASH BOOK

Date	Detail	Amount	Date	Detail	Amount
1	Opening balance	500.00	1	Bradley Software Ltd	106.78
4	Cash sales	390.00	4	Clee & Co.	690.00
10	Weelsby Partners	504.80	8	Halton Supplies	45.07
15	Cash sale	80.00	16	Tetney Merchandising	230.70
20	Atlantis Publishing plc	680.50	18	Bradley Software Ltd	305.75
27	Weelsby Partners	218.00	24	Vehicle Rentals plc	530.00
30	Cash sale	50.00	28	Corner Newsagency	12.43
			30	Halton Supplies	182.85

A few days later, Julia receives the following bank statement, dated 30 September, showing a balance of £733.32. By checking each item against her cash book, identify which items are not common to both records, and complete writing up the cash book as far as possible.

BANK STATEMENT

Date	Detail	Payments	Receipts	Balance
1	Balance b/f			500.00
4	Cheque 568	106.78		393.22
8	Counter credit		390.00	783.22
9	Cheque 569	690.00		93.22
10	Cheque 570	45.07		48.15
12	Counter credit		504.80	552.95
15	Charges for Sept.	25.00		527.95
19	Counter credit		80.00	607.95
20	Cheque 571	230.70		377.25
23	Counter credit		680.50	1057.75
27	Cheque 573	530.00		527.75
29	Counter credit		218.00	745.75
30	Cheque 574	12.43		733.32

(b) Prepare the bank reconciliation statement at 30 September.

10 **(a)** Peter Lee started business with £500 in his current account at Midclay Bank plc. He issued cheques totalling £3,638 during July, his first month of trading. He also banked cheques received totalling £4,003. Calculate the balance in Peter Lee's cash book at 31 July.

(b) A few days later, Peter receives a bank statement dated 31 July which shows a balance of £622. By checking each item against his cash book he is able to determine that:

▶ Bank charges of £232 entered on the bank statement had not been entered in the cash book.

▶ A cheque received for £240 and paid into the bank account during July had been returned by the bank marked 'No funds available'. The original receipt had been entered in the cash book, and is accordingly included in the total amount shown above, but no adjustment had been made in the cash book for the fact that the cheque has turned out to be worthless.

▶ A cheque paid for £87 had been incorrectly entered in the cash book as £78. The total for the month shown above therefore includes £78 in respect of this transaction.

Calculate the new balance shown by the cash book.

(c) Checking of the bank statement against the cash book also revealed some outstanding items, namely:

▶ Cheques written and sent to suppliers amounting to £843 had been entered in the cash book in July, and so are included in the totals for the month given above, but were not presented to the bank for payment until August.

▶ Cheques received totalling £605 had been entered in the cash book and paid into the bank, but had not been credited by the bank until 2 August.

Draft the Bank Reconciliation Statement at 31 July.

11 **(a)** Briefly explain the difference between the nature and purposes of internal and external audit.

(b) What is a qualified audit report? Outline the likely effect on the company of such a report.

12 Simon runs a small 'one man and a van' haulage business. He has asked you to help him prepare 'a set of accounts for the tax man showing what profit I've made', but he has not kept any significant accounting records during the year. You sit down with him and he tells you that he started his business a year ago by putting £5,000 of his own money into a business bank account and using more of his own money to buy a van for £14,000.

He says that he thinks the van is now worth about £12,000, customers still owe him £3,400, but he owes a garage £300 for diesel. He has kept his bank statements and the current one shows that he has £6,100 on a deposit account and a further £700 in a current account. He has drawn £1,300 per month from the business for his living expenses.

Prepare a statement of affairs at the beginning and end of the year and so calculate his profit for the year.

Answers to these questions can be found at the back of this book.

15

Information technology and accounting

Objectives

By the end of this chapter you should be able to:

▶ Explain the control issues applicable to accounting within an IT environment.

▶ Describe how accounting systems can be designed and implemented.

▶ Outline the main features of e-accounting.

Introduction

We noted in the previous chapter that accounting has become ever more reliant on the use of computers. In all but the smallest entities, it has now become most unusual to find an accounting system that is not computer-based to some degree. The purpose of this chapter is to consider the control issues in such systems, the design and use of those systems, and the development of e-accounting.

There is a danger that the role of information technology can be seen as something of an afterthought in the study of financial accounting. This is because your studies have focused on the traditional principles of accounting, such as double entry, the layout and role of the statement of financial position, the meaning of ratios, and so on, and it is not always obvious where information technology fits in. Nevertheless, it is important that you have some awareness of how information technology has changed, and is changing, accounting, both to understand accounting at this level and as a basis for any further study you may undertake.

The principles of double entry that you have learnt and applied in previous chapters underpin almost all current commercial accounting software. Increasingly, this may not be obvious on the surface as developers move towards greater ease of use, and away from requiring users to implement double entry bookkeeping. After all, if one of the advantages of accounting software that we identified in Chapter 3 is the automation of the double entry discipline, then it may well be helpful for such mechanics to be hidden behind simpler data entry screens. However, such a discipline still exists and provides a strong control against error within the accounting application.

To illustrate, we've constructed a typical screen below for a hypothetical accounting software application for a company called Newbolt Engineering Ltd. You'll notice that it presents a screen by function, that is, it allows the user to select an area of the accounting system, whether sending an invoice to customers, processing an invoice from a supplier, or whatever. At this stage there's no need for the user to know anything about double entry bookkeeping, only to know the job they want to do. A user will select the button for the function they want to undertake, which will open up that part of the software. For example, if we want to enter details of a purchase invoice from a supplier we will start by selecting 'Suppliers'.

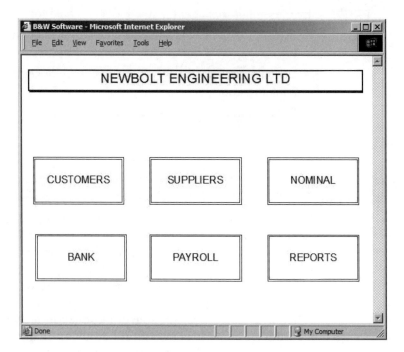

We saw back in Chapter 3 how information technology can help to make accounting both more reliable and richer in the information it provides. Chapter 14 gave us some further insight into how control techniques can enhance financial accounting, and this is especially true once we are operating within an information technology environment. The first section in this chapter expands this exploration of control and information technology.

Control issues

Chapter 14 outlined how controls within an accounting system can help to guard against fraud, mistakes and incompetence. This is no less true in a computer-based system. Think about what we need to achieve. We need an accounting system that at least minimises error and fraud, and certainly a system that detects it. One of the great benefits of a computer-based system is that arithmetic error should normally be eliminated, and the software should not allow entries which do not balance.

What this means in practice is that, as we saw in Chapter 3, the entry of, say, the debit for the purchase of inventory will always require a corresponding credit for the same amount. We know from the logic of the double entry system that such a correspondence is required, but we also know that it is easy to make a mistake in a manual system and forget to make a credit entry, to make an entry for the wrong amount, or to make a second debit entry, and so on. However, the use of accounting software inserts a check into the accounting system so that we at least enter the same total debit as credit, even where the transaction may be made up of more than one debit and/or more than one credit. Consider the screenshot below.

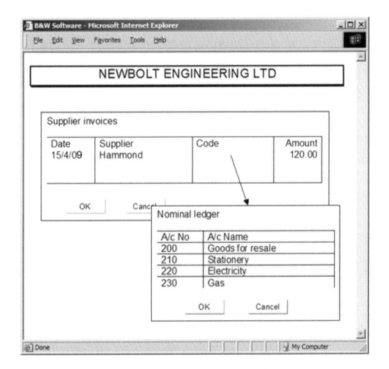

Having selected 'Suppliers' from the first screen we now want to enter details of a purchase invoice. We start by entering the name of the supplier. We won't have to type this in since we should be able to select it from a drop-down box in the 'Supplier' column. Note that, in double entry terms, what this does is credit Hammond in our purchase ledger. The debit is a matter of where we record the asset or expense, and this is the purpose of the 'Code' column. Clicking in this column will pop-up the box we can see above, listing all our nominal ledgers (scrolling up and down in this box will take you to other nominal ledger accounts). All we have to do now is click on one line in this pop-up box to tell the software which account should be debited with the £120. The essential point to notice here is that the software has made the debit and credit entries, and ensured that both entries are for £120. We could, of course, have used the software in this way without a knowledge of the double entry bookkeeping that we first met back in Chapter 3. However, it should be obvious to you that double entry bookkeeping underpins such software.

While this is a significant improvement, it will still be possible to make errors of principle, such as posting a repair invoice to an electricity account, or crediting the wrong customer with a receipt. Some of these errors may be deliberate.

Activity 15.1

Assume that you have used the cash receipt module of an accounting software package to record the receipt of £400 from Clark into the bank account, and the software then presents you with a screen asking where the money has come from, i.e. which account to credit. Which of the following separate errors would you normally expect to be detected and prevented by the computer-based accounting system?

(a) Entering the receipt as being from Clarkson.
(b) Entering the receipt as being £40.
(c) Entering the receipt as being a payment to Clark.
(d) Entering the receipt correctly and then entering it again correctly.
(e) Entering the receipt as being for sales of trading goods when it was for the sale of our old office computer.

Answer

At its simplest we would expect the computer-based accounting system to detect and prevent any error that violates the principles of double entry. This will be the case for event (b) where Clark's account will only be credited with £40, leaving the software to query the remaining £360. It will also be the case for event (c) since a payment to Clark cannot normally be dealt with through a cash receipt module.

Events (a), (d) and (e) will not be prevented by a simple software check on the validity of the double entry. However, it may be that other checks will detect a problem. For example, while we may enter the receipt as being from Clarkson, as in (a), this does mean that both Clark's and Clarkson's ledger accounts will be wrong and periodic inspection of the accounts would highlight a problem to be investigated. This could be the case, for example, if we periodically review payments to detect bad debts and for credit control purposes. A similar technique may help us to pick up error (d). Error (e), on the other hand, may only be detected if and when we try to agree our physical computers with book records.

The lesson to be drawn is that no single control can be relied on to detect and prevent all types of errors. What is required is a range of controls, and information technology can provide some of them. In other words, what we need is a coherent system which relies on much more than simply the blind logic of double entry. One element in such a broader system is the audit trail.

Audit trails

An **audit trail** is simply a listing of transactions, including a note of who entered the transaction. This enables both the organisation and its auditors to trace the accounting treatment of a transaction, to ensure that it has been dealt with correctly. Alternatively, it allows the identification of an error and who made it. For routine transactions, this may mean no more than the software attaching a number to each transaction and keeping a record of who logged in to make that transaction. This, of course, implies that there must be some way of ensuring that only the correct person is able to log in with their personal identification.

The usual answer to this control problem is to use a password. This has the additional benefit of preventing anyone other than the nominated person from writing up the accounts. It is possible to set various levels of password protection so that, for example, the sales ledger clerk can only access the sales ledger and cash book receipts, the assistant accountant can access any ledger, but only the chief accountant can access the software which allows the preparation of final accounts. Passwords cannot be relied on by themselves, since people tend to forget their passwords, tell them to those helping them 'temporarily', use easy-to-guess words, or leave their PC unattended after logging in.

A second benefit of an audit trail is then to at least trace what entries have been made. As we've seen, accounting software takes care of one leg of the double entry. Recording the cash book receipt of £100 from a customer called Jack, for example, would automatically also credit Jack's account in the sales ledger. Nevertheless, a mistake, such as entering the receipt as being from Jill, would still require an explicit double entry to correct the error, in this case debiting Jill's account and crediting Jack's. In other words, it should not be possible to simply go back to Jill's account and cross out the entry and then make it in Jack's instead. This has ensured that the audit trail was always very clear, if rather laboured.

Activity 15.2   Assuming we have kept a good audit trail of transactions, what else is required for the audit trail system to be effective?

Answer   The use of nominated persons, passwords and an audit trail should protect reasonably well against accidental or deliberate fraud. However, an audit trail is only of use if someone reads it, and picks up any anomalies. In a larger organisation, this will usually be included within the internal audit function. In a smaller organisation, it may only be done by exception, when a problem becomes apparent for other reasons. The point is that an audit trail is of no value unless it is reviewed, at least by exception, and preferably routinely.

It should be obvious from all of the above that controls in an accounting system are something that should be considered when designing that system, rather than something that is bolted on afterwards. Indeed, designing a system which copes with all the inputs we throw at it and still produces the useful information we require, while building in appropriate controls, is a significant part of accounting, and accordingly we now turn our attention to a brief review of design.

Designing an accounting system

You will probably be aware of the current pace of change in computing, in terms of the power of hardware, the sophistication of software, and the spectacular growth in the ability to interconnect with other computing systems. This implies that any description of current practices would be seriously out of date before you came to read this. We will therefore deal less with the current practicalities and more with the principles of designing an accounting system.

The basic principles of designing an accounting system will be the same whether we intend that system to be implemented using computers or not. The starting point should be to be very clear about exactly what we want from that system. This means making our accounting needs and wants explicit in terms of:

▶ Sources of, and types of, data to be dealt with.

▶ The information to be extracted from the system by way of management information, financial statements (e.g. a statement of financial position), statutory returns (e.g. a VAT return), and anything else we think might be useful to any of the people we might regard as having a right to such information.

▶ An acceptable level of costs for running this accounting system.

Hence, two of the key influences on how we plan and implement an accounting system are the type of raw data and the requirements of the end users. There will be many types of raw data, ranging from delivery notes to bank statements and from time sheets to petty cash vouchers.

Activity 15.3

(a) List five source documents for accounting information that you think would be relevant to a trading company. You may find it helpful to think about an organisation you are familiar with, and the types of documentation it has to deal with.

(b) Identify three separate reports or statements that you would want to extract from the accounting system, other than final accounts such as the statement of financial position.

Answer

This is a deliberately open-ended activity, since any answer will be dependent on the particular organisation. Nevertheless, you could have suggested, among other things, that source documents would include:

- ▶ sales invoices, giving details of amounts charged to customers
- ▶ sales credit notes, showing amounts due to customers because of goods returned, overcharges, etc.
- ▶ purchase invoices and credit notes, giving the same details as the equivalent sales documents, but in respect of our purchases from suppliers
- ▶ bank statements, showing bank charges, interest received, etc.
- ▶ cheque stubs, recording details of amounts paid
- ▶ paying-in slips, detailing amounts received into our bank account.

The information statements that we might want could include, for example:

- ▶ a list of outstanding trade receivables
- ▶ a list of outstanding trade payables
- ▶ a forecast of cash flows in and out of our bank account over the next few months
- ▶ a statement of inventory in hand
- ▶ a summary of actual expenditure, compared with budgeted expenditure.

Once we are clear about the need for a comprehensive system, have clarified the data to be dealt with, and have decided on the information statements we want from our accounting system, then we can move on to consider implementation.

The options at this point are to have a system custom-written for us or to buy a general system 'off the peg'. The latter will obviously be much cheaper and is, therefore, the usual approach. Occasionally, a specialist software supplier will be able to customise a standard package marginally, and this may achieve the best of both worlds.

Many accounting systems were designed originally as modular systems. This means that they were divided into separate, self-contained programs for different parts of the total accounting system. Thus there was one module available for dealing with the sales ledger, and other, separate, modules for purchases, nominal, inventory, etc. This had advantages in that users only had to buy those parts of the system that they needed. A business which only sells for cash would therefore not need to acquire the sales ledger module. This approach also had the incidental benefit of reducing the demands on the hardware.

As hardware power has risen and prices have fallen, however, the rationale for modular systems has become less obvious. It is now more common to find that accounting software is integrated, so that all functions are, in principle at least, part of a whole. This is obviously a simpler approach and ought to make the software easier to use.

Implementation

Once we have decided on the general approach, it only remains to successfully implement such a package. This will require not only suitable hardware and software, but also an organised approach to the **implementation of an**

accounting system. In particular, we must consider how the data can be accurately transferred from any old system to the new, and contingency plans in case the new system fails in any unforeseen way. Data loss is a serious problem and could result in the collapse of the organisation.

A typical process for the transfer of an accounting system from an old system, whether manual or an older computer-based system, to our newly specified system would include:

1 Ensuring that the old system is up to date.

2 Installing hardware and software as determined by the issues considered above. This might include spare hardware and back-up software, preferably on a separate site, to be used in case of damage to, or failure of, the main hardware. These issues are considered in more detail later in this chapter.

3 Entering all existing data onto the software. Given the importance of this step, it should preferably be verified, even though this is an expensive process. This could be done, for example, by re-entering all data and comparing the two sets. Where we are transferring data from an older computer-based system, this step should be relatively straightforward, given common formats between accounting packages, but it should still be verified.

4 Running both the old system and the new system for a period. Again, this is expensive, but it is essential to be sure that the new system works adequately before ending the old system. This process is known as parallel running.

5 Once the new system is running reliably, the old system can be discontinued. Note that the new system must include suitable control procedures before it can be considered to be satisfactory.

Activity 15.4

Arturo Ltd is considering changing from its existing accounting system to a newer system with greater functionality. Outline the procedures that you will implement in order to ensure that there is no loss of data, and no subsequent failure of the new system. You may find it most effective to organise your answer as a list of points – we have.

Answer

Our suggested answer summarises much of what has been covered earlier in this chapter. For more detail on any of these points you should therefore refer back.

▶ Identify the data sources and required outputs, and so clarify the required system. This should help to ensure that the system will be sufficiently comprehensive to accurately deal with all data.

▶ Similarly, suitable software, i.e. that with a data format common with the old system (or at least a proven data transfer program), and the necessary hardware will improve the chances of avoiding data loss, especially in the transfer period.

▶ Parallel running will provide some reassurance about the reliability of the new system before the old system is discontinued.

▶ Once the new system is running, it is essential that frequent and regular back-up copies are taken of the data. If done conscientiously, this should ensure that any data loss is restricted to only whatever data have been input since the last back-up.

▶ Contingency plans for back-up hardware and software will guard against the effects of a disaster, such as a major fire. This is covered in more detail in the next section.

Contingency planning

There remains the major control problem of what to do if the computer system breaks down. The usual method used to control for this possibility is the use of back-ups. This means that there must always be at least two sets of the same data, and many organisations will use three sets of data. At the start of the day, there will thus be, say, two sets of data, A and B. Set A will be used as the working set for that day's transactions, so that by the end of the day it will not only include the transactions that are on B, but will also have had that day's transactions added on to it. If there is any disaster during the day and data set A is lost, set B can be used, and all that will have been lost will be the transactions for the day up to the time of the disaster. It would not be a major issue to re-enter these on set B. If all goes well, then set B can be backed up from set A at the end of the day so that we again start the next day with two sets of data. It will improve the level of control if set B is kept off-site until needed. There is obviously a danger from, for example, fire if set B is located on the same site as set A, as both sets could then be lost. This is why some organisations work with three sets of data, thus allowing the third set to always be off-site. Sets B and C can then be backed up in rotation, and the worst that could happen is that we would lose one day's entry of transactions.

A further back-up issue is the use of parallel hardware, so that there is something to run the software on in the case of a major disaster. It will obviously be expensive to keep otherwise redundant hardware, so one alternative would be to come to a mutual arrangement with another organisation running the same software, so that each could use the other's facilities, perhaps overnight, and so maintain processing of accounts pending replacement of its own facilities. This may, of course, not be possible, but there are a number of commercial firms which offer such facilities to a number of companies in exchange for a fee.

The next part of this chapter deals briefly with e-accounting. Although the focus is on the impact of communications and information technology on accounting, bear in mind that any changes to accounting systems to incorporate the benefits of e-accounting are an extension of what we have covered so far, not a replacement. In other words, e-accounting offers new opportunities for accounting systems to process data in order to provide and disseminate useful information, but the basic principles of design and control remain the same.

E-accounting

Electronic accounting, or just **e-accounting**, can be defined as the application of communications and information technology to accounting. This covers many of the issues we have already dealt with, but the focus is usually on the transmission and sharing of data and information, and especially on the use of the internet in accounting.

The increasing power of the PC has gradually shifted computing towards processing by the end user, so that individuals can carry out much of their work locally. This has advantages in terms of flexibility, but can cause difficulties in terms of shared data. In the days when there was only a single, central computer, it was implicit that everyone used their terminals to access the same data on the single central computer. Once PCs acquired the power to process data locally, the question arose of how to ensure that many different versions of the same data were not created. The answer usually adopted is the network.

A network is a number of computers connected together. Their interconnection allows for a single set of data to be maintained, since all will use and update the one set of data. This single data set will be held on one of the computers in the network. This means, for example, that the organisation's list of employees for payroll purposes – name, rate of pay, method of payment, etc. – should always be up to date and correct. Contrast this with what could happen if a number of payroll clerks all started with the same set of data, but then each amended it as they processed the payroll over the weeks and months. The organisation would be generating multiple sets of data for the same employee, with no assurance over which was the most reliable.

The technology of how the network is constructed, and how the accounting software and operating system software ensures that only one set of data is maintained, is beyond the scope of this brief description. All we need to note for our purposes is that there is a significant control issue here. From the point of view of design and implementation of an accounting system we can normally rely on the software controls to ensure that only one set of data is maintained and used by all users. However, we also need to consider controls over such issues as: who is authorised to be a user?; whether some users only need to be able to read the data and not be allowed to change it; the distribution of reports around the organisation, and so on.

Sharing of data has become a more high-profile issue with the development of the internet. In concept, this is simply a network of networks. Connection to any one network allows access to all other computers connected to any of the other networks. In this regard, one notable development is the use of 'internet-enabled' accounting packages. Potentially this means packages which use ordinary browsers to interface with the accounting software. A browser is itself software which allows the user to look at pages on the world wide web, and has the advantage of being widely available and probably already familiar to users. A saleswoman, for example, could use a laptop to connect to the main company system to check customer details such as credit limits. The browser could then be used to run a small application program, known as an 'applet', from within the browser to, for example, enter details of the day's orders from those customers. The applet would link to the main accounting software, without the saleswoman having to learn how to use the main accounting package or to have it loaded on her laptop. Training and software costs should therefore both be reduced.

Of potentially greater value to the accountant is the use of the internet to allow for transmission of accounting data and information between an organisation and any other. To appreciate the importance of this consider the following activity.

Activity 15.5

Company A sends a sales invoice for goods to company B. List the steps that would typically be taken within company A and company B to process this invoice. Highlight the points at which the same data is copied.

Answer

Company A will prepare the invoice from a record of the goods sold. This could be, for example, a copy of a delivery note. This assumes that the delivery note has been correctly prepared as a record of the goods delivered. Preparation of the invoice will then involve copying data from the delivery note to the sales invoice. Company A will then often post the paper invoice to company B.

When company B receives the invoice it will enter it into the accounting system as a purchase invoice. At its simplest this will involve copying the details from the invoice into the purchase ledger. When company B eventually pays the invoice the payment details will follow the reverse route with a similar number of points at which the same details must be manually entered into the two accounting systems.

When the process is highlighted in this way it should be apparent that it is wasteful to process the same data not only more than once within a company but also across companies. We have already seen how computers can reduce the need to enter more data than once within a company's accounting system. This is a major step, but shouldn't it be possible to take the data that has already been entered within company A and use it to write up the ledgers in company B as well? What is required is the transmission of data from the accounting system of company A to that of company B, and vice versa when we deal with the payment.

Activity 15.6

Outline two problems that you can foresee with such an approach.

Answer

The problems that occur to us are that the two accounting systems may well not produce data in the same format, and that there are surely problems of security. Allowing a third party access to your accounting system must have implications for control within that system.

On the question of security, bear in mind what we said above, that the basic principles of control will still apply in the world of e-accounting. This implies that the techniques we explored, such as passwords and audit trails, should still help us to maintain controls over our systems. In this case, for example, company B could give company A a password which allows access only to the company A account in company B's purchase ledger.

The question of compatibility of data formats is more difficult. Each writer of accounting software has historically tended to store data in their own format, and building in the facility to import and export data from and to other software packages has been laborious and expensive. This is unfortunate because the potential gains if accounting systems were compatible are very significant.

To illustrate this point, consider the above activity again. If company A could send its invoice to company B, either over the internet or as an e-mail attachment, in a format that was understandable by the accounting system of company B there would be no need for re-entering of the details in company B. Similarly, the payments details could be sent direct from the accounting system of company B to that of company A. The savings in time, error correction, and hence in cost, should be obvious. Such a single format is being developed within accounting systems, and is known as XML.

XML

XML stands for eXtensible Mark-up Language, and an understanding of XML can be gained by looking at this name. A mark-up language is a set of labels ('tags') which can be attached to content to describe that content. The current language of the web is a mark-up language known as the hypertext mark-up language, or HTML. This allows the content of a web page, that is, the words and pictures you see on screen, to be described by attaching a tag to each picture, word, or group of words such as a paragraph. This description may be of the paragraph's meaning, such as the CITE tag which marks that paragraph as a citation. More usually within HTML the tag is a description of the formatting of the paragraph, such as the BGCOLOR tag, which can be used to set the background colour behind the paragraph.

XML takes a more rigorous approach to marking up with tags, in that it is strict about only using tags which describe the meaning of the content – formatting is dealt with separately. This means that each piece of content is marked with a description of what it is. For example, a figure of £10,000 could be tagged as being the share capital for the current year, or as the sales ledger balance for company B, or as anything else we want. What this implies, of course, is that we must have a large set of tags, one for every item we might ever deal with in an accounting system. Whereas the tags for HTML are centrally defined, for our XML accounting to work we must be able to define our own tags. In other words, the mark-up language must be eXtensible, hence XML.

Two things follow. First, if the accounting software of both company A and company B can read a common set of XML tags then the data is interchangeable and we have the possibility of integrating our accounting systems with those of our customers, supplier, lenders, etc. in the way we explored above.

Second, financial reporting is about producing financial statements for a variety of purposes. Certainly, this will include the production of a statement of cash flows for publication, but we might also want a revised format of the cash flow information as part of an application for a loan. Once all the underlying data has been tagged with its XML tag this revision becomes an easy process. We can set up a template, perhaps in our accounting software, perhaps in a spreadsheet or word-processor, so that the necessary figures are extracted from the accounting system and placed in the correct place in the template. The template will know which piece of data is the right one because, of course, each piece of data carries its own unique tag. This might seem laborious but next time we need the same report we have only to run the template again and it will extract the corresponding data from the updated accounting system.

Activity 15.7   List at least two advantages for a company of having its accounting data held in XML format.

Answer   The potential advantages are principally the ability to exchange accounting data with other organisations, leading to faster, less error-prone and therefore cheaper routine accounting, and the 're-purposing' of accounting information. This second point means that information, such as the net profit will, of course, appear in the statement of comprehensive income, but could also be useful in a loan application, a report to employees, a tax return, a marketing web page, etc. Without XML tags, re-using the profit figure implies manually extracting it from the statement of comprehensive income and entering it into each of the other documents. Not only is there potential for error each time this is done, but it is also time-consuming. Multiplied over every figure we report to any user this is a significant cost. With XML tags a template can be prepared once for each purpose and re-used indefinitely.

The advantages that we have considered above have resulted in a major effort to implement XML as the key data format within accounting. In particular, software companies and firms of accountants and professional bodies have combined to develop an agreed set of tags for use within accounting. Such a common set is, of course, essential if there is to be the required commonality of tags to describe each item of accounting data and to allow for the interchange of that data. For example, it is essential that we all agree to tag the inventory figure as, say INVENTORY, and not as, say, STOCK.

This common effort has resulted in a set of tags specific to the world of accounting, known as the eXtensible Business Reporting Language, or XBRL. XBRL can be thought of as a sub-set of XML, and it is actually XBRL which will almost certainly form the basis of data formats in accounting in the future.

The wider picture

The final part of this chapter is concerned with uses of information technology other than accounting software that may still be of relevance to the accountant. Much of this is likely to deal with applications that are familiar to you, but what we are focusing on here is the use of those applications in accounting.

The first area to look at is other applications software, especially spreadsheets and databases. Spreadsheets are an electronic version of the accountant's traditional working paper with many columns and rows. You have already seen one major example of such a working paper in the use of the extended trial balance in Chapter 7. A spreadsheet not only allows text and numbers to be placed in the cells of the spreadsheets, but then also enables formulae to be included, which refer to that text and, more usually, to those numbers. This then means that totals and other calculated figures can be automatically computed, and then recomputed if any underlying figure changes. This ability to very quickly recalculate enables the user to try out 'what if?' scenarios, i.e. changing figures, perhaps as a result of changing underlying assumptions, so that alternative courses of action can be tested. Most of the more modern spreadsheets allow calculations to include references to more than one spreadsheet.

A database is a collection of data stored on a computer system. However, constructing a useful database is a much more complex matter than constructing a spreadsheet to automatically add up a budget, or using a word processor to write the notes to the accounts. Accordingly, it is far less common to find databases being seriously used by end users. Note that the maintenance of supplementary accounting records, such as a register of all our non-current assets, or our inventory records, may well be implemented using a database package.

The other significant area of the common use of information technology by accountants is the acquisition and communication of information. First, e-mail is the transfer of messages between computers, either over a permanent network or over a phone line. There is usually the facility to attach files to the message, and this allows the easy transmission of financial data on an *ad-hoc* basis, or more routinely, as we saw above.

Second, there are the on-line information sources. Some of these are commercial and concerned specifically with data about UK companies, usually including the full annual report and accounts. Saving such data in spreadsheet format would, for example, enable the user to calculate ratios for a number of companies, and so make the sort of inter-firm comparisons we covered earlier in this book. More simply, it is an effective method of acquiring names of directors, addresses of registered offices, discovering who the auditors are, and so on. They may also provide ready calculated ratios, share prices, etc. and often present that information graphically. Being commercial, there is usually a substantial charge for using such services.

Summary

This chapter has been concerned with computer-based accounting and particularly with.

▶ the control issues in an IT environment

▶ the design of an accounting system

▶ the use of a computer-based accounting system.

This has been the last chapter that introduces new material. Chapter 16 attempts to pull together much of what this book has been about, through the use of one large case study. Accounting is about synthesising data and communicating it in a way meaningful to the users. The case study is one way of synthesising your knowledge and understanding acquired so far, and then using it to produce useful information. We strongly recommend that you try it.

Key terms

audit trail (p. 319)

designing an accounting system
(p. 320)

implementation of an accounting
system (p. 321)

back-ups (p. 323)

e-accounting (p. 324)

XML (p. 326)

Self-assessment questions

For each of the following questions, choose the single most appropriate answer.

1 The main advantage of a networked computer system is that it allows for:

(a) Maintenance of a single set of data.
(b) Sharing of scarce or expensive hardware.
(c) Exchange of data.
(d) All of the above.

2 Operating system software is primarily software to:

(a) Network computers in a wide area network.
(b) Give commands to the hardware.
(c) Record and extract accounting data.
(d) Allow computer hardware to be designed efficiently.

▶

3 Customised application software is:

(a) Software to record our customers' details and accounting transactions.
(b) Software that can be applied to any computer.
(c) Software developed to suit a particular organisation's needs.
(d) Software used to develop products and services for our customers.

4 Errors in a computer-based accounting system can be eliminated by the use of:

(a) An audit trail.
(b) Passwords used by nominated staff.
(c) Software that checks that all entries balance.
(d) None of the above.

5 The main advantage of keeping one set of data off-site at all times is:

(a) To minimise deliberate error and fraud.
(b) To ensure one set of data survives in case of a major disaster on-site.
(c) To allow for parallel running of two independent accounting systems.
(d) Effective compliance with any software licence agreement.

6 The importance of the internet to accountants is that it allows relatively easy access to:

(a) Different types of spreadsheet.
(b) Operating systems software.
(c) A wide range of information.
(d) Parallel running of accounting systems.

7 Which of the following are usually regarded as outputs from a computer-based accounting system?

(i) List of trade receivables.
(ii) Purchase invoices.
(iii) Summary of inventory in hand.
(iv) Statement of financial position.
(v) Audit trail.

(a) (i), (iii) and (v)
(b) (ii), (iii), (iv) and (v)
(c) (iii), (iv) and (v)
(d) None of the above

8 The transfer of accounting data from a manual system to a computer-based system can be verified by:

(a) Parallel running of both systems.
(b) Frequent back-ups, with one set of data always kept off-site.
(c) Ensuring that the accounting software includes the facility to check that all entries balance.
(d) Re-entering all transferred data and comparing with the first-entered set.

9 Are you familiar with accounting software? You may have used such software at work, but many of you are likely to be studying accounting before starting full-time work. Nevertheless, most higher educational establishments have some sort of accounting software for use by students. While it is often older versions of popular commercial packages such as Sage or Pegasus, it is still useful to try setting up accounts, entering a few transactions and extracting the results. Only in this way will you properly grasp many of the issues raised in this chapter, especially in relation to control.

When you use the package, try entering deliberate mistakes, and see which the software will pick up, and which it will not. Think about how your wider accounting system could prevent or detect the latter errors. Would a bank reconciliation help, for example? Wider still, what would you do now if the disk or other storage device on which you have just saved your transactions were to be lost or corrupted?

Even if you cannot get access to such a package, try to get hold of one of the newer generation of accounting packages, such as Quicken or Money, which are aimed at use in the small business, or for domestic accounting. Restricted or evaluation editions of such packages are occasionally available online, or given away with computing magazines. At the very least, browse such magazines looking for reviews of accounting packages.

Your overall aim is to get a feel for what accounting software can do, and how it typically does it. It is only through getting as close to the use of accounting software as your circumstances permit that you will be able to relate the practicalities of accounting to the inevitably rather general points that have been covered in this chapter.

10 Hyperion Landscaping Ltd currently keeps its accounting records in a manual system, but now intends to move to a computer-based system. Put the following items in the correct chronological order in which Hyperion should deal with them:

▶ Investigate suitable software.

▶ Get the manual system up to date.

▶ Monitor the audit trail for the computer system.

▶ Determine the information required from the system, e.g. budgets, statement of comprehensive income.

▶ Transfer the account balances from the manual system to the computer system.

▶ Back-up the computer records.

▶ Determine the source documents and other data to be processed by the system.

▶ Investigate suitable hardware.

▶ Move wholly to the computer system.

▶ Decide on back-up and security arrangements.

▶ Run both systems in parallel.

Answers to these questions can be found at the back of this book.

16

The finale

Objectives

By the end of this chapter you should be able to:

▶ Prepare a statement of comprehensive income from cash flows and appropriate statement of financial position information for a company.

▶ Redraft financial statements prepared using non-UK accounting practices.

▶ Prepare a report to users analysing and comparing non-UK and UK companies.

Introduction

The style of this chapter is somewhat different from previous chapters in that there is no new information to learn. If you work through this chapter diligently it will identify for you those items that you have not thoroughly understood.

This chapter also has something of an international flavour and is in essence a case study.

Case study

Bairstow Holdings plc is investigating the possibility of investing in one of two companies. The first, Hamilton Engineering Ltd, is a UK company, and the accounts for the year ended 31 December 20X9 are available. In line with current UK practice, these accounts have been prepared in line with International Accounting Standards (IASs). The second is an overseas competitor to Hamilton Engineering, called Kriton Manufacturers SA. Kriton is incorporated in the (imaginary) central European country of Ecudia. Bairstow Holdings has also obtained the annual report and accounts for Kriton, but has found that the accounts are significantly different from those of Hamilton.

In particular, the accounting regulations in Ecudia do not require the publication of a statement of comprehensive income. However, they do require a statement of cash flows, although in a non-IAS format, and a statement of financial position. As assistant accountant for Bairstow Holdings, you have been asked to use the available information about Kriton to redraft the Kriton accounts in a format consistent with generally accepted accounting practice according to international accounting standards. Having thus prepared accounts for Kriton which are comparable to those of Hamilton, you are also required to analyse their respective positions and prospects, and so to recommend which company, if either, Bairstow should invest in.

Accounts for Kriton Manufacturers SA

All amounts are expressed in the local currency, the euro (€).

STATEMENT OF CASH FLOWS
FOR THE YEAR ENDED 31 DECEMBER 20X9

	€
Receipts	
From customers	654,836
Interest received	12,900
Non-current assets sold	105,040
Debentures issued	150,000
	922,776
Payments	
To suppliers for goods purchased	362,573
To suppliers for other expenses	151,353
Purchases of non-current assets	278,200
Costs of debenture issue	2,150
Tax paid	63,045
Dividends paid	40,257
Interest paid	5,238
	902,816
Increase in bank balance	19,960

STATEMENT OF FINANCIAL POSITION

	20X9 (€)	20X8 (€)
Non-current assets		
Land and buildings	588,933	465,287
Machinery	659,314	590,721
Vehicles	34,941	54,020
	1,283,188	1,110,028

Current assets				
Inventory	90,200		86,582	
Trade receivables	44,877		43,084	
Bank	39,532		19,572	
	174,609		149,238	
Current liabilities				
Trade payables	(31,613)		(33,365)	
Other creditors	(5,045)		(4,502)	
Tax	(42,919)		(63,045)	
Dividends	(42,300)		(40,257)	
Contingencies	(56,000)		–	
		(3,268)		8,069
		1,279,920		1,118,097
Debentures		450,000		300,000
		829,920		818,097
Share capital		500,000		500,000
General reserve		329,920		318,097
		829,920		818,097

Notes to the accounts

Non-current assets

You discover that the non-current assets of Kriton are depreciated in accordance with the fiscal policy in operation in Ecudia. Thus depreciation for the year to 31 December 20X9 of €85,343 has been reflected in the Kriton accounts. If the depreciation charge had been based on the same policy as in Hamilton, then the depreciation charge would have been €103,445 for the year, i.e. an additional €18,102.

The non-current asset figures in the statement of financial position of Kriton reflect the depreciation charged over the years, that is, they are at net book value, in accordance with Ecudian generally accepted accounting practices. If the total provision for depreciation brought forward at the beginning of 20X9 had been calculated on the same basis as for Hamilton, it would have been an extra €46,578. In other words, the net book value as at 1 January 20X9 would have been reduced by that amount.

Other expenses

Research and development costs of Kriton are written off to the statement of comprehensive income as and when they are incurred. They form part of the other expenses on the statement of cash flows.

All contingencies, no matter how remote, are also included in this statement of comprehensive income. You estimate that €56,000 in expenses has been accrued for. It is very unlikely to ever become due. You also note that this type of contingency would not normally be accrued for in the UK, i.e. according to international accounting standards.

Dividends

These are interim dividends declared at the year end and the company is committed to pay them on 7 January.

Inventory

Standard accounting practice in Ecudia is to value inventory at selling price. The valuations at historical cost for Kriton would be €65,900 at 31 December 20X8 and €67,250 at 31 December 20X9.

Issue costs

Debenture issue costs are written off in the year in Ecudia.

HAMILTON ENGINEERING LTD FINANCIAL STATEMENTS
STATEMENT OF FINANCIAL POSITIONS AS AT 31 DECEMBER

		20X9 (£)		20X8 (£)
Non-current assets		850,976		793,465
Current assets				
Inventory	23,472		26,574	
Trade receivables	36,457		38,563	
Bank	6,453		–	
		66,382		65,137
		917,358		858,602
Share capital		600,000		600,000
General reserves		101,815		1,324
		701,815		601,324
Non-current liabilities				
Debentures		150,000		200,000
Current liabilities				
Trade receivables	29,756		27,463	
Tax	35,787		29,465	
Bank	–		350	
		65,543		57,278
		917,358		858,602

STATEMENT OF COMPREHENSIVE INCOME
FOR THE YEAR ENDED 31 DECEMBER

		20X9		20X8
		(£)		(£)
Sales		524,536		395,764
Cost of sales		284,657		269,472
Gross profit		239,879		126,292
Depreciation	65,655		59,685	
Expenses	32,657		28,675	
Interest paid	7,500		10,000	
		105,812		98,360
Net profit before tax		134,067		27,932
Taxation		33,576		29,465
Retained profit for the year		100,491		(1,533)

Note of retained earnings

	20X9	20X8
Retained profit b/f	1,324	2,857
Profit (loss) for the year	100,491	(1,533)
Retained profit c/f	101,815	1,324

Notes

▶ No non-current assets were sold during the year but £124,844 were bought.

▶ Research and development expenditure is charged to the statement of comprehensive income.

▶ Inventory is valued at historical cost.

▶ The debentures were redeemed at nominal value.

Required

1 Draft a statement of comprehensive income for Kriton Manufacturers SA for the year ended 31 December 20X9. Refer to Chapter 7 if you need to refresh your knowledge of how to do this.

2 Redraft the statement of comprehensive income for Kriton prepared in answer to (1) above in accordance with international generally accepted accounting practice (i.e. the same accounting practices as Hamilton Engineering Ltd).

3 Redraft the statement of financial position at both 31 December 20X9 and 31 December 20X8 for Kriton, in accordance with international generally accepted accounting practice (i.e. the accounting practice of Hamilton Engineering Ltd).

4 Redraft the statement of cash flows for the year ended 31 December 20X9 in accordance with best international practice, adopting the indirect method of reporting. Refer to Chapter 10 if you need to refresh your knowledge of how to do this.

5 Calculate the following ratios for both Kriton, using your newly drafted accounts, and for Hamilton, for both 20X8 and 20X9, as far as the information allows:

(a) Gross profit.

(b) Net profit.

(c) Return on capital employed.

(d) Return on owner's equity.

(e) Gearing.

(f) Current.

(g) Quick.

(h) Trade receivables' collection.

(i) Trade payables' payment.

(j) Inventory turnover.

(k) Sales to capital employed.

Refer to Chapter 12 if you need to refresh your knowledge of how to do this.

6 Use the ratios as a basis for your recommendation to the directors of Bairstow Holdings plc on which company, if either, they should invest in. Refer to Chapter 12 if you need to refresh your knowledge of how to do this.

Answers

1 To draw up the statement of comprehensive income for Kriton we need to convert the cash flows to accruals-based accounting. Generally, you have completed the reverse of this exercise when drawing up the statement of cash flows from the statement of comprehensive income in Chapter 10. For the sales calculation we take the receipts (cash) from customers and adjust it for opening and closing trade receivables. Opening trade receivables we will assume are all paid during the period and therefore have been included in the cash received and thus we need to deduct €43,804. Closing trade receivables have obviously not paid and therefore these will increase the cash received by €44,877. The other calculations for purchases, expenses, taxation and dividends work in a similar way as you can see below. For interest payable and receivable we have no other information available and must assume that these equate to interest paid and received.

KRITON MANUFACTURERS SA
STATEMENT OF COMPREHENSIVE INCOME FOR THE YEAR ENDED
31 DECEMBER 20X9

	€	€
Sales (654,836 − 43,084 + 44,877)		656,629
Opening inventory	86,582	
Purchases (362,573 − 33,365 + 31,613)	360,821	
	447,403	
Less closing inventory	90,200	357,203
Gross profit		299,426
Expenses (151,353 − 4,502 + 5,045)	151,896	
Depreciation	85,343	
Contingency	56,000	
Profit on sale of assets (note 1)		
(105,040 − 19,697)	(85,343)	
Debenture issue costs	2,150	
Interest received	(12,900)	
Interest paid	5,238	
		202,384
Net profit before tax		97,042
Tax		42,919
Net profit after tax		54,123
Dividends		42,300
		11,823
Retained profit b/f		318,097
Retained profit c/f		329,920

Note 1

Opening assets valuation	1,110,028
Add purchase new assets	278,200
	1,388,228
Less depreciation for the year	85,343
	1,302,885
Closing asset valuation	1,283,188
Thus net book value assets sold	19,697

2 We now have to look at all the accounting policies of Kriton and convert to IAS accounting policies where necessary. For example, we are told that the depreciation policy of Kriton is different from that of international GAAP and if IAS policy had been used the depreciation charge would have increased to €103,445. We need to make changes for inventory, historical cost not selling price, and remove the contingency. We also have to remember that the retained profits of Kriton will have been calculated using Ecudia GAAP and we therefore need to amend the retained profit brought forward.

KRITON MANUFACTURERS SA
STATEMENT OF COMPREHENSIVE INCOME FOR THE YEAR ENDED 31 DECEMBER
20X9 IN ACCORDANCE WITH INTERNATIONAL GAAP

	€	€
Sales		656,629
Opening inventory	65,900	
Purchases	360,821	
	426,721	
Less closing inventory	67,250	
		359,471
Gross profit		297,158
Expenses	151,896	
Depreciation	103,445	
Contingency	–	
Debenture issue costs	2,150	
Interest received	(12,900)	
Interest paid	5,238	
Profit on sale of assets	(85,343)	
		164,486
Net profit before tax		132,672
Taxation		42,919
Net profit after tax		89,753

STATEMENT OF CHANGES IN EQUITY
FOR THE YEAR ENDED 31 DECEMBER 20X7
IN ACCORDANCE WITH INTERNATIONAL GAAP

	€
Retained profit b/f (note 1)	250,837
Retained profit for the year	89,753
Dividends	(42,300)
Retained profit c/f	€298,290

Note 1: Adjustment to retained profit b/f

	€
Retained profit b/f as per statement of financial position	318,097
Less previous years' depreciation	(46,578)
Less revaluation of closing inventory 31 December 20X8	(20,682)
Retained profit b/f	250,837

3 Changes, to convert to international GAAP will be required to non-current assets, inventory and liabilities (contingencies).

KRITON MANUFACTURERS SA
STATEMENT OF FINANCIAL POSITION AS AT 31 DECEMBER 20X9 UNDER INTERNATIONAL GAAP

	€	€
Non-current assets (1,283,188 – 46,578 – 18,102)		1,218,508
Current assets		
Inventory	67,250	
Trade receivables	44,877	
Bank	39,532	151,659
		1,370,167
Share capital		500,000
General reserve		298,290
		798,290
Non-current liabilities		
Debentures		450,000
Current liabilities		
Trade payables	31,613	
Other creditors	5,045	
Taxation	42,919	
Dividends	42,300	
		121,877
		1,370,167

KRITON MANUFACTURERS SA
STATEMENT OF FINANCIAL POSITION AS AT 31 DECEMBER 20X8 AS PER INTERNATIONAL GAAP

	€	€
Non-current assets		1,063,450
Current assets		
Inventory	65,900	
Trade receivables	43,084	
Bank	19,572	128,556
		1,192,006
Share capital		500,000
General reserve		250,837
		750,837
Non-current liabilities		
Debentures		300,000

Current liabilities

Trade payables	33,365	
Other creditors	4,502	
Tax	63,045	
Dividends	40,257	141,169
		1,192,006

4 This activity should be quite straightforward as you are now working from the international GAAP prepared statement of comprehensive income and statement of financial positions as we did in Chapter 10.

KRITON MANUFACTURERS SA

STATEMENT OF CASH FLOWS FOR THE YEAR ENDED 31 DECEMBER 20X9

	€	€
Cash inflow from operating activities (note 1)		140,910
Interest paid		(5,238)
Tax paid		(63,045)
Net cash paid in investing activities		
Purchase of assets	(278,200)	
Proceeds of sale of assets	105,040	
Interest received	12,900	
		(160,260)
Net cash from financing activities		
Debenture issue	147,850	
Dividends paid	(40,257)	
		107,593
Change in cash and bank		19,960

Note 1

Operating profit for the year before tax, interest and dividends		
(132,672 + 5,238 − 12,900)		125,010
Add back:		
Depreciation	103,445	
Issue costs	2,150	
Less profit on sale	(85,343)	20,252
		145,262
Increase in inventory	(1,350)	
Increase in receivables	(1,793)	
Decrease in trade payables	(1,752)	
Increase in other creditors	543	
		(4,352)
		140,910

5 We have shown our ratios in two separate tables for ease of reference. The first table shows the ratios themselves, while the subsequent table shows the underlying calculations. Note that not all ratios can be calculated for Kriton, in the absence of a statement of comprehensive income for 20X8. Such restrictions are often a feature of accounts analysis, and conclusions and recommendations have to be determined from what information is available. Note also that the fact that Kriton's accounts are in a different currency does not impact on the calculation of the ratios; the currency is 'cancelled out'.

	Kriton		Hamilton	
	20X9	20X8	20X9	20X8
Gross profit	45.3%		45.7%	31.9%
Net profit	0.7% (note 1)		25.6%	7.1%
Return on capital employed	0.8% (note 1)		12.7%	1.1%
Return on shareholders' funds	0.6% (note 1)		14.3%	(0.3)%
Gearing	36.0%	28.5%	17.6%	25.0%
Current	1.24	0.91	1.01	1.14
Quick	0.69	0.44	0.65	0.67
Trade receivables' collection	25 days		25 days	35 days
Trade payables' payment	32 days (note 2)		38 days	37 days
Inventory turnover	68 days		30 days	36 days
Sales to capital employed	0.53		0.62	0.49

Note 1

The 'raw' net profit figure is €89,753. Using this gives a net profit to sales percentage of 13.7%. However, our view is that this would be an unreliable figure, since it includes a very substantial profit on the sale of non-current assets, which is unlikely to be repeated, and is therefore a poor guide to future performance. The figure we have used for profit therefore excludes this profit on sale of non-current assets, and is consequently €4,410. The same figure has then also been used for the next two ratios. Note that our identification of a sustainable profit here is a contentious issue – the essential thing is to be consistent in any such adjustment policy.

Note 2

Since only the cost of sales figure is available for Hamilton, we have also used the cost of sales figure for Kriton's ratio calculation. Strictly, the denominator should, of course, be the purchases figure, but our approach has the key merit of consistency.

The answers above have been calculated from the following fractions. You should be able to identify the amounts involved below from the accounts.

	Kriton 20X9	Kriton 20X8	Hamilton 20X9	Hamilton 20X8
Gross profit	$\frac{297{,}158}{656{,}629}$		$\frac{239{,}879}{524{,}536}$	$\frac{126{,}292}{395{,}764}$
Net profit	$\frac{4{,}410}{656{,}629}$		$\frac{134{,}067}{524{,}536}$	$\frac{27{,}932}{395{,}764}$
Return on capital employed	$\frac{9{,}648}{1{,}248{,}290}$		$\frac{107{,}991}{851{,}815}$	$\frac{8{,}467}{801{,}324}$
Return on shareholders' funds	$\frac{4{,}410}{798{,}290}$		$\frac{100{,}491}{701{,}815}$	$\frac{(1{,}533)}{601{,}324}$
Gearing	$\frac{450{,}000}{1{,}248{,}290}$	$\frac{300{,}000}{1{,}050{,}837}$	$\frac{150{,}000}{851{,}815}$	$\frac{200{,}000}{801{,}324}$
Current	$\frac{151{,}659}{121{,}877}$	$\frac{128{,}556}{141{,}169}$	$\frac{66{,}382}{65{,}543}$	$\frac{65{,}137}{57{,}278}$
Quick	$\frac{84{,}409}{121{,}877}$	$\frac{62{,}656}{141{,}169}$	$\frac{42{,}910}{65{,}543}$	$\frac{38{,}563}{57{,}278}$
Trade receivables' collection	$\frac{44{,}877}{656{,}629} \times 365$		$\frac{36{,}457}{524{,}536} \times 365$	$\frac{38{,}563}{395{,}764} \times 365$
Trade payables' payment	$\frac{31{,}613}{359{,}471} \times 365$		$\frac{29{,}756}{284{,}657} \times 365$	$\frac{27{,}463}{269{,}472} \times 365$
Inventory turnover	$\frac{67{,}250}{359{,}471} \times 365$		$\frac{23{,}472}{284{,}657} \times 365$	$\frac{26{,}574}{269{,}472} \times 365$
Sales to capital employed	$\frac{656{,}629}{1{,}248{,}290}$		$\frac{524{,}536}{851{,}815}$	$\frac{395{,}764}{801{,}324}$

6 Analysis and recommendations

The following points should be included in any report you prepare for Bairstow plc:

▶ The absence of an statement of comprehensive income for Kriton for 20X8 means that some ratios cannot be calculated.

▶ The net profit figure to be used for Kriton for 20X9 is subject to debate over the repeatability of the profit on the sale of the non-current assets.

▶ The gross profit percentages for 20X9 are very similar between the two companies, but the net profit percentages indicate that Kriton's expenses are substantially more than Hamilton's, in relation to their respective turnovers. This indicates that serious attention needs to be given to Kriton's expenses.

▶ The poor net profit in Kriton is also reflected in return on capital and on shareholders' funds ratios; that is, they are much lower for Kriton than for Hamilton. It is also worth noting that Hamilton's ratios have improved since 20X8. Kriton thus appears a less attractive possibility as an investment than Hamilton, if the objective is a high return on that investment.

▶ The gearing ratio has increased in Kriton, while it has fallen in Hamilton. The high gearing implies high interest charges, which is likely to leave little profit as a return for investors. Again, the implication is that Kriton is unattractive as an investment, relative to Hamilton.

▶ The relative positions of the two companies as regards liquidity show Kriton to be in the stronger position. Both its current and quick ratios have improved significantly over 20X9, while Hamilton's position has worsened, as evidenced by the same two ratios. This may imply a concern over the future ability of Hamilton to meet its obligations in the short term, despite its relatively good profitability.

▶ Both trade receivable collection and trade payable payment periods are similar for the two companies, as far as can be determined from the limited information available for Kriton. Credit management policies and practices are probably therefore similar in the two companies.

▶ The inventory turnover period, however, is much longer in Kriton than in Hamilton. This is surprising, given that they are in the same industry, albeit operating in different countries. It may be that Kriton's relative inability to move its inventory quickly is a cause of its relatively poor profitability.

▶ The similarity of the sales to capital employed ratios suggest that both companies are similar in their ability to generate sales from a given level of investment.

▶ Overall, Kriton's problems seem to stem from its high level of expenses, relative to turnover, compared with what Hamilton has been able to achieve. This area should certainly be investigated before any decision to invest in Kriton is made. Furthermore, it may well be productive to investigate why Kriton has been unable to shift its inventory as quickly as its competitor.

▶ The better investment would therefore appear to be Hamilton. However, any decision to invest should take into account the alternative investments open to Bairstow. At its simplest, these could include, for example, placing the money in a deposit account. This would, of course, probably be a significantly safer investment than putting money into Hamilton, and the question of relative risk should be considered alongside that of relative return.

Summary

This final chapter has attempted to pull together many of the issues that you have studied in this book. It has been an extensive case study, and it is likely that you did not find it very easy. However, we recommend that you return to it at least once more – you should find it an excellent way to revise and consolidate your understanding.

Answers to self-assessment questions

Chapter 1 What is accounting?

Answers to Questions 1–8

1 (c) 2 (a) 3 (d) 4 (c) 5 (b) 6 (b) 7 (b) 8 (b)

Question 9

Statement of comprehensive income	A summary of gains and losses by the organisation during the past year
Statement of financial position	A summary of the assets, liabilities and capital applicable to the organisation at the end of the year
Statement of cash flows	A summary of liquid funds that flowed in and out of the organisation in the past year

Question 10

1 List and consider the users, and their needs. In particular, financial statements in the UK are mostly used by existing and potential investors and lenders.

2 Such users are concerned with whether the entity is now, and/or is likely to be in future, a good source of financial return and security. This means that they are looking to the statements for, in the words of the Framework for the Preparation and Presentation of Financial Information, 'information about the financial position, performance and changes in financial position of an enterprise that is useful to a wide range of users in making economic decisions'.

3 Other users' needs should also be considered, in terms of the decisions they need to make about the entity. For example, employees' use of the financial statements could be considered in relation to decisions about whether to join or leave the entity, or pay rises.

4 Note the shortcomings of UK financial statements in that they only provide historical information, while decision making is inherently forward looking.

5 Nevertheless, the usefulness of historical information for confirmatory purposes should be considered in relation to specific users. However, stewardship is not specifically highlighted in the Framework.

6 The generally accepted conclusion, then, is that the main rationale for financial accounting and reporting in the UK is to aid users in decision making, but that the confirmatory stewardship role, while secondary, is also valid.

Chapter 2 The statement of financial position

1 (a) 2 (c) 3 (b) 4 (c) 5 (c) 6 (d)

Question 7

MORTLAKE LTD
STATEMENT OF FINANCIAL POSITION AS AT 31 DECEMBER

Non-current assets		
Building		42,000
Vehicle		13,000
Current assets		55,000
Inventory	6,000	
Trade receivables	4,000	10,000
		65,000
Equity		60,000
Current liabilities		
Trade payables		
		5,000
		65,000

Notes:

1 The non-current assets have been valued at historical cost, rather than at the higher market value, since the market value is uncertain, and it is, in any case, more prudent (cautious) to apply the lower figure to the valuation. Prudence is a concept that we will look at in more detail in Chapter 4.
2 The inventory has similarly been valued at the lower of the possible valuations. This is our best estimate of the economic benefit that it represents to Mortlake.
3 The equity can be taken as the balancing figure because the statement of financial position equation defines equity as the difference between assets and liabilities.

Question 8

(a) The total historical cost of the building is £380,000 and this is the figure that should be used in the company's statement of financial position. The repairs have not improved the building and have no continuing existence, so should be treated as an expense and not as part of the value of the building.
(b) The key point here is that the car was written off after the statement of financial position date, and so did exist at that point. If we are to report the state of affairs at the statement of financial position date we must include that car. Valuing both cars, therefore, at the usual historical cost valuation gives a figure of £27,000.
(c) There are three valuations possible here, historical cost of £19,000, net realisable value of £8,000 and replacement cost of £15,000. Historical cost does have the key advantage of being objective – both the other valuations must be guesses, albeit good ones. The figure to be used here would therefore be £19,000. If you are unhappy about this choice then we can only say that many accountants would agree with you, since it is an obviously out of date, and therefore arguably irrelevant, figure. Nevertheless, as we have seen, standard practice is normally to use historical cost.

(d) The only debtor we can rely on to pay us, and thus to provide some economic ben-efit, is the first, i.e. the one for £2,000. The others would not be shown as trade receivables in the statement of financial position because they are both unlikely to result in our receiving cash.

Question 9

(a)

YEOVIL ELECTRONICS

STATEMENT OF FINANCIAL POSITION AT 31 DECEMBER 20X9

Non-current assets		
Premises		345,000
Plant and machinery		104,800
		449,800
Current assets		
Inventory	67,250	
Trade receivables	46,200	113,450
		563,250
Capital		371,470
Non-current liabilities		
Long-term loan		120,000
Current liabilities		
Trade payables	56,780	
Bank overdraft	15,000	71,780
		563,250

(b)

YEOVIL ELECTRONICS

STATEMENT OF FINANCIAL POSITION AT 31 DECEMBER 20X9

Non-current assets		
Premises		480,000
Plant and machinery		95,000
		575,000
Current assets		
Inventory	61,000	
Trade receivables	46,200	107,200
		682,200
Capital		493,600
Non-current liabilities		
Long-term loan		120,000
Current liabilities		
Trade payables	53,600	
Bank overdraft	15,000	68,600
		682,200

(c)

YEOVIL ELECTRONICS
STATEMENT OF FINANCIAL POSITION AT 31 DECEMBER 20X9

Non-current assets		
Premises		450,000
Plant and machinery		40,000
		490,000
Current assets		
Inventory	83,650	
Trade receivables	44,000	127,650
		617,650
Capital		425,870
Non-current liabilities		
Long-term loan		120,000
Current liabilities		
Trade payables	56,780	
Bank overdraft	15,000	
		71,780
		617,650

(d) There is no absolute answer to this question, of course. Feedback centres around the following points:

1 The historical cost statement of financial position (a) has the key merit of relative objectivity.

2 Historical cost is out of date, i.e. none of the figures represent the fair value position at the statement of financial position date, except by coincidence, even though the title of the statement of financial position says that they do.

3 The replacement cost statement of financial position (b) is a current valuation.

4 There are, however, problems with the objective determination of the replacement costs. These make the method both relatively subjective and relatively expensive to implement.

5 It could be argued that the method rests on an assumption that assets will be replaced with something similar. This may not be the case in times of changing technologies and changing working methods.

6 The net realisable value use in statement of financial position (c) is also a current method of valuation, and preferable to historical cost on that ground.

7 It has similar drawbacks to those of replacement cost, namely the difficulties of objective determination and cost.

8 It has been objected that the use of realisable value implies the intention to liquidate the organisation in the foreseeable future. This is probably even less supportable than the automatic replacement assumption implicit in the use of the replacement cost method.

Any decision on which statement of financial position gives the most true and fair view should be justified by reference to the above points. While there is no correct answer, note that the IASB still effectively assumes historical cost. However, IAS 16 does allow for a move towards replacement cost, or even deprival value, where historical cost is no longer considered true and fair.

Chapter 3 The statement of comprehensive income

Question 1

Our answer starts with the calculation of closing inventory, i.e.:

5,000 + 2,000 – 3,000 = 4,000 units in inventory

Under FIFO, those sold are deemed to be from the first delivery, leaving 2,000 units at £12, and the other 2,000 units therefore being from the delivery at £13. The closing inventory valuation is therefore:

(2,000 × 12) + (2,000 × 13) = 50,000.

We can now calculate the cost of sales, being purchases less closing inventory – there is no opening inventory to worry about in this case. The calculation is 531,946 – 50,000 = 481,946.

Next we need to allocate the expenses to their Companies Act categories. This is best set out as a table.

	Cost of sales	Selling	Administration
Cost of sales, as above	481,946		
Wages	87,388	87,388	43,694
Transport	21,790	21,790	10,895
Rent and insurance	12,310	12,310	6,155
	£603,434	£121,488	£60,744

Finally, we can put all the above together into our statement of income, as follows:

ANARKHI LTD
STATEMENT OF INCOME
FOR THE YEAR ENDED 31 DECEMBER

Sales		794,062
Cost of sales		603,434
Gross profit		190,628
Selling and distribution expenses	121,488	
Administration expenses	60,744	
		182,232
Net profit		8,396
Tax		3,900
Retained profit		£4,496

Question 2

TAYSIDE GLASS LTD
STATEMENT OF INCOME
FOR THE YEAR ENDED 31 MARCH 20X9

Sales		80,007
Cost of sales:		
Purchases	62,419	
Less: closing inventory	4,200	
		58,219
Gross profit		21,788
Wages	9,650	
Rent	4,600	
Telephone	627	
Light and heat	1,629	
Office expenses	1,127	
		17,633
Net profit, transferred to reserves		4,155

TAYSIDE GLASS LTD
STATEMENT OF FINANCIAL POSITION AT 31 MARCH 20X9

Non-current assets		
Shop fittings		6,000
Delivery van		4,000
		10,000
Current assets		
Inventory	4,200	
Trade receivables	1,215	
Bank	370	5,785
		15,785
Share capital		10,000
Reserves		4,155
		14,155
Current liabilities		
Trade payables		1,630
		15,785

Question 3

	FIFO		AVCO	
Sales		575,200		575,200
Cost of sales				
Opening inventory	11,000		11,000	
Purchases	501,000		501,000	
	512,000		512,000	

Closing inventory				
30 computers	18,000			
at £600				
30 computers			18,020	
at £602 (note 1)		494,000		493,980
		81,200		81,220

Note 1

	Quantity	AVCO	Value
Opening stock	20	550	11,000
Bought	300	550	165,000
Sold	(260)	550	(143,000)
End January	60	550	33,000
Bought	240	650	156,000
	300	630	189,000
		(189,000 / 300)	
Sold	(280)	630	(176,400)
		(from above)	
End February	20	630	12,600
Bought	300	600	180,000
	320	602	192,600
		(192,600 / 320)	
Sold	(290)	602	174,580
Closing stock	30	602	18,020

Question 4

The arguments in favour of a receipts and payments account for the cricket club would include:

▶ Simplicity; it is a relatively easy statement to prepare.
▶ Understandability; being based solely on cash in and out it should be easier for non-accountant members of the club to understand.
▶ Objectivity; it doesn't rely on the estimates that are inherent in accruals accounting.

The arguments in favour of using an statement of income would include:

▶ It arguably provides a more useful report since it takes into account events that have not resulted in a cash flow in the current year, such as goods purchased for fund raising activities but not yet paid for.
▶ Consistency with performance reports of most other organisations.

Chapter 4 Concepts and characteristics

Answers to Questions 1–5
1 (b)   2 (d)   3 (b)   4 (c)   5 (d)

Question 6

1 The essay should start with a consideration of the stated purposes of the IASB. The idea that the Board exists to establish and improve standards of financial accounting and reporting is widely accepted.

2 The key question is how to achieve this. One major method is the publication of accounting standards, that is, by specifying clear accounting practices.

3 Some consideration could be given to whether existing standards actually do this, and, if not, why not.

4 One possible reason for perceived lack of clarity in the specification of accounting standards is arguably the lack of general agreement on fundamental questions, such as the purposes of financial accounting.

5 If this is accepted, then practical accounting standards can only be specified once such underlying issues have been largely resolved. In other words, the theoretical principles must be established in order to guide the determination of what practical standards should be specified.

Question 7

	UK	*French*
Relevance	Each company operates differently and in a different environment. Accounts that reflect this will be more relevant for users than those which ignore such differences.	The question should be asked relevant for whom? If we accept the list of users in the Framework then we note that many may not be financially literate, and the relative simplicity of French accounting will be an advantage.
Reliability	The question should be asked reliable for what? If we accept decision making as the purpose then it is necessary to prepare accounts that reflect the real differences between companies.	Clear rules consistently applied result in reliability.
Comparability	Accounts are arguably more comparable if they have been prepared in the way most appropriate for each company.	Requiring all companies to prepare their accounts in the same way means that the user can be sure that the same item has been dealt with in exactly the same way in different companies' accounts.
Understandability	Attempting to reach a true and fair view may result in more complex accounts, but they will still be understandable if users are financially literate.	A single method leads to simpler accounts, which must result in more understandable accounts.

Question 8

1 The overall purpose of the Statement is to provide a coherent framework for the determination of standard accounting practice.
2 The first part states the purposes of accounting as to aid decision making and also to confirm the results of past activities. It also lists the legitimate users of financial statements. The purpose is to define the aims of accounting, and so to set the general direction for the following parts.
3 The second part deals with the qualitative characteristics of accounting, namely reliability, relevance, comparability and understandability. It thus defines the hallmarks of a 'good' set of financial statements.
4 The next part defines the 'elements' of financial accounting, thereby setting the parameters of accounting. In other words, its purpose is to define the scope of financial accounting. This complemented by recognition rules which limit recognition of items in financial statements to those which both fall within the definitions of elements and are capable of objective measurement.
5 Accordingly, the next part is concerned with valuation. It effectively focuses on deprival value as the ideal, but the general purpose is more to provide a framework within which decisions about the most appropriate valuation method can be decided.
6 Finally, the Framework explores the issue of capital maintenance, and the issue of what we mean by 'capital' and the net worth of an organisation.

Chapter 5 The double entry system

Question 1

CAPITAL ACCOUNT

30.4.	Bal c/d	20,000	1.4.	Bank	20,000
			1.5.	Bal b/d	20,000

BANK ACCOUNT

1.4.	Capital	20,000	1.4.	Premises etc	17,000
12.4.	Cash	1,305	2.4.	Cash	500
17.4.	A. Britton	400	17.4.	R. Sevier	500
22.4.	S. Boatman	50	22.4.	P. Ocean	900
25.4.	Cash	570	30.4.	Bal c/d	3,425
		22,325			22,325
1.5.	Bal b/d	3,425			

PREMISES ACCOUNT

1.4.	Bank	8,000	30.4.	Bal c/d	8,000
1.5.	Bal b/d	8,000			

CASH ACCOUNT

2.4.	Bank	500	2.4.	Stationery	175
3.4.	Sales	450	5.4.	Wages	160
5.4.	Sales	250	9.4.	Sundries	80
9.4.	Sales	340	12.4.	Wages	160
12.4.	Sales	340	12.4.	Bank	1,305
18.4.	Sales	550	18.4.	Sundries	60
22.4.	Sales	850	19.4.	Wages	160
			24.4.	Wages	160
			24.4.	Sundries	50
			24.4.	Drawings	400
			25.4.	Bank	570
		3,280			3,280

DRAWINGS ACCOUNT

24.4.	Cash	400	30.4.	Bal c/d	400
1.5.	Bal b/d	400			

FIXTURES ACCOUNT

1.4.	Cash	5,000	30.4.	Bal c/d	5,000
1.5.	Bal b/d	5,000			

INVENTORY ACCOUNT

1.4.	Bank	4,000	30.4.	Statement of comprehensive income	4,000
30.4.	Statement of comprehensive income	3,500	30.4.	Bal c/d	3,500
1.5.	Bal b/d	3,500			

WAGES ACCOUNT

5.4.	Cash	160			
12.4.	Cash	160			
19.4	Cash	160			
24.4.	Cash	160	30.4.	Statement of comprehensive income	640
		640			640

PURCHASES ACCOUNT

8.4.	R. Sevier	950			
16.4.	P. Ocean	1,500	30.4.	Statement of comprehensive income	2,450
		2,450			2,450

STATIONERY AND SUNDRIES ACCOUNT

2.4.	Cash	175			
9.4.	Cash	80			
18.4.	Cash	60			
24.4.	Cash	50	30.4.	Statement of comprehensive income	365
		365			365

SALES ACCOUNT

			3.4.	Cash	450
			4.4.	A. Britton	650
			5.4.	Cash	250
			9.4.	Cash	340
			10.4	R. Sewell	440
			12.4.	Cash	340
			15.4.	S. Boatman	260
			18.4.	Cash	550
30.4.	Statement of comprehensive income	4,130	22.4.	Cash	850
		4,130			4,130

S. BOATMAN ACCOUNT

15.4	Sales	260	22.4.	Bank	50
			30.4.	Bal c/d	210
		260			260
1.5.	Bal b/d	210			

P. OCEAN ACCOUNT

22.4.	Bank	900	16.4.	Purchases	1,500
30.4.	Bal c/d	600			
		1,500			1,500
			1.5.	Bal b/d	600

A. BRITTON ACCOUNT

4.4.	Sales	650	8.4.	Returns		100
			17.4.	Bank		400
			30.4.	Bal c/d		150
		650				650
1.5.	Bal b/d	150				

R. SEVIER ACCOUNT

11.4.	Returns	230	8.4.	Purchases	950
17.4.	Bank	500			
30.4.	Bal c/d	220			
		950			950
			1.5.	Bal b/d	220

R. SEWELL ACCOUNT

10.4.	Sales	£440	30.4.	Bal c/d	£440
1.5.	Bal b/d	440			

RETURNS INWARDS ACCOUNT

8.4.	A. Britton	£100	30.4.	Statement of comprehensive income	£100

RETURNS OUTWARDS ACCOUNT

30.4.	Statement of comprehensive income	230	11.4.	R Sevier	230

TRIAL BALANCE AS AT 30.4.X1

	Dr	Cr
Capital		20,000
Premises	8,000	
Fixtures	5,000	
Inventory	4,000	
Wages	640	
Purchases	2,450	
S. Boatman	210	
A. Britton	150	
P. Ocean		600
Returns inwards	100	
Returns outwards		230
Bank	3,425	
Stationery	365	

Sales		4,130
R. Sevier		220
R. Sewell	440	
Drawings	400	
	25,180	25,180

STATEMENT OF COMPREHENSIVE INCOME FOR THE MONTH ENDED 30.4.X1

Sales		4,130	
Less returns inwards		100	4,030
Opening inventory		4,000	
Add purchases	2,450		
Less returns outwards	230	2,220	
		6,220	
Less closing inventory		3,500	2,720
Gross profit			1,310
Wages		640	
Stationery		365	1,005
Net profit			305

STATEMENT OF FINANCIAL POSITION AS AT 30.4.X1

Non-current assets			
Premises		8,000	
Fixtures		5,000	13,000
Current assets			
Inventory		3,500	
Trade receivables: S. Boatman	210		
A. Britton	150		
R. Sewell	440	800	
Bank		3,425	7,725
Total assests			20,725
Capital			20,000
Add net profit	305		
Less drawings	400		(95)
			19,905
Current liabilities			
Creditors: P. Ocean	600		
R. Sevier	220		820
Total capital and liabilities			20,725

Question 2

CAPITAL ACCOUNT

5.6.	Balance c/d	50,000	1.6.	Bank	50,000
			6.6.	Balance b/d	50,000
					50,000

BANK ACCOUNT

1.6.	Capital	50,000	1.6.	Premises etc.	25,000
5.6.	Roberts	60	1.6.	Furn & fitt	2,000
5.6.	Cash	1,440	1.6.	Purchases	10,000
			2.6.	Cash	400
			5.6.	Davids	250
			5.6.	Balance c/d	13,850
		51,500			51,500
6.6.	Balance b/d	13,850			

PREMISES ACCOUNT

1.6.	Bank	19,000	5.6.	Balance c/d	19,000
6.6.	Balance b/d	19,000			

FURNITURE & FITTINGS ACCOUNT

1.6.	Bank	6,000			
1.6.	Bank	2,000	5.6.	Balance c/d	8,000
		8,000			8,000
6.6.	Balance b/d	8,000			

PURCHASES ACCOUNT

1.6.	Bank	10,000			
3.6.	Davids	600			
5.6.	Cash	250	5.6.	Balance c/d	10,850
		10,850			10,850
6.6.	Balance b/d	10,850	6.6.	Statement of comprehensive income	10,850

CASH ACCOUNT

2.6.	Bank	400	2.6.	Sundries	90
2.6.	Sales	300	4.6.	Office	70
3.6.	Sales	550	5.6.	Purchases	250
4.6.	Sales	400	5.6.	Bank	1,440
5.6.	Sales	200			
		1,850			1,850

SUNDRIES ACCOUNT

2.6.	Cash	90	5.6.	Balance c/d	90
6.6.	Balance b/d	90	5.6.	Statement of comprehensive income	90

OFFICE ACCOUNT

4.6.	Cash	70	5.6.	Balance c/d	70
6.6.	Balance b/d	70	5.6.	Statement of comprehensive income	70

SALES ACCOUNT

			2.6.	Cash	300
			2.6.	Roberts	100
			3.6.	Cash	550
			4.6.	Cash	400
			4.6.	Richards	350
			5.6.	Cash	200
5.6.	Balance c/d	2,380	5.6.	Martins	480
		2,380			2,380
6.6.	Statement of comprehensive income	2,380	6.6.	Balance b/d	2,380

ROBERTS DEBTOR ACCOUNT

2.6.	Sales	100	6.6.	Bank	60
			5.6.	Balance c/d	40
		100			100
6.6.	Balance b/d	40			

RICHARDS DEBTOR ACCOUNT

4.6.	Sales	350	5.6.	Balance c/d	350
6.6.	Balance b/d	350			

MARTIN DEBTOR ACCOUNT

5.6.	Sales	480	5.6.	Balance c/d	480
6.6.	Balance b/d	480			

DAVIDS CREDITOR ACCOUNT

5.6.	Bank	250	3.6.	Purchases	600
5.6.	Balance c/d	350			
		600			600
			6.6.	Balance b/d	350

INVENTORY ACCOUNT

5.6.	Statement of comprehensive income	9,500	

TRIAL BALANCE AS AT 5.6.X1

	Dr	Cr
Capital		50,000
Bank	13,850	
Premises	19,000	
Furniture and fittings	8,000	
Purchases	10,850	
Sundries	90	
Office	70	
Sales		2,380
Roberts debtor	40	
Richards debtor	350	
Davids creditor		350
Martin debtor	480	
	52,730	52,730

STATEMENT OF COMPREHENSIVE INCOME FOR THE WEEK ENDED 6.6.X1

Sales		2,380
Purchases	10,850	
Inventory	9,500	1,350
Gross profit		1,030
Sundries	90	
Office	70	160
Net profit		870

STATEMENT OF FINANCIAL POSITION AS AT WEEK ENDED 6.6.X1

Non-current assets				
Premises			19,000	
Furniture and fittings			8,000	27,000
Current assets				
Inventory			9,500	
Trade receivables:	Roberts	40		
	Richards	350		
	Martin	480	870	
Bank			13,850	24,220
Total assets				51,220
Capital				50,000
				870
				50,870
Current liabilities				
Davids creditor			350	350
Total capital and liabilities				51,220

Question 3

To maintain orderly recording of all business transactions in such a way that errors (but not all of them) are avoided. To enable the extraction at a point in time of balances to identify the position of the business.

Question 4

Duality.

Question 5

Assets = Capital + Liabilities

Question 6

An asset or expense.
A credit balance b/d is a liability, income or capital.

Question 7

The trial balance checks that the system has been correctly maintained in that for every debit an equal and opposite credit entry has been made and that accounts have been added correctly.

Question 8

Similar question to Activity 5.11 but well worth the revision.

▶ An entry completely missing.
▶ An entry in the wrong account.
▶ Errors that cancel.
▶ Transposed debit and credit entries.

STATEMENT OF COMPREHENSIVE INCOME FOR NARN
FOR THE YEAR ENDED 31 MARCH 200X

Sales		79,000
Opening inventory	2,700	
Purchases	32,000	
	34,700	
Closing inventory	4,200	30,500
Gross profit		48,500
Salaries and wages	15,600	
Heating and lighting	3,600	
Motor expenses	4,500	
Rent	10,400	
Other expenses	2,300	36,400
Net profit		12,100

STATEMENT OF FINANCIAL POSITION FOR NARN AS AT 31 MARCH 200X

Non-current assets		
Fixtures and fittings	5,600	
Vehicles	10,900	16,500
Current assets		
Inventory	4,200	
Debtors	6,600	
Bank and cash	5,500	16,300
Total assets		32,800
Capital injection by Narn	15,000	
Net profit	12,100	27,100
Current liabilities		
Trade payables	5,700	5,700
Total capital and liabilities		32,800

Question 10

CORRECTED TRIAL BALANCE FOR NARN 31 MARCH 200X

Sales (79,000 + 900)		79,900
Purchases	32,000	
Inventory	2,700	
Salaries and wages	15,600	
Heating and lighting	3,600	
Rent	10,400	
Other expenses (2,300 + 450)	2,750	
Fixtures and fittings	5,600	
Vehicles	10,900	
Motor expenses	4,500	
Trade receivables		
(Trade receivables) (6,600 + 900)	7,500	
Trade payables (Trade payables)		5,700
Capital injection		15,000
Bank and cash (5,500 − 225 − 225)	5,050	
	100,600	100,600

STATEMENT OF COMPREHENSIVE INCOME FOR NARN FOR THE YEAR ENDED 31 MARCH 200X

Sales		79,900
Opening inventory	2,700	
Purchases	32,000	
	34,700	
Closing inventory	4,200	30,500
Gross profit		49,400
Salaries and wages	15,600	
Heating and lighting	3,600	
Motor expenses	4,500	
Rent	10,400	
Other expenses	2,750	36,850
Net profit		12,550

STATEMENT OF FINANCIAL FOR NARN AS AT 31 MARCH 200X

Non-current assets		
Fixtures and fittings	5,600	
Vehicles	10,900	16,500
Current assets		
Inventory	4,200	
Debtors	7,500	
Bank and cash	5,050	16,750
Total assets		33,250

Capital injection by Narn		15,000	
Net profit		12,550	27,550
Current liabilities			
Creditors		5,700	5,700
Total net assets			33,250

Chapter 6 Adjustments, including entries in ledger accounts

Question 1

STATIONERY ACCOUNT

X5	Cash	450			
31.12.X5	Bal c/d	50	31.12.X5	Statement of comprehensive income	500
		500			500
			1.1.X6	Bal b/d	50

INSURANCE ACCOUNT

X5	Cash	600	31.12.X5	Statement of comprehensive income	300
			31.12.X5	Bal c/d	300
		600			600
1.1.X6	Bal b/d	300			

MOTOR EXPENSES ACCOUNT

X5	Cash	550	1.1.X4	Bal b/d	70
31.12.X5	Bal c/d	90	31.12.X5	Statement of comprehensive income	570
		640			640
			1.1.X6	Bal b/d	90

RENTS PAID ACCOUNT

1.1.X5	Bal b/d	600	31.12.X5	Statement of comprehensive income	1,350
X5	Cash	1,500	31.12.X5	Bal c/d	750
		2,100			2,100
1.1.X6	Bal b/d	750			

RENTS RECEIVABLE ACCOUNT

31.12.X5	Statement of comprehensive income	600	X5	Cash	500
			31.12.X5	Bal c/d	100
		600			600
1.1.X6	Bal b/d	100			

Question 2

(a) False. An accrued expense will increase the charge for expenses to the statement of comprehensive income so if it is ignored the profit will be overstated.

(b) True. An accrued expense brought forward from a previous period will reduce the charge to the statement of comprehensive income in the current year so if this is ignored the charge will be increased and profit understated.

(c) False. An accrued expense has not been paid but has been used up in generating revenue.

(d) True. Refer to rents paid above.

(e) True. Refer to stationery above.

(f) False. An accrued expense has not been paid and therefore is a liability.

(g) True. This is income due in the period and therefore a form of debtor.

Question 3

Matching.

Question 4

Office expenses accrue £75, statement of comprehensive income charge £1,500.

Rents prepaid £1,200, statement of comprehensive income charge £3,600. Students may well ask where the charge is for the period 1 January 20X5 to 31 March 20X5. This should have been identified as a prepayment of the previous period.

Sales accrue £2,500 = statement of comprehensive income charge. Raise a debtor of £2,500 also.

Of the insurance payment of £3,600, £900 relates to the previous period £2,700 to this. Accrue £990 for the period 30 September to 31 December. Charge to statement of comprehensive income £3,690.

Question 5

Reliability. This is to ensure that assets – trade receivables (debtors) – are not overstated in the statement of financial position.

Question 6

False. There is still a possibility that further debts could turn bad.

Question 7

BAD DEBTS ACCOUNT

A. Bloggs	780		
B. Swift	320		
P. Trent	750	Statement of comprehensive income	1,850
	1,850		1,850

PROVISION FOR BAD DEBTS ACCOUNT

		Balance b/d	2,100
		Statement of comprehensive income	495
Balance c/d	2,595		
	2,595		2,595
		Balance b/d	2,595

Calculation of required provision:

Trade receivables (Trade receivables)	54,500	
Bad debts written off	1,850	
	52,650	
Less: Debt to be paid	750	
	51,900	
Provision at 5%	2,595	
Statement of financial position extract:		
Trade receivables (trade receivables)	52,650	
Less: Provision	2,595	50,055

Question 8

Bad debts to be written off £450 + £650 + £216 = £1,316.
Trade receivables figure after write-off £45,680 − £1,316 = £44,364 but £24 requires no further provision for bad debt therefore provision for bad debt is calculated as

$$(£44,364 − £24) * 4\% = £1,774$$

Charge to statement of comprehensive income bad debts £1,316, provision for bad debts £1,774.
Trade receivables balance £42,590.

Question 9

Cost of the asset, estimate of useful life to the business, estimate of residual value at the end of that useful life at current prices, assessment of method of use of asset in the business.

Question 10

(a) False. Depreciation is the measure of the use of the asset in generating revenues. This may or may not equate to net realisable value.

(b) True.

(c) False. They may use the asset differently therefore the method will be different and also residual value and estimated life may be different.

(d) False. The method used should equate to how the asset is used, not the type of asset. However, in many businesses vehicles are depreciated by reducing balance and buildings by straight line.

(e) True.

(f) True. Depreciation is an expense so if omitted expenses will be understated and therefore profit overstated.

Question 11

BUILDINGS ACCOUNT

1.1.X0	Bank	60,000	31.12.X0	Bal c/d	60,000
1.1.X1	Bal b/d	60,000	31.12.X1	Bal c/d	60,000
1.1.X2	Bal b/d	60,000	31.12.X2	Bal c/d	60,000

VEHICLES ACCOUNT

1.1.X0	Bank	12,000	31.12.X0	Bal c/d	12,000
1.1.X1	Bal b/d	12,000	31.12.X1	Bal c/d	12,000
1.1.X2	Bal b/d	12,000	1.12.X2	Sale	12,000

EQUIPMENT ACCOUNT

1.1.X0	Bank	9,000	31.12.X0	Bal c/d	9,000
1.1.X1	Bal b/d	9,000	31.12.X1	Bal c/d	9,000
1.1.X2	Bal b/d	9,000	1.1.X2	Sale	1,500
			31.12.X2	Bal c/d	7,500
		9,000			9,000

PROVISION FOR DEPRECIATION OF BUILDINGS ACCOUNT

31.12.X0	Bal c/d	1,000	31.12.X0	Statement of comprehensive income	1,000
			1.1.X0	Bal b/d	1,000
31.12.X1	Bal c/d	2,000	31.12.X1	Statement of comprehensive income	1,000
		2,000			2,000

			1.1.X2	Bal b/d	2,000
31.12.X2	Bal c/d	3,000	31.12.X2	Statement of comprehensive income	1,000
		3,000			3,000

PROVISION FOR DEPRECIATION OF VEHICLES ACCOUNT

31.12.X0	Bal c/d	3,000	31.12.X0	Statement of comprehensive income	3,000
			1.1.X1	Bal b/d	3,000
31.12.X1	Bal c/d	5,250	31.12.X1	Statement of comprehensive income	2,250
		5,250			5,250
1.12.X2	Sale	5,250	1.1.X2	Bal b/d	5,250

PROVISION FOR DEPRECIATION OF EQUIPMENT ACCOUNT

31.12.X0	Bal c/d	820	31.12.X0	Statement of comprehensive income	820
			1.1.X1	Bal b/d	820
31.12.X1	Bal c/d	1,640	31.12.X1	Statement of comprehensive income	820
		1,640			1,640
1.12.X2	Sale	280	1.1.X2	Bal b/d	1,640
31.12.X2	Bal c/d	2,040	31.12.X2	Statement of comprehensive income	680
		2,320			2,320

SALE OF VEHICLES ACCOUNT

1.12.X2	Asset	12,000	1.12.X2	Cash	6,500
			1.12.X2	Depreciation	5,250
			31.12.X2	Statement of comprehensive income	250
		12,000			12,000

SALE OF EQUIPMENT ACCOUNT

1.12.X2	Asset	1,500	1.12.X2	Cash	1,200
			1.12.X2	Depreciation	280
			31.12.X2	Statement of comprehensive income	20
		1,500			1,500

STATEMENT OF COMPREHENSIVE INCOME FOR THE YEAR ENDED 31.12.X2

Depreciation of buildings	1,000
Depreciation of equipment	680
Loss on sale of vehicles	250
Loss on sale of equipment	20

STATEMENT OF FINANCIAL POSITION AS AT 31.12.X2

	Cost	Depreciation	Net book value
Buildings	60,000	3,000	57,000
Equipment	7,500	2,040	5,460
	£67,500	£5,040	£62,460

Question 12
Workings
Fixture and fittings

As at 1.10.X5 these are three years old, therefore depreciation provided as at this date is

$$3 \times (25,000 - 1,800)/8 = 8,700$$

The new fixtures and fittings will be depreciated by $15,200/8 = 1,900$ per annum. Therefore depreciation charge for the year ended 30.9.X6 and for 30.9.X7 is 4,800.

Vehicles

The van as at 1.10.X5 is three years old and depreciation charges of:

▶ Year 1: 4,000, net book value 12,000
▶ Year 2: 3,000, net book value 9,000
▶ Year 3: 2,250, net book value 6,750

will have been made.

The depreciation charge for year ended 30.9.X6 will be £1,688 and net book value at this date will be £5,062.

In December the van is destroyed and £3,200 received in settlement – this can be treated as a sale and thus loss on disposal is £1,862.

The new van will require depreciation of £4,625 in the year ended 30.9.X7.

FIXTURES AND FITTINGS

1.10.X5	Balance b/d	25,000			
1.11.X5	Bank	15,200	30.9.X6	Balance c/d	40,200
		40,200			40,200
1.10.X6	Balance b/d	40,200	30.9.X7	Balance c/d	40,200

VEHICLES

1.10.X5	Balance b/d	16,000	30.9.X6	Balance c/d	16,000
1.10.X6	Balance b/d	16,000	31.12.X6	Disposal	16,000
5.1.X7	Bank	18,500	30.9.X7	Balance c/d	18,500
1.10.X7	Balance b/d	18,500			

DISPOSAL OF VEHICLE ACCOUNT

31.12.X6	Vehicle	16,000	31.12.X6	Bank	3,200
			31.12.X6	Depreciation	10,938
			30.9.X7	Loss on disposal	1,862
		16,000			16,000

PROVISION FOR DEPRECIATION F&F

30.9.X6	Balance c/d	13,500	1.10.X5	Balance b/d	8,700
			30.9.X6	Statement of comprehensive income	4,800
		13,500			13,500
			1.10.X6	Balance b/d	13,500
30.9.X7	Balance c/d	18,300	30.9.X7	Statement of comprehensive income	4,800
		18,300			18,300
			1/10/X7	Balance b/d	18,300

PROVISION FOR DEPRECIATION VEHICLES

			1.10.X5	Balance b/d	9,250
30.9.X6	Balance c/d	10,938	30.9.X6	Statement of comprehensive income	1,688
		10,938			10,938
31.12.X6	Disposal	10,938	1.10.X6	Balance b/d	10,938
30.9.X7	Balance c/d	4,625	30.9.X7	Statement of comprehensive income	4,625
		15,563			15,563
			1.10.X7	Balance b/d	4,625

EXTRACT STATEMENT OF FINANCIAL POSITION AS AT 30.9.X6

	Cost	Depreciation	NBV
Fixtures and fittings	40,200	13,500	26,700
Vehicles	16,000	10,938	5,062

EXTRACT STATEMENT OF FINANCIAL POSITION AS AT 30.9.X7

	Cost	Depreciation	NBV
Fixtures and fittings	40,200	18,300	21,900
Vehicles	18,500	4,625	13,875

Question 13

An assessment of the amount of an asset used up in generation of revenue for a given period.

Question 14

Cost, residual value, useful life to the business, method of usage (i.e. equal amount each period or some other method of usage).

Question 15

Depreciation charges are as follows:

31 December 20X0 buildings £4,000, equipment £8,000 and vehicles £11,000.

31 December 20X1 buildings £4,000, equipment £7,200 and vehicles £9,900.

From the information given buildings should be depreciated on a straight line basis as follows:

$$\frac{400,000 - 190,000}{40} = 5,250, \text{ i.e. } 1.3\%$$

Equipment percentage depreciation is calculated from the following:

$$\frac{1 - 8/1,000}{80,000} = 42\%$$

and vehicles

$$\frac{1 - 6/6,000}{110,000} = 38\%$$

Black is underestimating the depreciation charges.

Question 16

ADJUSTED STATEMENT OF COMPREHENSIVE INCOME TOSUSO YEAR ENDED 31.12.200X

Unadjusted profit		10,870
Depreciation (54,000 − 5,400)/10	4,860	
Bad debts	6,700	
Provision for bad debts (63,000 − 6,700) × 5% − 3,000	(185)	
Electricity accrual	1,500	
Prepayment of rent	(4,500)	8,375
Adjusted profit		2,495

Chapter 7 Preparation of statement of comprehensive income and statement of financial position from trial balance and adjustments

Question 1

STATEMENT OF COMPREHENSIVE INCOME FOR THE YEAR ENDED 31.12.X5 FOR RODNEY

Sales		71,230
Opening inventory	4,340	
Purchases	29,760	
	34,100	
Less closing inventory	4,870	29,230
Gross profit		42,000
Rates	800	
Heat and light	2,770	
General expenses	2,420	
Motor expenses	3,240	
Wages	8,250	
Bad debts	360	
Depreciation: Premises	600	
Fixtures and fittings	800	
Vehicles	1,320	
Provision for bad debts	40	
Loan interest	600	21,200
Net profit		20,800

STATEMENT OF FINANCIAL POSITION AS AT 31.12.X5 FOR RODNEY

	Cost	Depreciation	Net book value
Non-current assets			
Premises	30,000	3,000	27,000
Fixtures and fittings	8,000	2,400	5,600
Vehicles	12,000	6,720	5,280
	50,000	12,120	37,880
Current assets			
Inventory		4,870	
Trade receivables	6,400		
Less bad debts provision	320	6,080	
Bank		820	
		11,770	11,770
			49,650
Capital			15,500
Add net profit		20,800	

Less drawings	4,660	16,140
		31,640
Non-current liabilities		12,000
Current liabilities		
Creditors	5,210	
Accruals	800	6,010
Total capital and liabilities		49,650

Workings

1 The following adjustments are required to the trial balance as given:

Debit heat and light account	120	
Credit accruals account		120
Debit expenses account	80	
Credit accruals account		80
Debit loan interest account	600	
Credit accruals account		600

2 The depreciation charges are calculated as follows:

Premises £30,000 × 2% = £600
Fixtures and fittings £8,000 × 10% = £800
Vehicles £(12,000 − 5,400) × 20% = £1,320

3 The adjustment for bad debts is as follows:

Debit bad debts account	130
Credit debtors account	130

The trade receivables (trade receivables) balance now becomes:

£6,530 − 130 = £6,400

The provision for bad debts is required to be set at:

5% × £6,400 = £320

The provision already in the trial balance is £280 therefore an additional provision of £40 is required.

Question 2

**STATEMENT OF COMPREHENSIVE INCOME FOR THE YEAR
ENDED 31.12.X9 FOR ATEC**

Sales		53,500
Opening inventory	5,400	
Purchases	29,200	
	34,600	
Closing inventory	6,200	28,400
Gross profit		25,100
Rents receivable		600
Profit on sale of asset		12,100
		37,800

Other expenses		120
Electricity		930
Salaries and wages		12,330
Rates		600
Telephone		370
Office expenses		150
Provision for depreciation: Premises		300
	Equipment	1,200
	Vehicles	2,250
	New vehicles	1,250
Bad debts		120
Provision for bad debts		4	19,624
Net profit			18,176

STATEMENT OF FINANCIAL POSITIONS AS AT 31.12.X9 ATEC

	Cost	Depreciation	Net book value
Non-current assets			
Premises	15,000	2,400	12,600
Equipment	12,000	9,600	2,400
Vehicles	17,000	6,500	10,500
	44,000	18,500	25,500
Current assets			
Inventory		6,200	
Trade receivables	4,680		
Provision for bad debts	94	4,586	
Rents		50	
Cash		90	
			10,926
Total assets			36,426
Capital			21,500
Profit		18,176	
Drawings		11,000	7,176
			28,676
Current liabilities			
Trade payables	5,200		
Accruals	550		
Bank	2,000		7,750
Total capital and liabilities			36,426

Workings

Premises

The trial balance figure for depreciation of £4,200 implies a useful life of 50 years (i.e. 30,000/50 × 7 years).

Premises left after sale cost £15,000 thus depreciation for the year is £300.

Premises sold cost	£15,000
Dep.	£2,100
NBV	£12,900
Price	£25,000
Profit	£12,100

Equipment

The trial balance figure for depreciation implies a useful life of ten years (i.e. 12,000/10 × 7).

Thus depreciation for the year is £1,200.

Vehicles

These were bought a year ago and NBV at 1.1.X9 is £9,000. Depreciation is calculated at the rate of 25% reducing balance, thus current year charge is £9,000 × 25% = £2,250. The van bought 1.2.X9 needs to be recorded as an asset of the business not a charge against drawings. Using 25% reducing balance as depreciation policy gives a charge for this asset for the current year of £1,250.

Question 3

Statement of comprehensive income for Celia for the year ended 31.3.20X8

Sales	295,500	
Less sales returns	1,800	293,700
Purchases	154,500	
Less purchase returns	750	
	153,750	
Opening inventory	18,000	
	171,750	
Less closing inventory		
(18,750 – 2,000 + 600)	17,350	154,400
Gross profit		139,300
General expenses	16,750	
Wages (32,500 + 700)	33,200	
Rent and rates (12,000 – 400)	11,600	
Provision for doubtful debts		
(49,250*2% – 1,970)	(985)	
Depreciation plant and equipment		
(92,000*20%)	18,400	
Depreciation for vehicles		
((15,000 – 6,000)25%)	2,250	
Interest on loans (25,000*8%)	2,000	83,215
Net profit		56,085

STATEMENT OF FINANCIAL POSITION FOR CELIA AS AT 31.3.20X8

	Cost	Depreciation	NBV
Non-current assets			
Plant and equipment	92,000	55,200	36,800
		(36,800 +	
		18,400)	
Vehicles	15,000	8,250	6,750
		(6,000 +	
		2,250)	
	107,000	63,450	43,550
Current assets			
Inventory		17,350	
Trade receivables	49,250		
Less provision			
for doubtful debts	985	48,265	
Prepayments		400	
Bank		12,175	78,190
Total assets			**121,740**
Capital		10,000	
Retained profits b/f	15,525		
Add net profit for year	56,085		
	71,610		
Less drawings	19,750	51,860	61,860
Non-current liabilities			
Loan			25,000
Current liabilities			
Trade payables		32,180	
Accruals			
(wages 700 + interest 2,000)		2,700	34,880
Total capital and liabilities			**121,740**

Question 4

INCOME AND EXPENDITURE ACCOUNT FOR THE YEAR ENDED 31.3.20X8 FOR FOOTBALL CLUB

Gross profit on bars		5,600
Gross profit on events	8,200	
Less invoice not yet submitted	2,800	5,400
Subscriptions (12,300 + 2,300)		14,600
		25,600
General expenses	2,300	
Insurances	667	
Heat and light	2,650	

Provision for depreciation clubhouse		1,000	
Provision for depreciation furniture and fittings		340	
Provision for bad debts (1% × 1,200)		12	6,969
Surplus			18,631

STATEMENT OF FINANCIAL POSITION AS AT 31.3.20X8
FOR FOOTBALL CLUB

	Cost	Depreciation	NBV
Non-current assets			
Clubhouse	25,000	2,000	23,000
Furniture and fittings	3,400	680	2,720
	28,400	2,680	25,720
Current assets			
Inventory		550	
Trade receivables	1,200		
Less provision for bad debts	12	1,188	
Subscriptions due		2,300	
Bank and cash		1,680	5,718
Total assets			31,438
Accumulated fund		8,400	
Add surplus for the year		18,631	27,031
Current liabilities			
Trade payables		3,790	
Accruals		617	4,407
Total funds and liabilities			31,438

Chapter 8 Accounts of limited companies and other organisations

Question 1

	Sole trader	Company
(a)	No	Yes – Companies Acts
(b)	The sole trader	The shareholders
(c)	The sole trader	The directors appointed by the shareholders
(d)	No	Yes
(e)	Yes	No
(f)	No	Yes
(g)	Drawings	Dividends
(h)	No	Possible if a plc

Question 2
Options available:

(a) Issue of further share capital either ordinary or preference.
(b) Issue of long-term loans, for example debentures.

The company would probably find it relatively easy to raise further capital by the issue of debentures given there are no long-term loans in existence.

Question 3

(a) Par value is £1.
(b) Book value is 37/20 = £1.85.
(c) Interest payable on the debentures is 5% that is £400,000.
(d) Lower.

Question 4

CUDDLY TOY LTD PUBLISHED STATEMENT OF COMPREHENSIVE INCOME FOR THE YEAR ENDED 31.12.X5

		£000
Turnover		1,562
Cost of sales		1,005.8
Gross profit		556.2
Distribution expenses	114.65	
(98 + 4.9 + 11.75)		
Administration expenses (24 + 4.9)	28.9	143.55
Operating profit		412.65
Interest		21
Profit before taxation		391.65
Taxation		200
Profit after taxation		191.65
Interim dividends		54
Retained profits for the year		137.65
Retained profits b/f		185
		322.65

Cost of sales calculation:		
Opening inventory	660	
Purchases	885	
	1,545	
Less closing inventory	560	
		985
Depreciation: Equipment	11	
Premises	9.8	20.8
		1,005.8

STATEMENT OF FINANCIAL POSITION AS AT 31.12.X5

	Cost	Depreciation	Net book value
	(£000)	(£000)	(£000)
Non-current assets			
Land	1,010		1,010
Buildings	980	409.6	570.4
Equipment	55	29	26
Vehicles	72	36.75	35.25
	2,117	475.55	1,641.65
Current assets			
Inventory		560	
Debtors		180	
Bank		121	861
TOTAL ASSETS			2502.65
Capital and reserves			
Ordinary £1 shares			900
Share premium			350
Retained profits			322.65
			1,572.65
Non-current liabilities			
5% debentures			420
Current liabilities			
Trade payables			
Taxation		200	
Debenture interest		21	
Interim dividends		54	510
Total equity and liabilities			2,502.65

Question 5

GERRY LTD STATEMENT OF COMPREHENSIVE INCOME FOR THE YEAR ENDED 31.3.X6

Sales		271,700
Opening inventory	14,167	
Purchases	186,000	
	200,167	
Closing inventory	23,483	
Cost of sales		176,684
Gross profit		95,016
Depreciation	21,000	
Provision for bad debts	226	
General expenses		

(1,5840 + 1,437 − 925)	16,352	
Wages and salaries	31,862	69,440
		25,576
Debenture interest		2,400
Net profit before taxation		23,176
Taxation		9,700
Net profit after taxation		13,476
Dividends: Preference paid	1,200	
		1,200
Retained profit for the year		12,276
Retained profit b/f		976
		13,252
Transfer to general reserve		3,000
Retained profit c/f		10,252

STATEMENT OF FINANCIAL POSITION AS AT 31.3.X6

	Cost	Depreciation	Net book value
Non-current assets	210,000	40,000	170,000
Current assets			
Inventory		23,483	
Trade receivables		10,450	
Prepayments		925	
Bank		9,731	44,589
Total assets			214,589
Capital and reserves			
Ordinary shares of £1			100,000
6% preference shares			20,000
Share premium			9,500
Revaluation reserve			10,000
General reserve			15,000
Retained profit			10,252
			164,752
Non-current liabilities			
8% debentures			30,000
Current liabilities			
Trade payables	7,500		
Accruals	2,637		
Taxation	9,700		19,837
Total equity and liabilities			214,589

Question 6

HOBO LTD: STATEMENT OF COMPREHENSIVE INCOME FOR
THE YEAR ENDED 30.9.X6

Turnover		623,300
Cost of sales		459,675
Gross profit		163,625
Distribution expenses	56,635	
Administration expenses	44,038	100,673
Operating profit		62,952
Interest		6,650
Profit before taxation		56,302
Taxation		22,680
Profit after taxation		33,622
Retained profit b/f 1.10.X5		26,000
		59,622

Calculations
Cost of sales:

Opening inventory		18,950
Purchases		426,500
		445,450
Less: Closing inventory		20,650
		424,800
Production wages	32,900	
Depreciation: Premises	1,375	
Equipment	600	34,875
		459,675

Distribution expenses:

Warehouse wages	30,200
Delivery expenses	22,060
Depreciation buildings	1,375
Equipment	600
Vehicles	2,400
	56,635

Administration expenses:

Audit fee	1,200
Bad debts	5,320
Provision for bad debts	4,618
Salaries	15,200
Rents	12,100
Other	5,600
	44,038

STATEMENT OF FINANCIAL POSITION AS AT 30.9.X6

	Cost	Depreciation	Net book value
Non-current assets			
Premises	275,000	6,500	268,500
Equipment	12,000	4,800	7,200
Vehicles	18,500	8,900	9,600
	305,500	20,200	285,300
Current assets			
Inventory		20,650	
Trade receivables		87,742	
Prepayments		500	
Bank		51,810	160,702
TOTAL ASSETS			446,002
Capital and reserves			
Ordinary 50p shares			100,000
Share premium			50,000
Retained profits			59,622
			209,622
Non-current liabilities			
7% debentures			95,000
Current liabilities			
Trade payables	111,450		
Taxation	22,680		
Debenture interest	6,650		
Accruals	600		141,380
Total equity and liabilities			446,022

Question 7
Workings

Production expenses		Distribution expenses	
Opening inventory	6,230	Warehouse wages	10,100
Purchases	15,260	Warehouse expenses	950
	21,490	Depreciation: Premises	1,000
Closing inventory	4,560	Equipment	1,250
	16,930	Vehicles	1,126
Production wages	12,320		14,426
Production expenses	7,210		
Depreciation: Premises	2,000	Administration expenses	
Equipment	2,500	Debenture discount	500
	40,960	Provision for bad debts	412
		Administration salaries	14,200
		Administration expenses	950

Depreciation calculations:

Premises

200,000 * 2% = 4,000

Equipment

50,000 * 10% = 5,000

Vehicle 4,503 * 25% = 1,126

Depreciation: Premises	1,000
Equipment	1,250
	18,312

Vehicle sale	Cost	Depreciation	NBV
Balance	15,000	6,560	8,440
Sale	7,000	3,063	3,937
Balance	8,000	3,497	4,503

BURN LTD PUBLISHED STATEMENT OF COMPREHENSIVE INCOME FOR THE YEAR ENDED 31.12.X9

Sales		79,710
Production costs		40,960
Gross profit		38,750
Distribution expenses	14,426	
Administration expenses	18,312	32,738
Operating profit		6,012
Loss on sale of vehicle		187
Profit before interest and taxation		5,825
Interest 6% debentures	3,000	
5% debentures	500	3,500
Profit before tax		2,325
Taxation		1,200
Profit after tax		1,125
Retained profits b/f (62,000 – 9,500)		52,500
Retained profits c/f		53,625

BURN LTD PUBLISHED STATEMENT OF FINANCIAL POSITION AS AT 31.12.X9

Non-current assets	Cost	Depreciation	NBV	
Premises	200,000	24,000	176,000	
Equipment	50,000	20,000	30,000	
Vehicles	8,000	4,623	3,377	
	25,800	48,623	209,377	
Current assets				
Inventory		4,560		
Trade receivables	8,240			
Provision bad debts	412	7,828		
Bank		103,520		
Cash		250	116,158	
Total assets			325,535	

Capital and reserves		
Ordinary shares £1		140,000
Share premium		60,000
Retained profits		53,625
		253,625
Non-current liabilities		
6% debentures	50,000	
5% debentures	10,000	60,000
Current liabilities		
Trade payables	7,210	
Debenture interest	3,500	
Taxation	1,200	11,910
Total equity and liabilities		325,535

Question 8

BLACK LTD STATEMENT OF COMPREHENSIVE INCOME
FOR THE YEAR ENDED 31.12.20X5

Sales		537,600
Less returns inwards		2,450
		535,150
Opening inventory	22,300	
Purchases	321,700	
	344,000	
Less returns outwards	4,670	
	339,330	
Less closing inventory	22,000	
	317,330	
Production wages	74,000	
Depreciation	5,500	396,830
Gross profit		138,320
Distribution expenses	41,708	
Administration expenses	80,670	
Profit on sale	(3,000)	119,378
Profit before interest		18,942
Interest on debentures		3,000
Profit before tax		15,942
Taxation		9,860
Profit after tax		6,082
Retained profits b/f		9,870
Retained profits c/f		15,952

BLACK LTD STATEMENT OF FINANCIAL POSITION AS AT 31.12.20X5

Non-current assets	Cost	Depreciation	NBV
Premises	150,000	13,100	136,900
Equipment	50,000	29,500	20,500
Vehicles	85,000	43,188	41,812
	285,000	85,788	199,212

Current assets			
Inventory	22,000		
Trade reveivables	41,990		
Prepayments	5,600		
			69,590
Total assets			268,802

Capital and reserves			
Ordinary shares £1			150,000
Retained profits			15,952
			165,952
Non-current liabilities			
Debentures		50,000	50,000

Current liabilities			
Trade payables	34,200		
Debenture interest	3,000		
Accruals	3,500		
Bank overdraft	2,290		
Taxation	9,860		52,850
Total equity and liabilities			268,802

Question 9

Rights issue is a pro-rata issue of shares to current shareholders at a value below market value of the shares. Cash is brought into the company from the rights issue.

Bonus issue is a pro-rata issue of shares to current shareholders which is free and capitalises existing reserves. No extra cash is brought into the company.

Question 10

GAMMA EXTRACT FROM STATEMENT OF FINANCIAL POSITION AS AT 31.12.X6

Ordinary share capital (1,000,000 + 400,000 RI + 400,000 BI)	1,800,000
Share premium (RI 200,000 × £2.25)	450,000
Accumulated profits (456,000 – 400,000 BI)	56,000
	2,306,000

Net assets before share issues was	1,456,000
Cash raised from rights issue 200,000 ×4.25 =	850,000
Net assets after share issues	2,306,000

STATEMENT OF COMPREHENSIVE INCOME (PROFIT AND LOSS ACCOUNT) FOR RIA FOR THE YEAR ENDED 31 DECEMBER 20X0

	£000s	£000s
Revenue		285,100
Cost of sales	191,700	
Adjustment to closing stock	400	
Depreciation (2,000 + 1,600)	3,600	
		195,700
Gross profit		89,400
Rental income from investment properties		1,600
		91,000
Operating expenses	39,500	
Depreciation	3,600	
Investment property loss in value	3,300	
Bank interest	1,030	47,430
Net profit before tax		43,570
Taxation		12,000
Net profit after tax		31,570
Preference dividends	1,330	
Ordinary dividends	5,340	6,670
Retained earnings for the year		24,900

STATEMENT OF FINANCIAL POSITION FOR RIA AS AT 31 DECEMBER 20X0

	Cost	Depreciation	nbv
	(£000s)	(£000s)	(£000s)
Assets			
Non-current assets			
Land	20,000		20,000
Property	64,000	4,000	60,000
Plant and equipment	48,000	25,600	22,400
	132,000	29,600	102,400
Investment properties			18,000
			120,400
Current assets			
Inventories		13600	
Trade receivables		18,000	
			31,600
Total assets			152,000

Equity and liabilities

Equity

Share capital: Ordinary 25p shares		26,700
Preference shares £1		13,300
Revaluation reserve		28,000
Retained earnings (23,300 + 24,900)		48,200
		116,200
Current liabilities		
Trade payables	15,700	
Tax	12,000	
Bank overdraft	8,100	35,800
Total equity and liabilities		152,000

Working

1 adjustment to closing stock:

Net realisable value of damaged stock 1,27.0,000 – 600,000 = 670,000
Loss on damaged stock 1,070,000 – 670,000 = 400,000

2 Depreciation buildings 64m/16 years = 4m
3 Depreciation plant and equipment (48,000 – 22,400) ×12.5% = 3,200
4 Loss on investment properties 21.3m – 18m = 3.3m

Question 12

STATEMENT OF COMPREHENSIVE INCOME FOR JACOB, HENRY AND ISAAC
FOR THE YEAR ENDED 31 DECEMBER 20X0

Sales		623,430
Opening inventory	32,300	
Purchases	323,700	
	356,000	
Closing inventory	34,250	321,750
		301,680
Wages	114,000	
Rates and insurance	22,300	
Electricity and gas	19,450	
Vehicle expenses	8,450	
Depreciation: Premises	2,200	
Furniture and fittings	1,640	
Vehicles	5,216	
		173,256
		128,424
Salaries: Jacob	30,000	
Henry	25,000	
Isaac	33,000	

Interest on capital accounts: Jacob 3,200
 Henry 2,600
 Isaac 2,400
Interest charged on drawings: Jacob (480)
 Henry (1,100)
 Isaac (675)
Profit share: Jacob 10,344
 Henry 10,344
 Isaac 13,791

 128,424

CAPITAL ACCOUNTS

		Jacob	Henry	Isaac			Jacob	Henry	Isaac
31.12.X0	Eliminate goodwill		100,000	150,000	1.1.X0	Bal.b/d	80,000	65,000	60,000
31.12.X0	Cash	93,000			31.12.X0	Goodwill introduced	75,000	75,000	100,000
	Loan	62,000							
31.12.X0	Balance c/d		40,000	10,000					
		155,000	140,000	160,000			155,000	140,000	160,000
					1.1.X0	Bal/b/d		40,000	10,000

CURRENT ACCOUNTS

		Jacob	Henry	Isaac			Jacob	Henry	Isaac
1.1.X0	Bal. b/d	980		1,450	1.1.X0	Bal. b/d		2,880	
31.12.X0	Interest on drawings	480	1,100	675	31.12.X0	Salaries	30,000	25,000	33,000
31.12.X0	Drawings	9,600	22,000	13,500	31.12.X0	Interest on capital accounts	3,200	2,600	2,400
31.12.X0	Jacob cash loan	19,490 12,994							
31.12.X0	Bal. c/d		17,724	33,566	31.12.X0	Share of profits	10,344	10,344	13,791
		43,544	40,824	49,191			43,544	40,824	49,191
					1.1.X0	Bal. b/d		17,724	33,566

CASH ACCOUNT

31.12.X0	Balance b/d	36,870	31.12.X0	Cash to Jacob	112,490
31.12.X0	Loan from bank	185,000	31.12.X0	Balance c/d	109,380
		221,870			221,870
1.1.X0	Balance b/d	109,380			

STATEMENT OF FINANCIAL POSITION FOR JACOB, HENRY AND ISAAC AS AT 31 DECEMBER 20X0

	Cost	Depreciation	NBV
Premises	220,000	30,800	189,200
Furniture and fittings	16,400	8,200	8,200
Vehicles	32,600	11,736	20,864
	269,000	50,736	218,264
Inventory		34,250	
Trade receivables		11,870	
Cash		109,380	155,500
			373,764
Capital accounts: Henry		40,000	50,000
Isaac		10,000	
Current accounts: Henry		17,724	51,290
Isaac		33,566	
Loan Jacob			74,994
Loan bank			185,000
Trade payables			12,480
			373,764

Chapter 9 Group accounting

Question 1

It is a basic idea in accounting that, where there is a conflict between the legal form and the economic substance of a transaction, that we always prefer the economic substance. In the case of group accounting, we therefore consider whether the acquisition of shares gives us full control of the other company in practice, even though it may not give us full ownership.

Where we acquire most of the shares this will normally give us full control of the other company, meaning that both companies are now subject to a single point of day to day control, i.e. the management of the holding company. In other words, there is, in substance, a single entity and the accounting should reflect this by preparing a single set of financial statements, in addition to those of the individual companies.

Question 2

HARPER LTD
STATEMENT OF FINANCIAL POSITION AT 31 DECEMBER 20X9

Non-current assets	100,000
Goodwill	76,000
Inventory	140,000
Bank	80,000
	396,000
Share capital	240,000
Reserves	52,000
Non-controlling interest	104,000
	396,000

Goodwill calculation

Investment in S	220,000
Shares acquired (200,000 × 60%)	(120,000)
Pre-acquisition reserves (40,000 × 60%)	(24,000)
Goodwill	76,000
Non-controlling interest	
Shares (200,000 × 40%)	80,000
Pre-acquisition reserves (40,000 × 40%)	16,000
Post-acquisition reserves (20,000 × 40%)	8,000
	104,000
Reserves	
Harper	40,000
Sharpe	
Share of post acquisition (60%× 20,000)	12,000
	52,000

Question 3

O'MALLEY
CONSOLIDATED STATEMENT OF FINANCIAL POSITION

Non-current assets	200,000
Goodwill	21,000
Inventory	210,000
Bank	120,000
	551,000
Share capital	420,000
Reserves	87,000
Non-controlling interest	44,000
	551,000

Goodwill calculation

Investment in S	390,000
Shares acquired (300,000 × 90%)	(270,000)
Revaluation reserve (50,000 × 90%)	(45,000)
Pre-acquisition reserves (60,000 × 90%)	(54,000)
Goodwill	21,000

Note: The revaluation reserve is the difference between the book value of £150,000 and the fair value of £200,000.

Non-controlling interest

Shares (300,000 × 10%)	30,000
Revaluation reserve (50,000 × 10%)	5,000
Pre-acquisition reserves (60,000 × 10%)	6,000
Post-acquisition reserves (30,000 × 10%)	3,000
	44,000

Reserves

O'Malley	60,000
Tamworth	
Share of post acquisition (90% × 30,000)	27,000
	87,000

Note: This answer does not include a restatement of the statement of financial position of the subsidiary after the revaluation of the non-current assets. In a relatively simple example, such as this, it probably isn't necessary, but you can do one prior to the above calculations if you find it helpful.

Question 4

HAMMONDS LTD

CONSOLIDATED STATEMENT OF COMPREHENSIVE INCOME

Revenue	3,900
Expenses	2,710
Profit before tax	1,190
Tax	150
Profit after tax	1,040
Attributable to non-controlling interest	100
Attributable to shareholders of H	940

Workings

	H	S	Inter-co adjustment	Total
Revenue	3,000	1,200	(300)	3,900
Expenses	(2,150)	(860)	300	(2,710)
	850	340		1,190
Tax	(60)	(90)		(150)
Profit	790	250		1,040

The non-controlling interest will be 40% of the profit after tax of S Ltd, hence 40% of 250, so 100.

Chapter 10 Statement of cash flows

Question 1

The statement of cash flows identifies net cash inflows from operations, net cash inflows from investments in non-current assets, net flows from financing activities and payments in respect of interest, dividends and taxation. None of these are identifiable from the statement of comprehensive income or statement of financial position.

It also identifies the extent to which reported profit is matched by cash flows. Thus the distinction between profit and cash flow is clearly made. The user of the statement has more relevant information on which to assess the solvency of the business.

Question 2

Reconciliation of operating profit and net cash flows from operating activities:

		£000
Net profit for the year before tax		158
Add interest charged		12
Net profit before interest and tax		170
Amortisation	15	
Depreciation	187	
Profit on sale	(45)	
		157
		327
Increase in inventory	(26)	
Increase in trade receivables	(58)	
Increase in trade payables	6	
		(78)
Net cash inflows from operating activities		249

STATEMENT OF CASH FLOWS FOR SPARROW LTD
FOR THE YEAR ENDED 31.12.X5

Net cash flow from operating activities		249
Interest paid	(12)	
Taxation paid	(64)	(76)
Net cash used in investing activities		
Payments to acquire tangible non-current assets	(376)	
Payments to acquire investments	(20)	
Sale of non-current assets	133	(263)

Net cash used in financing activities		
Equity dividends paid	(60)	
Issue of shares	150	
Issue of debentures	50	140
Increase in cash balances		50

This increase in cash balances equates to the change shown on the statement of financial positions – balance at bank of £26,000 from an overdrawn balance of £24,000.

Question 3

The statement of cash flows identifies the following in respect of the financial operations and position of Sparrow Ltd for the year ended 31.12.X5:

▶ Tax, dividend and interest payments were more than covered by the net cash inflow from operating activities.
▶ The outflow of cash in respect of the acquisition of non-current assets and investments has been covered by cash generated from operating, cash generated from sale of assets and the rest from new capital raised by way of share and loan.
▶ Cash raised from new capital has cleared the overdrawn bank balance and left £26,000 in the bank.
▶ Working capital has increased substantially.
▶ It appears that Sparrow Ltd has been expanding its activities by its investment in increased working capital and new assets. Management must ensure that cash flows from operating also increase in line with this expansion.

Question 4

Reconciliation of operating profit to net cash flow from operating activities:

		£m
Operating profit		238
Add depreciation		38
Less profit on disposal of asset		(4)
Add reduction in inventory		24
Less increase in trade receivables		(33)
Increase in trade payables		99
Net cash inflow		362

Statement of cash flows for the year ended 30.9.0Y		
Net cash inflow from operations		362
Returns on investment and servicing of finance:		
Interest paid	(10)	
Taxation paid	(38)	(48)
Net cash used in investing activities		
Purchase tangible non-current assets	(313)	
Sale of tangible non-current assets	35	
Interest received	6	(272)

Net cash used in financing activities

Equity dividends paid	(39)	
Issue of ordinary shares	42	
Redemption of debentures	(17)	(14)
Increase in cash and cash equivalents		28

Cash equivalents included 30-day government bond

Question 5

(a) Reconciliation of operating profit to net cash flow from operating activities:

Net profit for the year before tax	48,590	
Less interest and dividends received	22,500	26,090
Add interest charged		7,500
Net profit before interest and tax		33,590
Depreciation on buildings	38,600	
Depreciation other	25,000	
Loss on sale	9,600	73,200
		106,790
Increase in inventory	(1,000)	
Decrease in trade receivables	5,550	
Decrease in trade payables	(27,990)	(23,440)
Net cash inflows from operating activities		83,350

STATEMENT OF CASH FLOWS FOR PEAK LTD FOR THE YEAR ENDED 31.12.X5

Net cash flow from operating activities		83,350
Interest paid	(7,500)	
Taxation paid	(10,500)	(18,000)
Net cash used in investing activities		
Payments to acquire tangible non-current assets	(161,350)	
Payments to acquire investments	(86,000)	
Sale of non-current assets	17,900	
Interest received	15,000	
Dividends received	7,500	(206,950)
Net cash used in financing activities		
Issue of shares	60,000	
Issue of debentures	105,000	
Equity dividends paid	(35,000)	130,000
Decrease in cash balances		11,600

(b) The cash flow shows that:

- ▶ The amount generated from operating activities more than covered the net interest, dividends and tax paid for the company during the year ended 31 December 20X5.
- ▶ Non-current assets were purchased in excess of sales of £229,450. This was financed by the issue of shares and debentures of £165,000 cash. The remaining £64,450 was financed from internal resources of the company resulting in a cash reduction of £11,600.
- ▶ The interest and dividends received on the investments are at a good level.
- ▶ Questions should be asked in respect of the fall in the profit for the year.
- ▶ Gearing has increased during the year but does not appear to be at a high risk level.
- ▶ The company has expanded its assets by the use of long-term capital resources in the main.

(c) The statement of cash flows:

- ▶ Identifies the factors which have caused the change in the cash and cash equivalent position.
- ▶ Identifies the extent to which profits result in inflows of cash.
- ▶ Is more objective and verifiable than the statement of comprehensive income as it has no need for accruals and other estimates.
- ▶ Provides information on something familiar to users – cash. Profit is not universally understood by users.
- ▶ Provides information on the financial adaptability of a business and its liquidity.

However:

- ▶ The information provided is all historical. Will this provide an indication of the future that can be relied on?
- ▶ The format presentation, many would say, is cluttered and lacks clarity.

Question 6

(a) Reconciliation of operating profit to net cash flow from operating activities:

Net profit for the year before tax	32,590	
Less interest and dividends received	(20,500)	
Add interest charged	7,500	
Net profit before interest and tax		19,590
Depreciation on buildings	119,600	
Depreciation other	25,000	
Loss on sale	5,600	150,200
		169,790
Increase in inventory	(11,000)	
Decrease in trade receivables	15,550	
Decrease in trade payables	(6,990)	(2,440)
Net cash inflows from operating activities		167,350

STATEMENT OF CASH FLOWS FOR THE YEAR ENDED 31.12.X5

Net cash flow from operating activities		167,350
Interest paid	(7,500)	
Taxation paid	(18,500)	(26,000)
Net cash used in investing activities		
Payments to acquire tangible		
non-current assets	(478,350)	
Payments to acquire		
investments	(106,000)	
Sale of non-current assets	21,900	
Interest received	12,000	
Dividends received	8,500	(541,950)
Net cash used in financing activities		
Issue of shares	304,000	
Issue of debentures	105,000	
Equity dividends paid	(25,000)	384,000
Decrease in cash balances		16,600

(b) The statement of cash flows shows that:

▶ The amount generated from operating activities more than covered the net interest, dividends and tax paid for the company during the year ended 31 December 20X5.

▶ Non-current assets were purchased in excess of sales of £562,450. This was financed by the issue of shares and debentures of £409,000 cash. The remaining £153,450 was financed from internal resources of the company resulting in a cash reduction of £16,600.

▶ The interest and dividends received on the investments is at a good level.

▶ Questions should be asked in respect of the fall in the profit for the year.

▶ Gearing has increased quite substantially during the year.

▶ The company has expanded its assets by the use of long-term capital resources in the main.

(c) As per Question 5.

Question 7

(a) B entity

Reconciliation of operating profit to net cash flow from operating:

	£m	£m
Profit before interest and tax		
(190 + 6 net interest)		196
Depreciation (from IS)	60	
Impairment (from IS)	40	
Profit on sale (from IS)	(16)	84
		280
Increase in inventory (from BS changes)	(8)	
Decrease in trade receivables		
(from BS changes)	4	
Increase in trade payables		
(from BS changes)	8	4
Net cash flow from operating activities		284

Working

Purchase of property, plant and equipment

Net change in assets on balance sheet (778 − 640)	= 138
nbv item sold (72 −16 profit on sale)	= 56
Depreciation	60
	254

STATEMENT OF CASH FLOWS FOR THE YEAR ENDED 30 SEPTEMBER 20X7

	£m	£m
Net cash inflow from operating activities	284	
Tax paid (90 + 80 − 80)	(90)	
Interest paid	(16)	178
Net cash used in investing activities		
Payments to acquire intangible		
non-current assets		
(280 − 240 + 40 impairment)	(80)	
Payments to acquire property,		
plant and equipment	(254)	
Sale of non-current assets	72	
Interest received	10	(252)
Net cash used in financing activities		
Dividends paid (30 + 80 − 40)	(70)	
Issue of shares (660 − 540		
ordinary shares and premium)	120	
Non-current liabilities raised		
(240 − 200)	40	90
Increase in cash balances		16

(b) Cash is the lifeblood of an organisation but the statement of cash flows is histori-cal. If we are concerned over the liquidity of a business, the ability to pay its debts, then a cash flow forecast would be more useful.

Cash flow from operating activities is derived by either the direct or indirect method. Indirect method uses information from the accruals based accounting system. The direct method reflects cash transactions and therefore should be used. The indirect method has the potential to confuse uses.

Cash flow bottom line is change in cash and cash equivalents. The definition of cash equivalents may not be precise.

Question 8
(a) T entity

Reconciliation of operating profit to net cash flow from operating:

	£m	£m
Profit before interest and tax		
(285 + 9net interest)		294
Depreciation (from IS)	90	
Impairment (from IS)	60	
Profit on sale (from IS)	(24)	126
		420
Increase in inventory (from BS changes)	(12)	
Decrease in trade receivables		
(from BS changes)	6	
Increase in trade payables		
(from BS changes)	12	6
Net cash flow from operating activities		426

Working
Purchase of property, plant and equipment

Net change in assets on balance sheet (1,167 – 960)	207
nbv item sold (108 – 24 profit on sale)	84
Depreciation	90
	381

STATEMENT OF CASH FLOWS FOR THE YEAR ENDED 31 DECEMBER 20X7

	£m	£m
Net cash inflow from operating activities	426	
Tax paid (135 + 120 – 120)	(135)	
Interest paid	(24)	267
Net cash used in investing activities		
Payments to acquire intangible non-current assets (420 – 360 + 60 impairment)	(120)	
Payments to acquire property, plant and equipment	(381)	
Sale of non-current assets	108	
Interest received	15	(378)
Net cash used in financing activities		
Dividends paid (45 + 120 – 60)	(105)	
Issue of shares (900 – 750 + 90 – 60 ordinary shares and premium)	180	
Non-current liabilities raised (360 – 300)	60	135
Increase in cash balances		24

(b) Cash flow statements identify:
- ▶ net cash inflows from operations
- ▶ net cash inflows from investments in non-current assets
- ▶ net flows from financing activities
- ▶ payments in respect of interest, dividends and taxation.

None of the above are identifiable from the income statement and balance sheet.

Also identifies the extent to which reported profit is matched by cash flows and thus the distinction between cash and profit is clearly made.

The user of the statement of cash flows has more relevant information on which to assess the solvency of the entity.

Chapter 11 Regulatory framework, corporate social responsibility and corporate governance

Question 1

The determinants of accounting practice tend to be:

- ▶ providers of finance
- ▶ accounting profession
- ▶ economic environment
- ▶ type of law – common or codified
- ▶ other countries' influences.

Question 2

Only those countries that are members of the EU are required by the EU Fourth Directive to incorporate the concept of true and fair into their legislation. The interpretation placed on this phrase may be different in each country. Given the difficulty we have in understanding this phrase in the UK, translating it into another language will increase those difficulties.

Question 3

Discussion should revolve around want constitutes influence. Worldwide influence here would seem to imply that IASB standards should be adopted by all countries. However influence could be assumed to be that over world stock markets. Given the rise of China's economy in the global market place then the IASB will not exert world influence unless the major stock markets and the major companies in China report under IASs. However, this influence could still exist even if the other (non-quoted) companies in China report under China's standards. To date, China has more or less adopted IASs as it has developed its accounting framework.

Question 4

The list is probably endless and we identify only a few here:

▶ The growth of SRI means entities will have to report on their social and environmental impact or risk losing investors.
▶ Environmental disasters caused by entities are now widely reported through the global media and entities are thus under greater scrutiny and pressure to disclose information.
▶ An entity's value in the market can be damaged if it does not take on board social and environmental risk factors. Its brand and reputation are likely to be damaged.
▶ An entity's reputation as a good 'corporate citizen' can have a positive effect on employee recruitment and retention.
▶ Good corporate citizenship can also generate customers and forge better links with suppliers.

Question 5

This can be applied to the environment because if we continue to consume the environment we will impoverish perhaps not ourselves, but certainly future generations. Economic activity affects the environment as natural resources are depleted or polluted through, for example, usage, the effects of global warming and acid rain. There is a need to look forward, as the theory of capital maintenance does, to ensure natural wealth – the environment – is maintained and therefore a system of stewardship and maintenance of this natural wealth is a necessity. Reporting in respect of stewardship and maintenance of assets is the accountant's domain. If the objective of financial statements is to provide useful information to users in order for them to assess the stewardship of management and for making economic decisions then, in the view of many, financial statements will need to incorporate the issue, certainly, of environmental reporting and possibly CSR to meet this objective. This will not be an easy task as systems will be difficult to design, but, through their training, accountants are ideally placed to play a leading role in this area. As you may have noticed from the CSR examples we gave many of these reports are assured by accountancy firms.

Chapter 12 Interpretation, including ratio analysis and consideration of additional information required

Question 1

▶ Trade receivables – Supermarket: Does not normally have trade receivables as most business is conducted by cash.
– Manufacturer: Supplies goods on credit therefore its trade receivables will be quite high.

▶ Inventory – Supermarket: Inventory turnover periods will be short as items have a limited life.
– Manufacturer: A large amount of money may be tied up in inventory and inventory turnover periods may be quite long.

▶ Cash – Supermarket: Probably quite low as cash will flow through the business daily, but will then be invested so as to earn interest.
– Manufacturer: May have reserves of cash to meet unforeseen events.

▶ Current liabilities – Supermarket: Trade payables may be quite high and form a major part of the liabilities of the business.
– Manufacturer: Trade payables turnover period will normally be of the order of 40 days. However, as he will take a long time to turn these goods into finished products he will need cash available to go on purchasing goods.

In conclusion, the current assets of the supermarket may well be much lower than its current liabilities and therefore its current ratio may well be less than 1:1. This is not unsafe for the supermarket, as the supermarket has cash flowing through the tills every day, but would be for the manufacturer. It would therefore not be appropriate to compare a supermarket with a manufacturer. Like must be compared with like in any assessment of the performance, financial status and investment potential of a business.

Question 2

OLIVET LTD

Ratios	20X4	20X5
Return on capital employed	$\frac{20 + 5}{88.5} = 28.2\%$	$\frac{10 + 7.5}{129.5} = 13.5\%$
GP percentage	50%	40%
NP percentage	20%	10%
Sales to capital employed	1.13	0.77
Return on owners' equity	52%	18.3%
Gearing ratio	56.5%	57.9%
Current ratio	49/30 = 1.6:1	57.5/42 = 1.37:1
Acid test	0.72:1	0.6:1
Trade receivables' turnover period	73 days	91 days
Trade payables' turnover period	146 days	182.5 days
Inventory turnover period	201 days	198 days
Dividend cover	2	1
Interest cover	5	2.3

From the information given in the question we can identify that:

▶ Sales have remained static but cost of sales has increased.
▶ Expenses other than interest have been slightly reduced.
▶ Dividend has remained at 20X4 level even though profits were reduced. In fact in 20X5 all the profit earned has been paid out in dividend.
▶ Land appears to have been revalued as the revaluation reserve has increased by £10,000.
▶ Further buildings, equipment and investments have been purchased during 20X5.
▶ Inventory, trade receivables and trade payables have all increased in 20X5.
▶ There is a bank overdraft in 20X5.

The above would seem to suggest that Olivet has attempted to expand by the purchase of further non-current assets but this does not appear to have produced extra sales.

Ratios of all types have worsened, indeed the ROCE has halved as has the net profit percentage. The return on owners' equity has fallen sharply and the current dividend policy appears somewhat imprudent.

It is possible, of course, that Olivet increased its investment in non-current assets towards the end of the year and therefore these non-current assets will not have generated revenue for a full year. However, even if this is the case the decline in the profit percentages is still a potentially dangerous situation.

Question 3

RATIO CALCULATIONS

	A Ltd	B Ltd
R on CE	470/2370 = 19.8%	174/876 = 19.9%
R on SHF	450/2170 = 20.7%	114/276 = 41.3%
GP/Sales	720/2150 = 33.5%	364/1512 = 24.1%
NP/Sales	470/2150 = 21.9%	174/1512 = 11.5%
Sales/CE	2150/2370 = 0.91 times	1512/876 = 1.73 times
Current ratio	1360:760 = 1.79:1	1020:1040 = 0.98:1
Acid test	940:760 = 1.24:1	680:1040 = 0.65:1
Trade receivables period	900/2150×365 = 153 days	680/1512×365 = 164 days
Trade payables period	360/1430×365 = 92 days	400/1148×365 = 127 days

(calculated using cost of sales as proxy for purchases)

	A Ltd	B Ltd
Gearing	200/2370 = 8.4%	600/876 = 68.5%
Interest cover	470/20 = 23.5 times	174/60 = 2.9 times
Dividend cover	350/200 = 1.75 times	84/80 = 1.05 times

Return on capital employed is very similar for both companies but B's return on shareholders' funds is double that of A, reflecting the high gearing of B at 68.5%. B is borrowing at 10% and earning at 19.9% with the difference going to shareholders.

A earns a much better gross and net profit margin than B but B operates on higher efficiency, i.e. B's capital employed earns 1.73 times sales to A's 0.91.

B's liquidity is much lower than A's due to the large bank overdraft of B. This overdraft could be regarded as long term rather than short term, thus increasing B's liquidity ratio to 1020:480 = 2.125:1.

B is high geared and thus potentially at risk if profits decrease. B is also paying most of its earnings in the form of dividends thus reducing the potential for reinvestment in the company. This could be risky as the assets of B are currently 74% depreciated implying they are reaching the end of their useful life and will need replacing. A's assets are only 36% depreciated. Note also that if the overdraft is regarded as long term this increases B's gearing.

B is high risk but currently earning good returns for shareholders. B's vulnerability must be monitored.

A is low geared and appears stable.

Question 4

OCEAN LTD

(a) (i)   Cost of sales has increased by 76% on 20X0 levels.
(ii)   All expenses have increased.
(iii) Profit after tax increased by 50%.
(iv)   Debenture interest payable in 20X1.
(v)   Debentures and shares issued 20X1, more capital raised.
(vi)   Non-current assets increased substantially.
(vii) Net current assets reduced but inventory, trade receivables, trade payables all increased in value.

(b) (i) *ROCE*

	20X0	20X1
	$\dfrac{94}{730} = 12.8\%$	$\dfrac{186}{982} = 18.9\%$

This indicates an increase in profitability of the business from the increased investment.

(ii) *Net profit margin* $\dfrac{94}{1,168} = 8\%$ $\dfrac{186}{1,944} = 9.6\%$

Increase in margins due to control of expenses or increased sales prices

(iii) *Volume of trade* $\dfrac{1,168}{730} = 1.6$ times $\dfrac{1,944}{982} = 1.98$ times

Ocean is earning more sales per pound of net assets or capital employed in 20X1 than 20X0.

(iv) *Gross profit margin* $\dfrac{390}{1,168} = 33.4\%$ $\dfrac{574}{1,944} = 29.53\%$

This reduction in the ratio is probably due to a decrease in sales prices which has generated more sales or an increase in costs of goods sold.

(v) *Expenses to sales* $\dfrac{296}{1,168} = 25.3\%$ $\dfrac{388}{1,944} = 20\%$

This decrease indicates better control of expenses.

(vi) *Non-current assets to sales* $\dfrac{560}{1,168} = 0.48$ $\dfrac{856}{1,944} = 0.44$

Invert   2.08   2.27

Non-current assets are earning 2.27 times their value in sales in X1 compared to 2.08 times in X0.

(vii) *NCA to sales*

$$\frac{170}{1,168} = 0.15 \qquad \frac{126}{1,944} = 0.06$$

Invert   6.87   15.4

NCA are earning more sales in X1 than X0.

(viii) *Inventory turnover*

$$\frac{98 \times 365}{778} = 46 \text{ days} \qquad \frac{109 \times 365}{1,370} = 29 \text{ days}$$

Inventory has increased in turnover showing greater efficiency.

(ix) *Trade receivables turnover*

$$\frac{120 \times 365}{1,168} = 37 \qquad \frac{226 \times 365}{1,370} = 29 \text{ days}$$

Trade receivables are paying quicker which indicates greater efficency in debt collection.

(x) *Trade payables' turnover*

$$\frac{69 \times 365}{778} = 46 \text{ days} \qquad \frac{148 \times 365}{1,370} = 39 \text{ days}$$

Ocean is .taking longer to pay suppliers which may indicate it is using creditors to finance their business operations.

(xi) *Wages/sales*   13.3%   10.4%

Amount of wages to generate £1 of sales has decreased.

(xii) *Other expenses/sales*   9.3%   6.4%

Shows better control of expenses in 20X1.

(xiii) *Depreciation/sales*   2.7%   3.2%

Depreciation has marginally increased as a proportion of sales possible due to an increase in assets.

(xiv) *ROOE*

$$\frac{94}{730} = 20\% \qquad \frac{170}{822} = 20.7\%$$

The shareholders in 20X1 have benefited by the return to debenture holders being constrained to 10% whereas their capital earned (see ROCE at (i)) 18.9%.

(xv) *Current ratio*   312:142 = 2.2:1   468:342 = 1.4:1

Substantial reduction but still appears viable.

(xvi) *Acid ratio*   218:142 = 1.5:1   344:342 = 1:1

Again reduced but remains viable with careful monitoring.

(xvii) *Gearing ratio*   not relevant   160:822 = 19.5%

Gearing of Ocean Ltd is low.

(xviii) *Interest cover*   not relevant

$$\frac{186}{16} = 11.6$$

The interest payable in fixed capital debentures is more than adequately covered by earnings.

Overall the company has performed well in raising capital to finance expansion in assets which had resulted in increased sales and greater return on earnings.

Question 5

No answer provided

Question 6

(a)

		30/09/X7		30/09/X6	
(ii)	*Gross profit*	$\dfrac{279}{1,644} \times 100 = 16.97\%$		$\dfrac{225}{1,495} \times 100 = 15.05\%$	
(ii)	*Net profit*	$\dfrac{173}{1,644} \times 100 = 10.52\%$		$\dfrac{151}{1,495} \times 100 = 10.10\%$	
(iii)	*Current ratio*	$\dfrac{152}{123} = 1.24{:}1$		$\dfrac{151}{99} = 1.53{:}1$	
(iv)	*Acid test (Quick ratio)*	$\dfrac{106}{123} = 0.86{:}1$		$\dfrac{100}{99} = 1.01{:}1$	

(b) The bank will be interested in the profitability of the company and will therefore calculate both gross profit and net profit ratios. If a company wishes to be successful it must sell its products for more than it costs to acquire or produce them. The bank would expect the gross profit percentage to remain stable. If the net profit falls then it may suggest that the company is not controlling its costs, which could indicate potential problems.

It is important to understand that even though a company is making profits this does not mean that it has a healthy cash flow. The bank will be interested in liquidity ratios such as current ratio and acid test ratio because these identify whether the company can meets its current liabilities from its current assets. The bank will not lend any company money if it believes that the loan will not be repaid.

(c)

▶ *Present and potential investors* – to decide whether or not to invest in the company
▶ *Suppliers* – to decide whether the company will be able to pay for goods supplied, and how quickly the company pays its suppliers
▶ *Customers* – to determine whether the company is likely to remain in business to continue supplying goods. This may be important if the product is supplied with a warranty.
▶ *Management* – to assess the financial performance and financial stability of the company
▶ *Employees* – to assess whether the company is likely to remain in business; to check profit related pay calculations
▶ *Government* – to determine whether sufficient taxes have been paid.

(d)

	£000
Operating profit	173
Adjustments for:	
Depreciation for year	20
Decrease in stock	5
Increase in debtors	(16)
Increase in creditors	17
Net cash inflow from operating activities	199

Question 7

(a)

United

(i)   *Gross profit* $\dfrac{18,600 - 10,230}{18,600}$ × 100   = 45.00%

(ii) *Current ratio* $\dfrac{1,800 + 1,740 + 500}{2,140}$ = 1.89:1

(iii) *Acid test (quick ratio)* $\dfrac{1,740 + 500}{2,140}$ = 1.05: 1

(iv) *Debtors collection period* $\dfrac{1,740}{18,600}$ × 365   = 34.15 days

(v)   *Creditors payment period* $\dfrac{2,140}{10,400}$ × 365   = 75.10 days

(vi) *ROCE* $\dfrac{2,720}{2,000 + 4,720 + 1,000}$ × 100   = 35.23%

Prince

(i)   *Gross profit* $\dfrac{22,000 - 14,300}{22,000}$ × 100   = 35.00%

(ii) *Current ratio* $\dfrac{2,640 + 2,200 + 268}{3,528}$ = 1.45:1

(iii) *Acid test (quick ratio)* $\dfrac{2,200 + 268}{3,528}$ = 0.70:1

(iv) *Debtors collection period* $\dfrac{2,200}{22,000}$ × 365   = 36.5 days

(v)   *Creditors payment period* $\dfrac{3,528}{13,800}$ × 365   = 93.31 days

(vi)   *ROCE* $$\frac{1,640}{4,000 + 3,000 + 3,340} \times 100 \quad = 15.86\%$$

(b) It is recommended that Camber invest in United for the following reasons:

▶ United has a higher gross profit and higher ROCE than Prince.

▶ Both companies take approximately the same amount of time to collect their debts.

▶ Prince takes 18 days longer to pay its creditors, which could jeopardise its relationship with suppliers and risk problems with supplies.

▶ Both companies have a current ratio in excess of 1, which means that they can meet their current liabilities from current assets.

▶ When inventory is removed, United can still meet its current liabilities but Prince would need to convert its inventory to cash to meet its current liabilities.

Overall Prince is a more risky investment.

(c) Other methods (apart from ratio analysis) could include:

▶ company search agencies

▶ press/ journal reports

▶ visits to the company

▶ internet site access

▶ cash flow analysis

▶ share price tracking

▶ audit reports.

Chapter 13 Valuation and performance measurement

Question 1

This is a difficult and contentious area. Nevertheless, the answer attempts to outline the main points for and against such a development. You should have listed some or all of the same points.

For change

1 The meaning of the statement of financial position figure is uncertain, given that it is not only subject to subjective amounts of depreciation but also out of date.

2 Periodic revaluations depend on the decisions of individual companies, and there is thus little consistency between the statement of financial positions of different companies. This makes any comparative analysis very difficult, if not meaningless. A requirement for all to adopt another valuation could largely remove the inconsistency.

3 It is theoretically incorrect to add together amounts for assets bought at different times, which, as a result of inflation, are thus not expressed in the same currency.

For retaining historical cost

1 Historical cost is objective, and hence relatively easily audited.

2 The simplicity of historical cost makes it a cheaper method to implement, since no time need be spent in determining an alternative valuation.

3 It is probably more easily understood by non-accountants.

4 Its widespread acceptance allows for better comparison between companies.

Question 2

(a)

		Historical cost	Deprival value
Freehold land		3,600,000	4,700,000
(no depreciation)			
Vehicles			
cost	1,300,000	1,100,000	
depreciation	325,000	275,000	
		975,000	825,000
		4,575,000	5,525,000

The recoverable amount of the land is the greater of the economic value of £5,000,000 and the net realisable value of £4,200,000, i.e. £5,000,000. Deprival value is then the lower of the £5,000,000 and the replacement cost of £4,700,000, i.e. £4,700,000. Following the same logic, the recoverable amount of the vehicles is the greater of £800,000 and £1,100,000, and this is compared with the replacement cost, which is still the same as the historical cost of £1,300,000. The lower of these is the deprival value of £1,100,000.

Depreciation is simply a quarter of the valuation.

(b)

REVALUATION ACCOUNT

		Land	1,100,000
		Vehicles	125,000
			1,225,000

The vehicle revaluation is the difference between the present historical cost carrying value of £975,000 and the undepreciated deprival value of £1,100,000.

Question 3

(a) All figures in £000s.

ASSET COST

1/1/X7	Bank	520			
31/12/X8	Revaluation	280			
		800	1/9/X9	Sale of asset	800

PROVISION FOR DEPRECIATION

31/12/X8	Revaluation	26	31/12/X7	Income statement	26
1/9/X9	Sale of asset	40	31/12/X8	Income statement	40

REVALUATION

			31/12/X8	Asset cost	280
			31/12/X8	Prov for depn	26
1/9/X9 Revenue reserve		306			306

SALE OF ASSET

1/9/X9 Asset cost	800	1/9/X9	Prov for depn	40
		1/9/X9	Bank (proceeds)	750
		1/9/X9	Income statement (loss)	10

(b) At 31 December 20X9 the Asset Cost and Provision for Depreciation accounts both carry a nil balance, having been cleared by transfer to the Sale of Asset account. The balance on the Revaluation account of £306,000 is dealt with by direct transfer to the Revenue Reserve account, or equivalent. Finally, the debit balance of £10,000 on the Sale of Asset account represents the loss on sale, and is taken as a charge to the income statement part of the statement of comprehensive income for the year.

(c) Holderness Ltd could have adopted either the net realisable value (NRV) or the economic value (EV) methods of valuation, as alternatives to the replacement cost basis used on revaluation. NRV is the amount which the building could be sold for at arm's length on the open market, net of any direct selling expenses. EV sums the present values of the future additional net revenues expected to be received by Holderness Ltd as a result of its use of the building. It involves estimating such future inflows, and the selection of a suitable discount rate. Both these issues are problematic, and the method is therefore not widely found in practice.

Reasons for revaluation include the desire to show a more current valuation of the company's worth, in the interests of a true and fair view. More practically, the revaluation will usually, as in this case, increase the valuation of the company, making it seem more attractive to less financially literate potential investors and lenders.

Question 4

(a) Problems with historical cost accounting may be listed as:

▶ It results in out-of-date valuations in the statement of financial position.
▶ The valuations will usually be lower than a current value, so that the net worth of the organisation will be understated.
▶ The same physical amount of inventory will be valued more highly at the year end than at the start of the year, because we will have paid more for it. This real overstatement of closing inventory will result in the consequent understatement of the cost of sales, and hence in the overstatement of gross profit.
▶ The understatement of non-current assets will lead to the understatement of the depreciation charge for the year, and hence to the overstatement of net profit.
▶ Decisions based on the accounts will therefore be questionable, since they are based on non-current data.

(b)

Sales		400,000
Purchases	340,000	
Closing inventory	65,000	
		275,000
Gross profit		125,000

(c) There is no absolute, correct answer to this, but a good answer might be expected to include the following points:

▶ Historical cost is simpler, and hence more understandable.
▶ Historical cost takes no account of the fact that prices are changing.
▶ Current cost is more up to date, and takes some account of changing prices.
▶ Being more up to date, current cost may be a better basis for decisions about the future.
▶ Current cost arguably maintains the real, physical capital need for the business to continue to be a going concern.
▶ Historical cost is more objective and thus more easily audited.
▶ Current cost inevitably involves some estimation of current values and may therefore be less reliable.

Chapter 14 Control of accounting systems

Answers to Questions 1–8
1 (c)　2 (c)　3 (a)　4 (d)　5 (a)　6 (a)　7 (b)　8 (b).

Question 9
(a) The items you should have identified are:

▶ The cheques paid out dated 18th (£305.75) and 30th (£182.85) are not on the bank statement.
▶ The £50.00 paid in on the 30th was not shown on the bank statement.
▶ The bank statement did show bank charges of £25.00. This has not yet been entered in the cash book. The amended cash book will be as follows:

CASH BOOK

Date	Detail	Amount	Date	Detail	Amount
1	Opening balance	500.00	1	Bradley Software Ltd	106.78
4	Cash sales	390.00	4	Clee & Co.	690.00
10	Weelsby Partners	504.80	8	Halton Supplies	45.07
15	Cash sale	80.00	16	Tetney Merchandising	230.70
20	Atlantis Publishing plc	680.50	18	Bradley Software Ltd	305.75
27	Weelsby Partners	218.00	24	Vehicle Rentals plc	530.00
30	Cash sale	50.00	28	Corner Newsagency	12.43
			30	Halton Supplies	182.85
			30	Bank charges	25.00
			30	Balance c/f	294.72
		2,423.30			2,423.30

(a)

JULIA
BANK RECONCILIATION STATEMENT AT 30 SEPTEMBER

Balance per bank statement		733.32
Less: Unpresented cheques:		
18 May, Bradley Software Ltd	305.75	
30 May, Halton Supplies	182.85	
		488.60
		244.72
Add: Uncredited lodgement:		
30 May, cash sale		50.00
Balance per cash book (as updated)		294.72

Question 10

(a)

Opening balance	500
Add: Cheques banked	4,003
	4,503
Less: Cheques issued	3,638
Cash book balance at 31 July	865

(b)

Balance as above	865
Less: Bank charges	232
	633
Less: Worthless cheque previously added	240
	393
Less: Error in entry	9
Cash book balance, as adjusted	384

(c)

PETER LEE
BANK RECONCILIATION STATEMENT AT 31 JULY

Balance per bank statement	622
Less: Unpresented cheques	843
Overdrawn	221
Add: Uncredited lodgements	605
Balance per cash book, as adjusted	384

Question 11

(a) An external audit is an independent, expert examination of the records and financial statements of an organisation, to enable the auditor to form an opinion on whether the accounts show a true and fair view or not. External auditors report primarily to the shareholders of a company, and are nominally appointed by them. External audit is not an attempt to find fraud, and it is not a management control.

An Internal audit is an expert investigation of financial, and sometimes other, systems within an organisation. The purpose is for the internal auditors to be able to report to the management of the organisation on the effectiveness of those systems, and on how they might be improved. Internal audit may be directed towards detecting fraud, and is part of management control.

(b) A qualified audit report is one in which the auditor has reservations which have a material effect on the financial statements. The circumstances giving rise to a qualification will be either:

▶ where there is a limitation on the scope of the audit, and hence an unresolvable uncertainty, which prevents the auditor from forming an opinion, or

▶ where the auditor is able to form an opinion, but, even after negotiation with the directors, disagrees with the financial statements.

The likely effect of a qualified audit report will be to significantly reduce the reliability of the financial statements in the eyes of any user of those statements. This may well then impact on the company's ability to raise finance or trade credit from such users. This may make trading conditions more difficult for the company and lead to a fall in the share price.

Question 12

Statement of affairs at the start of the year:

Van	14,000
Bank	5,000
	19,000
Capital	19,000

Statement of affairs at the end of the year:

Van	12,000
Trade receivables	3,400
Deposit account	6,100
Current account	700
Trade payable	(300)
	21,900
Capital	21,900

Profit for the year:

Closing capital	21,900
Opening capital	19,000
Increase in capital	2,900
Drawings (12 × 1,300)	15,600
Profit for the year	18,500

Chapter 15 Information technology and accounting

Answers to Questions 1–8

1 (d) 2 (b) 3 (c) 4 (d) 5 (b) 6 (c) 7 (d) (correct choice is 1, 3, 4 and 5) 8 (d)

Question 9

The nature of the activity means that there is no formal feedback to this question.

Question 10

1 Determine the information required from the system, e.g. budgets, statement of comprehensive income.
2 Determine the source documents and other data to be processed by the system.
3 Decide on back-up and security arrangements.
4 Investigate suitable software.
5 Investigate suitable hardware.
6 Get the manual system up to date.
7 Transfer the account balances from the manual system to the computer system.
8 Back-up the computer records.
9 Run both systems in parallel.
10 Monitor the audit trail for the computer system.
11 Move wholly to the computer system.

Glossary

Account The named place in the ledger system where one side of the double entry involved in recording a financial transaction of an organisation will be made, e.g. an expense of wages paid by cash will be entered in the wages account and the cash account.

Accounting Standards Board (ASB) The body which sets the accounting standards in the UK under the auspices of the FRC. Now works in conjunction with the International Accounting Standards Board (see below)

Accounts payable New title for creditors. Amounts owed by an organisation.

Accounts receivable New title for debtors. Amounts due to an organisation.

Accruals Amounts owed by the business to a supplier of a service at the balance sheet date. When preparing the income statement, revenue and profits are matched with the associated costs and expenses incurred in earning them. This is often also referred to as the 'matching' concept.

Alternative methods of valuation There are three alternatives to historical cost. These are replacement cost, net realisable value and economic value. They may be synthesised using the deprival value model.

Annual report The report produced annually by a company, incorporating the format presentation of the financial statements and various other information required by law or deemed appropriate for companies to produce.

Appropriation account The last section of the income statement. It is a statement of what has happened to the net profit and usually consists of tax, dividends and retained profit.

Articles of Association These define the rights of shareholders, the rules of operation of the company, and the rights and duties of owners and employees of the company.

Assets An asset represents the control of future economic benefits as a result of past transactions or events. In most cases we can reduce this to 'an asset is what you own', but note that you do not always have to own an asset to control it; for example, a leased asset is controlled but not owned.

Audit External audit is the independent, expert scrutiny of an entity's financial statements and supporting information, usually to assess whether or not those statements give a true and fair view, and reporting to the funders. Internal audit is a tool of management intended to assess the effectiveness of control systems within an organisation, and reporting to that management.

Audit trail The record of entries to record, process and present a particular transaction or event.

Back-ups Duplicate records of accounting data and information, prepared on a regular basis as a precaution against problems with the originals.

Bad debts Those debts that will not be paid by the debtor to the organisation. The debt will never be received and therefore must be written off as an expense of trading.

Balance off To balance off is the process by which we extract a debit or credit balance from a ledger account.

Balance sheet – see 'Statement of financial position'.

Balance sheet equation Assets = Equity + Liabilities. The equation can be expressed in different ways.

Bank reconciliation A statement proving that the entity's bank balance agrees with the balance according to the bank, subject to items legitimately in transit.

Benchmarks Indicators against which an item or items can be measured.

Cash flows Cash that is flowing into or out of an organisation.

Cash flow statement – see 'Statement of cash flows'.

Characteristics The features which distinguish good accounting from bad. They are held to be relevance, reliability, comparability and understandability.

Charity accounts Financial statements prepared by those organisations operating under the Charities Act.

Closing inventory The value of the inventory at the end of the accounting period.

Closing inventory account The ledger account used to record the value of the remaining inventory left with the organisation at a specific date, generally the balance sheet date.

Concepts The ideas which underpin the practice of accounting.

Consolidated statement of comprehensive income A statement which combines statements of comprehensive income for a number of companies in a group.

Consolidated statement of financial position A statement which combines statements of financial position for a number of companies in a group.

Control accounts Statements to prove that the total balance of individual debtors or creditors agrees with a total balance calculated from global postings. It is a control over the completeness and accuracy of the debtors and creditors accounting.

Corporate entity The notion of corporate entity means that several people can band together as owners of a business, by investing capital in the business, and the business will be a legal entity separate from the owners. It also means that the owners – the investors of capital – can be changed without the need also to change the legal entity of the company.

Corporate governance System by which corporate entities are directed and controlled.

Corporate social responsibility (CSR) Entities taking account of social and environmental impact of their decisions when making decisions.

Credit transactions Financial transactions of an organisation that do not involve the immediate payment of cash, e.g. a sale made by an organisation where payment will be received in two weeks' time.

Current cost accounting (CCA) A system of inflation accounting which attempts to maintain the ability of the entity to do the same things from one year to the next.

current purchasing power A system of inflation accounting which attempts to maintain the purchasing power of the owners of a business, despite the falling value of their investment in the entity.

Dearing Committee A committee established by government to review the working of the Accounting Standards Committee.

Debentures Capital raised by the company in the form of long-term loans.

Decision making The main purpose of accounting is deemed to be to provide useful information to a range of users so that they can make economic decisions based on that information.

Depreciation The measure of the amount of an asset that is used up in generating revenues.

Deprival value The lower of replacement cost and recoverable amount, which is the greater of net realisable value and economic value. It provides a single, logically coherent, alternative to historical cost.

Designing an accounting system The process of specifying what we want an accounting system to be able to do (the outputs), what data it must cope with (the inputs), and how the two can be most effectively and efficiently connected.

Determinants The factors that determine the accounting framework of a particular country.

Direct method A method of determining the net cash flows from operating activities by recording the flows by function or activity, e.g. receipts from customers, payments to suppliers.

Dividend The cash payment made to shareholders as their return on their investment. The dividend is appropriated out of the profits made and available for distribution by the company. The dividend paid is shown as a change in equity

Double entry The method by which financial transactions of an organisation are entered into the ledger accounts; for every debit entry there will be an equal and opposite credit entry.

E-accounting (electronic accounting) The use of information technology to aid accounting practice.

Earnings per share (EPS) A key ratio for measuring the performance of a company. Compares the earnings in a period to the number of ordinary shares issued.

Economic value Economic value is arrived at by summing the present values of the inflows attributable to an asset; in other words, it is the present value of those inflows.

Environmental reporting Reporting on an entity's impact on the environment.

Extended trial balance A working paper on which the adjustments to the double entry accounts will be made. This speeds up the process of producing an income statement and balance sheet without having to wait for all the ledger accounts to be adjusted.

External audit – see 'Audit'.

Financial Accounting Standards Board (FASB) The USA accounting standards board.

Financial Reporting Council (FRC) The supervisory body which ensures that the UK accounting standards setting system is working.

Format presentation The Companies Act refers to regulations for four formats that can be used for the presentation of the income statement of a company and two for the balance sheet.

Fourth and Seventh Directives Directives on company law issued by the European Union.

Funds flow The flow of funds in and out of the organisation, such as share capital, working capital, etc. Funds are not necessarily flows of cash.

Gearing ratio The fixed-term capital in a company compared to the shareholders' capital.

Goodwill The value of a company as a whole over and above the net assets reported on a statement of financial position.

Goodwill in partnerships The difference between the fair vale of the partnership if sold and the book value according to the statement of financial position at the date of sale.

Going concern There is an assumption that the business will continue to operate for the foreseeable future.

Group accounting. The construction of a single set of financial statements to report on a group of companies under a single point of control

Harmonised reporting framework An attempt to produce a framework that will serve the purposes of all countries.

Implementation of an accounting system The practice of turning the designed accounting system into a functioning, live system.

Income and expenditure account The equivalent of an income statement used by non-profit making entities.

Income statement – see 'Statement of comprehensive income'.

Incomplete records Any bookkeeping records which are less than full double entry records. This can vary from double entry which doesn't quite balance to no systematic records at all.

Indicators – see 'Benchmarks'.

Indirect method A method of determining the net cash flows from operating activities by adjusting the income statement balance for such entries as changes in working capital and depreciation provision.

Information technology In the context of accounting, the use of hardware and software to aid in the recording, processing, presentation and even in the interpretation of financial information.

Inter-company transactions Transactions between group companies, which should be cancelled out as part of group accounting.

International Accounting Standards Board (IASB) The independent body that sets international accounting standards.

Inventory valuation The method chosen for valuing inventory, usually first-in, first-out (FIFO).

Ledger The place where double entry accounts are recorded.

Ledger adjustments All adjustments necessary to the ledger accounts to take account of such things as accruals, prepayments, bad debts, depreciation, etc.

Liabilities A liability is the obligation to transfer benefits to someone else as a result of past transactions or events. 'Obligation' is interpreted very strictly, so that it means being unable to avoid the transfer out, not just that the payment is commercially sensible.

Limited company An organisation established as a company whose owners, the shareholders, have limited liability.

Limited liability Shareholders' loss is limited to that of their initial investment in the company.

Matching – see 'Accruals'.

Measurement bases The particular valuation basis chosen from among historical cost, replacement cost, net realisable value and economic value.

Memorandum of Association Defines the relationship between the company and any external parties and states the objectives of the company, i.e. what sort of trade it will undertake. It also identifies the maximum capital to be invested in the company by the owners, known as the share capital.

Needs and objectives The needs and objectives of users of financial statements as defined by the Framework for the Preparation and Presentation of Financial Statement, issued by the IASB. In the UK the equivalent statement from the ASB is the Statement of Principles.

Net cash flow from operating activities Cash flow, inflow and outflow, resulting directly from the operating activities of the organisation, e.g. sale and purchase of inventory for cash.

Net profit margin (NPM) A ratio comparing net profit to sales.

Net realisable value Valuing what the asset could be sold for today, less any costs of selling.

Net worth The amount that the organisation is worth according to the statement of financial position.

Non-controlling interest. The minority stake in a subsidiary company.

Non-current assets Previously in the UK known as fixed asset but under the influence of international standards these are referred to as non-current assets. Non-current assets are assets with a life of more than one year which are not held for sale or consumption in the normal operating cycle.

Opening inventory The value of the inventory (stock of goods for sale or use within the organisation) at the start of the accounting period.

Partnerships Entities formed by the coming together of two or more people to form unregistered businesses with the aim of making and sharing profits in accordance with a legal agreement.

Partners' capital accounts The ledger accounts to record the capital contributed to the business by each partner.

Partners' current accounts The ledger accounts to record all business transactions with and between partners involved in the partnership except for the contribution of capital.

Period-end adjustments Ledger adjustments made to the ledger accounts but at a period end (this is likely to be the balance sheet date), e.g. accruals, prepayments, bad debts, depreciation.

Premium The amount paid by the purchaser of a share which is over and above the nominal value of the share.

Prepayment An amount paid in advance to the provider of a service to the organisation at the balance sheet date.

Presentation Publishing economic information about the business entity in a form which complies with any applicable rules, such as those given by law and accounting standards.

Price/earnings (P/E) ratio A ratio comparing earnings per share to the price of a share on the stock market.

Processing Turning the raw data that we have recorded into useful information that can be presented to those interested in knowing about the organisation.

Profit and loss account Since the advent of international accounting standards into the UK this statement is more properly known as the statement of comprehensive income. However, the use of the term 'profit and loss account' is likely to continue for a few years yet, especially in relation to small and medium-sized companies.

Provision for bad debts A charge made in the income statement for those debts that might go bad (remain unpaid) in the future. The provision is normally made at so many per cent of the total debtors outstanding at the balance sheet date based on past experience of the amount that goes bad.

Realisation Only recognising, i.e. making an accounting entry for, those transactions where the money has changed hands, or is almost certain to do so in the near future.

Receipts and payments account A summary of monies in and out of an entity's bank account. Often used instead of an income statement for small, simple organisations, such as clubs.

Recording The gathering of raw economic data into a structured form, such as double entry bookkeeping.

Reducing balance method A method for the calculation of depreciation. It assumes the same percentage of the net book value of the asset is used up each period.

Regulatory framework The framework of accounting specified by the ASB and by company law in the UK. On the international stage the IASB sets the international accounting standards which form the backbone of the regulatory framework.

Replacement cost Valuing an asset at what it would cost to replace today.

Reserves Accumulated profits and capital gains available to shareholders. These reserves can be termed realised and unrealised.

Return on capital employed (ROCE) A ratio to measure the return made on the capital invested in a business. It generally refers to profit before tax and interest, compared to shareholder capital plus long-term capital employed in the business.

Return on shareholders' funds (ROSHF) (or return on owner's equity (ROOE)) A ratio that compares the return made by the business with the shareholder funds invested in the business. It generally refers to profit after tax but before ordinary shareholder dividends, compared with ordinary shares and reserves.

Revaluation on acquisition The process of bringing valuation of the net assets of a subsidiary up to date immediately before the main part of group accounting is carried out.

Revenue recognition Revenue is the inflow of economic benefits arising from ordinary activities. Its recognition should be made only when it both arises from ordinary activities and is reasonably certain to be realised.

Roadmap for convergence Plan by which the USA standards will converge with the international standards of accounting.

Rules based Accounting systems based on extant rules rather than principles.

Sale of a non-current asset account The ledger account to record the sale of a non-current asset. The proceeds of the sale are recorded on the credit side and the net book value of the asset in the books at the time of the sale is transferred to the debit side of the account.

Shares The capital of a company is divided into shares which are issued to the shareholders as collateral for their investment. The shares can have various nominal values and be of several types, e.g. ordinary, preference.

Sources and applications of funds Sources are where the money has come from, for example previous profits, share issues and amounts borrowed. Applications are where the money has gone, either spent on expenses or on assets. Given this definition, total sources must always equal total applications.

Statement of cash flows The new title for the cash flow statement. A statement showing the cash inflows and outflows. A summary of cash received and paid during a period, usually of one year.

Statement of changes in equity A summary of all gains and losses accounted for ('recognised') during a period, usually of one year. It differs from an income statement by including unrealised gains as well as the realised gains that will appear in an income statement. In the UK, until the advent of international accounting standards, the equivalent statement was the 'statement of total recognised gains and losses'.

Statement of comprehensive income. The new title of the income statement. List of expenses incurred by an organisation set against its revenues plus unrealised gains and losses. It covers a specific period which is generally one year.

Statement of financial posititon. The new title for the balance sheet. This is a summary of the assets and liabilities of the organisation at a specific time.

Stewardship A secondary purpose of accounting is to record the economic events relevant to an entity, so that those who provided the finance can see what has been done with their money. In other words, the managers of the entity are held to be stewards of the money.

Straight line method A method by which the provision for depreciation is calculated. It assumes that the asset is used up in equal amounts in each period.

Taxation The charge levied by government authorities on the profits of a company.

Time value of money The operation of interest means that money has a value, not only in terms of the absolute amount, but also in terms of when it is received. The sooner it is received, the better, since it can be placed on deposit and earn interest. This value according to when the money is received is its time value.

Trading account The first part of what is loosely called the income statement. It consists of sales, cost of sales and hence gross profit.

Trial balance The check on the double entry system whereby each debit balance and each credit balance is extracted from the ledgers, listed in either a debit or credit column, and the two columns totalled to see if they agree.

True and fair view This term is the over-riding legal requirement for financial reporting in the UK but is undefined by law. Accordingly, what it effectively means is whatever accountants have defined it to mean through compliance with the accounting standards. Note that the requirement is to show 'a true and fair view' not 'the true and fair view'.

Value in use What an asset is worth as it is being used, i.e. the benefits of its use for the entity. It is accordingly measured by its economic value.

Volume of trade (VofT) A ratio comparing sales to capital employed.

Working capital Current assets minus current liabilities. Also known as 'net current assets' or 'net current liabilities'.

XML (eXtensible Mark-up Language) A method of tagging each item of financial data with a label marking its meaning, to aid in processing that data.

Index